Supplements to Journal of Cell Science

From time to time *Journal of Cell Science* will publish supplementary volumes dealing with topics of outstanding interest to cell and molecular biologists. These volumes
are free to subscribers to the Journal and can also be purchased separately for £10
($19), plus postage, from The Biochemical Society, P.O. Box 32, Commerce Way,
Colchester CO2 8HP

Higher Order Structure in the Nucleus

Proceedings of the first British Society for Cell Biology – Company of Biologists Symposium held in Manchester, April 1984, organized and edited by:

P. R. COOK

Sir William Dunn School of Pathology
University of Oxford

and

R. A. LASKEY

Department of Zoology
University of Cambridge

Journal of **CELL SCIENCE SUPPLEMENT 1, 1984**

Published by
THE COMPANY OF BIOLOGISTS LIMITED
CAMBRIDGE

Published by The Company of Biologists Ltd
Department of Zoology, University of Cambridge, Downing Street
Cambridge CB2 3EJ

© The Company of Biologists Limited 1984

Typeset and Printed by the Pindar Group of Companies, Scarborough, North Yorkshire

HIGHER ORDER STRUCTURE IN THE NUCLEUS
CONTENTS   SUPPLEMENT 1   1984

J. Cell Sci. Suppl. 1, 1–20 (1984)
Printed in Great Britain © The Company of Biologists Limited 1984

THE HIGHER ORDER STRUCTURE OF CHROMATIN AND HISTONE H1

JEAN O. THOMAS

Department of Biochemistry, University of Cambridge, Tennis Court Road, Cambridge CB2 1QW, England

SUMMARY

The basic chromatin fibre (the 10 nm diameter fibre) is a linear repeating array of nucleosomes, or nucleosome filament. The core of each disk-like nucleosome is a wedge-shaped protein octamer containing two molecules of each of the four core histones (H3, H4, H2A and H2B) around which two turns of DNA are wound in a left-handed superhelix with about 80 base-pairs per turn. The two turns are sealed by a molecule of the fifth histone H1 (or H5 in nucleated erythrocytes). The linker DNA that connects one two-turn particle to the next varies from essentially zero to about 80 base-pairs in chromatins from different sources. The exact significance of this variation is unclear.

Interphase chromatin exists largely in the form of 30 nm fibres. Folding of the nucleosome filament into very similar 30 nm fibres, which is H1-dependent, occurs *in vitro* in the presence of monovalent cations or much lower concentrations of divalent cations. These higher-order structures probably arise by helical coiling of the nucleosome filament into a solenoid. Systematic studies of chromatin folding in solution, for a range of chromatin fragment sizes and ionic strengths, reveal two discontinuities in behaviour that reflect two structural transitions. One is interpreted as the formation of a turn of a solenoid with about six nucleosomes, at ionic strength 25 mM, and is a common feature of chromatin from three different sources, which differ in DNA repeat length, and type and amount of H1. The other transition is interpreted in terms of hydrodynamic shearing of long solenoids at low ionic strengths (below ~45 mM). It suggests a more stable higher-order structure for chicken erythrocyte chromatin than for rat liver chromatin (attributed largely to the presence of H5), and may prove to be a useful general assay for the relative stabilities of different chromatins, which might be relevant to their ease of unravelling for transcription. A study of short (165 base-pair) repeat chromatin from cerebral cortex neurons has led to the suggestion that in the general case the linker DNA might be located, perhaps with H1, in the central hole in the solenoid.

H1 molecules in both extended and condensed chromatin (although not when dissociated from it) are close enough to be chemically cross-linked with reagents of span 2–12 Å. This suggests an H1 polymer in chromatin, which might have a role in chromatin condensation. Chemical cross-linking studies using cleavable, bifunctional amino-group reagents have permitted the domains of H1 molecules that are in proximity in the extended and condensed states to be determined, and changes occurring on folding to be identified.

In another approach towards understanding the role and behaviour of H1 we have studied further the ability of H1 molecules to migrate between sites on different chromatin fragments. H1 and H5 (an extreme H1 variant) also exchange, but show differences in behaviour that may reflect their different abilities to stabilize higher-order structures, revealed in the sedimentation studies outlined above. In particular, H5 shows a greater preference than H1 for sites in higher-order structures.

INTRODUCTION

The condensation of DNA in the eukaryotic nucleus is brought about in stages. In the first and second of these, giving the 10 nm diameter fibre and the 30 nm diameter fibre, the histones play a major role. The 30 nm fibre, in which a compaction of about 40-fold in the length of the DNA is achieved, probably represents the bulk of (inactive) chromatin in the interphase nucleus. In transcribable chromatin the 30 nm fibre is almost certainly relaxed into the 10 nm form in which the compaction of the DNA is about sixfold. Differential stability of higher-order structures would provide an attractive coarse control of the accessibility of chromatin for transcription, and one possible mechanism for modulating stability might be through the use of H1 variants. This article will be concerned mainly with our studies of the interconversion of the 10 nm and 30 nm fibres *in vitro*, and of the role and behaviour of histone H1. The organization of the 30 nm fibres of interphase nuclei into loops or domains that may represent cytogenetic units, by association with non-histone proteins that may act as clamps (and may be part of the nuclear framework) will be discussed elsewhere in this volume, as will the further folding of the 30 nm fibre in the highly condensed metaphase chromosome.

THE NUCLEOSOME AND THE NUCLEOSOME FILAMENT

The 10 nm diameter fibre is a repeating linear array of nucleosomes, termed the nucleosome filament. Each nucleosome contains about 200 base-pairs (bp) of DNA (166–241 bp depending upon source) associated with an octameric protein core comprising pairs of each of four types of histone – the lysine-rich histones H2A and H2B, and the arginine-rich histones H3 and H4 (Kornberg, 1974). The DNA is organized in two turns of about 166 bp (see below), which are sealed by the binding of one molecule of the fifth histone, H1, at the entry and exit points of the DNA. The remaining 34 bp of DNA (if the repeat is 200 bp) comprises the linker DNA that connects one nucleosome to the next and contributes part of the H1 binding site. The length of the linker may vary from essentially zero to about 80 base-pairs in chromatins from different sources. The repeating nucleoprotein structure of chromatin is reflected in a beaded appearance in the electron microscope, and the alternation of highly protected (nucleosome core) DNA and more exposed (linker) DNA accounts for the differential susceptibility of the DNA to nucleases, e.g. micrococcal nuclease. (Further details and references may be found in several reviews (e.g. Kornberg, 1977; McGhee & Felsenfeld, 1980; Igo-Kemenes, Hörz & Zachau, 1982; Thomas, 1983).)

Complete digestion (at all linkers) gives rise to mononucleosomes, and partial digestion to populations of oligonucleosomes of various lengths, which may be fractionated by sedimentation through sucrose gradients. Mononucleosomes containing a full repeat length of DNA (e.g. 200 bp in rat liver) may be exonucleolytically trimmed by micrococcal nuclease in two discrete stages, first to 166 bp and finally to 146 bp, at which points histone–DNA interactions presumably provide obstacles to further digestion. The 166 bp and 146 bp particles are termed, respectively, chromatosomes and nucleosome core particles. The latter contain no H1, showing that the 10 bp at each end of the chromatosome DNA are involved in binding H1. X-ray diffraction of single crystals, combined with electron microscopy (Finch *et al.* 1977; Finch *et al.* 1981), and neutron diffraction (Bentley, Finch & Lewit-Bentley, 1981) have shown the core particle to be a slightly wedge-shaped disc, 11 nm in diameter and 5·5 nm high, containing two turns of DNA, with about 80 bp per turn. The relation between the nucleosome and its digestion products, the chromatosome and the nucleosome core particle, is shown in Fig. 1. The binding of H1 at the entry and exit points of the DNA on the nucleosome, through its central globular domain (see below) (Allan, Hartman, Crane-Robinson & Aviles, 1980), accounts for the frequent zig-zag appearance in electron micrographs of the nucleosome filament at low ionic strength, in contrast with a beads-on-a-string appearance of the H1-depleted filament (Thoma, Koller & Klug, 1979).

Although the resolution currently available in X-ray diffraction studies of the nucleosome core particle (Finch *et al.* 1981) may not be sufficient to distinguish between the individual histones, the positions of the histones have been deduced by combination of various lines of evidence. A low-resolution model for the core histone octamer, obtained from an image reconstruction analysis of regular aggregates of the protein free of DNA at high ionic strength (Klug *et al.* 1980), showed the octamer to be wedge-shaped, with a series of ridges on its surface forming a left-handed helical ramp (Fig. 2A). Assignment of the DNA to this ramp, as in Fig. 2(B,C), has since been shown to be correct by neutron diffraction studies of single crystals (Bentley *et al.* 1981). The histone–histone proximities determined by chemical cross-linking (Thomas & Kornberg, 1975*a,b*) and the order of the histones along the DNA determined by histone–DNA cross-linking (Mirzabekov, Shick, Belyavsky & Bavykin, 1978; Shick, Belyavsky, Bavykin, & Mirzabekov, 1980) were then used to assign regions of the octamer to particular histones, making the assumption that histones are single-domain proteins and taking into account the shape of the octamer. The histone assignment is shown in Fig. 2(B,C). Dissection of the octamer model according to the

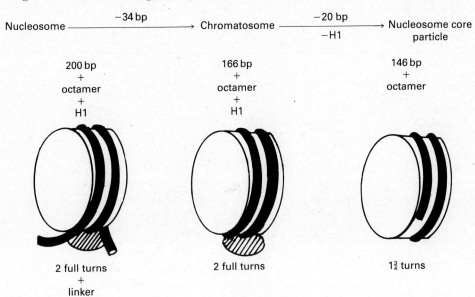

Fig. 1. The relationship between the nucleosome, and the chromatosome and core particle generated from it by 'trimming' with micrococcal nuclease.

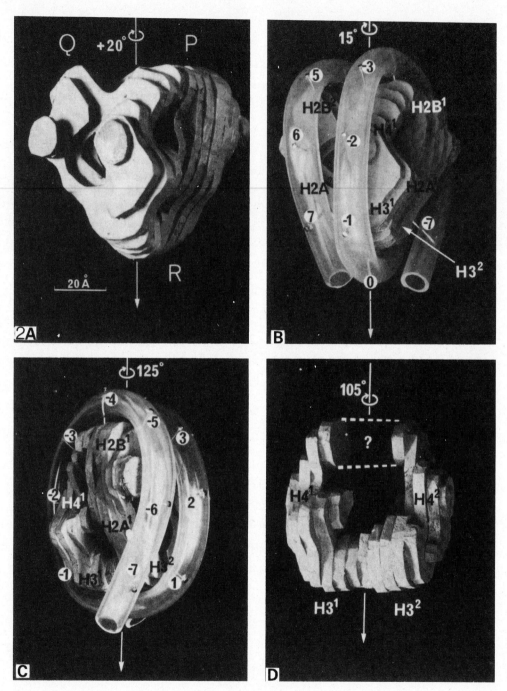

Fig. 2

known dissociation pattern for the octamer in solution, namely into a tetramer $(H3)_2(H4)_2$ and two H2A-H2B dimers, reveals that the tetramer has the form of a 'dislocated horseshoe' (Fig. 2D), and has a critical role in the nucleosome, as originally suggested (Kornberg & Thomas, 1974; Kornberg, 1974). Specifically, it organizes a central turn of about 80 bp of DNA, leaving two H2A-H2B dimers each to stabilize a further half-turn of DNA above and below the plane of the tetramer.

COILING OF THE NUCLEOSOME FILAMENT

Electron micrographs of metaphase chromosomes and of thin sections of interphase nuclei in the absence of chelating agents (see, e.g. Ris & Korenberg, 1979; Davies & Haynes, 1976), as well as of Miller spreads of fibres from metaphase chromosomes (Rattner & Hamkalo, 1978), suggest that the next level of folding of the nucleosome filament (the 'higher-order structure') is the 25–30 nm diameter fibre. The nature of this folding has been the subject of some debate but there is general agreement that H1 is essential. Most of the evidence supports the solenoid model, in which the 10 nm fibre is wound continuously into a contact helix with about six nucleosomes per turn (Finch & Klug, 1976). There is little hard evidence that discontinuous clusters of nucleosomes termed 'superbeads' have any structural significance, especially in view of their apparent size heterogeneity (for further discussion and references, see Butler & Thomas, 1980; Thomas, 1983; Butler, 1983). Since they are prevalent in electron micrographs of samples fixed at intermediate ionic strengths, superbeads could well be due to 'detached' non-interacting turns, or multiples of turns, of a solenoidal structure.

Most physical studies of chromatin folding have been carried out on higher-order structures reconstructed from the extended nucleosome filament (prepared at low ionic strength) by the addition of NaCl (60–100 mM) or $MgCl_2$ (0·3–3 mM). Electron microscopy of samples fixed at a range of ionic strengths from 1 to 100 mM shows gradual compaction of the zig-zag arrangement of nucleosomes through a family of more compact intermediate structures (perhaps open helices of decreasing pitch; perhaps contact helices with increasing numbers of nucleosomes per turn) to a fibre of 25–30 nm diameter, interpreted as a solenoid, at ionic strength 60 mM and above (Thoma *et al.* 1979). In the absence of H1 regular folding does not occur, pointing to a critical role of H1 in folding. The basic N-terminal regions of the core histones

Fig. 2. The structure of the nucleosome core particle. A. A model of the histone octamer obtained by image reconstruction analysis. The arrow indicates the dyad axis. P, Q and R are the three ridges (see text). B,C. Two views of the histone octamer structure with two turns of a DNA superhelix wound on it. (The DNA diameter is actually slightly larger than indicated.) Distances along the DNA are indicated by numbers -7 to $+7$, taking the dyad axis as origin, to mark the 14 repeats of the double helix contained in the 146 bp of DNA in the nucleosome core particle, which correspond to sites of DNase I attack. D. The $(H3)_2(H4)_2$ tetramer dissected out of the octamer model. The region marked '?' is a no-man's land that cannot be assigned unambiguously to one or other of the H4 and H2B molecules bordering it. The periphery of the tetramer constitutes about one turn, or somewhat less, of a flat left-handed helix. The views in A–D are related by rotation about the dyad axis as indicated. Adapted from Klug *et al.* (1980). (From Thomas (1983).)

(the 'tails'), some or all of which may be bound only loosely, if at all, in the core particle, may also be involved (Allan, Harborne, Rau & Gould, 1982) but definitive evidence for the role of these regions is at present lacking. The degree of hyperacetylation of the 'tails' that may be achieved by butyrate treatment of HeLa cells does not affect the ability of the chromatin to fold in an essentially normal fashion, although there is some indication that the degree of compaction might be marginally lower in the acetylated material (McGhee, Nickol, Felsenfeld & Rau, 1983).

It is an attractive possibility that higher-order structures of different stability may be generated using the repertoire of H1 variants that occur in a cell (whose proportions may change dramatically in different developmental stages and in different cell types), perhaps in conjunction with changes in repeat length, histone post-translational modification, and even core histone variants, the significance of all of which are poorly understood. Since unravelling of the higher-order structure is almost certainly a prerequisite for gene expression, an understanding of the factors that determine the stability of higher-order structures is likely to be an important step in understanding the relation of chromatin structure to gene activity. Electron microscopy of fixed samples tells us nothing about the *stability* of higher-order structures, and in an attempt to gain some insight into this, and other features of the higher-order structure, we have studied chromatin folding in solution. In two studies we compared chromatin from rat liver (a moderately active tissue), which has a repeat length of 200 bp and ~1 molecule of H1 per nucleosome, and chromatin from transcriptionally inert chicken erythrocytes. This has a repeat length of 212 bp, H5 has largely replaced H1, and there are 1·3 molecules of (H5+H1) per nucleosome (Bates & Thomas, 1981). Using increased sedimentation coefficient as an index of increased folding we studied a range of fragment sizes from very small to very large, over a wide range of ionic strengths from 5 mM to 120 mM (Butler & Thomas, 1980; Thomas & Butler, 1980; Bates, Butler, Pearson & Thomas, 1981). The sedimentation measurements confirmed a gradual compaction with increasing ionic strength as seen in electron micrographs. In addition, two discontinuities in behaviour revealed further details of the higher-order structure. In a series of short fragments, a change in behaviour observed for fragments about six nucleosomes long (Fig. 3) suggested that about six nucleosomes are required to form a complete unit of higher-order structure, and that this occurs at ionic strength ~25 mM. This transition at 6-mer was found both for rat liver chromatin (Butler & Thomas, 1980), and for chicken erythrocyte chromatin (Bates *et al.* 1981). A unit of higher-order structure is therefore the same, or very similar, in both cases – at least as assessed *in vitro* – despite the differences in repeat length and histone composition. The absence of any further discontinuity in the sedimentation behaviour of increasingly larger fragments up to 50 nucleosomes (see below) suggested strongly that the folding process is continuous, as would be expected for helical folding (e.g. into a solenoid). These sedimentation studies are therefore fully consistent with a solenoidal model for chromatin higher-order structure, with about six nucleosomes per turn.

A second discontinuity in behaviour is observed for much larger fragments (>50 nucleosomes for rat liver chromatin), namely a jump in sedimentation coefficient

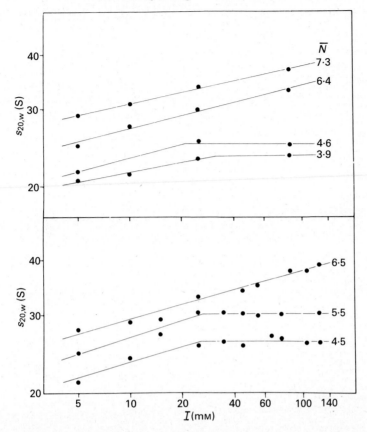

Fig. 3. Dependence of sedimentation coefficient upon ionic strength and and oligomer size for small nucleosome oligomers from chicken erythrocyte chromatin. $\bar{N}$ is the weight-average size of the oligomer, expressed in numbers of nucleosomes. (From Bates *et al*. (1981).)

between ionic strengths 45 mм and 55 mм as the ionic strength is increased (Fig. 4A) (Butler & Thomas, 1980; Thomas & Butler, 1980). When sedimentation coefficients are plotted as a function of oligomer size at two ionic strengths, one below and the other above that at which the jump is observed (Fig. 4B), it is apparent that the break in behaviour at 50 nucleosomes, which is the size for the onset of the jump, is at *low* ionic strength. In other words, large fragments at low ionic strength (<45 mм), but not at higher ionic strength, sediment slower than expected from extrapolation of the behaviour of smaller fragments (<50 nucleosomes). This has been attributed to failure of the interactions between the turns of longer solenoids to withstand hydro-dynamic shear, which has a greater effect on longer than on shorter solenoids with smaller axial ratios (Thomas & Butler, 1980; Bates *et al*. 1981).

Since the discontinuity in behaviour at ionic strength ~45 mм appears to reflect the 'break point' of the solenoid as the ionic strength is decreased, it may prove to be a useful parameter for comparison of the stability of higher-order structures of chromatins of different types (e.g. with different repeat lengths, H1 variants, and

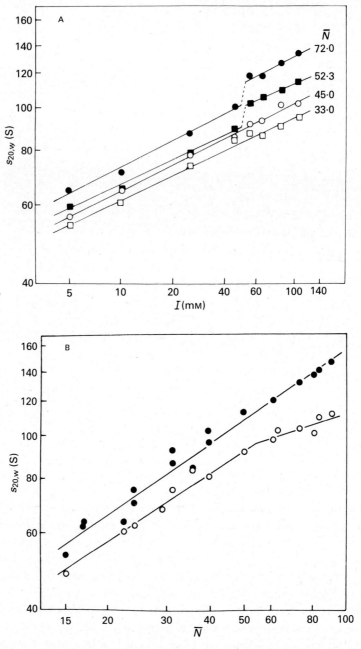

Fig. 4. Dependence of sedimentation coefficient upon ionic strength and oligomer size for nucleosome oligomers from rat liver chromatin. A. Ionic strength dependence for various sizes. B. Size dependence at ionic strengths 25 mM (○) and 65 mM (●) i.e. below and above the ionic strength for the jump. (From Thomas & Butler (1980).)

different states of histone post-translational modification). Some support for this comes from the finding that in chicken erythrocyte chromatin the critical size for the onset of the jump is about 10 nucleosomes (almost two turns of solenoid) longer than it is for rat liver chromatin (Bates *et al*. 1981). A more stable higher-order structure, which this suggests, is indeed consistent with the transcriptional inactivity of chicken erythrocyte chromatin. The extents to which the extreme H1 variant, H5, and the longer repeat length (212 bp), separately or in concert, contribute to this stability is not yet clear. Some aspects of the behaviour of H5 that may be relevant to its occurrence in more stable higher-order structures are discussed below (section entitled 'Exchange of H1 between chromatin fragments').

Further sedimentation studies suggest that the folding of chromatin (at least *in vitro*) may be relatively indifferent to the actual length of the linker DNA. Chromatin from cerebral cortex neurons (repeat length ~165 bp), which has no linker DNA, shows the same transition at ~6-mer as rat liver and chicken erythrocyte chromatins (Pearson, Butler & Thomas, 1983). Moreover, longer lengths (up to about 30-mer; larger fragments have not yet been examined) condense with increasing ionic strength into short solenoids indistinguishable from those from other sources. Since there is no linker, the DNA in this short-repeat chromatin must be wound directly from one nucleosome to the next, and this may be achieved by having the exit and entry points for the DNA on adjacent nucleosomes close together on the inside of the solenoid. In solenoids that *do* have linker DNA, but have the same gross morphology and sedimentation behaviour as short-repeat brain chromatin, the linker (and, possibly, by implication H1) seems likely to be on the *inside* of the solenoid i.e. in the central 'hole' (Pearson *et al*. 1983). Models in which a supercoiled linker connects exit and entry points (sealed by H1), which are alternately inside and outside on successive nucleosomes (McGhee, Rau, Charney & Felsenfeld, 1980), seem less likely, and are certainly ruled out for short-repeat brain chromatin where there is no linker DNA. The lack of any appreciable linker may account for the substoichiometric H1 content of this chromatin (Pearson, Bates, Prospero & Thomas, 1984), which can nonetheless form higher-order structures, at least *in vitro*; less linker means that less counterion (H1) is needed to offset electrostatic repulsions and permit folding. It remains to be seen, however, what the consequences are *in the cell* of a short DNA repeat and low H1 content – and whether these features perhaps lead to a less stable higher-order structure that correlates with the elevated transcriptional activity of neuronal nuclei as measured *in vitro*.

In summary, therefore, there is considerable evidence for the view that the 30 nm diameter chromatin fibre is a contact helix or solenoid with about six nucleosomes per turn. On the basis of the cross-striations seen in electron micrographs (Finch & Klug, 1976), and the 11 nm reflection in the X-ray pattern of folded chromatin fibres (Sperling & Klug, 1977), it has been proposed that the disk-shaped chromatosomes are arranged in edge-to-edge contact in the solenoid, with their faces projecting radially from the solenoid axis, and aligned roughly parallel to the axis, as shown in Fig. 5 (Thoma *et al*. 1979). The results of electric dichroism studies (Lee, Mandelkern & Crothers, 1981; McGhee *et al*. 1980; Yabuki, Dattagupta & Crothers, 1982) and neutron scattering studies (Suau, Bradbury & Baldwin, 1979) are largely in accord with this picture, as are earlier laser-light-scattering studies (Campbell, Cotter & Pardon, 1978). The internal location of H1 and linker DNA shown in Fig. 5 is

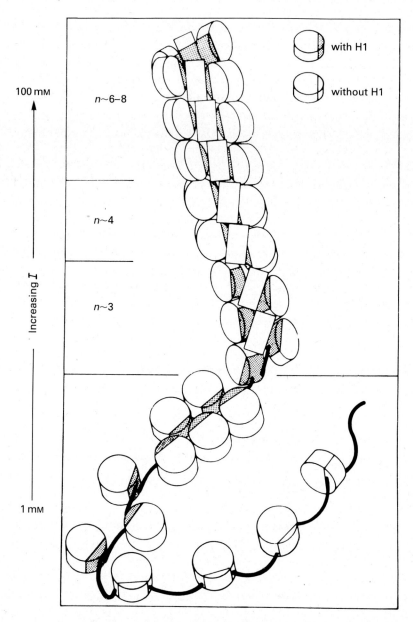

Fig. 5. A model for chromatin condensation. An idealized drawing of helical superstructures formed by chromatin containing H1 with increasing ionic strength. The open zig-zag of nucleosomes (bottom left) closes up to form helices with increasing numbers of nucleosomes per turn (n). The solenoid formed at high ionic strength probably has ~six nucleosomes per turn (see text). When H1 is absent (bottom right), no zig-zags or definite higher-order structures are found. (From Thoma *et al.* (1979).)

certainly compatible with the conclusions drawn above from the studies of three different types of chromatin, which showed gross similarities in their folding behaviour despite considerable diversity in linker length, and H1-type and content. The role and arrangement of H1 molecules in the superstructure will be discussed in greater detail below.

H I PROXIMITIES IN CHROMATIN

Some years ago we reported that H1 forms cross-linked homopolymers very readily on treatment of nuclei or chromatin with bifunctional amino-group reagents such as bisimidoesters (Fig. 6), whereas no such polymers are observed for H1 free in solution, indicating that the regions of the molecules that are cross-linked in chromatin are in close proximity (within 12 Å, or less, of each other) (Thomas & Khabaza, 1980). The H1 polymers also become cross-linked to several of the core histones, giving rise to the bands labelled $(H1)_n-X$ in Fig. 6. Close proximity between H1 molecules is incorporated into the model proposed for the solenoid (Thoma *et al.* 1979), and salt-driven helix formation by H1 was suggested as a possible driving force controlling solenoid formation. Evidence for a salt-induced conformational change in H1 (Smerdon & Isenberg, 1976), and for a change from a non-cooperative to a cooperative interaction with DNA at ionic strength 20–40 mM (Renz & Day,

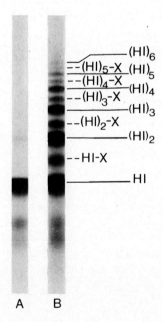

A   B

Fig. 6. H1 proximities in rat liver chromatin revealed by chemical cross-linking. Chromatin was cross-linked with dimethylsuberimidate at pH 8·5 and the H1 extracted with 5 % perchloric acid and analysed in SDS/polyacrylamide gels. (For details see Thomas & Khabaza (1980).) A. Cross-linking at ionic strength ~520 mM; H1 is dissociated and is not cross-linked. B. Cross-linking at ionic strength ~20 mM; H1 is bound in chromatin and becomes cross-linked to other H1 molecules and to core histones (X).

1976) gave some support to this idea, since 20 mM is the ionic strength at which higher-order structures begin to form. However, cautious interpretation of these experiments might be wise until, for example, the possibility that the effects are due to the renaturation of denatured (acid-extracted) H1 has been excluded.

The formation of cross-linked H1 polymers for chromatin in the extended state at low ionic strength, and for short oligonucleosomes, as well as for condensed chromatin and nuclei, suggests strongly that H1 molecules are already in close proximity or in contact *along* the nucleosome filament and do not make contact exclusively within the solenoid. However, additional types of interactions between H1 molecules (or H5 molecules in the case of chicken erythrocytes) might form in the folded state, and this has been examined by an analysis of the regions of the molecules cross-linked in the extended and condensed states. H1 and H5 both consist of a central globular domain (G) of about 80 residues flanked by two basic regions (N and C) that are less structured, at least in H1 (H5) in solution, and it is useful to focus attention on these different regions in attempting to identify possible changes in the nature of the H1–H1 (H5–H5) cross-links.

The strategy that we (A. C. Lennard & J. O. Thomas, unpublished results) and others (Nikolaev, Glotov, Itkes & Severin, 1981; Nikolaev *et al.* 1983) have adopted is to use cleavable (S–S containing) cross-linking agents, and to examine cross-linked dimers of H5 or H1. Cuts are introduced specifically with proteases (e.g. chymotrypsin cuts at the single phenylalanine almost at the junction of the globular domain and C-terminal tail giving NG and C fragments), and fragments cross-linked to each other are identified by 'diagonal' two-dimensional electrophoresis in sodium dodecyl sulphate (SDS)/polyacrylamide gels, with thiolysis of the cross-links between the two dimensions. In the case of *nuclei*, in which the chromatin is condensed, cross-links were found between all combinations of the half-molecules, namely C–C, NG–NG and NG–C (Nikolaev *et al.* 1981; A. C. Lennard & J. O. Thomas, unpublished results). The pattern was no simpler for isolated extended chromatin (Nikolaev *et al.* 1983; A. C. Lennard & J. O. Thomas, unpublished results), suggesting a random orientation (head-to-tail, head-to-head, tail-to-tail) of H1 or H5 molecules along the nucleosome filament. However, it seemed to us possible that random collisions in solution, for example between distant parts of the same chain, arising from the inherent flexibility of the nucleosome filament, or incipient formation of higher-order structures, might account for this, so we examined the cross-linked H5 dimers formed from fractionated dinucleosomes and found only NG–C cross-linked products, implying a head-to-tail orientation of successive H5 molecules along the nucleosome filament, and suggesting that C–C, and to a lesser extent NG–NG contacts are formed upon folding. Results obtained with short ('zero length') cross-linking reagents suggest that in beef kidney nuclei the C-terminal regions of adjacent H1 molecules are actually within 2 Å of each other, as are adjacent NG and C-terminal regions; NG–NG contacts were not detected (Ring & Cole, 1983). Precisely how the folding brings different regions of H1 into proximity remains for the moment unclear, as do the consequences of site-specific H1 phosphorylations in *S* and *M* phases of the cell cycle (Ajiro *et al.* 1981). However, the architectural details revealed by the use of cross-linking reagents of different chemical types and span lengths will be invaluable in any attempts to construct models.

What is the possible structural significance of H1–H1 (or H5–H5) contacts unique to the folded state? Such contacts might be important for its stability; higher-order structures of different stability might then result from the presence of different H1 subtypes produced, for example, at different developmental stages. The idea of 'lattices' of H1-subtypes, giving rise to regions of differential stability along a chromosome is attractive, but the distribution of H1 subtypes in the chromosome remains for the moment unknown.

EXCHANGE OF H1 BETWEEN CHROMATIN FRAGMENTS

At the ionic strengths required to condense chromatin with monovalent cations, for example at the Na^+ concentrations used in the electron microscopy and sedimentation studies described above, H1 molecules migrate rapidly and freely between chromatin fragments. This was first shown (Caron & Thomas, 1981) by mixing two chromatin fragments of different length (one radiolabelled *in vivo* with [^{14}C]lysine and the other unlabelled), separating them by centrifugation in sucrose density gradients, and analysing the histone content by sodium dodecyl sulphate/polyacrylamide gel electrophoresis and fluorography. Unlike the core histones, which showed no tendency to leave their parent fragments, the H1 molecules had already begun to rearrange at an

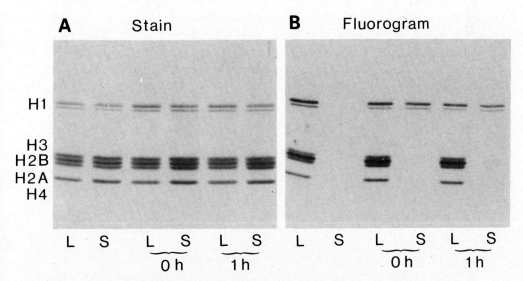

Fig. 7. Exchange of H1 between two chromatin fragments from P3K mouse myeloma cells. The longer fragment (L) is labelled with [^{14}C]lysine and is ~11 nucleosomes long. The short fragment (S) is unlabelled and is ~3·5 nucleosomes long. In this experiment (see text) the fragments were mixed at ionic strength 75 mM, separated again by sedimentation in sucrose density gradients and the histones analysed in SDS/polyacrylamide gels. A, The stained gel; and B, its fluorogram. The first two tracks contain the starting materials. The next two pairs contain the fragments subjected to centrifugation immediately after mixing (0 h), and those separated after 1 h. (From Caron & Thomas (1981).)

ionic strength of 30 mM, and had equilibrated completely between the two fragments at ionic strength 75 mM (Fig. 7), as shown by the distribution of ^{14}C-labelled H1, without change in the overall H1 content as determined by staining intensity in a gel.

Is there a paradox in that higher-order structures are H1-dependent, and yet – at the ionic strengths required for formation of higher-order structures with monovalent cations – H1 molecules exchange rapidly between sites? There is no contradiction, since the overall structure is likely to be maintained provided most of the H1 binding sites are occupied most of the time. An analogous situation exists in the two-layer disk aggregate of tobacco mosaic virus protein, in which a dynamic microequilibrium exists between free subunits and those assembled in disks, even though the macroequilibrium between the assembled disk and its component subunits strongly favours the assembled structure (Butler & Durham, 1977). Exchange of the components of an assembled structure between different sites in the structure is therefore certainly not impossible.

Does exchange occur between heterologous as well as homologous H1 types? This may be relevant to the investigation of the distribution of H1 variants in chromatin and in particular to the question of whether there is clustering of H1 types in the chromosome, which might perhaps be obliterated by exchange. We chose to examine H5 in chicken erythrocyte chromatin as an extreme H1 variant, which is bound more tightly to chromatin than is H1, as indicated by the higher ionic strength required to wash it off ($\sim$0·7 M compared with $\sim$0·5 M for H1). We also wondered whether the higher stability of chicken erythroctye chromatin discussed above might not be due to an absence of migration of H5 between sites. However, as Fig. 8, for example, shows, H1 and H5 from chicken erythrocyte chromatin and H1 from rat liver chromatin show broadly the same exchange characteristics with respect to ionic strength as the homologous H1 molecules studied earlier (Thomas & Rees, 1983). All four H1 types (two from rat chromatin, two from chicken) begin to exchange at a slightly lower ionic strength (25 mM) than H5 (35 mM); beyond 75 mM there is no appreciable change in the distribution of H1 or H5. Similar results were found when the rat fragment was the shorter one and the chicken the longer.

Although there was no net gain of lysine-rich histones by either fragment – the phenomenon being simply one of exchange – certain fragment combinations clearly revealed a small but definite preference of H5 for fragments long enough to form higher-order structures. This was reflected in a higher H5:H1 ratio in the longer fragment. Fig. 9 shows the results of exchange between a long rat liver chromatin fragment and a series of short fragments from chicken erythrocytes. Most of the H5 from trinucleosomes has migrated to the long rat fragment in exchange for H1, so the H5:H1 ratio is higher for the rat fragment. The effect is less apparent when the chicken fragment is seven nucleosomes long, possibly because the formation of a stable element of higher-order structure at this fragment length (see above) leads to binding modes for H5 approaching those in longer higher-order structures.

Differences between H1 and H5 were also revealed in competition experiments between occupied H1 or H5 binding sites on chromatin fragments from rat liver or chicken erythrocytes and empty sites on H1-depleted rat chromatin (Thomas & Rees,

A

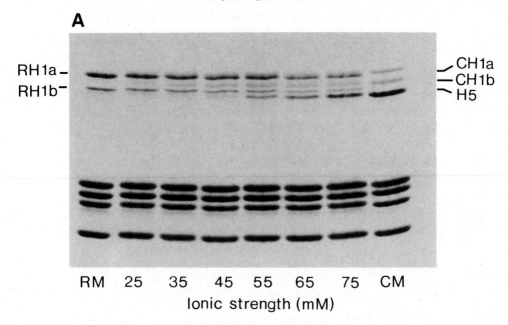

RH1a —

RH1b —

CH1a
CH1b
H5

RM   25   35   45   55   65   75   CM

Ionic strength (mM)

B

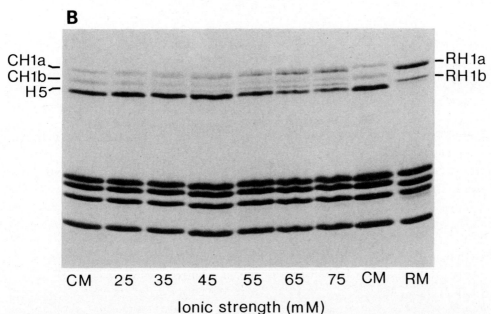

CH1a
CH1b —
H5

RH1a
RH1b

CM   25   35   45   55   65   75   CM   RM

Ionic strength (mM)

Fig. 8. Exchange of H1 and H5 between rat liver chromatin and chicken erythrocyte chromatin as a function of ionic strength. A long rat chromatin fragment and a short chicken fragment were mixed at various ionic strengths, separated by sedimentation in sucrose gradients, and the histone contents analysed in SDS/polyacrylamide gels. A. The rat fragments; B, the chicken fragments. RM and CM are the original rat or chicken fragments run as markers. (From Thomas & Rees (1983).)

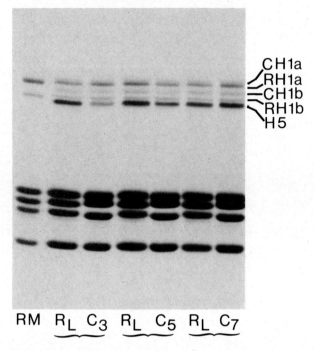

CH1a
RH1a
CH1b
RH1b
H5

RM   R$_L$ C$_3$ R$_L$ C$_5$ R$_L$ C$_7$

Fig. 9. Exchange of H1 and H5 between long rat liver chromatin and short chicken erythrocyte chromatin fragments of various lengths. The bracketed tracks in the SDS/polyacrylamide gel show the histones in the pairs of fragments separated in a sucrose gradient after mixing at ionic strength 75 mM. The rat fragment contains ~43 nucleosomes (weight-average size) and the chicken fragment 3, 5 or 7 nucleosomes as shown. RM is a rat histone marker. (From Thomas & Rees (1983).)

1983). Rat H1 does not distinguish between the two types of site and equilibrates freely, whereas H5 discriminates in favour of sites on native chromatin. This is so even when the chicken fragments are too short to form higher-order structures, probably due to the absence of high-affinity 'higher-order' sites on the H1-depleted chromatin, which cannot fold. In contrast, when the challenging rat fragment had not been depleted of H1, the H5 was equally shared as described earlier (Fig. 8); H5 thus seems to bind best to preformed binding sites. This may reflect the situation during the terminal stages of erythropoiesis, when H5 largely replaces H1 in erythrocyte chromatin. H5 may be specially designed to compete successfully with H1 for binding-sites in the higher-order structure, thus stabilizing the structure and ensuring the transcriptional inactivity of chromatin in the mature avian erythrocyte. This increased stabilization must presumably relate in some way to the molecular differences between H1 and H5 (a shorter N-terminal basic region, a more arginine-rich C-terminal region and a slightly more basic central globular domain in H5), and may possibly be mediated through H5–H5 interactions (see above), although at present this is purely speculative. H5 is an extreme variant of H1. Subtle differences probably also exist between more homologous H1 types, with possible implications for differential stability of higher-order structures.

The finding that H1 and its variants migrate between sites in chromatin at ionic strengths well below physiological and well within the normal working range, has considerable practical implications – not least for the feasibility of studies (chemical, immunochemical) to determine the distribution of H1 variants along the chromatin fibre. Exchange might lead to rearrangement, although this might not occur if 'lattices' of H1 molecules in contact exist in chromatin, since energetic considerations might constrain an H1 of a given type to return to its parent lattice.

Although, as argued earlier, the gross morphology of higher-order structures is not affected by exchange of H1 (H5), it became important for our purposes that we should be able to study higher-order structures in various ways under conditions in which H1 cannot exchange and thus possibly rearrange. We have recently found that this is possible, if the higher-order structures are condensed at low ionic strength with submillimolar concentrations of Mg^{2+} instead of with 70 mM-NaCl (J. O. Thomas & C. Rees, unpublished results). The possibility that exchange of H1 subtypes occurs during the conditions of nuclear isolation must also be confronted – although (see above) it will not necessarily lead to rearrangement – but it is less easy to test convincingly. Mg^{2+}-containing isolation buffers at low ionic strength, which are commonly used, seem likely to be fairly safe, in view of the findings for chromatin. However, buffers approaching physiological ionic strength may merit closer scrutiny.

There is some indication that bound H1 molecules are naturally in dynamic equilibrium within the cell. For example, there is strongly suggestive evidence for exchange of H1 and H5 between the rat myoblast nucleus and the chicken erythrocyte nucleus of a heterokaryon generated by cell fusion, which may be linked to the mutual and reciprocal alterations in genetic activity of the nuclei (Appels, Bolund & Ringertz, 1974; Linder, Zuckerman & Ringertz, 1982). Redistribution of H1 molecules may also be involved in the 're-modelling' of chromatin that must occur in nuclei from differentiated cells after microinjection into enucleated *Xenopus* eggs (Gurdon, Laskey & Reeves, 1975), and in the reprogramming of gene expression in somatic nuclei injected into *Xenopus* oocytes (De Robertis & Gurdon, 1977). A naturally dynamic occupancy of H1 sites would indeed facilitate such effects, although the migration of H1 to heterologous chromatin is not obviously compatible with the 'lattice argument' mentioned earlier.

CONCLUSION

The structures of the nucleosome and the nucleosome filament are known in broad outline and in the next year or two we can expect a structure for the nucleosome core particle at 5 Å resolution*. The next level of folding is almost certainly helical coiling, probably into a contact helix or solenoid with about six nucleosomes per turn. Beyond this, our detailed knowledge of this level of folding is rather limited. What is the relationship between one nucleosome and the next in the higher-order structure? What is the path of the linker DNA? Is the suggestion regarding an internal location

---

* See note added in proof.

for the linker correct? Is H1 located inside or outside the solenoid? What are the roles of its N- and C-terminal basic regions in higher-order structure? And does the globular domain of H1 do any more than seal the two turns of DNA around the nucleosome? Is there a role for the basic N-terminal regions of the core histones in higher-order structure? These are just a few of the immediate questions to which answers are needed before we can build a detailed model for the solenoid.

The location, exposed or otherwise, in the solenoid of the basic N-terminal regions of the core histones and the C-terminal half of H1 are of some interest, since these regions contain sites of enzymic modifications that might modulate the stability of the structure. Antibodies to these regions, particularly the N-terminal 20 residues of H2B and the C-terminal 'half' of H1, are common in the sera of patients with systemic lupus erythematosus (Hardin & Thomas, 1983; Thomas, Wilson & Hardin, 1984) and these should prove useful probes for the accessibility or otherwise of these regions in the higher-order structure.

A more detailed understanding of the higher-order structure of chromatin in its inactive state will surely provide a firm basis for understanding the early events of gene activation, which probably include those involved in relaxation of the solenoid to the nucleosome filament. Further alterations to the structure that may be necessary to permit active transcription fall outside the scope of this article.

Note added in proof. The structure of the nucleosome core particle at 7Å resolution has recently been published (T. J. Richmond, J. T. Finch, B. Rushton, D. Rhodes & A. Klug (1984). *Nature, Lond.* **311**, 532–537).

REFERENCES

AJIRO, K., BORUN, T. W., SHULMAN, S. D., MCFADDEN, G. M. & COHEN, L. H. (1981). Comparison of the structures of human histones 1A and 1B and their intramolecular phosphorylation sites during the HeLa S-3 cell cycle. *Biochemistry* **20**, 1454–1464.
ALLAN, J., HARBORNE, N., RAU, D. C. & GOULD, H. (1982). Participation of core histone 'tails' in the stabilization of the chromatin solenoid. *J. Cell Biol.* **93**, 285–297.
ALLAN, J., HARTMAN, P. G., CRANE-ROBINSON, C. & AVILES, F. X. (1980). The structure of histone H1 and its location in chromatin. *Nature, Lond.* **288**, 675–679.
APPELS, R., BOLUND, L. & RINGERTZ, N. R. (1974). Biochemical analysis of reactivated chick erythrocyte nuclei isolated from chick/HeLa heterokaryons. *J. molec. Biol.* **87**, 339–355.
BATES, D. L., BUTLER, P. J. G., PEARSON, E. C. & THOMAS, J. O. (1981). Stability of the higher-order structure of chicken erythrocyte chromatin in solution. *Eur. J. Biochem.* **119**, 469–476.
BATES, D. L. & THOMAS, J. O. (1981). Histones H1 and H5: one or two molecules per nucleosome? *Nucl. Acids Res.* **9**, 5883–5894.
BENTLEY, G. A., FINCH, J. T. & LEWIT-BENTLEY, A. (1981). Neutron diffraction studies on crystals of nucleosome cores using contrast variation. *J. molec. Biol.* **145**, 771–784.
BUTLER, P. J. G. (1983). The folding of chromatin. *CRC Crit. Rev. Biochem.* **15**, 57–91.
BUTLER, P. J. G. & DURHAM, A. C. H. (1977). Tobacco mosaic virus protein aggregation and the virus assembly. *Adv. Protein Chem.* **31**, 187–251.
BUTLER, P. J. G. & THOMAS, J. O. (1980). Changes in chromatin folding in solution. *J. molec. Biol.* **140**, 505–529.
CAMPBELL, A. M., COTTER, R. I. & PARDON, J. F. (1978). Light scattering measurements supporting helical structures for chromatin in solution. *Nucl. Acids Res.* **5**, 1571–1580.
CARON, F. & THOMAS, J. O. (1981). Exchange of histone H1 between segments of chromatin. *J. molec. Biol.* **146**, 513–537.

DAVIES, H. G., MURRAY, A. B. & WALMSLEY, M. E. (1974). Electron-microscope observations on the organization of the nucleus in chicken erythrocytes and a superunit thread hypothesis for chromosome structure. *J. Cell Sci.* **16**, 261–299.

DE ROBERTIS, E. M. & GURDON, J. B. (1977). Gene activation in somatic nuclei after injection into amphibian oocytes. *Proc. natn. Acad. Sci. U.S.A.* **74**, 2470–2474.

FINCH, J. T., BROWN, R. S., RHODES, D., RICHMOND, T., RUSHTON, B., LUTTER, L. C. & KLUG, A. (1981). X-ray diffraction study of a new crystal form of the nucleosome core showing higher resolution. *J. molec. Biol.* **145**, 757–769.

FINCH, J. T. & KLUG, A. (1976). Solenoidal model for superstructure in chromatin. *Proc. natn. Acad. Sci. U.S.A.* **73**, 1897–1901.

FINCH, J. T., LUTTER, L. C., RHODES, D., BROWN, R. S., RUSHTON, B., LEVITT, M. & KLUG, A. (1977). Structure of nucleosome core particles of chromatin. *Nature, Lond.* **269**, 29–36.

GURDON, J. B., LASKEY, R. A. & REEVES, O. R. (1975). The developmental capacity of nuclei transplanted from keratinized skin cells of adult frogs. *J. Embryol. exp. Morph.* **34**, 93–112.

HARDIN, J. A. & THOMAS, J. O. (1983). Antibodies to histones in systemic lupus erythematosus: Localization of prominent autoantigens on histones H1 and H2B. *Proc. natn. Acad. Sci. U.S.A.* **80**, 7410–7414.

IGO-KEMENES, T., HÖRZ, W. & ZACHAU, H. G. (1982). Chromatin. *A. Rev. Biochem.* **51**, 89–121.

KLUG, A., RHODES, D., SMITH, J., FINCH, J. T. & THOMAS, J. O. (1980). A low resolution structure for the histone core of the nucleosome. *Nature, Lond.* **287**, 509–516.

KORNBERG, R. D. (1974). Chromatin structure: a repeating unit of histones and DNA. *Science* **184**, 868–871.

KORNBERG, R. D. (1977). Structure of chromatin. *A. Rev. Biochem.* **46**, 931–954.

KORNBERG, R. D. & THOMAS, J. O. (1974). Chromatin structure: oligomers of the histones. *Science* **184**, 865–868.

LEE, K. S. & CROTHERS, D. M. (1982). Influence of ionic strength on the dichroism properties of polynucleosomal fibres. *Biopolymers* **21**, 101–116.

LEE, K. S., MANDELKERN, M. & CROTHERS, D. M. (1981). Solution structural studies of chromatin fibres. *Biochemistry* **20**, 1438–1445.

LINDER, S., ZUCKERMAN, S. H. & RINGERTZ, N. R. (1982). Distribution of histone H5 in chicken erythrocyte – mammalian cell heterokaryons. *Expl Cell Res.* **140**, 464–468.

MCGHEE, J. D. & FELSENFELD, G. (1980). Nucleosome structure. *A. Rev. Biochem.* **49**, 1115–1156.

MCGHEE, J. D., NICKOL, J. M., FELSENFELD, G. & RAU, D. C. (1983). Histone hyperacetylation has little effect on the higher order folding of chromatin. *Nucl. Acids Res.* **11**, 4065–4075.

MCGHEE, J. D., RAU, D. C., CHARNEY, E. & FELSENFELD, G. (1980). Orientation of the nucleosome within the higher order structure of chromatin. *Cell* **22**, 87–96.

MIRZABEKOV, A. D., SHICK, V. V., BELYAVSKY, A. V. & BAVYKIN, S. G. (1978). Primary organization of nucleosome core particles of chromatin: sequence of histone arrangement along DNA. *Proc. natn. Acad. Sci. U.S.A.* **75**, 4184–4188.

NIKOLAEV, L. G., GLOTOV, B. O., DASHKEVICH, V. K., BARBASHOV, S. F. & SEVERIN, E. S. (1983). Mutual arrangement of histone H1 molecules in extended chromatin. *FEBS Lett.* **163**, 66–68.

NIKOLAEV, L. G., GLOTOV, B. O., ITKES, A. V. & SEVERIN, E. S. (1981). Mutual arrangement of histone H1 molecules in chromatin of intact nuclei. *FEBS Lett.* **125**, 20–24.

PEARSON, E. C., BATES, D. L., PROSPERO, T. D. & THOMAS, J. O. (1984). Neuronal nuclei and glial nuclei from mammalian cerebral cortex: nucleosome repeat lengths, DNA contents and H1 contents. *Eur. J. Biochem.* **144**, 330–360.

PEARSON, E. C., BUTLER, P. J. G. & THOMAS, J. O. (1983). Higher-order structure of short-repeat chromatin. *EMBO J.* **2**, 1367–1372.

RATTNER, J. B. & HAMKALO, B. A. (1978). Higher order structure in metaphase chromosomes. I. The 250 Å fiber. *Chromosoma* **69**, 363–372.

RENZ, M. & DAY, L. A. (1976). Transition from non-cooperative to cooperative and selective binding of histone H1 to DNA. *Biochemistry* **15**, 3220–3228.

RING, R. & COLE, R. D. (1983). Close contacts between H1 histone molecules in nuclei. *J. biol. Chem.* **258**, 15361–15364.

RIS, H. & KORENBERG, J. (1979). Chromosome structure and levels of chromosome organization. In *Cell Biology*, vol. 2 (ed. D. M. Prescott & L. Goldstein), pp. 267–361. New York: Academic Press.

SHICK, V. V., BELYAVSKY, A. V., BAVYKIN, S. G. & MIRZABEKOV, A. D. (1980). Primary organization of the nucleosome core particles: sequential arrangement of histones along DNA. *J. molec. Biol.* **139**, 491–517.

SMERDON, M. J. & ISENBERG, I. (1976). Conformational changes in sub-fractions of calf thymus histone H1. *Biochemistry* **15**, 4233–4242.

SPERLING, L. & KLUG, A. (1977). X-ray studies on 'native' chromatin. *J. molec. Biol.* **112**, 253–263.

SUAU, P., BRADBURY, E. M. & BALDWIN, J. P. (1979). Higher-order structures of chromatin in solution. *Eur. J. Biochem.* **97**, 593–602.

THOMA, F., KOLLER, TH. & KLUG, A. (1979). Involvement of histone H1 in the organization of the nucleosome and of salt-dependent superstructures of chromatin. *J. Cell Biol.* **83**, 403–427.

THOMAS, J. O. (1983). Chromatin structure and superstructure. In *Eukaryotic Genes: Their Structure, Function and Regulation* (ed. N. Maclean, S. P. Gregory & R. A. Flavell), pp. 9–30. London: Academic Press.

THOMAS, J. O. &BUTLER, P. J. G. (1980). Size-dependence of a stable higher-order structure of chromatin. *J. molec. Biol.* **144**, 89–93.

THOMAS, J. O. & KHABAZA, A. J. A. (1980). Cross-linking of histone H1 in chromatin. *Eur. J. Biochem.* **112**, 501–511.

THOMAS, J. O. & KORNBERG, R. D. (1975a). An octamer of histones in chromatin and free in solution. *Proc. natn. Acad. Sci. U.S.A.* **72**, 2626–2630.

THOMAS, J. O. & KORNBERG, R. D. (1975b). Cleavable cross-links in the analysis of histone–histone associations. *FEBS Lett.* **58**, 353–358.

THOMAS, J. O. & REES, C. (1983). Exchange of histones H1 and H5 between chromatin fragments. A preference of H5 for higher-order structures. *Eur. J. Biochem.* **134**, 109–115.

THOMAS, J. O., WILSON, C. M. & HARDIN, J. A. (1984). The major core histone antigenic determinants in systemic lupus erythematosus are in the trypsin-sensitive regions. *FEBS Lett.* **169**, 90–96.

YABUKI, H., DATTAGUPTA, N. & CROTHERS, D. M. (1982). Orientation of nucleosomes in the thirty-nanometer chromatin fiber. *Biochemistry* **21**, 5015–5020.

J. Cell Sci. Suppl. 1, 21–29 (1984)
Printed in Great Britain © The Company of Biologists Limited 1984

DNA SUPERCOILING AND ITS EFFECTS ON THE STRUCTURE OF DNA

JAMES C. WANG

Department of Biochemistry and Molecular Biology, Harvard University,
7 Divinity Avenue, Cambridge, Massachusetts 02138, U.S.A.

SUMMARY

In prokaryotic organisms, there is strong evidence that the DNA is underwound or negatively supercoiled. The degree of supercoiling of intracellular DNA is less certain, and various estimates that can be made from existing data place the specific linking difference (superhelical density) of intracellular DNA in prokaryotes around -0.04. The effects of negative supercoiling on DNA structure are illustrated by the flipping of alternating C-G or T-G sequences from right-handed *B*-helical form to the left-handed *Z*-helical form. For a plasmid containing a 42 base-pair alternating C-G insert, the *B*-to-*Z* transition occurs at a specific linking difference of -0.031 in a dilute aqueous buffer; the same transition occurs at a specific linking difference of -0.041 for a plasmid containing a 42 base-pair alternating T-G insert. The probing of the structure of a particular sequence of intracellular DNA is discussed.

INTRODUCTION

In discussing the higher order structure of chromatin, the term 'supercoiling' has two connotations. In one it describes the spatial path of the DNA: the coiling of the DNA around the histone core in a nucleosome, the coiling of a string of nucleosomes into a superstructure, etc. In the other it describes torsional and flexural changes of the DNA when its structure and spatial path deviate from that assumed by the most stable structure of DNA when it is associated with other small and large molecules in the cellular milieu. It is the latter that will be discussed below.

THE SUPERCOILED STATE OF DNA IN PROKARYOTES

In a bacterium, it is generally accepted that the DNA is negatively supercoiled. Here 'negatively supercoiled' specifically refers to a lower than expected linking number. The linking number of closed circular DNA or a constrained DNA loop is dependent on both its helical structure and its spatial path (see Crick, 1976; Bauer, Crick & White, 1980), both of which are influenced by the association of various cellular contents to DNA. Although it has been known since 1965 that closed duplex DNA rings from natural sources have linking numbers lower than those expected for pure DNA (reviewed by Bauer, 1978), for a decade it remained uncertain whether the differences could be accounted for by the binding of proteins or other cellular contents. The discovery of DNA gyrase, an ATP-dependent enzyme that catalyses the negative supercoiling of DNA *in vitro*, however, suggests strongly that intracellular bacterial DNA is in a metastable 'underwound' state (Gellert, Mizuuchi, O'Dea & Nash, 1976a). This implication is fully supported by the finding that inhibition of the enzyme by drugs or the use of temperature-sensitive mutants results in an increase in the linking number of intracellular DNA (Gellert, O'Dea, Itoh & Tomizawa, 1976b; Drlica & Snyder, 1978; Orr & Staudenbauer, 1981; Lockshon & Morris, 1983).

Additional evidence supporting the underwound state of intracellular DNA comes from studies of psoralen binding to intact and broken DNA *in vivo* (Pettijohn & Pfenninger, 1980; Sinden, Carlson & Pettijohn, 1980). Psoralen, which penetrates cells readily, can form covalent adducts with DNA when irradiated with ultraviolet (u.v.) light. Under a given set of conditions of irradiation, the amount of covalent adducts formed is proportional to the amount of total DNA-bound psoralen; thus the relative levels of psoralen binding *in vivo* can be determined by the relative amounts of covalent adducts formed during irradiation. Since the binding of psoralen reduces the helical twist of DNA (Wiesehahn & Hearst, 1978), the thermodynamics of DNA supercoiling predict a higher affinity of psoralen for intact intracellular DNA if it is underwound, relative to that of intracellular DNA broken by γ-ray irradiation. Pettijohn & Pfenninger (1980) found that the intact DNA binds psoralen better by about a factor of 2.

Genetic evidence suggests that the degree of negative supercoiling *in vivo* is maintained by a dynamic balance between the actions of DNA gyrase and DNA topoisomerase I. It is found that mutations in *top*A, the structural gene encoding DNA topoisomerase I, is often accompanied by compensatory mutations in *gyr*A or *gyr*B, the structural genes encoding the gyrase subunits. These compensatory mutations are believed to be down-mutations that decrease the intracellular level of gyrase activity to counterbalance the reduction in topoisomerase I activity (DiNardo *et al.* 1982; Pruss, Manes & Drlica, 1982).

Although the genetic finding of compensatory mutants supports the idea that intracellular supercoiling is regulated by a dynamic balance of the actions of topoisomerases, the very existence of compensatory mutants makes it difficult to test the idea directly through measurements of the linking number of intracellular DNAs in mutants with a single defective topoisomerase. We have therefore turned to the construction of mutants in which DNA topoisomerase I is under the control of a regulated promoter (Wang, Peck & Becherer, 1983).

In one experiment, the promoter of *Escherichia coli* DNA topoisomerase I is replaced by the isopropyl-β-D-thiogalactoside (IPTG)-induceable *lac* promoter, and the gene is cloned into a single-copy plasmic pDF41 (Kahn *et al.* 1979). An *E. coli* $cysB^+trpE^-$ strain is then transformed with the plasmid. In the presence of IPTG, so that the plasmid *top*A gene is turned on, the chromosomal copy of the *top*A gene is deleted by phage Pl transduction, using Pl grown on strain DM700 ($\Delta cysB\Delta top$-$A trpE^+$) and selecting for $TrpE^+$ transductants. The transductants are then checked for the *cys*B marker. Because *top*A is located between *cys*B and *trp*E (Wang & Becherer, 1983), transductants that are $cysB^-trpE^+$ have acquired the $\Delta cysB\Delta topA$-$trpE^+$ region of DM700. Furthermore, since a functional *top*A gene is present on the plasmid throughout these genetic manipulations, no compensatory mutations occur.

We can therefore examine the effect on the degree of supercoiling of intracellular DNA when IPTG is removed.

Using pACYC184 (Chang & Cohen, 1978) as a test plasmid in the strain described above, it is found that its negative specific linking difference $-(\alpha-\alpha^\circ)/\alpha^\circ$, where α is the linking number of the DNA and α° is that of the pure DNA when completely relaxed, is increased by about 0·02 when IPTG is removed (L. Snyder & J. C. Wang, unpublished results). Detailed results will be reported elsewhere.

The above result is consistent with the involvement of multiple topoisomerase in the regulation of DNA supercoiling *in vivo*. Because the gene encoding DNA topoisomerase III (Dean *et al.* 1983) has not been identified, the role of the new topoisomerase in supercoiling regulation is at present unknown.

HOW SUPERCOILED IS INTRACELLULAR DNA INSIDE AN *E. COLI* CELL?

Specific linking differences of plasmid and phage DNAs isolated from *E. coli* are generally in the range between $-0·05$ and $-0·08$, when the linking number α° of the relaxed state is taken as that of the pure DNA in a dilute aqueous buffer containing about 100 mM monovalent salt and a few millimolar Mg^{2+} (see, for example, Wang, 1969; published values are corrected for the change in the unwinding angle of ethidium from 12° to 26°). The larger intracellular phage λ DNAs have negative specific linking differences closer to the lower end of the range; *E. coli* DNA itself appears to be supercoiled to the same extent as intracellular phage λ DNA (Worcel & Burgi, 1972). Since DNA *in vivo* is associated with proteins and other molecules, the linking number α° of the relaxed state *in vivo* is likely to be significantly different from that *in vitro*. It is known that intracellular DNAs isolated from cells upon inhibition of gyrase have specific linking differences that are with 15–30% of those from cells that normal levels of gyrase (Gellert *et al.* 1976b; Drlica & Snyder, 1978). Taking an average of 25% and assuming that this residual level of supercoiling is due to the difference between α° values *in vivo* and *in vitro*, then the specific linking difference of DNA in *E. coli*, with respect to a relaxed state *in vivo*, can be estimated to be in the range from $-0·04$ to $-0·06$; the lower value ($-0·04$) is probably the better estimate (the higher values come primarily from measurements with small plasmids).

The intracellular degree of supercoiling has also been estimated from the psoralen binding experiments described earlier (Pettijohn & Pfenninger, 1980; Sinden *et al.* 1980). A factor of 2 in the affinity of psoralen binding to intact and broken DNA corresponds to a specific linking difference of $-0·05$, which is in agreement with estimates based on linking number measurements. Both kinds of estimates are subject to fairly large errors, however.

SUPERCOILING INDUCED STRUCTURAL CHANGES IN DNA

With pure DNA, it is now well-established that supercoiling can induce dramatic structural changes such as the flipping of alternating C-G and T-G sequences from the right-handed B-helix form to the left-handed Z-helix form (Singleton, Klysik,

J. C. Wang

Stirdivant & Wells, 1982; Peck, Nordheim, Rich & Wang, 1982; Haniford &
Pulleyblank, 1983*a*; Nordheim & Rich, 1983), and the formation of a cruciform
structure from a palindromic sequence (Gellert *et al.* 1979; Mizuuchi, Mizuuchi &
Gellert, 1982). An example is shown in Fig. 1. Here two families of topoisomers, one
containing a 42 base-pair alternating C-G insert and the other a 42 base-pair T-G
insert, were run on the same two-dimensional gel at room temperature in a buffer
containing 90 mм-Tris·borate (pH 8·3) and 2·5 mм-Na₂EDTA, as described
previously (Wang *et al.* 1983; Peck & Wang, 1983). The group of spots on the right
half of the gel are topoisomers with the C-G insert; counting counterclockwise from
the apex of the arch of spots, as described previously, shows that the *B–Z* transition
occurs around $\alpha - \alpha° = -13$ (where α is the linking number of the topoisomer and
$\alpha°$ is that of the relaxed DNA). The plasmid is 4400 base-pairs in size, and thus $\alpha°$

Fig. 1. Two-dimensional gel electrophoresis patterns of DNA topoisomers containing a
42 base-pair (bp) alternating C-G insert (right half) and a 42 bp alternating T-G insert (left
half). The two mixtures of topoisomers were run on the same gel; as described earlier
(Peck & Wang, 1983); 1·6 % agarose gel was used. The plasmid pLP42 containing the
(C-G)₂₁ insert has been described previously (Peck & Wang, 1983); the (T-G)₂₁ insert is
between the *Eco*RI and *Bam*HI sites of pBR322. The T-G sequence is derived from
pAC42, a plasmid with a (T-G)₂₁ segment derived from a herpes simplex virus DNA
segment (pAC42 DNA was a gift from Dr Leroy F. Liu, Johns Hopkins Hospital).

is calculated to be $4400/10 \cdot 5$ or 419. The specific linking difference at which the B–Z transition apparently occurs is therefore $(\alpha - \alpha°)/\alpha°$ or $-0 \cdot 031$. The group of spots on the left half of the gel are topoisomers with the T-G interest. The B–Z transition apparently occurs at a linking difference around -16, which corresponds to a specific linking difference of $-0 \cdot 041$ (the size of this $(T\text{-}G)_{21}$-containing plasmid is 4050 base-pairs). This transition occurs in a region where the gel electrophoretic mobilities of the neighbouring topoisomers are only slightly different; thus making it difficult to analyse the energetics of the transition quantitatively, as we did for the transition with alternating C-G inserts (Peck & Wang, 1983). Nevertheless, qualitatively it is apparent that the B–Z transition can occur with alternatig T-G at a negative superhelical density somewhat higher than than for alternating C-G of the same length. This is in agreement with the findings of others (Haniford & Pulleyblank, 1983a,b; Nordheim & Rich, 1983).

DOES THE Z STRUCTURE EXIST *IN VIVO*?

Although the formation of the Z-helix is evident in a moderately negatively super-coiled DNA containing alternating C-G or T-G inserts, whether the Z structure is present *in vivo* is less certain. For fairly long alternating C-G inserts in pure DNA, in a dilute buffer containing 100 mM-NaCl the B–Z transition occurs around a value for specific linking difference of $-0 \cdot 04$. With the rather large uncertainty in the degree of supercoiling of intracellular DNA, it is not possible to predict whether alternating C-G inserts would exist in the B or Z form *in vivo*, even when the possible complications of preferential binding of cellular components to one or the other form are neglected.

In *E. coli*, experiments have been carried out to measure the difference in the linking numbers of a pair of plasmids of the same size, one with and the other without an alternating C-G or T-G insert. The basic assumption is that if the insert is a left-handed helical form, the plasmid containing it should have a lower linking number corresponding to the difference in helical twists between the inserts in the right-handed and left-handed helical forms. No difference is observable under physiological conditions (M. Gellert & G. Felsenfeld, personal communication; Haniford & Pulleyblank, 1983b). Haniford & Pulleyblank (1983b) were able to observe, however, the expected difference in the linking numbers of plasmids with and without alternating C-G inserts when chloramphenicol was added to cells harbouring the plasmids for 18 h. Since blockage of protein synthesis by chloramphenicol greatly perturbs cellular physiology, it is desirable to examine the linking difference under less drastic conditions. It remains to be seen whether increasing the degree of negative supercoiling *in vivo* by switching off the *top*A gene might drive C-G inserts into the Z structure.

PROBING THE DNA STRUCTURE *IN VIVO* WITH LIGHT

The question regarding the existence of Z structure *in vivo* points to the general problem of probing the structure of a particular sequence of intracellular DNA.

We have recently explored the use of light in probing DNA structure and DNA–protein interactions *in vivo* (Becker & Wang, 1984). Basically, when DNA is irradiated with u.v. light, photochemical lesions are introduced into the bases with frequencies that depend on the photochemical cross-sections of the bases. Suppose we have a 200 base-pair DNA fragment that is uniquely labelled at one of its ends. If the extent of irradiation is low so that for each DNA fragment less than one base is photochemically reacted, then the distribution of photochemical lesions along the DNA sequence should reflect the photochemical cross-sections of the bases in the sequence. Chemical treatment of the irradiated DNA can be carried out to cleave the DNA backbone at the site of the photolesion. This converts a unique pattern of photochemical lesions to a unique distribution of end-labelled fragments of different sizes, which can be analysed directly on a DNA-sequencing gel. Since light penetrates cells, the strategy can be readily adapted to *in vivo* studies. Here the indirect end-labelling approach for sequencing genomic DNA directly, described in the recent work of Church & Gilbert (1984), provides a way of examining the pattern of photochemical lesions in any sequence.

The photochemical approach described above can also be extended to the combined use of light with wavelengths outside the range of absorption by DNA and a photo-sensitizer. In such an experiment, the photosensitizer becomes a probe that senses the DNA structure and its interactions with other molecules. Preliminary results using these approaches are quite encouraging. A 'photo-footprint' of *lac* repressor *in vivo* has been obtained and the photochemical cross-sections of bases also appears to depend on the structure (Becker & Wang, 1984).

THE POSSIBILITY OF OTHER SUPERCOILING-INDUCED STRUCTURAL CHANGES

B–Z transition and cruciform formation are two of the best-known examples of supercoiling-induced structural changes. In general, any structural change that alters the linking number of a duplex DNA ring in its relaxed state is affected by supercoiling, whether the structural change is associated with a change in the twist or writhe, or a combination of the two.

Recent mapping of S_1 nuclease-sensitive sites in negatively supercoiled DNA (Shen, 1983; Schon, Evans, Welsh & Efstratiadis, 1983) has led to the interesting suggestion that homopurine-homopyridine stretches might assume a novel structure in a negatively supercoiled DNA (Schon *et al.* 1983). How could one test such a hypothesis?

In the cases of *B–Z* transition and cruciform formation, two types of gel electrophoresis experiments have been carried out. In one, the structural change is detected by an abrupt change in electrophoretic mobility (Singleton *et al.* 1982; Peck *et al.* 1982; Wang *et al.* 1983; Peck & Wang, 1983; Lyamichev, Panyutin, Frank-Kamenetskii, 1983; Courey & Wang, 1983; Haniford & Pulleyblank, 1983*a,b*; Gellert, O'Dea & Mizuuchi, 1983). In the other, supercoiled topoisomers of a family of plasmids containing different lengths of the sequence are examined by the topoisomer band-shift technique (Wang, 1979), and the helical repeat and the hand-edness of the helical structure are deduced from the observed shifts (Peck & Wang, 1983). The limitation in these experiments is the resolution of topoisomers in gels. As illustrated in Fig. 1, topoisomers with absolute values of specific linking differences greater than 0·05 are not resolved by gel electrophoresis in the first dimension; thus any transition that occurs at a higher degree of supercoiling is not observable. It is plausible, however, that by using rings a few hundred base-pairs in length the range of resolution can be extended. With a 210 base-pair ring, it has been observed that topoisomers with $\alpha = 20$ to 16 are resolved by polyacrylamide gel electrophoresis (D. Horowitz & J. C. Wang, unpublished data).

CONCLUDING REMARKS

The large effects of DNA supercoiling on the helical structure of DNA are readily demonstrated by the formation of Z-helix and cruciform in negatively supercoiled DNA. These structural changes illustrate beautifully the polymorphic nature of DNA structure. The physiological effects of DNA supercoiling, however, may not be related to such dramatic structural changes. Searches for the cruciform *in vivo* have yielded negative results so far (Sinden *et al.* 1983; Courey & Wang, 1983; Gellert *et al.* 1983; Borst *et al.* 1984), and the search for the Z structure *in vivo*, as summarized in an earlier section, has also been unsuccessful. Continued search in this direction is needed to provide a firmer conclusion; the ability to manipulate the degree of super-coiling and to measure structural changes *in vivo* should be helpful. There are also ample examples suggesting that the subtler effects of DNA supercoiling may have profound physiological consequences. For example, the binding of a *lac* repressor to its operator, though making only a small change in the twist or writhe of the DNA, is sensitive to the degree of supercoiling of the DNA (Wang, Barkley & Bourgeois, 1974); many processes of biological importance, such as transcription by purified polymerases, the phage λ integrase and transposon $\gamma\delta$ resolvase-catalysed site-specific recombination and the phage ϕX174 gene A protein-catalysed initiation of replication are strongly affected by the supercoiling of the DNA (reviewed by Gellert, 1981). These biochemical observations, together with the genetic evidence that in prokary-otes mutations in genes encoding topoisomerases that affect supercoiling result in a broad spectrum of physiological effects, strongly implicate the importance of DNA supercoiling *in vivo*, at least in prokaryotes (Gellert, 1981). With the recent identifica-tion of genes encoding DNA topoisomerases in the lower eukaryote, yeast (DiNardo, Voelkel & Sternglanz, 1984; Goto & Wang, 1984), there is also hope that the question of whether DNA supercoiling occurs in eukaryotes can now be subjected to genetic as well as biochemical tests.

Work of this group on DNA supercoiling has been supported by grants from the U.S. Public Health Service, the National Science Foundation, and the American Cancer Society.

REFERENCES

BAUER, W. R. (1978). Structure and reactions of closed duplex DNA. *A. Rev. Biophys. Bioengng* **7**, 287–313.

BAUER, W., CRICK, F. H. C. & WHITE, J. H. (1980). Supercoiled DNA. *Scient. Am.* **243**, 118–133.

BECKER, M. M. & WANG, J. C. (1984). Footprinting DNA in living cells with light. *Nature, Lond.* **309**, 682–687.

BORST, P., OVERDULVE, J. P., WEIJERS, P. J., FASE-FOWLER, F. & VAN DEN BERG, M. (1984). DNA circles with cruciforms from *Isospora (Toxoplasma) gondii. Biochim. biophys. Acta* **781**, 100–111.

CHANG, A. C. Y. & COHEN, S. N. (1978). Construction and characterization of amplifiable multi-copy DNA cloning vehicles derived from the P15A cryptic miniplasmid. *J. Bact.* **134**, 1141–1156.

CHURCH, G. & GILBERT, W. (1984). Genomic DNA sequencing. *Proc. natn. Acad. Sci. U.S.A.* **81**, 1991–1995.

COUREY, A. J. & WANG, J. C. (1983). Cruciform formation in a negatively supercoiled DNA may be kinetically forbidden under physiological conditions. *Cell* **33**, 817–829.

CRICK, F. H. C. (1976). Linking numbers and nucleosomes. *Proc. natn. Acad. Sci. U.S.A.* **73**, 2639–2643.

DEAN, F., KRASNOW, M. A., OTTER, R., MATZUK, M. M., SPENGLER, S. J. & COZZARELLI, N. R. (1983). *Escherichia coli* type-I topoisomerases: Identification, mechanism, and role in recombination. *Cold Spring Harbor Symp. quant. Biol.* **47**, 769–777.

DINARDO, S., VOELKEL, K. & STERNGLANZ, R. (1984). DNA topoisomerase II mutant of *S. cerevisiae*: Topoisomerase II is required for segregation of daughter molecules at the termination of DNA replication. *Proc. natn. Acad. Sci. U.S.A.* **81**, 2616–2620.

DINARDO, S., VOELKEL, K. A., STERNGLANZ, R., REYNOLDS, A. E. & WRIGHT, A. (1982). *Escherichia coli* topoisomerase I mutants have compensatory mutations in gyrase genes. *Cell* **31**, 43–51.

DRLICA, K. & SNYDER, M. (1978). Superhelical *Escherichia coli* DNA: Relaxation by coumermycin. *J. molec. Biol.* **120**, 145–154.

GELLERT, M. (1981). DNA topoisomerases. *A. Rev. Biochem.* **50**, 879–910.

GELLERT, M., MIZUUCHI, K., O'DEA, M. H. & NASH, H. A. (1976a). DNA gyrase: An enzyme that introduces superhelical turns into DNA. *Proc. natn. Acad. Sci. U.S.A.* **73**, 3872–3876.

GELLERT, M., MIZUUCHI, K., O'DEA, M. H., OHMORI, H. & TOMIZAWA, J. (1979). DNA gyrase and DNA supercoiling. *Cold Spring Harbor Symp. quant. Biol.* **43**, 35–40.

GELLERT, M., O'DEA, M. H., ITOH, T. & TOMIZAWA, J. (1976b). Novobiocin and coumermycin inhibit DNA supercoiling catalyzed by DNA gyrase. *Proc. natn. Acad. Sci. U.S.A.* **73**, 4474–4478.

GELLERT, M., O'DEA, M. H. & MIZUUCHI, K. (1983). Slow cruciform transitions in palindromic DNA. *Proc. natn. Acad. Sci. U.S.A.* **80**, 5545–5549.

GOTO, T. & WANG, J. C. (1984). Yeast DNA topoisomerase II is encoded by a single-copy, essential gene. *Cell* **36**, 1073–1080.

HANIFORD, D. B. & PULLEYBLANK, D. E. (1983a). Facile transition of poly(d(T-G)·d(C-A)) into a left-handed helix in physiological conditions. *Nature, Lond.* **302**, 632–634.

HANIFORD, D. B. & PULLEYBLANK, D. E. (1983b). The *in-vivo* occurrence of Z-DNA. *J. biomolec. Struct. Dynam.* **1**, 593–609.

KAHN, M., KOLTER, R., THOMAS, C., FIGURSKI, D., MEYER, R., REMAUT, E. & HELINSKI, D. R. (1979). Plasmid cloning vehicles derived from plasmids ColEl, F, R6K, and RK2. *Meth. Enzym.* **68**, 268–280.

LOCKSHON, D. & MORRIS, D. R. (1983). Positively supercoiled plasmid DNA is produced by treatment of *Escherichia coli* with DNA gyrase inhibitors. *Nucl. Acids Res.* **11**, 2999–3017.

LYAMICHEV, V. I., PANYUTIN, I. G. & FRANK-KAMENETSKII, M. D. (1983). Evidence of cruciform structures in superhelical DNA provided by two-dimensional gel electrophoresis. *FEBS Lett.* **153**, 298–302.

MIZUUCHI, K., MIZUUCHI, M. & GELLERT, M. (1982). Cruciform structures in palindromic DNA are favored by DNA supercoiling. *J. molec. Biol.* **156**, 229–243.

NORDHEIM, A. & RICH, A. (1983). The sequence $(dC\text{-}dA)_n \cdot (dG\text{-}dT)_n$ forms left-handed Z-DNA in negatively supercoiled plasmids. *Proc. natn. Acad. Sci. U.S.A.* **80**, 1821–1825.

ORR, E. & STAUDENBAUER, W. (1981). An *Escherichia coli* mutant thermosensitive in the B subunit of DNA gyrase: Effect on the structure and replication of the Colicin El plasmid *in vitro. Molec. gen. Genet.* **181**, 52–56.

PECK, L. J., NORDHEIM, A., RICH, A. & WANG, J. C. (1982). Flipping of cloned $d(pCpG)_n \cdot d\text{-}(pCpG)_n$ DNA sequences from right- to left-handed helical structure by salt, Co(III), or negative supercoiling. *Proc. natn. Acad. Sci. U.S.A.* **79**, 4560–4564.

PECK, L. J. & WANG, J. C. (1983). Energetics of B-to-Z transition in DNA. *Proc. natn. Acad. Sci. U.S.A.* **80**, 6206–6210.

PETTIJOHN, D. E. & PFENNINGER, O. (1980). Supercoils in prokaryotic DNA restrained *in vivo. Proc. natn. Acad. Sci. U.S.A.* **77**, 1331–1335.

PRUSS, G. J., MANES, S. H. & DRLICA, K. (1982). *Escherichia coli* DNA topoisomerase I mutants: increased supercoiling is corrected by mutations near gyrase genes. *Cell* **31**, 35–42.

SCHON, E., EVANS, T., WELSH, J. & EFSTRATIADIS, A. (1983). Conformation of promoter DNA: fine mapping of S_1-hypersensitive sites. *Cell* **35**, 837–848.

SHEN, C.-K. J. (1983). Superhelicity induces hypersensitivity of a human polypyrimidine·polypurine DNA sequence in the human $\alpha 2$-$\alpha 1$ globin intergenic region to S_1 nuclease digestion–high resolution mapping of the clustered cleavage sites. *Nucl. Acids Res.* **11**, 7899–7910.

SINDEN, R. R., CARLSON, J. O. & PETTIJOHN, D. E. (1980). Torsional tension in the DNA double helix measured with trimethylpsoralen in living *E. coli* cells: analogous measurements in insect and human cells. *Cell* **21**, 773–783.

SINGLETON, C. K., KLYSIK, J., STIRDIVANT, S. M. & WELLS, R. D. (1982). Left-handed Z-DNA is induced by supercoiling in physiological ionic conditions. *Nature, Lond.* **299**, 312–316.

WANG, J. C. (1969). Degree of superhelicity of covalently closed cyclic DNAs from *Escherichia coli. J. molec. Biol.* **43**, 263–272.

WANG, J. C. (1979). Helical repeat of DNA in solution. *Proc. natn. Acad. Sci. U.S.A.* **76**, 200–203.

WANG, J. C., BARKLEY, M. D. & BOURGEOIS, S. (1974). Measurements of unwinding of *lac* operator by repressor. *Nature, Lond.* **251**, 247–249.

WANG, J. C. & BECHERER, K. (1983). Cloning of the gene *top*A encoding for DNA topoisomerase I and the physical mapping of the *cys*B-*top*A-*trp* region of *Escherichia coli. Nucl. Acids Res.* **11**, 1773–1790.

WANG, J. C., PECK, L. J. & BECHERER, K. (1983). DNA supercoiling and its effects on DNA structure and function. *Cold Spring Harbor Symp. quant. Biol.* **47**, 85–91.

WIESEHAHN, G. & HEARST, J. E. (1978). DNA unwinding induced by photoaddition of psoralen derivatives and determination of dark-binding equilibrium constants by gel electrophoresis. *Proc. natn. Acad. Sci. U.S.A.* **75**, 2703–2707.

WORCEL, A. & BURGI, E. (1972). On the structure of the folded chromosome of *Escherichia coli. J. molec. Biol.* **71**, 127–147.

J. Cell Sci. Suppl. 1, 31–41 (1984)
Printed in Great Britain © The Company of Biologists Limited 1984

DNA SEQUENCES AND CHROMOSOME STRUCTURE

EDWIN M. SOUTHERN

MRC Mammalian Genome Unit, King's Buildings, West Mains Road, Edinburgh EH9 3JT, U.K.

SUMMARY

In this review evidence for the possible relationship between higher order chromosome structure and the distribution of tandem and dispersed repeated sequences in DNA has been examined. Evidence from studies of chromosome diminution in lower eukaryotes suggests that simple sequence DNAs may have a germ-line function and, in mammals, changes in simple sequence methylation, associated with changes in chromosome condensation, support the idea that the centromeric and telomeric heterochromatin may have a function in germ-line cells. For the major families of dispersed repeats, the weight of available evidence suggests that if they do play a role in chromosome organization, it is not an important one. Cytosine methylation is suggested as a candidate for a role in organizing the chromatin. Long-range patterns of methylation in vertebrates, the relationship of this to gene structure, and the association of changes in methylation with gene activity accord with current evidence linking specific nuclear structures to defined points in coding regions.

INTRODUCTION

The complex functions of the eukaryotic genome can be divided in to two broad groups: one set of functions is concerned with the expression of genes and another is concerned with replicating the genome and ensuring a proper division between replication cycles. Changing patterns of chromatin folding and, in particular, the condensation of the chromatin into the apparently simple structures seen in metaphase and other chromosomes, show that an apparatus has evolved to permit the nucleus to cope with the complex process of organizing the enormous DNA molecule of the genome throughout the division cycles.

Many structural features of chromosomes and their biological roles are understood from microscope studies. It is clear that they have specific sites that attach them to other structures; for example, centromeres, which attach to the mitotic spindle, and telomeres, which attach to the nuclear envelope. These interactions clearly help to shape and organize the DNA molecule into a more compact and manageable structure, and to position this structure within the overall architecture of the cell. In addition to interactions with other structures, it is also possible that the chromatin is shaped by intrinsic properties of the DNA sequence, of the kind discussed by Dr Wang (Wang *et al.* 1979, and this symposium) with or without specific interaction with proteins or other molecules.

Rapid progress is being made in the study of chromosomal properties in the lower eukaryotes. It has been possible to exploit recombinant DNA methods to isolate sequences that function as centromeres from yeast DNA, and others that function as telomeres from yeast, *Tetrahymena* and trypanosomes. Progress in understanding the larger chromosomes of higher eukaryotes has been less rapid. Although there are good methods for introducing recombinant DNA molecules into *Drosophila* and mammalian cells, none has yet been produced that behaves as a centromere or as a telomere in these cells. However, progress in methods for analysing the structure of DNA has produced abundant information about the sequences that make up the complex genomes of the higher eukaryotes, and it is worthwhile examining this information to see if it gives any insight into relationships between sequence and function. Two features of eukaryotic DNA sequences that may have some bearing on chromosome structure or function are covered in this review. These are the repeated sequences and cytosine methylation. I shall concentrate on bulk fractions of nuclear DNA, rather than dealing with specific topics such as the relationship of these features to gene activity, or the properties of simpler systems such as the genomes of viruses and organelles. Although these are relevant to the topic of this symposium, they justify a separate review. The topic is treated from the point of view of the molecular biologist studying the structure of DNA fractions, seeking to link them to a biological role. Other reviews in this symposium tackle the problem from the other side.

MOLECULAR STRUCTURE AND EVOLUTION

Repeated sequences in long tandem arrays

The satellite sequences in eukaryotic DNA, which were described more than 20 years ago (Kit, 1961; Sueoka, 1961), were the first repeated sequences to be discovered. They were discovered as density fractions when total DNA was analysed in caesium chloride gradients. Subsequent studies of their reassociation behaviour showed that these DNAs consisted of highly repeated sequences, in long tandem arrays (Britten & Kohne, 1966). Such long stretches of tandemly repeated sequences are now known to be of common occurrence. The simplest known – the satellite DNA of crab – consists of poly(dA-T), with a measurable content of other sequences (Swartz, Trautner & Kornberg, 1962). Other tandemly organized repeats are based on more complex units, ranging up to thousands of base-pairs (bp). For almost all sequences of this class, restriction fragment analysis, or sequence analysis shows that the sequences are made up of multiple copies of diverged repeats. For example, mouse satellite DNA has a dominant 234 bp repeat revealed by restriction enzymes. Sequence analysis shows that this unit is made up of four related 58 and 60 bp segments, and each of these sub-segments contains two variant 28 and 30 bp sequences (Horz & Altenburger, 1981). Other tandemly repeated sequences are more complex in their organization, with repeating units thousands of base-pairs in length; others are more simple.

These fractions of DNA often show related but distinct forms within an organism. For example, different satellite DNAs from *Drosophila virilis* (Gall, Cohen & Artherton, 1973) show sequence relationships. Relationships are also found between sequences of related organisms, as in the *Mus* species (Sutton & McCallum, 1971, 1972). All sequence relationships between and within species, and within one family of sequences, can be explained by a simple evolutionary scheme, in which cyclical rounds of multiplication and divergence take up a short segment from a pre-existing sequence and amplify this segment to the predominant form. Interspecies comparisons suggest that, in rodents, the time taken for one form to become predominant could be around 5×10^6 years (Southern, 1975).

The nature of the multiplication process is not known. Unequal crossing-over by sister chromatid exchange could certainly explain most of the observed features (Smith, 1973). In particular, the type B distribution of restriction enzyme sites (Horz & Zachau, 1977) is just what is expected of unequal recombination. But it seems unlikely that this is the sole mechanism of propagating the sequence, as it cannot readily explain how the sequence is spread between non-homologous chromosomes. Indeed, there is no good explanation of how this occurs. It is most likely that non-homologous chromosomes exchange sequences in regions that come together in certain states of the nucleus (Manuelidis, 1982).

Apart from the simple nature of their structure, there is no common feature to be found in the sequences of the satellite DNAs: some are A+T-rich, others are G+C-rich; some have a strong strand bias in purine/pyrimidine content, others have a bias towards alternating purine/pyrimidine sequences. Most relationships between satellite DNA sequences can be accounted for by common ancestry, rather than by selection acting to conserve function. However, the kind of relationship that could give some hint of function has been noted in the sequences of the alpha satellites of the guinea pig (Southern, 1970) and of the kangaroo rat (Salser *et al.* 1976). The satellite DNAs from these two distantly related rodents, both have C-C-C-T-A-A as a major component. This sequence is also found at the telomeres of chromosomes from trypanosomes (Blackburn & Challoner, 1984; van der Ploeg *et al.* 1984). It cannot be inferred from these relationships that these sequences behave as telomeres in the two rodent species, and this emphasizes the inadequacy of structural studies as against direct biological methods. Fortunately, methods are now being developed that may allow us to examine the function of these sequences more directly.

The dispersed repeats

Structural studies were possible on satellite DNAs because they could be purified on density gradients. Cloning has not added much information to the earlier studies, though the new sequencing methods have confirmed and extended the conclusions based on less precise methods of examining the sequences. Cloning has, however, had a significant impact on studies of the dispersed repeats, as it has made it possible to isolate individual copies; before the cloning techniques became available these could only be studied as mixed fractions.

Unlike the tandemly repeating sequences, each copy of a dispersed repeat is bounded not by copies of itself, but by unrelated sequences. Like the tandem repeats, the dispersed repeats can make up a substantial fraction of the genome, and in some organisms they make up the bulk of the DNA. It was clear, from early measurements of their reassociation rates, that the dispersed repeats in many organisms are dominated by a few major families. A recent detailed analysis of the major repeated families in human DNA (Sun *et al.* 1984) shows that there are just three, which are present in more than approximately 50 000 copies: these are known as the Alu and the

Kpn families, and the conserved sequence poly(C-A). Together they could account for 20 % of the DNA. Also described in this article are two minor repeats present in relatively few copies. It is not known how many minor families there are, but there are probably very many. In *Drosophila melanogaster*, the dispersed repeats make up about 10 % of the total DNA and are represented in around 50 different sequence families (Finnegan, 1984). Most of these families are widely dispersed through the *Drosophila* genome as compared to, for example, the Alu family in mammals; the less-abundant families in mammalian genomes could have a similarly wide distribution. The patterns of organization ascribed to different species from studies of the bulk repeated sequences (Britten & Davidson, 1969) become more complex when examined family by family, within each species.

Sequence analysis shows that, like the tandem repeats, the dispersed repeats can have widely different complexities, ranging from polymers of one or two base-pairs to sequences that consist of several kilobases of complex sequence. The detailed structure of these sequences is beyond the scope of this article, but the sequences that have been studied at the molecular level can be placed into five main classes: sequences that have retrovirus-like structure with long terminal repeats flanking the insert; elements that are flanked by short inverted repeats; elements that resemble pseudogenes in having a poly(A) sequence; and families of long inverted repeats that behave as 'foldback' sequences on reassociation; stretches of simple sequence DNA that resemble the satellite DNAs in sequence type but differ in that short runs of simple sequence are flanked by more complex sequences – poly(C-A) is an example of a dispersed simple sequence. These classes are not exclusive, and some sequences have more than one of the properties listed above. The structures are relevant to the origins of the sequence, as well as to their possible functions.

The first four categories have structural features that are similar to known mobile elements, and it is thought that such dispersed repeats are formed by a mechanism that could place them in almost any position in the genome. One such mechanism copies a sequence and introduces the copy into the genome. The sequence that is copied may be a sequence that is already present in the genome. Several copying mechanisms are possible. For example, the genomic copy of the sequence may be transcribed into RNA, which is then reverse transcribed to DNA, which is subsequently introduced into the genome. Other mechanisms include excision of a sequence from the genome by recombination followed by extrachromosomal replication, and reinsertion into the genome. The more complex and abundant sequences, of which the Alu and Kpn families in human DNA are examples, have properties that suggest that they may be generated by a process that starts with transcription of an RNA molecule. This mechanism is favoured because transcripts of the repeated sequences are found in cellular RNA, because tracts of poly(A) are found in association with the genomic copies of the sequences, and because the genomic copies are flanked by short direct repeats (reviewed by Rogers, 1984). The several families of dispersed repeats in *Drosophila* DNA have features that suggest that they too are produced by trans-position mechanisms, and that they are indeed mobile in the genome is shown by studies of their location, discussed below.

A second kind of mechanism, not requiring insertion of a copy, could generate repeated sequences *de novo* at the site that they occupy in the genome. The short tandem repeats, such as poly(C-A) could arise by 'slippage' replication of a short sequence (Burd & Wells, 1970) already present at the site.

These seem reasonable proposals for mechanisms of production of repeated sequences, and mechanisms are also known that could serve to maintain repeated sequences against erosion by mutation. Gene conversion is one mechanism that could operate on either dispersed or clustered sequences. The question as to whether selection acts to conserve the dispersed repeats is unresolved. Interspecies comparisons show the presence of families related to the human Alu and Kpn families in many mammals (Singer *et al.* 1983). The sequence poly(C-A) is even more widespread in the higher eukaryotes (Miesfeld, Krystal & Arnheim, 1981). However, there is no indication from these comparisons that the sequences serve a function that is dependent on the precise base sequence. The relationships can be explained as readily by constraints imposed by the mechanisms of producing repeated sequences as they can by selection for a desirable property.

CHROMOSOMAL LOCATION

So far we have dealt with the short-range analysis of the repeated sequences, with the kind of structure that is revealed by looking at restriction fragments by gel electrophoresis or by sequence analysis. What about the longer range? To address the question as to whether the repeated sequences are actively involved in determining the pattern of folding chromosomes or simply carried along as passengers, we shall first need a view of their distribution at the chromosome level, to bridge the gap between the cytological description of the chromosome, where fine detail corresponds to roughly 10^6 base-pairs, and the molecular level, where the longest clones cover less than 10^5 base-pairs.

Tandem repeats

For the long arrays of tandemly repeated sequences, the picture is fairly clear. *In situ* hybridization reveals that the major satellite DNAs are clustered together in 'specific' chromosomal locations. These locations are usually centromeric, as for the major and minor mouse satellite DNAs (Jones, 1970; Pardue & Gall, 1970), or telomeric, as for the Y-specific repeat of human DNA (Cooke, Schmidtke & Gosden, 1982). They may occur in these highly localized regions because the means of their production only functions at centromeres or telomeres; they may, of course, have a selectable function at these locations. It has been shown convincingly that the sequences that act as telomeres in the trypanosomes are multiple copies of the sequence C-C-C-T-A-A (Blackburn & Challoner, 1984; van der Ploeg *et al.* 1984), but there is no evidence that telomeric function requires the enormously long stretches of repeating sequences found in some organisms. It may be relevant that the trypanosome telomere seems to grow by one unit of the repeating subunit at each generation (Bernards, Michels, Lincke & Borst, 1983). Perhaps the long tracts of simple sequences that are found at some telomeres are a result of growth, which is a normal part of telomere function, continuing unchecked.

Dispersed repeats

For the dispersed repeats, the questions are more difficult to generalize because there are several structural categories, and because they occupy a more varied range of positions in the chromosome. In a full treatment we should consider their relationship to genes as well as possible roles in chromosomal functions; we should bear in mind that some are genes, whose products, such as ribosomal DNAs, have well-established functions. This discussion considers only the question of their chromosomal location and possible roles in chromosome functions.

The distribution of repeated sequences in *Drosophila* is readily seen by *in situ* hybridization to polytene chromosomes. The dispersed repeats are seen to be scattered widely throughout the genome, although there is some clustering in the heterochromatic regions (reviewed by Finnegan, 1984). Furthermore, their location is different in different strains of *Drosophila*. Another repeated sequence has been described that is located close to the telomeres (Rubin, 1977). Thus, there are two distinct types of repeated sequences in *Drosophila* DNA: there are sequences that move about the genome, and these sequences account for the major part of the moderately repeated sequences; there are sequences that have fixed locations at the centromeres and telomeres.

The dispersed sequences in *Drosophila* DNA are present in few copies, which are very widely scattered, but in mammals the major repeating sequence families are very dense. The average spacing of the Alu family members in human DNA is 3000 base-pairs. There is no equivalent of the polytene chromosome in mammals that would allow for the kind of resolution by *in situ* hybridization that has been achieved in *Drosophila*, and for this reason there have been few descriptions of *in situ* hybridizations carried out with dispersed repeated sequences in mammals. Manuelidis (1982) studied the distribution of the HindIII family using a biotin-labelled probe and immunofluorescent detection to give higher resolution. Her results suggest that this family, which forms part of the Kpn family described above, is clustered on the human chromosomes. A clustered distribution of a related family in mouse DNA is suggested by density gradient analysis. Meunier-Rotival *et al.* (1982) have shown that mouse DNA, like that of other mammals, can be separated into distinct density classes. These are not the classical density satellites. They are much less clearly defined. The important point, as far as this discussion is concerned, is that the BamHI/EcoRI family is confined to the light fractions of the main band, even when quite high molecular weight DNA is examined. Clustering of the repeated sequences would obviously lead to structurally distinct domains, but it is not clear whether the bands produced by staining chromosomes are related to these inhomogeneities in the distribution of the dispersed repeats.

The dispersed repeats are not excluded from the tandem repeats. Singer and her colleagues (1982) have shown the presence of Alu repeats within the primate satellites.

Several dispersed repeats have also been found in association with genes (e.g. see Shen & Maniatis, 1980).

The structure of major dispersed repeated sequence families and what we know about their chromosomal location give few clues as to whether they have a function that is relevant to the genome that carries them and, in particular, whether they have a role in determining the structure or function of chromosomes. This is a difficult issue because it has not been possible to address the question directly by putting ideas to experimental tests. There have been many suggestions for functions for these sequences, and few of them can be discarded from current knowledge. The weight of the evidence would suggest that if the repeated sequences that make up a high propor- tion of the DNA do have a function, it cannot be an important one. This is especially true of the more complex sequences, which are mobile in the genome, and which are longer than needed for specific protein binding sites. However, it is possible that some of the minor families have a function and it is possible that they have more than one function; as has been emphasized above, they belong to more than one structural class.

For the long tandem clusters, there is indirect evidence that they may have a germ- line function, as chromosome diminution, accompanied by a loss of repeated sequences, appears to occur frequently in going from germ-line to somatic cells during the development of many lower eukaryotes (reviewed by Bostock, 1980). No parallel loss of repeated sequence DNA has been seen in the vertebrates, but, as will be discussed below, there is an interesting change in the methyl cytosine content.

DNA METHYLATION AND ITS RELATIONSHIP TO GENOME ORGANIZA- TION

If the organization of the nucleus is likely to involve specific interactions with proteins, or specific alterations to DNA structures, it is worth looking at the pattern of methylation of the DNA, because this modification can both induce specific interaction with proteins and also induce the change from *B* to *Z*-form DNA.

The DNA of most higher eukaryotes is highly methylated; vertebrate DNA is methylated at the 5-position of cytosine in the sequence CpG. The DNAs are mostly resistant to restriction enzymes like *Hpa*II and *Hha*I, which have CpG as part of their recognition site and whose activity is blocked if the C in this sequence is methylated. It has been found, however, that there is a fraction in all vertebrate DNAs that is sensitive to these enzymes, and is therefore non-methylated (Cooper, Taggart & Bird, 1983): it is a minor fraction of the DNA (about 1 % in mammals) and it is unusually rich in G+C and the normally rare doublet CpG. Several non-methylated regions of the type described here have been found in the close proximity of genes, at the 5' end (Doerfler, 1983). Bird (personal communication) has shown that these unusual regions are scattered between regions with the more familiar properties of vertebrate DNA, throughout a high proportion of the genome, and though the distribution has not been analysed precisely, the relative amounts of the two fractions and the size of the methylated regions suggest that the average length of the non-methylated regions is only a few kilobases, and that in the mammalian genome, these are separated by 50 kb or more of methylated DNA. This interesting distribution of methyl cytosine has been discovered only recently, and much remains to be done in analysing the detailed pattern of distribution. However, it is already apparent that it could have important implications for the organization of the genome. As Riggs (1975) has emphasized, methylation has a strong effect on interactions between proteins and DNA; one possibility is that the non-methylated regions and the methylated regions interact differently with DNA binding proteins.

The non-methylated fraction is not changed in development; it is non-methylated in sperm DNA and in the DNA from all somatic cells that have been analysed. However, some of the methylated sequences are changed, and there are two quite different types of change. It is now well-established that genes that are active in any given cell type are often associated with regions of DNA that have lost methylated groups from cytosines that were methylated in sperm DNA. The reason for this association is not clear. But it is in marked contrast to changes in the methylation pattern of the simple sequence DNAs. It has been shown now that satellite DNAs in several organisms are undermethylated in sperm DNA, and that during development the sequences gain methylation. This is true of the major satellites in calf DNA (Sturm & Taylor, 1981), of the major and minor satellites in mouse DNA (Sandford *et al.* 1984), and of the satellites in human DNA, including one of the Y-chromosome-specific repeated sequences (Cooke *et al.* 1982).

As far as we are aware, this is the only difference found in these sequences in sperm and somatic cells, and it is therefore of considerable interest that the regions of the chromosomes with which these sequences are associated have quite different staining properties in chomosomes from somatic cells, as compared to chromosomes from sperm. Rudak, Jacobs & Yanagimachi (1978) noted that when chromosomes from human spermatozoa were 'reactivated' in hamster eggs, the pericentric regions of chromosomes 1, 9 and 16, and the long arm of the Y chromosome, were light-staining and extended as compared to the rest of the chromatin. In chromosomes from lymphocytes, these regions are relatively condensed and dark-staining. It is also known that these regions are the major sites of the human satellite DNAs. Thus there is a change in the state of chromosome condensation, which correlates with the methylation of the DNA, and it is possible that the change is brought about by either the interaction of the methyl groups with specific proteins, or by methyl groups directly affecting the conformation of the DNA within the chromatin.

CONCLUSION

The picture of the eukaryotic genome that can be drawn from the molecular analysis described here does not add much detail to the cytologist's view of the genome. Indeed it is difficult from present knowledge to relate any but the long repeated sequence domains to visible features in the nucleus. It is clear that the highly condensed heterochromatin is often associated with the presence of highly repeated simple sequences; in particular, these are found in regions around the centromeres. Now the work described by Dr Carbon (this symposium) shows clearly that only a short sequence is needed to specify an interaction with the mitotic spindle in yeast, and although the higher eukaryotes have a more complex centromere it seems unlikely that the large amounts of DNA contained in the heterochromatin are required for direct interaction with the spindle. Similarly, it seems unlikely that interaction with the scaffold requires the number of contact points that could be specified by a sequence of the major repeating sequence families, which punctuate the genome at intervals of only a few kilobases. If the major classes of repeated sequences do have a function in the genome it is not likely to be one that is specified by the base sequence; it is unlikely that they are involved in specific interaction with proteins, as this would demand conservation of the sequence and this is not seen. Furthermore, specific interaction between a protein and a DNA sequence makes contact with only a few bases in the DNA; the repeated sequence elements found in the eukaryotic genome by molecular reassociation are much longer than the length required to define a protein binding site. The information we have on the major interspersed repeats points to their being parasitic rather than essential components of the genome, and it is possible to take this view of the simple sequences, too. If they do have a function, they could serve a function in the host genome that depends more on the length of the sequence than the base sequence, or a function that depends on a particular secondary structure; they may, for example, provide passive building blocks or spacers, which allow for correct shaping of the nucleus and chromosomes mediated by more positive centres. As Cavalier-Smith (1978) has argued, the eukaryotic cell is large, and the need to fill out the nucleus to match the size of its cellular environment may provide the drive needed to expand the genome with otherwise neutral DNA. The sequences that undoubtedly do serve a role in specific interactions that shape the chromosome and nucleus are more likely to be discovered by the kind of approach described by Drs Laemmli and Carbon (this symposium).

Methylation of DNA has a profound effect on its interaction with proteins and it has been shown that methylation of cytosine facilitates the transformation of the helix into left-handed Z-DNA. Examination of patterns of methylation of vertebrate DNA, especially the ways in which the patterns differ in different cells, suggests that methylation may have an important role to play in genome organization. However, studies of these interesting modifications of the DNA are still at an early stage, and as for the repeated sequences, their role is enigmatic.

REFERENCES

BERNARDS, A., MICHELS, P. A. M., LINCKE, C. R. & BORST, P. (1983). Growth of chromosome ends in multiplying trypanosomes. *Nature, Lond.* **303**, 592–597.
BLACKBURN, E. H. & CHALLONER, P. B. (1984). Identification of a telomeric DNA sequence in *Trypanosoma brucei*. *Cell* **36**, 447–457.
BOSTOCK, C. J. (1980). A function for satellite DNA? *Trends Biochem. Sci.* **5**, 117–119.
BRITTEN, R. J. & DAVIDSON, E. H. (1969). Gene regulation for higher cells: A theory. *Science* **165**, 349–357.
BRITTEN, R. J. & KOHNE, D. E. (1966). Nucleotide sequence repetition in DNA. *Carnegie Instn Wash. Yb.* **65**, 78–106.

BURD, J. F. & WELLS, R. D. (1970). Effect of incubation conditions on the nucleotide sequence of DNA products of unprimed DNA polymerase reactions. *J. molec. Biol.* **53**, 435–459.

CAVALIER-SMITH, T. (1978). Nuclear volume control by nucleoskeletal DNA, selection cell volume and cell growth rate and the solution of the DNA C value paradox. *J. Cell Sci.* **34**, 247–278.

COOKE, H. J., SCHMIDTKE, J. & GOSDEN, J. R. (1982). Characterisation of a human Y chromosome repeated sequence and related sequences in higher primates. *Chromosoma* **87**, 491–502.

COOPER, D. N., TAGGART, M. H. & BIRD, A. P. (1983). Unmethylated domains in vertebrate DNA. *Nucl. Acids Res.* **11**, 647–658.

DOEFLER, W. (1983). DNA methylation and gene activity. *A. Rev. Biochem.* **52**, 93–124.

FINNEGAN, D. J. (1984). Genome evolution of prokaryotes and eukaryotes. *Int. Rev. Cytol.* (suppl. 17), (in press).

GALL, J. G., COHEN, E. H. & ARTHERTON, D. D. (1973). The satellite DNAs of *Drosophila virilis*. *Cold Spring Harbor quant. Biol.* **38**, 417–421.

HORZ, W. & ALTENBURGER, W. (1981). Nucleotide sequence of mouse satellite DNA. *Nucl. Acids Res.* **9**, 683–696.

HORZ, W. & ZACHAU, H. G. (1977). Characterization of distinct segments in mouse satellite DNA by restriction nucleases. *Eur. J. Biochem.* **73**m, 383–392.

JONES, K. W. (1970). Chromosomal and nuclear location of mouse satellite DNA in individual cells. *Nature, Lond.* **225**, 912–915.

KIT, S. (1961). Equilibrium sedimentation in density gradients of DNA preparations from animal tissues. *J. molec. Biol.* **3**, 711–716.

MANUELIDIS, L. (1982). Repeated DNA sequences and nuclear structure. In *Genome Evolution* (ed. G. A. Dover & R. B. Flavell), pp. 263–286. New York, London: Academic Press.

MEUNIER-ROTIVAL, M., SORIANO, P., CUNY, G., STRAUSS, F. & BERNARDI, G. (1982). Sequence organisation and genomic distribution of the major family of interspersed repeats of mouse DNA. *Proc. natn. acad. Sci. U.S.A.* **79**, 355–359.

MIESFELD, R., KRYSTAL, M. & ARNHEIM, N. (1981). A member of a new repeated sequence family which is conserved throughout eucaryotic evolution is found between human δ and β globin genes. *Nucl. Acids Res.* **9**, 5931–5947.

PARDUE, N. L. & GALL, J. G. (1970). Chromosomal localization of mouse satellite DNA. *Science* **168**, 1356–1358.

RIGGS, A. D. (1975). X-inactivation, differentiation and DNA methylation. *Cytogenet. Cell Genet.* **14**, 9–25.

ROGERS, J. H. (1984). Genome evolution of prokaryotes and eukaryotes. *Int. Rev. Cytol.* (suppl. 17), (in press).

RUBIN, A. M. (1977). Isolation of a telomeric DNA sequence from *Drosophila melanogaster*. *Cold Spring Harbor Symp. quant. Biol.* **42**, 1041–1046.

RUDAK, E., JACOBS, P. A. & YANAGIMACHI, R. (1978). Direct analysis of the chromosome constitution of human spermatozoa. *Nature, Lond.* **274**, 911–913.

SALSER, W., BOWEN, S., BROWNE, D., ADLI, F. E., FEDEROFF, N., FRY, K., HEINDELL, H., PADDOCK, G., POON, R., WALLACE, B. & WHITCOMBE, P. (1976). Investigation of the organisation of mammalian chromosomes at the DNA sequence level. *Fedn Proc. Fedn Am. Socs exp. Biol.* **35**, 23–35.

SANDFORD, J., FORRESTER, L., CHAPMAN, V., CHANDLEY, A. & HASTIE, N. (1984). Methylation patterns of respective DNA sequences in germ cells of *Mus musculus*. *Nucl. Acids Res.* **12**, 2823–2836.

SHEN, C. J. & MANIATIS, T. (1980). The organisation of repetitive sequences in a cluster of rabbit β-like globin genes. *Cell* **19**, 379–391.

SINGER, M. F. (1982). Highly repeated sequence in mammalian genomes. *Int. Rev. Cytol.* **76**, 67–112.

SINGER, M. F., THAYER, R. E., GRIMALDI, G., LERMAN, M. I. & FANNING, T. G. (1983). Homology between the *Kpn*I primate and *Bam*HI (M1F-1) rodent families of long interspersed repeated sequences. *Nucl. Acids Res.* **11**, 5739–5745.

SMITH, G. P. (1973). Unequal crossover and the evolution of multigene families. *Cold Spring Harbor Symp. quant. Biol.* **38**, 507–513.

SOUTHERN, E. M. (1970). Base sequence and evolution of guinea pig α-satellite DNA. *Nature, Lond.* **227**, 794–798.

SOUTHERN, E. M. (1975). Long-range periodicities in mouse satellite DNA. *J. molec. Biol.* **94**, 51–69.

STURM, K. S. & TAYLOR, J. H. (1981). Distribution of 5-methylcytosine in the DNA of somatic and germline cells from bovine tissues. *Nucl. Acids Res.* **9**, 4537–4546.

SUEOKA, N. (1961). Variation and heterogeneity of base composition of deoxyribonucleic acids: a compilation of old and new data. *J. molec. Biol.* **3**, 31–40.

SUN, L., PAULSON, K. E., SCHMID, C. W., KADYK, L. & LEINWAND, L. (1984). Non-Alu family interspersed repeats in human DNA and their transcriptive activity. *Nucl. Acids Res.* **12**, 2669–2690.

SUTTON, W. D. & McCALLUM, M. (1971). Mismatching and the reassociation rate of mouse satellite DNA. *Nature, Lond.* **232**, 83–85.

SUTTON, W. D. & McCALLUM, M. (1972). Related satellite DNAs in the genus *Mus*. *J. molec. Biol.* **71**, 633–656.

SWARTZ, M. N., TRAUTNER, T. A. & KORNBERG, A. (1962). Enzymatic synthesis of deoxyribonucleic acid. II. Further studies on nearest neighbour base sequences in deoxyribonucleic acid. *J. biol. Chem.* **237**, 1961–1967.

VAN DER PLOEG, L. H. T., LIN, A. Y. C. & BORST, P. (1984). The structure of the growing telomeres of trypanosomes. *Cell* **36**, 459–468.

WANG, A. H.-J., QUIGLEY, G. J., KOLPAK, F. J., CRAWFORD, J. L., VAN BOON, J. H., VAN DER MAREL, G. & RICH, A. (1979). Molecular structure of a left-handed double helical DNA fragment at atomic resolution. *Nature, Lond.* **282**, 680–686.

J. Cell Sci. Suppl. 1, 43–58 (1984)
Printed in Great Britain © The Company of Biologists Limited 1984

STRUCTURAL AND FUNCTIONAL ANALYSIS OF A YEAST CENTROMERE (*CEN3*)

JOHN CARBON AND LOUISE CLARKE

Department of Biological Sciences, University of California, Santa Barbara, CA 93106, U.S.A.

SUMMARY

Structure–function analysis of a yeast (*Saccharomyces cerevisiae*) centromere (*CEN3*) has been carried out by altering the nucleotide sequence of the DNA within and surrounding the centromere of yeast chromosome III, and observing the behaviour of the resulting altered chromosomes during mitotic and meiotic cell divisions. A centromere substitution vector (pJC3-13) was constructed, which contains in the proper orientation: the DNA sequences that normally flank the chromosome III centromere, a wild-type *URA3* gene for selection, and a unique *Bam*HI restriction site for insertion of various DNA sequences to be assayed for centromere activity. Cleavage of the plasmid DNA with *Eco*RI generates a linear DNA fragment whose ends are homologous with the regions flanking the centromere. Transformation of the appropriate homozygous *ura3* diploid yeast strain with this linear DNA results in *URA3*$^{+}$ transformants in which the *CEN3* region on one copy of chromosome III has been replaced by the *URA3* gene and the DNA sequence previously inserted into the vector. These studies identify a 289 base-pair (bp) DNA fragment from the *CEN3* region that retains full centromere function when used to replace the normal *CEN3* sequence. Centromeres function equally well in either orientation, and the chromosome XI centromere (*CEN11*) can be used to replace *CEN3*, with no observable effect on mitotic or meiotic chromosome segregation. Various DNA restriction fragments occurring within the *CEN3* region were used alone or in combinations to replace the normal *CEN3* sequence. Yeast centromeres contain a high A+T region about 82–89 bp in length (element II) flanked by a highly conserved 11 bp sequence (III) and a less-conserved 14 bp sequence (I). The experiments demonstrate that both regions II and III are necessary for normal centromere function, although centromeres containing III plus truncated or rearranged portions of the high A+T region II retain partial activity. Chromosomes of the latter type often give abnormal segregation patterns through meiosis, including separation and random segregation of sister chromatids during the first meiotic division.

INTRODUCTION

The centromere is responsible for the stable maintenance and accurate segregation of eukaryotic chromosomes during both mitotic and meiotic cell divisions. In addition, we know that the centromere controls the behaviour of the paired sister chromatids during the first and second meiotic divisions; during meiosis I the paired chromatids segregate together, whereas in meiosis II, the sister chromatids segregate individually to the daughter cells. In most higher eukaryotic chromosomes, the centromere is seen as a constricted region that contains a complex structure, known as the kinetochore, to which the spindle fibres attach during mitosis. Although a bundle of fibres attaches to the kinetochore in most organisms, it is thought that each yeast (*Saccharomyces cerevisiae*) chromosome binds to only a single microtubule at the centromere (Peterson & Ris, 1976). The macromolecular composition and architecture of the kinetochore are poorly understood.

The common yeast, *S. cerevisiae*, is a powerful experimental system for the study of eukaryotic cell division. Many mutant strains are available that contain conditional genetic lesions in proteins necessary for proper cell division (*cdc* mutants, for a review see Pringle & Hartwell, 1982). Extensive genetic maps of the 17 chromosomes are available, and the position of each centromere is known with respect to nearby genetic markers (Mortimer & Schild, 1980). In addition, yeast is easily transformed by exogenous DNAs, and many plasmid vectors are available that will replicate in both yeast and in *Escherichia coli* (shuttle vectors). Many yeast genes have been isolated by selecting for complementation of various yeast mutations by yeast DNA segments sealed into these shuttle vectors. These favourable properties of the yeast system have been exploited by several laboratories in developing experimental strategies for the isolation and analysis of yeast centromeres.

ISOLATION AND GENERAL PROPERTIES OF YEAST CENTROMERES

In contrast to most higher eukaryotic chromosomes, which contain considerable quantities of highly repetitive DNA sequences in the centromere regions, yeast chromosomal DNA consists almost entirely of unique sequences, even at the centromeres. Thus, it is possible to isolate a relatively large region of the genome as a set of overlapping DNA fragments by using overlap hybridization screening procedures (chromosome 'walking') to select suitable cloned DNA segments from genomic libraries. The chromosome III centromere region was isolated in this way by first cloning the centromere-linked genes, *LEU2, CDC10* and *PGK*, and then obtaining the flanking and intervening regions by overlap hybridization screening of plasmid genomic libraries (Chinault & Carbon, 1979; Clarke & Carbon, 1980*a,b*). The functional centromere (*CEN3*) was localized to a $1·6 \times 10^3$ base-pair DNA segment initially (Clarke & Carbon, 1980*b*); however, we now believe that the functional region is considerably smaller (scc below). Using similar strategies, functional centromere DNAs have been isolated from yeast chromosomes IV, VI and XI (*CEN4*, Stinchcomb, Mann & Davis, 1982; *CEN6*, Panzeri & Philippsen, 1982; *CEN11*, Fitzgerald-Hayes, Buhler, Cooper & Carbon, 1982).

A second method for the isolation of yeast centromere DNAs depends upon the ability of a functional centromere to stabilize various yeast plasmids against mitotic loss when the host cells are grown on media non-selective for the plasmid genetic marker (Hsiao & Carbon, 1981). Mitotic stabilizing sequences thus obtained are mapped to a particular chromosome by standard genetic methods. This technique was used for the isolation of *CEN5* (Maine, Surosky & Tye, 1984) and *CEN14* (M. Neitz & J. Carbon, unpublished results).

Circular plasmids containing a yeast DNA replicator (*ARS*), a genetic marker, and a DNA segment containing a functional centromere, display many of the properties of authentic chromosomes in dividing yeast cells (Clarke & Carbon, 1980*b*). These minichromosomes are relatively stable mitotically (loss rate = 0·01–0·03 per cell division), whereas *ARS* plasmids lacking a centromere are lost at higher frequencies (0·2–0·3 per cell division). A single copy of a *CEN* plasmid in a diploid yeast cell undergoes a pattern of meiotic segregation typical of an aneuploid yeast chromosome. The duplicated chromatids segregate together in the first division, and then segregate individually to the two sister spores that are formed after the second meiotic division. Linear minichromosomes containing telomeric ends plus a replicator and centromere also have many of the properties of natural chromosomes in yeast (Murray & Szostak, 1983).

Nucleotide sequence data are now available for four yeast centromere regions: *CEN3* and *CEN11* (Fitzgerald-Hayes, Clarke & Carbon, 1982); *CEN4* (C. Mann & R. Davis, personal communication); and *CEN6* (Panzeri & Philippsen, 1982). These DNAs contain no large regions of homology, and, in fact, DNA fragments containing centromeres from different yeast chromosomes do not cross-hybridize. However, these four *CEN* regions contain common structural features, as shown in Fig. 1. All four contain a high A+T region (93–94% A+T) of nearly uniform length (82–89 base-pairs (bp)), designated sequence element II in Fig. 1. This high A+T region is bounded on one side by a highly conserved 11 bp sequence (element III), and, on the other side, by a less highly conserved 14 bp sequence (element I). Element III varies by no more than a single A–T transversion in the group of four centromeres. Deletion of the element I–III sequences results in complete loss of centromere activity (Bloom, Fitzgerald-Hayes & Carbon, 1982), and certain single base changes in the element III region also affect centromere activity *in vivo* (R. Ng & J. Carbon, unpublished results; J. McGrew & M. Fitzgerald-Hayes, personal communication).

The conformation of the chromatin in the centromere regions has been analysed by making use of *CEN3* and *CEN11* hybridization probes to map the location of nuclease-

Sequence elements common to four yeast centromeres

	Element I	Element II	Element III
CEN3	ATAAGTCACATGAT	← 88 bp (93% A + T) →	TGATTTCCGAA
CEN11	ATAAGTCACATGAT	← 89 bp (94% A + T) →	TGATTTCCGAA
CEN4	AAAGGTCACATGCT	← 82 bp (93% A + T) →	TGATTACCGAA
CEN6	TTTCATCACGTGCT	← 89 bp (94% A + T) →	TGTTTTCCGAA
	(ATAAGTAAAATAAT)*		

* (40 bp to left of
I in *CEN6*)

Fig. 1. Sequence elements common to four yeast centromeres. Nucleotides that are identical to the element I and III consensus sequences (ATAAGTCACATGAT and TGATTTCCGAA, respectively) are underlined. In *CEN6*, a second sequence showing considerable homology to the element I consensus sequence occurs 40 bp to the left of the element I region. The sequence element IV regions (Fitzgerald-Hayes *et al.* 1982) are not shown, since that homology only occurs in *CEN3* and *CEN11*, and the region can be deleted without inactivation of the centromere. The data are taken from the following sources: *CEN3* and *CEN11* (Fitzgerald-Hayes *et al.* 1982); *CEN4* (C. Mann & R. Davis, personal communication); *CEN6* (Panzeri & Philippsen, 1982).

sensitive sites in the DNA surrounding the sequence element I–III region (Bloom & Carbon, 1982). These key sequences are contained within a 220–250 bp protected region that is bounded on each side by a hypersensitive cleavage site, whereas the normal internucleosomal spacing is 160 bp in yeast. It has been postulated that this aberrant region in the chromatin contains the yeast kinetochore, which binds to only a single microtubule (Bloom *et al.* 1982).

STRUCTURE–FUNCTION STUDIES BY GENOMIC SUBSTITUTION

The plasmid-based assay of DNA segments for centromere function has been quite useful, but it does suffer from the deficiency that the circular minichromosomes do not behave exactly like authentic chromosomes in yeast. For example, the mitotic loss rate of a *CEN* plasmid is usually about 10^{-2} to 10^{-3} per cell division, whereas the typical yeast chromosome is considerably more stable (loss rate = 10^{-5} per cell division). Also, the meiotic distribution of a *CEN* plasmid is often difficult to follow, since many tetrads with a $4+:0-$ or $0+:4-$ distribution of the minichromosome are usually obtained. For these reasons, a preferable approach towards examining centromere function is to make sequence alterations, deletions or substitutions directly in the parental yeast chromosome. Preliminary experiments demonstrating the feasibility of this approach have recently been described (Clarke & Carbon, 1983).

It is possible to alter the sequence of a particular region of the yeast genome by transformation with an appropriate segment of double-stranded linear DNA (Rothstein, 1983). If the DNA segment used in the transformation is homologous at both ends with the genome and contains a wild-type gene that can be used as a selective marker, it is observed in most of the transformants that a sequence conversion has occurred, and the DNA sequence of the linear DNA fragment substitutes for the sequence found at the site of homology in the genome (e.g., see Fig. 3A). To modify routinely the centromere region of yeast chromosome III, we have constructed the centromere substitution vector (pJC3-13) shown in Fig. 2B. This plasmid contains in the proper orientation the DNA sequences that normally flank *CEN3* (labelled regions A and B in Fig. 2), a wild-type *URA3* gene for selection, and a unique *Bam*HI site for insertion of various DNA sequences between the two flanking regions. Cleavage of the plasmid with *Eco*RI releases a linear restriction fragment whose ends are homologous with the regions flanking the chromosome III centromere. Transformation of the appropriate *ura3* mutant with this linear DNA results in *URA3*⁺ transformants in which the 624 bp *CEN3* region of one copy of chromosome III has been replaced by the *URA3* gene and the DNA sequence previously inserted into the unique *Bam*HI site (see Figs 2 and 3).

The usefulness of this method was demonstrated by carrying out the *CEN3* substitutions shown in Fig. 3 (Clarke & Carbon, 1983). The 624 bp *Bam*HI-*Sau*3A fragment that contains functional *CEN3*, as determined by the plasmid assay (Fitzgerald-Hayes *et al.* 1982), was deleted in construction 3-13, replaced with the same 624 bp fragment in both possible orientations (constructions 303-4 and 303-6),

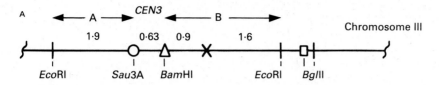

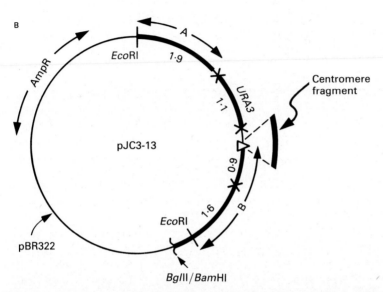

Fig. 2. A. Restriction map of the centromere region of *S. cerevisiae* chromosome III, giving the location of various restriction sites as shown. Numbers denote base-pairs$\times 10^{-3}$. B. Restriction map of the centromere substitution vector pJC3-13. The identity of the symbols is the same as given in A. Fragments of DNA to be tested for centromere function by substitution into chromosome III are inserted into the *Bam*HI site as indicated by the arrow. For details of the construction of plasmid pJC3-13, see Clarke & Carbon (1983).

and replaced with an 858 bp DNA fragment containing *CEN11* in both orientations (constructions 311-9 and 311-11). A diploid host was used for these transformations, since loss of one copy of chromosome III could readily be detected by the uncovering of recessive genetic markers (*his4, leu2,* and *MAT***a** or *MAT*α) located on both arms of chromosome III. In the particular diploid chosen (SB9882-4), loss of one copy of III results in a $2n-1$ strain that is mating-type **a**, Leu$^-$ and His$^-$; whereas loss of the other chromosome III gives a $2n-1$ strain that is mating-type α, Leu$^+$ and His$^+$ (see legend for Table 1 for further details). The transformants were demonstrated to possess the predicted structures around *CEN3* by using genomic Southern hybridization blots to measure the size of restriction fragments in the altered *CEN3* regions (Clarke & Carbon, 1983).

The transformants with altered chromosomes III were examined carefully with regard to rates of mitotic non-disjunction of III, distribution of appropriate genetic markers through the first and second meiotic divisions, haploid spore viability, and

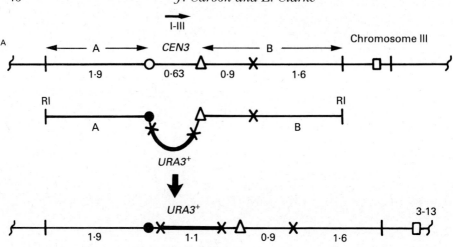

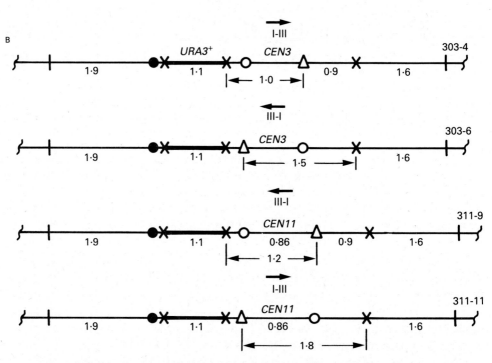

Fig. 3. A. Schematic representation of the conversion of the *CEN3* region of chromosome III to the acentric 3-13 construction. The sequence of the *Eco*RI restriction fragment used in the transformation completely replaces the normal sequence found between regions A and B. In this case, the centromere is replaced by only the *URA3* gene. B. Physical maps of the centromere region of chromosome III in various constructions produced using the pJC3-13 substitution vector. In these constructions, the 624 bp *CEN3* fragment is introduced in the two possible orientations, and the 858 bp *CEN11* fragment is substituted for *CEN3*, again in both possible orientations. See Clarke & Carbon (1983) for details.

Table 1. *Chromosome III non-disjunction in strains with altered centromeres*

Sequences at centromeres III of diploid	Structural alteration of *CEN3* (orientation)	Frequency of appearance of competent **a** or α cells (per cell division)
CEN3/*CEN3*(SB9882-4)	Wild-type	$0 \cdot 7 \times 10^{-5}$
CEN3/*CEN3*(SB9882-4CR)	Wild-type	$0 \cdot 1 \times 10^{-5}$
303-4/*CEN3*	624 bp *CEN3* (correct)	$0 \cdot 9 \times 10^{-5}$
303-6/*CEN3*	624 bp *CEN3* (reverse)	$0 \cdot 3 \times 10^{-5}$
303-9/*CEN3*	858 bp *CEN11* (reverse)	$1 \cdot 1 \times 10^{-5}$
303-11/*CEN3*	858 bp *CEN11* (correct)	$0 \cdot 6 \times 10^{-5}$
303-12/*CEN3*	289 bp *CEN3* (reverse)	$0 \cdot 2 \times 10^{-5}$
303-14/*CEN3*	289 bp *CEN3* (correct)	$0 \cdot 5 \times 10^{-5}$

The observed frequencies of appearance of mating-competent cells represent the sum of mitotic gene conversion and recombination at the *MAT* locus, plus non-disjunction of chromosome III to form $2n-1$ cells. Some of these data are taken from Clarke & Carbon (1983). See that reference for a more detailed description of experimental methods. The structures of the altered *CEN3* regions in these strains are given in Figs 3 and 4.

rates of mitotic and meiotic recombination around genetic markers on the altered chromosomes. As expected, complete deletion of the 624 bp *CEN3* region results in extreme instability of chromosome III, confirming that this DNA sequence contains all or an important portion of the functional centromere. The other alterations shown in Fig. 3B, all of which interrupt the normal DNA sequences on both sides of the 624 bp *CEN3* region, have no measurable effect on the mitotic or meiotic behaviour of chromosome III *in vivo* (see Table 1 and also Clarke & Carbon, 1983).

The results of this preliminary study demonstrated that the yeast centromeres are completely functional when placed in either orientation in the genome, even when in opposition to a centromere in the opposite orientation. Also, the insertion of the *URA3* gene immediately adjacent to *CEN3* has no observable effect on centromere function, although recombination frequencies measured across the centromere could be slightly altered (Clarke & Carbon, 1983). Finally, the results indicated that yeast centromeres are not necessarily chromosome-specific, since *CEN11* could substitute for *CEN3* with no detrimental effects, both in heterocentric (*CEN11* on one copy of III, *CEN3* on the other) or in homocentric (*CEN11* on both copies of III) diploids. Haploids containing *CEN11* in place of *CEN3* on the single copy of III also appear to be completely normal.

MOLECULAR DISSECTION OF A YEAST CENTROMERE

More recently, we have used the fragment-mediated transformation system to define more accurately the structural features necessary for proper functioning of *CEN3*. Various restriction fragments contained within the 624 bp *CEN3* *Bam*HI-*Sau*3A fragment were used individually or in various combinations as substitutes for the 624 bp *CEN3* region in the genome.

For example, cleavage of the 624 bp fragment with both *Rsa*I and *Alu*I yields a 289 bp segment that extends from a point 4 bp immediately to the left of element I through elements I–III, and ends 172 bp to the right of element III (see Fig. 4 for details of these constructions). Substitution of the 624 bp *CEN3* sequence in the genome with this 289 bp fragment effectively deletes sequences occurring on both sides of the key element I–III region. The 289 bp *Rsa*I-*Alu*I fragment was purified by polyacrylamide gel electrophoresis, and blunt-end ligated with plasmid pJC3-13 DNA that previously had been cleaved with *Bam*HI and the ends filled in using the *E. coli* DNA polymerase plus appropriate deoxynucleoside triphosphates. After transformation of *E. coli* to ampicillin-resistance with this DNA mixture, we identified individual clones that contained hybrid pJC3-13 plasmids with the 289 bp fragment

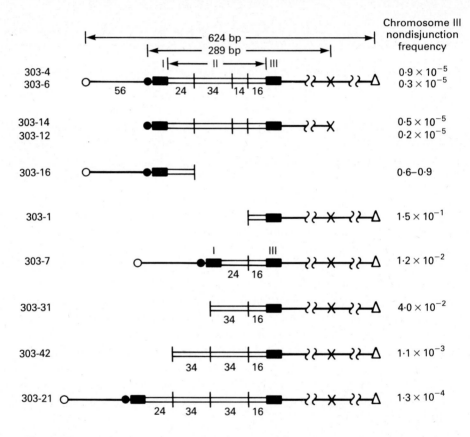

Fig. 4. Physical maps of the altered *CEN3* regions introduced into yeast chromosome III by the fragment-mediated transformation method. At the top is shown the normal 624 bp *Bam*HI-*Sau*3A fragment containing *CEN3*. The solid bars represent sequence elements I and III as indicated. The restriction sites are as follows: *Sau*3A (–O–); *Rsa*I (–●–); *Aha*III (–|–); *Alu*I (–×–); and *Bam*HI (–△–). Numbers are in base-pairs (bp). The double line represents the high A+T region, element II. The relative orientations of the 34 bp segments in constructions 303-31, 42 and 21 are unknown. The appropriate DNA fragments were sealed into the *Bam*HI site of plasmid pJC3-13 as described in the text. Methods for plasmid construction, procedures for yeast transformation, and the assays for rates of chromosome III loss were as described by Clarke & Carbon (1983).

sealed into the *Bam*HI site in either of the two possible orientations. Plasmid pJC303-14 contains the 289 bp sequence in the same orientation as occurs in the yeast genome, whereas the orientation is reversed in pJC303-12.

Plasmid pJC303-12 and pJC303-14 DNAs were individually cleaved with *Eco*RI, and the resulting DNA fragments were used to transform diploid yeast strain SB9882-4CR (see legend to Table 2 for genotype) to *URA3*$^+$. The transformant colonies (about 10^3 per μg transforming DNA) were normal in appearance and growth-rate, and the Ura$^+$ phenotype was mitotically quite stable. After growth of individual transformants in non-selective media for several generations, no Ura$^-$ cells could be detected among 1000 that were examined. The rate of loss of chromosome III in these transformants was measured more exactly by scoring for the number of mating-competent cells in a growing population. As described above, the loss of one copy of chromosome III in an **a**/α diploid (sterile) results in a competent mater, since the mating-type locus (*MAT***a** or *MAT*α) is located on that chromosome (see Clarke & Carbon, 1983, for details). As shown in Table 1 and Fig. 4, the chromosome III loss rate in these transformants was no greater than 10^{-5} per cell division, a value not significantly different from that obtained with the untransformed parent diploid strain.

The meiotic behaviour of the altered chromosomes III in the transformants of the 303-12 and 303-14 classes were examined by the classical methods of yeast genetic analysis. The diploid transformants were induced to sporulate, the individual spores in the tetrads separated by micro-dissection, and the resulting haploids scored for the distribution of appropriate genetic markers. In addition, haploid progeny containing the altered *CEN3* region (*URA3*$^+$) were back-crossed to examine the effect of having two altered *CEN3* regions in opposition. The results of these meiotic analyses, summarized in Table 2, indicate normal behaviour of the chromosomes III containing the 289 bp *CEN3* fragment in place of the normal 624 bp sequence. Spore viability was uniformly high (>90% in most cases), and the *URA3* marker on the altered chromosome III segregated as a centromere-linked gene, tightly linked to *LEU2* on chromosome III. Recombination frequencies between markers on chromosome III, and the number of gene conversions observed also fell within normal ranges. Finally, the predicted structure of the DNA in the *CEN3* region in the *URA3* haploids was verified by using a standard genomic Southern blot hybridization analysis (data not shown, see Clarke & Carbon (1983) for details).

The results described above suggest that the functional centromere is completely contained within the 289 bp *Rsa*I-*Alu*I fragment (unless sequences within flanking regions A and B are required and are able to function when physically separated from the centromere core). The importance of the physical integrity of the element I–III sequence region was examined by making use of the restriction enzyme, *Aha*III, which recognizes and cleaves at the midpoint of the sequence, T-T-T-A-A-A. This recognition site occurs at three positions in the A+T-rich element II region of *CEN3*, as shown in Fig. 4. Thus, cleavage of the 624 bp *Bam*HI-*Sau*3A fragment with *Aha*III produces four fragments: (a) a 98 bp fragment containing element I plus 24 bp of element II; (b) a 34 bp fragment from within element II; (c) a 14 bp fragment from

Table 2. Meiotic behaviour of chromosome III containing a 289 bp CEN3 substitution

a/α diploid strain	Tetrads scored	Spore viability (%)	Apparent map distance (centimorgans)			% Gene conversions		
			HIS4-LEU2	LEU2-URA3 / LEU2-CEN3	URA3-MAT	HIS4	LEU2	MAT
303-14/CEN3	33	95	21	9	33	10	6	0
303-12/CEN3	41	98	20	10	45	18	6	0
Back-crosses:								
303-14(29D) × BF305-18A	22	91	5	0	32	9	0	0
303-14(38A) × 303-14(18B)	26	95	21	9	31*	8	8	0
303-12(2A) × 303-14(18B)	13	77	29	8	21*	0	8	0
					*(LEU2-MAT)			
Literature values			9.9–19.9	3.4–11.6 (LEU2-CEN3)	20–23.1 (CEN3-MAT)	8.4	2.5	0.6

The URA3/ura3 heterozygous diploids, 303-14/CEN3 and 303-12/CEN3, were obtained by transformation of yeast strain SB9882-4CR (a ura3-52 trp1-289 leu2-3 leu2-112 his4-519 cry1/α ura3-52 trp1-289 can1) with the centromere-substitution EcoRI fragments as described in the text. The 303-14 construction contains the URA3 gene plus the 289 bp RsaI-AluI CEN3 fragment in the correct orientation, whereas the 303-12 construction contains the CEN3 sequence inserted in the orientation opposite from that seen in normal chromosome III. The back-cross diploids were constructed by mating selected Ura+ haploid progeny from the first two groups of tetrads. The genotypes are: 303-14(29D), α URA3(III) ura3(V) trp1 leu2 his4; BF305-18A, a arg5,6 ura3 met14 ade1; 303-14(38A), α URA3(III) ura3(V) trp1; 303-14(18B), a URA3(III) ura3(V) trp1 leu2 his4 met14 ade1; 303-12(2A), α URA3(III) ura3(V) trp1. As expected, URA3+ segregated 2+:2− always in sister spores in all tetrads from the first three diploids (URA3 thus maps 0 centimorgan from CEN3). In the homozygous URA3 back-cross diploids, URA3 segregated 4+:0− in all tetrads. For experimental details, see Clarke & Carbon (1983).

within element II; and (d) a 478 bp fragment containing the rightward 16 bp of II plus III and the remaining sequences to the right of III. We substituted the normal *CEN3* region with these fragments, either alone or in various combinations, to learn more about which DNA sequences are important in controlling the various centromere functions.

A small recombinant plasmid library, consisting of vector pJC3-13 with various combinations of the *Aha*III fragments sealed into the plasmid *Bam*HI site, was constructed as follows. The purified 624 bp *CEN3* fragment was cleaved with *Aha*III, mixed with one-tenth of the quantity of *Bam*HI-cleaved pJC3-13 DNA, and ligated overnight at room temperature in the presence of the bacteriophage T4 DNA ligase plus ATP, to seal annealed cohesive ends. Since the *Aha*III cleavage leaves blunt ends, the resulting mixture was treated with DNA polymerase plus deoxynucleoside triphosphates to fill in unreacted *Bam*HI ends, and then the ligation step was repeated. The DNA mixture was used to transform *E. coli* strain JA226 to ampicillin resistance, and the resulting colonies were screened by colony hybridization (Reed, 1982), using ^{32}P-labelled 624 bp *CEN3* fragment as hybridization probe. The colonies displayed different levels of radioactivity, depending upon the number of *Aha*III fragments cloned into the plasmid vector. Plasmid DNA preparations were examined by restriction mapping to determine the identity and arrangement of fragments cloned into the *Bam*HI site of pJC3-13.

Plasmids containing the inserts shown in Fig. 4 were chosen for *CEN3* replacement transformations. In the case of the inserts containing one or more copies of the 34 bp *Aha*III fragment plus other fragments, we have not determined the relative orientation of the various fragments with respect to each other (refers to pJC303-31, 303-42, and 303-21). The centromere replacement transformations were carried out in the usual manner, using *Eco*RI-cleaved plasmid DNAs to transform diploid yeast strain SB42583 (see legend to Table 3 for genotype) to *URA3*[+]. Several transformants of each class were colony purified and used for further studies.

The rates of chromosome III loss in these transformants were assayed as described above, using quantitative mating to determine the number of mating-component cells in a population (Clarke & Carbon, 1983), or, if chromosome III loss rates were greater than 10^{-3}, by assaying cell populations directly for Ura[−] cells using standard replica-plating techniques. The results of these assays, shown in Fig. 4, are quite clear. Fragment (a), containing element I plus 24 bp of the high A+T region, is completely inactive in terms of centromere function. On the other hand, fragment (d), which contains the highly conserved sequence element III plus 16 bp of element II, does show some very weak stabilizing activity, although the frequency of chromosome III loss in these strains (303-1) is about 5000 times greater than is observed in wild-type yeast. The importance of the high A+T region II for proper centromere function can be seen by comparing the results obtained with the substitutions labelled 303-7, 303-31, 303-42 and 303-21, which contain increasing amounts of high A+T DNA joined to element III. As additional A+T sequences are added, the non-disjunction frequency decreases from 10^{-1} through successive orders of magnitude to 10^{-4}. However, it is clear that the physical arrangement or total length of the high A+T

Table 3. *Meiotic behaviour of various diploids containing altered chromosome III centromeres*

a/α diploid strain	Mitotic non-disjunction	Spore viability (%)	Complete tetrads/total	URA3+ distribution in tetrads			Ura3:Met14			Map distance (cM)	
				4+:0−	3+:1−	2+:2−	PD	NPD	T	LEU2-URA3 / LEU2-CEN3	LEU2-HIS4
Heterocentrics											
303-1AD/CEN3	0·15	55	11/43	0	2	9	3	6	0	–	–
303-7A/CEN3	$1·2 \times 10^{-2}$	83	18/33	3	1	14	7	7	0	6·3	7·7
303-31A/CEN3	4×10^{-2}	84	20/34	1	2	17	9	11	0	6·7	17
303-42A/CEN3	$1·1 \times 10^{-3}$	89	25/35	0	0	25	14	11	0	6·3	14
303-21A/CEN3	$1·3 \times 10^{-4}$	91	27/33	0	0	27	16	11	0	6·8	31
							Leu2:Met14				
							PD	NPD	T		
Homocentrics											
303-7A(18A)/303-7A(21C)	10^{-2}	47	3/41	3	0	0	5	2	5	21	14
303-42A(32B)/303-42A(1D)	10^{-3}	70	14/46	14	0	0	4	7	4	17	15

The heterocentric (heterozygous URA3+/ura3) diploids were obtained by transformation of yeast strain SB42583 (a/α leu2/LEU2+ his4/HIS4+ cry1/CRY1+ ADE1+/ade1 MET14+/met14 trp1/trp1 ura3/ura3) with the various centromere-substitution EcoRI fragments as shown in Fig. 4 and described in the text. The homocentrics were obtained by back-crossing selected URA3+ hybrid progeny from the first group of tetrads. The genotypes are: 303-7A(18A), a URA3+(III) ura3(V) LEU2+ HIS4+ met14 ADE1+; 303-7A (21C), α URA3+(III) ura3(V) leu2 his4 MET14+ ADE1+; 303-42A(32B), a URA3+(III) ura3(V) leu2 his4 MET14+ ade1; 303-42A(1D), α URA3+(III) ura3(V) LEU2+ HIS4+ met14+ ADE1+. In the case of homocentrics, map distances are calculated from combined data including complete tetrads plus triads, assuming a normal distribution of markers into the non-viable spores. cM, centimorgans.

sequences must be important for proper mitotic function of the centromere, since all of these reconstructions show some degree of impairment of *CEN* function. It is interesting, however, that chromosome III containing replacement 303-21 is nearly normal in mitotic function, whereas the element II region has been grossly rearranged and is 20 bp longer than is seen in wild-type *CEN3*.

The results of standard meiotic tetrad analyses, carried out on these *CEN3* substitution strains, are summarized in Tables 3 and 4. Standard genetic theory would predict that a non-disjunction of chromosome III occurring during the first meiotic division would lead to a tetrad with two dead and two live spores, both disomic for chromosome III. A non-disjunction event occurring during meiosis II would lead to one dead and three live spores, of which one (the non-sister) would be disomic for III. If the sister chromatids of the altered chromosome III separate prematurely during meiosis I and segregate randomly, one could observe several different types of tetrads. One class would also include tetrads with one dead and three live spores, but the single chromosome III disome would be found in one of the two sister spores of the triad. For these reasons, the tetrads in which only two or three spores germinated to yield viable colonies were also examined carefully in these meiotic analyses.

Tetrad analysis of diploid transformants of the 303-16 class was not possible; these strains would not sporulate, probably because of the high rate of loss of chromosome III to yield *MAT***a** or *MAT*α $2n-1$ cells. Transformant class 303-1 diploids would sporulate, but spore viability was quite low (55 %) and complete tetrads were difficult to obtain. The transformants of the other four classes sporulated readily, however, and spore viability was reasonably high (83–91 %), as shown in Table 3. The heterocentric diploids showing rates of chromosome III loss equal to or greater than 10^{-2} (303-1, 303-7 and 303-31) produced a relatively high proportion of aberrant tetrads, in which the *URA3* marker on the altered chromosome segregated $4+:0-$ or $3+:1-$ (see Table 3). The origin of these unusual tetrads is unclear, although the $4+:0-$ tetrads could result from the presence of cells trisomic for chromosome III $(2n+1$

Table 4. *Occurrence of haploids disomic for chromosome III among meiotic progeny from diploids containing structurally altered centromeres III*

Diploid	Viable spores in tetrad	Total asci in class	Asci containing one **a**/α sterile spore	Mating-competent progeny	
				Sisters	Non-sisters
303-7A(18A)/303-7A(21C)	4	3	1	–	–
	3	10	6	3	3
	2	11	4	–	–
303-42A(32B)/303-42A(1D)	4	14	2	–	–
	3	16	3	0	3
	2	10	0	–	–

For genotypes, see legend to Table 3. The **a**/α chromosome III disome strains scored as both weak **a** and weak α due to non-disjunction of chromosome III during mitotic growth. Sister spores were identified by scoring the distribution of *met14* (centromere-linked on XI).

cells) among the sporulating diploids. However, in those cases where the *URA3* marker segregated normally $(2+:2-)$, it scored perfectly as a centromere-linked gene, giving only parental or non-parental ditype distributions with respect to the centromere-linked *MET14* gene. Thus, the altered chromosome III did not appear to be segregating randomly through meiosis in these heterocentric diploids. The segregation of *URA3* was perfectly normal in the heterocentrics whose mitotic chromosome III loss rate was 10^{-3} or less (303-42 and 303-21). As expected, *URA3* was closely linked to *LEU2* on chromosome III in all of the transformants (Table 3).

Homocentric diploids were constructed by back-crossing *URA3*+ haploid progeny from some of the tetrads described above. The most interesting results were obtained from the homocentric 303-7/303-7 and 303-42/303-42 diploids, as summarized in Tables 3 and 4. Even though the frequency of mitotic non-disjunction of chromosome III in these diploids is no greater than 10^{-2}, aberrant tetrads were seen at much higher frequencies and spore viability was much lower than was observed with the heterocentric diploids. A relatively large proportion of tetrads from the homocentric diploids yielded only two or three viable spores (Table 4). Significantly, many of the progeny from these aberrant tetrads were disomic for chromosome III (sterile *MATa/MATα* strains), as shown in Table 4. The number of progeny containing chromosome III disomes actually would be greater than is reflected by the data in Table 4, because for technical reasons the *MATa/MATa* and *MATα/MATα* disomes were not scored. Thus, these altered centromeres appear to function more poorly in meiosis than in mitosis, but only when they are in opposition to another chromosome containing an altered centromere.

DISCUSSION AND CONCLUSIONS

At the DNA level, at least, the structural complexity of the yeast centromere is somewhat simpler than might have been predicted, especially considering the rather large and complex kinetochore regions seen on chromosomes from higher eukaryotes. However, yeast chromosomes are two orders of magnitude smaller than chromosomes from animal cells, and are thought to bind to only a single spindle fibre, rather than to a large bundle of fibres. It appears from our studies that the functional centromere region is no larger than 289 bp, and, in fact, could be considerably smaller. At this writing, it is still uncertain how much of the DNA occurring immediately to the right of the element III region is required for proper *CEN* function.

All yeast centromeres examined to date contain the highly conserved sequence element III (11 bp), which has been observed to vary by no more than a single A–T transversion among the four yeast *CEN* DNAs that have been sequenced. The physical integrity of this region is absolutely critical with regard to centromere function, since various single base changes induced either within or closely adjacent to the *CEN3* element III can lead to drastically increased levels of non-disjunction of chromosome III. For example, changing either of the two C residues to a T within element III decreases *CEN3* activity (J. McGrew & M. Fitzgerald-Hayes, personal communication); and an A to C change at a position 7 bp to the right of element III on chromosome III results in a non-disjunction frequency of 10^{-4} for the altered chromosome (R. Ng & J. Carbon, unpublished results). It seems most likely that this critical region is a binding site for a protein (or group of proteins) that serves as an interface between the centromere DNA and the spindle fibre. The isolation of a protein fraction that binds with high selectivity to *CEN* DNA fragments has been reported (Bloom *et al.* 1982; Bloom *et al.* 1984), but direct evidence that these proteins are bound to the centromere *in vivo* or are important for centromere function is still lacking.

The high A+T region (element II) is clearly required for proper centromere function, since deletion of 48 bp within this region in *CEN3* (construction 303-7, Fig. 4) increases the chromosome III loss rate by three orders of magnitude (to 10^{-2} per cell division). However, the exact role played by element II with regard to centromere function is still unclear. The high A+T regions in the four centromeres that have been sequenced are of fairly uniform length (ranging from 82–89 bp) and base composition (93–94 % A+T), but no long regions of perfect homology are evident. The chromosomes III altered in the element II region of *CEN3* appear to be more defective in meiotic than in mitotic segregation processes. In fact, the homocentric 303-7/303-7 diploid, in which both *CEN3* regions contain the 48 bp deletion in element II, produces more aberrant than normal tetrads, even though the mitotic non-disjunction frequency is only 10^{-2} (see Table 4). There is reasonable evidence to conclude that, in the 303-7/303-7 diploid, the chromosome III sister chromatids are prematurely separating during the first meiotic division, and segregating randomly. This follows from the presence of triads in which one spore is disomic for chromosome III and the other two are non-sisters (Table 4), and also from the abnormally high number of tetrads in which the centromere III-linked *LEU2* marker appears in non-sister spores (Table 3). Thus, it seems reasonable to propose that the high A+T region II is intimately involved in the control of chromosome segregation through meiosis, especially in whatever mechanism operates to hold the sister chromatids together during the first meiotic division. It has been proposed that differential regulation of replication of the centromere DNA (perhaps in the element II region) could be involved in controlling chromatid separation (Tschumper & Carbon, 1982).

What is the relationship between the relatively simple structure that serves as the yeast centromere and the highly complex kinetochore structure seen at the centromere region of chromosomes from higher eukaryotes? This question can only be answered by the isolation and molecular characterization of centromere DNAs from other organisms, particularly from those with chromosomes that bind to several microtubules at the centromere. Given present technology, this task would be difficult or impossible using chromosomes from most higher eukaryotes, because their centromere regions include vast amounts of DNA, much of it consisting of long runs of highly repetitive sequences. It seems likely that other relatively 'simple' eukaryotes, whose chromosomes are somewhat larger than those from *S. cerevisiae* and thus might contain centromeres with more than one spindle fibre binding site, would represent the best experimental systems for extending these studies on centromeres and chromosome segregation.

We are grateful to Virginia Kuga for excellent technical assistance. This research was supported by a grant (CA-11034) from the National Cancer Institute, National Institutes of Health.

REFERENCES

BLOOM, K. S., AMAYA, E., CARBON, J., CLARKE, L., HILL, A. & YEH, E. (1984). Chromatin conformation of yeast centromeres. *J. Cell Biol.* (in press).

BLOOM, K. S. & CARBON, J. (1982). Yeast centromere DNA is in a unique and highly ordered structure in chromosomes and small circular minochromosomes. *Cell* **29**, 305–317.

BLOOM, K. S., FITZGERALD-HAYES, M. & CARBON, J. (1982). Structural analysis and sequence organization of yeast centromeres. *Cold Spring Harbor Symp. quant. Biol.* **47**, 1175–1185.

CHINAULT, A. C. & CARBON, J. (1979). Overlap hybridization screening: Isolation and characterization of overlapping DNA fragments surrounding the *leu2* gene on yeast chromosome III. *Gene* **5**, 111–126.

CLARKE, L. & CARBON, J. (1980*a*). Isolation of the centromere-linked *CDC10* gene by complementation in yeast. *Proc. natn. Acad. Sci. U.S.A.* **77**, 2173–2177.

CLARKE, L. & CARBON, J. (1980*b*). Isolation of a yeast centromere and construction of functional small circular chromosomes. *Nature, Lond.* **287**, 504–509.

CLARKE, L. & CARBON, J. (1983). Genomic substitutions of centromeres in *Saccharomyces cerevisiae. Nature, Lond.* **305**, 23–28.

FITZGERALD-HAYES, M., BUHLER, J.-M., COOPER, T. & CARBON, J. (1982). Isolation and subcloning analysis of functional centromere DNA (*CEN11*) from yeast chromosome XI. *Molec. cell. Biol.* **2**, 82–87.

FITZGERALD-HAYES, M., CLARKE, L. & CARBON, J. (1982). Nucleotide sequence comparisons and functional analysis of yeast centromere DNAs. *Cell* **29**, 235–244.

HSIAO, C.-L. & CARBON, J. (1981). A direct selection procedure for the isolation of functional centromeric DNA. *Proc. natn. Acad. Sci. U.S.A.* **78**, 3760–3764.

MAINE, G. T., SUROSKY, R. T. & TYE, B.-K. (1984). Isolation and characterization of the centromere from chromosome V (*CEN5*) of *Saccharomyces cerevisiae. Molec. cell. Biol.* **4**, 86–91.

MORTIMER, R. K. & SCHILD, D. (1980). The genetic map of *Saccharomyces cerevisiae. Microbiol. Rev.* **44**, 519–571.

MURRAY, A. W. & SZOSTAK, J. W. (1983). Construction of artificial chromosomes in yeast. *Nature, Lond.* **305**, 189–193.

PANZERI, L. & PHILIPPSEN, D. (1982). Centromeric DNA from chromosome VI in *Saccharomyces cerevisiae* strains. *EMBO J.* **1**, 1605–1611.

PETERSON, J. B. & RIS, H. (1976). Electron microscopic study of the spindle and chromosome movement in the yeast *Saccharomyces cerevisiae. J. Cell Sci.* **22**, 219–242.

PRINGLE, J. R. & HARTWELL, L. H. (1982). *S. cerevisiae* cell cycle. In *The Molecular Biology of the Yeast* Saccharomyces (ed. J. N. Strathern, E. W. Jones & J. R. Broach), pp. 97–142. New York: Cold Spring Harbor Laboratory Press.

REED, S. I. (1982). Preparation of product-specific antisera by gene fusion: Antibodies specific for the product of the yeast cell-division cycle gene, *CDC28. Gene* **20**, 255–265.

ROTHSTEIN, R. J. (1983). One-step gene disruption in yeast. *Meth. Enzym.* **101**, 202–211.

STINCHCOMB, D. T., MANN, C. & DAVIS, R. W. (1982). Centromeric DNA from *Saccharomyces cerevisiae. J. molec. Biol.* **158**, 157–179.

TSCHUMPER, G. & CARBON, J. (1983). Copy number control by a yeast centromere. *Gene* **23**, 221–232.

J. Cell Sci. Suppl. 1, 59–79 (1984)
Printed in Great Britain © The Company of Biologists Limited 1984

REPLICATION AND TRANSCRIPTION DEPEND ON ATTACHMENT OF DNA TO THE NUCLEAR CAGE

D. A. JACKSON[1], S. J. McCREADY[2] AND P. R. COOK[1]

[1] *Sir William Dunn School of Pathology, University of Oxford, South Parks Road, Oxford OX1 3RE, U.K.* and [2] *The Botany School, South Parks Road, Oxford OX1 3RA, U.K.*

SUMMARY

When living cells are lysed in a non-ionic detergent and 2 M-NaCl, structures are released that resemble nuclei. They contain naked nuclear DNA packaged within a flexible cage of RNA and protein. Since the DNA is supercoiled, it must be intact and looped by attachment to the cage. It is argued that this cage is the active site of the key nuclear functions, transcription and replication: outlying sequences are activated by attachment to polymerases at the cage. This thesis is supported by the close and specific association of nascent RNA with cages, the attachment of active viral sequences (in transformed and productively infected cells) and the attachment of nascent DNA during both normal and repair synthesis.

INTRODUCTION

It is an old idea that DNA and chromosomes are ordered within the eukaryotic nucleus (Comings, 1968; Dupraw, 1970) and that gene position affects function (Baker, 1968). However, it has only recently become possible to analyse the precise biochemical basis for this order, largely because methods have now been devised for isolating DNA in association with a sub-nuclear structure.

Since the first reports 20 years ago (Zbarsky, Dmitrieva & Yermolayeva, 1962; Smetana, Steele & Busch, 1963) many different sub-nuclear structures have been extracted from nuclei using high concentrations of salt. They share many basic constituents and include nuclear pore complexes, envelopes, ghosts, matrices, lamins, scaffolds and folded chromosomes (for reviews see Agutter & Richardson, 1980; Hancock, 1982; this volume). More or less degraded nucleic acid is attached to them. They can be isolated in association with *intact* DNA if cells – rather than nuclei – are lysed directly in a non-ionic detergent (e.g. Triton X-100), 2 M-NaCl and sufficient chelating agent to inhibit nucleases completely; then, structures are released that resemble nuclei (Fig. 1; Cook & Brazell, 1975, 1976; Cook, Brazell & Jost, 1976). These nucleoids can be made from a wide variety of cells (e.g. fibroblasts, lymphocytes, erythroblasts, teratocarcinoma and epithelial cells of men, rats, mice, birds, frogs and insects). They contain all the nuclear RNA and DNA but few proteins characteristic of chromatin (e.g. they contain no histones). They do contain elements of the matrix, the pore-complex/lamins and attached cytoskeletal actins and keratins. Four different approaches indicate that their DNA is intact; all involve the demonstration of supercoiling in nucleoid DNA.

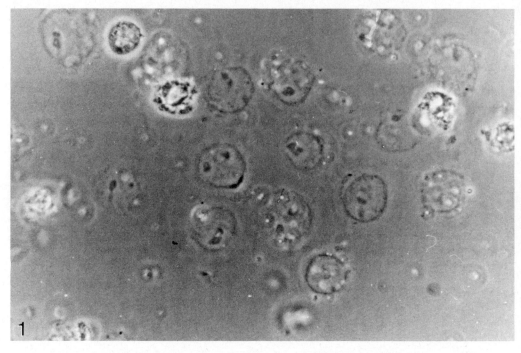

Fig. 1. HeLa nucleoids isolated in 1·95 M-NaCl and photographed in the phase-contrast microscope. The diameter of the nuclear region is about 12 μm (from Cook *et al.* 1976).

Supercoiling in nucleoid DNA

Supercoils can be maintained in circular, but not in free linear, DNA. Supercoiled molecules have distinctive properties (Bauer & Vinograd, 1974) and these are shared by nucleoids. For example, they sediment in gradients containing intercalating agents in a biphasic manner (Cook & Brazell, 1975, 1976) and they bind ethidium (Cook & Brazell, 1978) and scatter light (unpublished observation) like superhelical DNA. Perhaps the most striking demonstration comes from electron microscopy of nucleoids prepared using Kleinschmidt's procedure (Mullinger & Johnson, 1979; McCready, Akrigg & Cook, 1979). DNA, initially confined within a residual structure that we call the nuclear cage, is spread to form a huge skirt of supercoiled fibres attached to the collapsed cage (Fig. 2). All this evidence suggests that nuclear DNA is circular; however, as we believe that chromosomal DNA is linear, it must be looped, presumably by attachment at the base of the loops to the cage. Nicking one loop releases supercoils in that loop, but not in adjacent loops. We estimate there to be, on average, one supercoil every 90–180 base-pairs (Cook & Brazell, 1977) in loops of 220×10^3 base-pairs (Cook & Brazell, 1975, 1978). We have been unable to detect

Fig. 2. Part of a spread of a HeLa nucleoid. A tangled mass of superhelical fibres stretches from the collapsed cage to the edge of the field. The diameter of the cage is about 15 μm (see McCready *et al.* 1979).

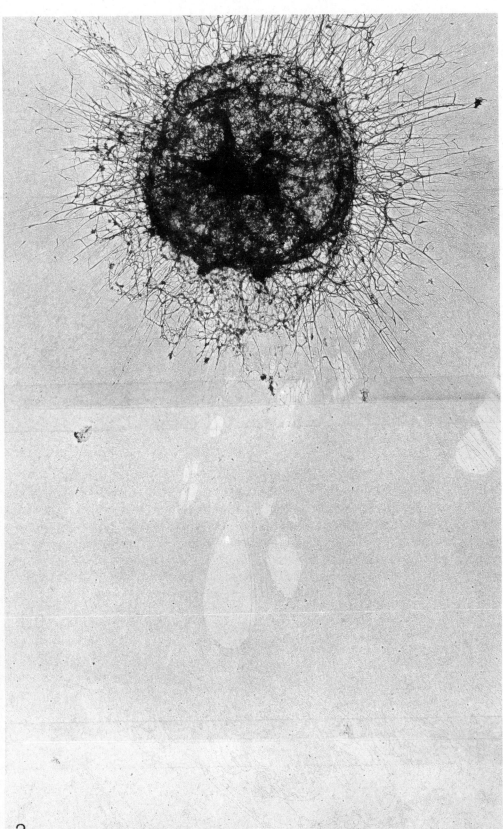

2

biophysically any changes in loop size as cells progress through mitosis (Warren & Cook, 1978). These loop sizes are very large – too large to represent one unit of transcription or replication.

The cage

The isolation of intact DNA packaged within the nucleoid cage has the important practical consequence that long and fragile DNA molecules can be pipetted without shearing them. Unfortunately, most primary diploid cells possess weak cages that break easily, releasing the DNA, which then shears (Cook & Brazell, 1976 and unpublished). Therefore, we have worked mainly with nucleoids that have robust cages and so contain DNA that remains superhelical on pipetting.

We will argue that the cage serves another – and most important – function: namely, that it is the *active site* of the key nuclear functions, replication and transcription. As a result, genes are positioned precisely within loops of nuclear DNA and their positions relative to the cage determine whether they are replicated or transcribed.

RNA IS SYNTHESIZED AT THE CAGE

It is now widely assumed that eukaryotic genes are transcribed by movement of an RNA polymerase along the DNA. The beautiful photomicrographs of 'genes in action' taken by Miller and colleagues strikingly illustrate this view (Miller & Beattie, 1969; Miller, 1975, and this volume), which is reinforced by the isolation of soluble polymerases. However, we hardly ever see transcription complexes in the skirts of nucleoid spreads; rather, all nascent RNA remains associated with the cage (Jackson, McCready & Cook, 1981). Furthermore, it is worth remembering that: (1) polymerases are only solubilized by sonication or incubation in the presence of Mg^{2+} (Beebee, 1979); (2) even then, the majority remain intractably associated with pelletable material (Beebee, 1979; Weil, Luse, Segall & Roeder, 1979; Kaplan, Kleinman & Horwitz, 1977; Klempnauer, Fanning, Otto & Knippers, 1980); (3) soluble RNA polymerases initiate inefficiently (e.g. in one relatively efficient system, the crude 'Manley' extract, RNA polymerase II polymerizes correctly initiated transcripts at <10 nucleotides/h (Manley *et al.* 1980) or 0·01 % of the rate *in vivo* (Cox, 1972). Our work with nucleoids led us to examine an alternative view: namely, that transcription occurs by movement of DNA past a fixed polymerase (Jackson *et al.* 1981).

Newly synthesized RNA is closely associated with the cage

When HeLa cells are incubated with [³H]uridine for 1 min to label only nuclear RNA, >95 % of the radioactivity initially present in the cells and insoluble in trichloroacetic acid subsequently cosediments with the nucleoids. It might do so, not because it is attached to the cage, but because it is entangled in DNA. We tested this possibility in two ways. First, when cells are pulse-labelled with [³H]uridine for 2·5 min, nucleoids are isolated and spread, and autoradiographs are prepared, >95 %

of the grains lie over the cage; even though DNA is spread, nascent RNA is not. A second experiment confirms that nascent RNA is not simply entangled in DNA. Cells were labelled with [^{14}C]thymidine for 24 h, followed by [^{3}H]uridine for 2·5 min. (Actinomycin D (0·08 μg/ml) was present during, and 30 min before, the ^{3}H pulse to suppress ribosomal RNA synthesis.) Nucleoids were isolated, incubated with the restriction endonuclease, *Eco*RI, and the amounts of the two labels remaining associated with cages were determined after filtration. In one typical experiment, when 90 % of ^{14}C (i.e. DNA) was detached, <15 % of the ^{3}H radioactivity (i.e. RNA) was lost.

The following control experiments demonstrate that RNA that *is* entangled in DNA *can* escape with the DNA from the cage. Entangled RNA was synthesized *in vitro* by incubating nucleoids with *Escherichia coli* RNA polymerase, [^{3}H]uridine and the appropriate precursors; presumably, the transcripts are initiated at sites scattered around the loops of naked DNA. In this case, spreading nucleoid DNA spreads labelled RNA; 34 % of the autoradiographic grains are found over the skirt. Furthermore, digestion with *Eco*RI detached this RNA. The RNA made *in vitro* is not so tightly associated with the cage as that synthesized *in vivo*. We next determined whether this tight association was specific.

Attachment of the 5′ end of nascent RNA

A 'cap' containing methylated bases is attached at the 5′ end of nascent RNA immediately transcription begins (Furuichi, 1978; Salditt-Georgieff, Harpold, Chen-Kiang & Darnell, 1980; Babich, Nevins & Darnell, 1980) so the 5′ end of such transcripts can be labelled with [^{3}H]methionine. This label is also incorporated into proteins, DNA and other methylated bases within RNA chains; only 8·3 % being incorporated into caps. If nascent RNA is attached at its 5′ end, caps should resist detachment by pancreatic ribonuclease. Therefore, we labelled cells with [^{3}H]-methionine for 15 min, isolated nucleoids and incubated them with sufficient ribonuclease to detach 75 % of nascent RNA. Now 8 % of the label was recovered with cages in caps. Therefore, removal of 75 % of the body of the chain detaches few, if any, caps.

Attachment of the 3′ end of nascent RNA

Any attachment at the 3′ end of the growing chain is technically much more difficult to demonstrate. Nevertheless, we have attempted to do so using doubly labelled nucleoids as follows. Cells were incubated (as before in the presence of actinomycin D) for 2 min with [^{14}C]uridine; then [^{3}H]uridine was added and the incubation continued for 1 min. The 3′ end will be richer in ^{3}H than ^{14}C and if attached, inspection of simple models indicates that the ^{3}H in nucleoids should be more resistant to detachment by ribonuclease than is the ^{14}C (Fig. 3A,B). Therefore, cells were doubly labelled, nucleoids were prepared and incubated with ribonuclease, the detached RNA was removed by filtration and the percentages of ^{14}C and ^{3}H remining associated with cages were determined. If RNA is attached at random to the cage, then ^{14}C and ^{3}H will be detached in equal proportions from the cages, i.e. the ratio of (% ^{3}H

D. A. Jackson, S. J. McCready and P. R. Cook

remaining) ÷ (% ^{14}C remaining) will remain at unity independently of the amount of ^{14}C remaining. On the other hand, if the 3' end is attached, then detachment of RNA will lead to a relative enrichment of ^{3}H, i.e. the ratio will increase above unity as the amount of ^{14}C remaining decreases. (Attachment at both ends would also cause

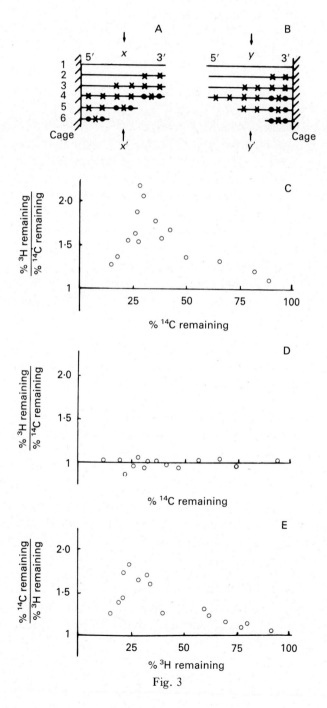

Fig. 3

this behaviour but we cannot distinguish such double attachment from 3' attachment using this labelling regime.) The results are consistent with attachment at the 3' end since the ^{3}H resists detachment; for example, removal of all but 30 % of the ^{14}C leaves leaves 54 % of the ^{3}H (i.e. the ratio is $54 \div 30 = 1 \cdot 8$) (Fig. 3c). When both labels are present together for 3 min there is no such variation in the normalized ratio so that these results cannot be due to a labelling artefact (Fig. 3D). This is confirmed by reversing the labels: in this case it is ^{14}C (the label added last) that is enriched (Fig. 3E).

Transcribed genes lie close to the cage

If nascent RNA is so closely associated with the cage, then so too must be the genes from which it is transcribed; DNA close to the cage should be richer in transcribed sequences than total DNA. Therefore, we prepared four types of DNA by incubating nucleoids with various amounts of *Eco*RI; then cages, and any associated DNA, were sedimented free of detached fragments to yield pellets that retained 100, 35, 14 and 5 % of the initial amount of cage-associated DNA. This cage-associated DNA was purified, labelled by 'nick-translation', denatured and the percentage of the DNA forming a hybrid with an excess of total nucleoid RNA was determined (Fig. 4); 13 % of nucleoid RNA hybridized with total DNA (i.e. sample 1). All the other samples of cage-associated DNA hybridized to greater extents, showing that they were richer in sequences complementary to nucleoid RNA. The result with the cages that retained 5 % of the total DNA (i.e. sample 4) is quite striking: 23 % of this DNA is complementary to nucleoid RNA. If we assume that only one strand is transcribed, then about half this sample of cage-associated DNA contains transcribed sequences – a remarkable enrichment.

These experiments suggest that both ends of nascent transcripts are attached to the cage and that transcribed sequences lie close to the cage. If so, transcripts must be generated as DNA passes through a fixed transcription complex at the cage (Fig. 5).

ATTACHMENT OF TRANSFORMING GENES

This model for transcription suggests that only attached genes can be transcribed.

Fig. 3. Nascent RNA is attached at the 3' end. A. A simple model for labelling and cutting RNA attached at the 5' end. 1. A completed strand of RNA (——) is attached at its 5' end to the cage. Cells are labelled for 2 min with [^{14}C]uridine ($\times$) followed by 1 min with [^{3}H]uridine ($\bullet$). 2–3. Some nascent RNA molecules complete synthesis after the addition of ^{14}C but before the addition of ^{3}H, so becoming only ^{14}C-labelled, whilst others (4–6), which initiate during the pulses, become labelled with both ^{14}C and ^{3}H. Digestion with ribonuclease (i.e. cutting between x and x') detaches ^{14}C and ^{3}H in roughly equal proportions. Therefore, on digestion, the ratio (% ^{3}H remaining) $\div$ (% ^{14}C remaining) remains at about unity. B. An array of molecules labelled as in A are attached at the 3' end. Cutting between y and y' detaches ^{14}C but not ^{3}H; therefore, the ratio is greater than unity. C. Cells were labelled with [^{14}C]uridine for 2 min followed by 1 min with [^{3}H]uridine, nucleoids were isolated, incubated with ribonuclease and the percentage of each label remaining associated with cages was determined. D. As C, except both labels were present together for 3 min. E. As C except labelling was for 2 min with [^{3}H]uridine followed by 1 min with [^{14}C]uridine (from Jackson *et al.* 1981).

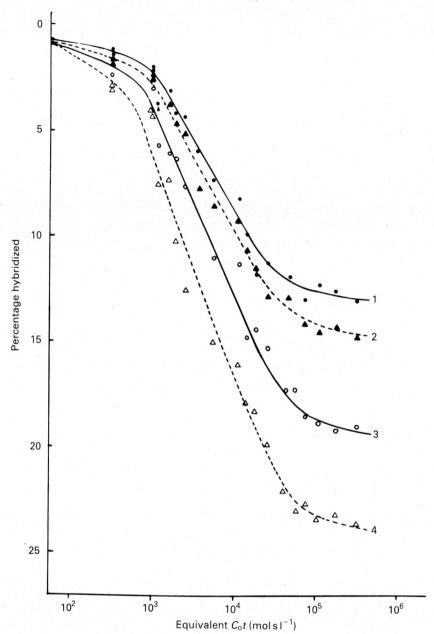

Fig. 4. Cage-associated DNA is enriched in sequences complementary to nucleoid RNA. Four different samples of cage-associated DNA containing 100 % (1), 35 % (2), 14 % (3) and 5 % (4) of the DNA associated with undigested nucleoids were labelled by nick-translation, denatured and the percentage of the DNA forming a hybrid with an excess of nucleoid RNA was determined (from Jackson *et al.* 1981).

We tested this using a series of rat cells transformed by polyoma and avian sarcoma virus (ASV) (Cook *et al.* 1982). On transformation these viruses integrate randomly within the genome so that we might expect viral sequences to integrate initially at

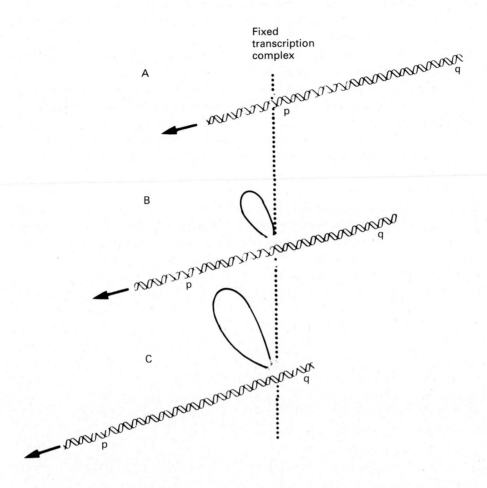

Fig. 5. A model for transcription. A. A fixed complex transcribes DNA between p and q. B,C. RNA is synthesized as DNA passes through the complex, the nascent RNA chain being attached at both ends, forming a loop (from Jackson *et al.* 1981).

random in the loops. However, if the cells express the transformed phenotype, we would predict that the integrated viral sequences, being transcribed, would lie close to the polymerase and so to the cage.

We map sequences relative to their point of attachment using our established procedure (Cook & Brazell, 1980). Nucleoids are partially digested with a restriction endonuclease; then cages, and any associated DNA, are sedimented free of detached DNA. The cage-associated DNA is purified and completely redigested using the same restriction endonuclease. Equal weights of this DNA are resolved into discrete fragments by gel electrophoresis and these are transferred to a filter and the relative amounts of any sequence on the filter are determined by autoradiography after hybridization with the appropriate probes. Following the first partial digestion, sequences lying close to the point of attachment will tend to co-sediment with the cages and so will be present in relatively greater abundance on the filter; therefore, they yield bands of greater intensity on autoradiography. The degree of enrichment is determined by reference to known amounts of total DNA run in adjacent channels in the gel.

Fig. 6 illustrates the mapping of polyoma sequences integrated into the cellular DNA in one transformed line, 82. Control DNA, undigested during the first partial digestion, yields three bands when subsequently digested completely with *Eco*RI and hybridized with a polyoma probe (Fig. 6A, channel 2; i.e. 100 % remaining). These correspond to the left and right-hand arms of the integrated virus – which also contain cellular sequences – and to an internal, and purely viral, sequence. If these nucleoids are partially digested with *Eco*RI to leave only 6 % of their DNA remaining attached to the cage and then their DNA is purified and completely fragmented with *Eco*RI, the bands obtained subsequently are three times more intense than those obtained with an equal weight of control DNA (compare channel 2 with 3, and 4 with 5). In contrast, hybridization of an albumin probe to the DNA of nucleoids that retain 6 % of the total DNA yields four bands, none of which are more intense than those obtained with the control DNA (Fig. 6B: compare channel 2 with 3, and 4 with 5; one band is probably a doublet). The enrichment of the viral, but depletion of the albumin, sequences can be highlighted by hybridizing a mixture of the two probes to the same filter (Fig. 6C). We conclude that there are fewer restriction sites between the integrated viral sequences and the point of attachment to the cage than there are between the albumin gene and its adjacent attachment sequence; i.e. the expressed viral sequences lie 'closer' to the cage than albumin sequences, which are – as far as we can judge – unexpressed in these fibroblasts.

The results obtain with the other transformed lines are summarized in Table 1. (Of course, comparisons between different cells should be made at the same levels of detachment.) In no case was the concentration of albumin sequences in the DNA that is closely associated with cages richer than that in the control. In every case the integrated viral sequences were enriched in the fraction of DNA that pellets with the cages.

Line 82 was analysed more extensively. In general, detaching more DNA from the nucleoids, whether with *Eco*RI or *Bam*HI, enriches the viral sequences to a greater extent (Table 1). We can assign the point of attachment to the left or right side of the viral sequence in line 82 by reference to the relative enrichments of each of the three viral bands. The left-hand junction sequence, which contains both cellular flanking sequences and viral sequences, is enriched more than the internal, and purely viral, sequence; both are enriched more than the right-hand junction sequence (Table 2 and fig. 7; compare channel 5 with the others). These differences increase as more DNA is detached. We interpret this as indicating that the left-hand fragment is closest to the attachment site or is attached more strongly. We note that the left-hand, internal and right-hand fragments contain 2, 1 and 0 enhancers, respectively.

Does the virus integrate selectively in sequences lying close to the cage or does it

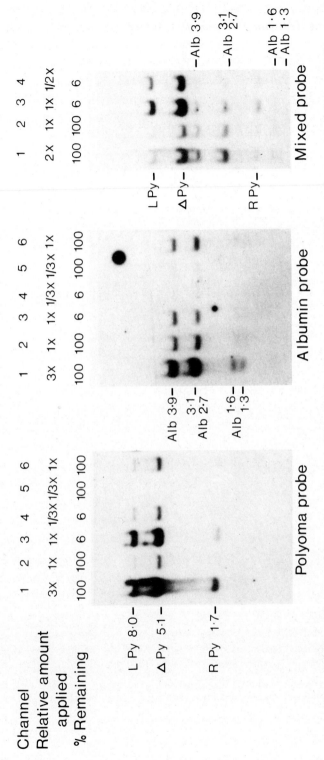

Fig. 6. Detachment mapping of albumin and polyoma viral sequences in the polyoma transformant, 82. Samples of total DNA (100 % remaining) and DNA that resists detachment by *Eco*RI (6 % remaining) were completely digested with *Eco*RI and various amounts were applied to three gels. After electrophoresis, blotting and hybridization with polyoma or albumin probes, autoradiographs were prepared and photographed. The sizes of the three polyoma bands (LPy, ΔPy, and RPy corresponding to the left-hand, internal and right-hand fragments, respectively) and the five albumin bands (two are not clearly resolved under these conditions) are given in base-pairs ×10⁻³. The polyoma, but not the albumin, sequences are enriched in the nucleoid samples that retained 6 % of the total DNA (from Cook *et al.* 1982).

D. A. Jackson, S. J. McCready and P. R. Cook

Table 1. *Detachment mapping of albumin, viral and junction sequences in various cell lines*

Cell	Percentage DNA remaining (relative enrichment)			
	Albumin	Polyoma	ASV	Polyoma junctions
Parent				
Rat–1	4 (1×)	100 (no bands)	100 (no bands)	9 (0·8×)[82J1]
				4 (1·6×([53C1]
				9 (1·0×)[7TL]
				4 (1·2×)[7TR]
Polyoma-transformed				
82	6 (0·9×)	14 (1·7×)		
		6 (3·5×)		
		5 (6·9×)*		
		4 (4·6×)†		
		1 (6·7×)		
		0·8 (18·0×)		
53		6 (2·3×)		
7axT	4 (0·9×)	4 (4·0×)		
Tsa 3T3	5 (0·7×)	5 (3·0×)		
ASV-transformed				
A+11	13 (0·6×)		13 (2·1×)	
A+22	3 (0·8×)		3 (3·9×)	
A23	6 (0·5×)		6 (>3·0×)	6 (0·6×)[7TR]
B31	5 (0·6×)		5 (3·9×)	5 (0·5×)[7TL]
A11 V1T	14 (0·8×)		17 (2·1×)‡	
	2 (1·0×)		14 (2·0×)	
			9 (3·0×)§	
			7 (3·0×)	
			5 (3·1×)‡	
			5 (>9·0×)†	
			4 (7×)	
			2 (>9·0×)	
Flat revertants of A11 VIT				
13N			3 (1·4×)	
21N	10 (1×)		17 (1·0×)†	
			10 (0·9×)	
			10 (1·5×)	
			4 (0·8×)	
			4 (2×)	
Aza-cytidine selected retransformants				
21 aza-C *trans* 1			8 (5·6×)	
			7 (5·1×)	
21 aza-C *trans* 3			8 (7·7×)	
			7 (6·0×)	
			6 (4·5×)	

Autoradiographs like those illustrated in Fig. 6 were prepared for each cell-line using polyoma, ASV, albumin or polyoma junction probes, scanned using a microdensitometer and peak heights were measured. The relative intensities of one of the strongest bands (and hence the relative enrichments) were determined by reference to similar bands obtained with varying weights of total DNA.

* Nucleoids were obtained from a population containing 75% mitotic cells obtained by successive thymidine and colcemid blocks.

† *Bam*H was used instead of *Eco*RI in both digestions.

‡ Nucleoids were incubated with ribonuclease to remove all but 4% or less of the RNA labelled in 15 min with [³H]uridine (10 μCi/ml) before the first *Eco*RI digestion.

§ Nucleoids were isolated from cells that had been subjected to 45 °C for 10 min, a procedure that reduced incorporation of pulse-labelled [³H]uridine into RNA by >95% (largely from Cook *et al.* 1982).

Table 2. *The left-hand* Eco *RI fragments of the integrated virus in cell line 82 lie closest to the cage*

Percentage DNA remaining	Relative enrichment of various fragments		
	Left	Internal	Right
14	1·7×	1·7×	1·6×
14	2·0×	1·4×	1·0×
6	3·5×	3·0×	2·2×
1	6·7×	5·5×	
0·8×	18·0×	13·7×	10·0×

Band intensities in autoradiographs prepared like those in Figs 6 and 7 were measured and the relative enrichments were determined (from Cook *et al*. 1982).

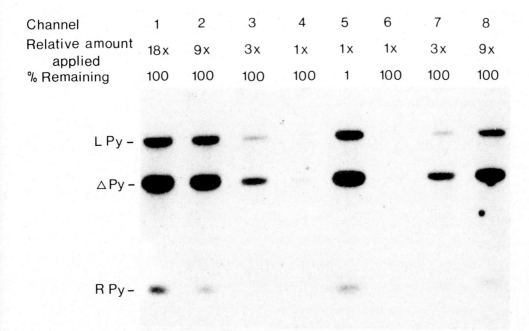

Channel	1	2	3	4	5	6	7	8
Relative amount applied	18x	9x	3x	1x	1x	1x	3x	9x
% Remaining	100	100	100	100	1	100	100	100

L Py –
△ Py –
R Py –

Polyoma probe

Fig. 7. Mapping the polyoma proviral sequence in cell line 82 with high levels of detachment. Various amounts (from 1 to 18x) of total DNA (100 % remaining) or DNA that resisted detachment by *Eco*RI (1 % remaining) were applied to the gel as indicated and an autoradiograph was prepared using the polyoma probe. The left-hand polyoma band (LPy) is enriched more than the right-hand band (RPy) (from Cook *et al*. 1982).

integrate randomly, inducing new attachments? Various viral sequences and contiguous cellular sequences have been cloned; therefore, we can test these possibilities by seeing whether cellular sequences that flank the inserted virus lie close to the cage in the parental Rat-1 cells (Table 1). Cellular sequences homologous to all four such polyoma junction probes tested (i.e. 82J1, 53C1, 7TL and 7TR) are readily detached from untransformed Rat-1 cages and cages prepared from ASV-transformants (i.e. the relative enrichments are <1·6; Table 1). By contrast, in the polyoma transformants these cellular sequences are attached to the integrated viral DNA and so are clearly associated with the cage. The attachment of outlying cellular sequences induced by viral integration can be highlighted as follows. The junction probe from the right side of the virus in 7axT (7TR) hybridizes with one major *Eco*RI fragment of $5·0 \times 10^3$ bases from parental Rat-1 cells. When the virus integrates, it does so into only one of the two homologous chromosomes, so that the junction probe now hybridizes to two fragments from the transformant 7axT: one of $5·0 \times 10^3$ base-pairs from the unaffected chromosome and another of $5·1 \times 10^3$ base-pairs, which contains viral sequences. With total DNA, the $5·0 \times 10^3$ base-pair band is the more intense (Fig. 8, channels 1, 2 and 5); however, when all but 4 % of the DNA is detached from

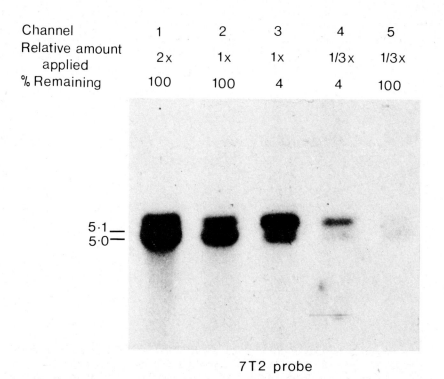

Channel	1	2	3	4	5
Relative amount applied	2x	1x	1x	1/3x	1/3x
% Remaining	100	100	4	4	100

5·1 —
5·0 —

7T2 probe

Fig. 8. Detachment mapping a junction sequence (7TR) in 7axT. Various amounts of total DNA or DNA that resisted detachment by *Eco*RI (4 % remaining associated with cages) were applied to the gel. Autoradiographs were prepared using the junction probe 7TR. The 5·1 and $5·0 \times 10^3$ base-pair bands are enriched 2·4 and 0·6 ×, respectively (from Cook *et al.* 1982).

7axT nucleoids, the band intensities are reversed (channels 3 and 4). The purely cellular $5 \cdot 0 \times 10^3$ base-pair band is depleted whilst the viral $5 \cdot 1 \times 10^3$ base-pair band is enriched. A similar enrichment of the viral bands but depletion of the purely cellular band is obtained when the junction probe 82J1 is used with 82 nucleoids.

Sub-clones of one of the ASV transformants (i.e. A11 VIT) present us with an opportunity to test the strength of this correlation between gene activity and proximity to the cage. Two sub-clones (i.e. 13N and 21N) have lost the transformed phenotype and contain no detectable viral transcripts. When these 'flat revertants' are treated with the antimetabolite, aza-cytidine (aza-C), and recloned, transformed colonies containing viral transcripts emerge at a high frequency. Two such clones derived from 21N (i.e. 21 aza-C *trans* 1 and 3) were analysed. As far as can be judged by restriction enzyme mapping, all cells in this series contain unchanged proviral sequences inserted in the same cellular sequence. However, they differ in whether or not the proviral sequence is expressed. Detachment mapping indicates that the ASV sequences, which are closely associated with the cage in the transformed VIT, are much less so in the untransformed 'flat revertants' (13N and 21N) but have regained their close association with the cage in the aza-C treated derivatives (Table 1). Again, gene activity correlates with proximity to the cage (see also Robinson, Nelkin & Vogelstein, 1982).

One trivial explanation of all these results is that nascent transcripts, which are presumably closely associated with their templates, prevent access of *Eco*RI to potential cutting sites in transcribing DNA. This possibility is unlikely since similar enrichments are seen when: (1) *Bam*HI replaced *Eco*RI in both digestions; (2) nascent RNA was detached before *Eco*RI digestion; (3) transcription is suppressed by heat-shock or during mitosis.

INFLUENZA VIRAL TRANSCRIPTS ARE ATTACHED

Our model also suggests that when a nuclear virus *productively* infects a cell it must first plug into the cage. Therefore, we studied the association of nascent transcripts of influenza, a virus known to require host nuclear activity (Jackson *et al.* 1982). Influenza virus is an RNA virus: infecting negative strands are first transcribed and the resulting positive strands then replicated into new virion RNA. After labelling infected chicken fibroblasts for $2 \cdot 5$ min with [^{3}H]uridine, we showed by hybridization that both nascent positive and negative strands were closely associated with the cage. In contrast, nascent RNA of a control rhabdovirus, whose reproduction is cytoplasmic, was not so associated.

ATTACHMENT DURING REPLICATION

It is now believed that DNA is replicated at the matrix or cage in the nucleus (Dijkwel, Mullenders & Wanka, 1979; Pardoll, Vogelstein & Coffey, 1980; McCready *et al.* 1980). Are sequences that initiate replication (i.e. origins) usually out in the loop, attaching only during *S*-phase (Fig. 9), or are they attached but

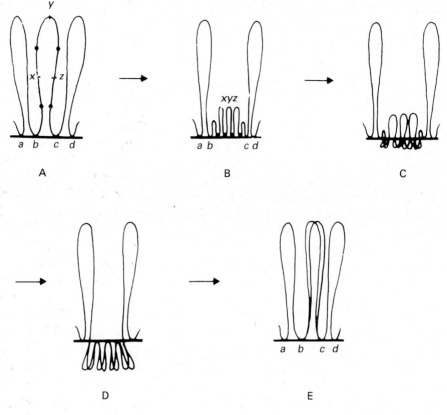

Fig. 9. A model for replication of nuclear DNA. A. Three adjacent structural loops (75 μm) are attached at the nuclear cage by specific base sequences (a,b,c,d). B. Before initiation, there is synchronous attachment, perhaps provoked by a change in degree of supercoiling in the loop, of four sequences (●) to form four replicons (bx, xy, yz and zc) each of about 20 μm. C,D. Bidirectional replication from each of the initiation points takes place as replicon loops move through the replication complex at the nuclear cage. E. When DNA synthesis is complete, the DNA detaches to form two newly replicated structural loops. It follows naturally from this model that the rate of replication could be controlled by varying the number of initial attachments and that adjacent replicons within a loop might attach and initiate replication synchronously (from McCready *et al.* 1980).

Fig. 10. Histograms of grain distributions over nucleoid spreads. A. 24 h label with [³H]thymidine, then ± irradiation; the unirradiated distribution reflects the total DNA distribution that is redistributed by irradiation. B. ± Irradiation (15 J/m²), then 5 min pulse, *S*-phase spreads; *S*-phase incorporation is cage-associated and somewhat redistributed by irradiation. C–F. Irradiation (15 (C,D) or 40 J/m² (E,F)), then 2·5 (C,E) or 5 min (D,F) pulse, non-*S* spreads; label is associated with cages. G. 15 J/m² irradiation, then 2·5 min pulse followed by 57·5 min chase, non-*S* spreads: some label remains associated with cages. H. *S*-phase spreads from G; label remains associated with cages. For C–H, medium was removed from HeLa cells growing logarithmically in Petri dishes, the cells were u.v.-irradiated and warm medium was added. After 30 min, [³H]thymidine was added for 2·5 or 5 min, the cells detached and lysed, nucleoids isolated and spread, autoradiographs prepared and photographed, and grains over each cage expressed as a percentage of the total over skirt and cage. Spreads were easily categorized as *S* or non-*S* according to grain density (from McCready & Cook, 1984).

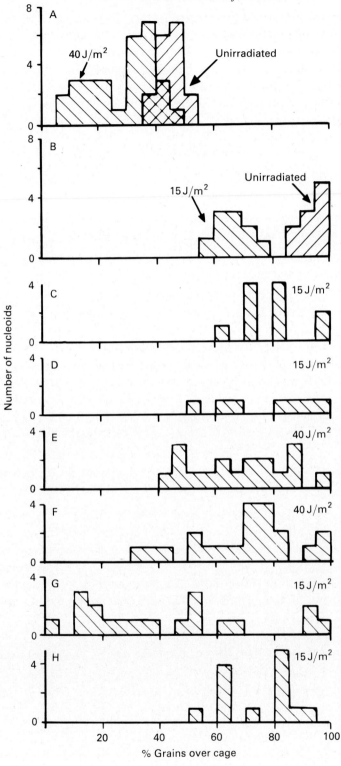

quiescent during most of the cell-cycle, awaiting activation during *S*-phase?

If origins are generally attached, even in the absence of DNA synthesis, they should be enriched in the fraction of total DNA that resists detachment by a nuclease from the sub-structure. The sites involved in initiating replication in nuclear DNA are poorly characterized but sequences that permit plasmids to replicate autonomously in yeast (i.e. ARSs) are likely candidates (see Monteil *et al.* 1984, for a review). Therefore, we compared the relative concentration of ARSs in total DNA and in DNA that resisted detachment and found that they were roughly similar. We also mapped the positions of four human ARSs relative to attachment points and found that all were located out in the loops (Cook & Lang, 1984) consistent with the model described in Fig. 9.

Repair of ultraviolet light-induced lesions

In principle, we can introduce damage randomly into DNA loops by ultraviolet (u.v.) irradiation of cells. Do repair enzymes operate like the fire brigade – rushing to the site of the fire (i.e. the damaged DNA) wherever it be – or are they, too, stuck to the cage requiring attachment of the damaged sequences?

We examined which is so by u.v.-irradiating HeLa cells (15 or 40 J/m^2), then growing them for 30 min before pulse-labelling (2·5 or 5 min) with [^{3}H]thymidine. Next, nucleoids were isolated and spread, autoradiographs were prepared, silver grains were counted over each spread and the proportion over the cage was calculated. The histograms of label distributions given in Fig. 10c–F for cells involved in unscheduled DNA synthesis (i.e. repair synthesis) clearly show that pulse-label is associated with the cage. Its distribution is quite unlike that of total DNA shown in Fig. 10A. Once again, enzymes work on DNA only when it is attached (McCready & Cook, 1984).

ACTIVE SITES OR ARTEFACTS?

Most of the experiments we have described involve associations of nucleic acids – usually nascent molecules – with cages. Might not these associations simply be artefacts induced by exposure to extreme conditions (i.e. detergents and 2 M-NaCl)? Simple calculations show that RNA and DNA are present at extraordinarily high concentrations in the nucleus (~100 mg/ml). Furthermore, single-stranded nucleic acids aggregate in high salt concentrations (Asano, 1975), so one might expect RNA and nascent DNA to precipitate onto any sub-nuclear structure. As only a fraction of the genome is being replicated or transcribed at any time only this fraction will precipitate, apparently specifically. If so, it would not be surprising to find that nascent DNA and RNA are associated, or that sequences can be mapped relative to these association points. However, nascent DNA cannot be solely responsible for the attachments since both loop size and the relative positions of genes within a loop remain constant even when no DNA is replicating during mitosis or G_1 (Warren & Cook, 1978; Cook & Brazell, 1980). The criticism that transcribing complexes are the mediators of artefactual attachments is more difficult to eliminate, but some telling observations on the *specificity* of the attachments of nascent RNA make this possibility unlikely. First, *all* the nascent RNA is attached specifically at its 5' end. Second, only RNA made *in vivo* is attached; pulse-labelled RNA does not associate with cages if first 'chased' into the cytoplasm, nor does nascent RNA if synthesized *in vitro* within the isolated nucleoid. Third, nascent transcripts of a nuclear virus, influenza virus, are all associated with cages, whereas those of a cytoplasmic rhabdovirus, are not. Fourth, the proximity of active viral genes in transformed cells to the cage cannot be an immediate consequence of transcription since they remain close to the cage when transcription stops during mitosis or heat-shock.

CONCLUSION

We have argued that a nuclear sub-structure that we call the cage not only organizes the DNA within the nucleus but is also the active site of transcription and replication. Attached polymerases generate nascent molecules, which are themselves attached. Replication might be initiated by attachment of origins or thymine dimers, transcription by attachment of 'enhancers' and viral infection by attachment of the incoming genome. It is easy to imagine how selective attachment might underlie selective gene activity during development or oncogenesis. Indeed, gross detachment and loss of supercoiling is correlated with total inactivation of the avian erythrocyte nucleus (Cook & Brazell, 1976) and oncogene attachments with transformation.

As anyone who has ever sailed on a boat knows, ropes of any length must be tied down at all times – otherwise they get tangled, preventing orderly operation; the same must be true of the long nucleic acid polymers in the nucleus. Then what is really remarkable – and fortunate – is that these attachments can remain stable during isolation in detergents and 2 M salt.

We thank the Science Research Council and the Cancer Research Campaign for their support. Figures and tables are reproduced with permission from *J. Cell Sci.*, the *E.M.B.O. J.* and *Nature*.

REFERENCES

AGUTTER, P. S. & RICHARDSON, J. C. W. (1980). Nuclear non-chromatin proteinaceous structures: their role in the organization and function of the interphase nucleus. *J. Cell Sci.* **44**, 395–435.

ASANO, K. (1975). Size heterogeneity of T2 messenger RNA. *J. molec. Biol.* **14**, 71–84.

BABICH, A., NEVINS, J. R. & DARNELL, J. E. (1980). Early capping of transcripts from the adenovirus major late transcription unit. *Nature, Lond.* **287**, 246–248.

BAKER, W. K. (1968). Position effect variegation. *Adv. Genet.* **14**, 133–169.

BAUER, W. & VINOGRAD, J. (1974). Circular DNA. In *Basic Principles in Nucleic Acid Chemistry* (ed. P. O. P. T'so), pp. 265–393. London: Academic Press.

BEEBEE, T. J. C. (1979). A comparison of methods for extracting ribonucleic acid polymerases from rat liver nuclei. *Biochem. J.* **183**, 43–54.

COMINGS, D. E. (1968). The rationale for an ordered arrangement of chromatin in the interphase nucleus. *Am. J. hum. Genet.* **20**, 550–560.

COOK, P. R. & BRAZELL, I. A. (1975). Supercoils in human DNA. *J. Cell Sci.* **19**, 261–279.

COOK, P. R. & BRAZELL, I. A. (1976). Conformational constraints in nuclear DNA. *J. Cell Sci.* **22**, 287–302.

COOK, P. R. & BRAZELL, I. A. (1977). The superhelical density of nuclear DNA from human cells. *Eur. J. Biochem.* **74**, 527–531.

COOK, P. R. & BRAZELL, I. A. (1978). Spectrofluorometric measurement of the binding of ethidium to superhelical DNA from cell nuclei. *Eur. J. Biochem.* **84**, 465–477.

COOK, P. R. & BRAZELL, I. A. (1980). Mapping sequences in loops of nuclear DNA by their progressive detachment from the nuclear cage. *Nucl. Acids Res.* **8**, 2895–2906.

COOK, P. R., BRAZELL, I. A. & JOST, E. (1976). Characterization of nuclear structures containing superhelical DNA. *J. Cell Sci.* **22**, 303–324.

COOK, P. R. & LANG, J. (1984). The spatial organization of sequences involved in initiation and termination of eukaryotic DNA replication. *Nucl. Acids Res.* **12**, 1069–1075.

COOK, P. R., LANG, J., HAYDAY, A., LANIA, L., FRIED, M., CHISWELL, D. J. & WYKE, J. A. (1982). Active viral genes in transformed cells lie close to the nuclear cage. *EMBO J.* **1**, 447–452.

COX, R. F. (1976). Quantitation of elongating form A and B RNA polymerases in chick oviduct nuclei and the effects of estradiol. *Cell* **7**, 455–465.

DIJKWEL, P. A., MULLENDERS, L. H. F. & WANKA, F. (1979). Analysis of the attachment of replicating DNA to a nuclear matrix in interphase nuclei. *Nucl. Acids Res.* **6**, 219–230.

DUPRAW, E. J. (1970). Suprachromosomal organization. In *DNA and Chromosomes, Molecular and Cellular Biology*, series II, pp. 186–204. New York: Holt Reinhart and Winston.

FURUICHI, Y. (1978). "Pretranscriptional capping" in the biosynthesis of cytoplasmic polyhedrosis virus mRNA. *Proc. natn. Acad. Sci. U.S.A.* **75**, 1086–1090.

HANCOCK, R. (1982). Topological organisation of interphase DNA: the nuclear matrix and other skeletal structures. *Biol. Cell* **46**, 105–122.

JACKSON, D. A., CATON, A. J., McCREADY, S. J. & COOK, P. R. (1982). Influenza virus RNA is synthesised at fixed sites in the nucleus. *Nature, Lond.* **296**, 366–368.

JACKSON, D. A., McCREADY, S. J. & COOK, P. R. (1981). RNA is synthesised at the nuclear cage. *Nature, Lond.* **292**, 552–555.

KAPLAN, L. M., KLEINMAN, R. E. & HORWITZ, M. S. (1977). Replication of adenovirus type 2 DNA *in vitro. Proc. natn. Acad. Sci. U.S.A.* **74**, 4425–4429.

KLEMPNAUER, K-H., FANNING, E., OTTO, B. & KNIPPERS, R. (1980). Maturation of newly replicated chromatin of simian virus 40 in its host cell. *J. molec. Biol.* **136**, 359–374.

MANLEY, J. L., FIRE, A., CANO, A., SHARP, P. A. & GEFTER, M. L. (1980). DNA-dependent transcription of adenovirus genes in a soluble whole-cell extract. *Proc. natn. Acad. Sci. U.S.A.* **77**, 3855–3859.

McCREADY, S. J., AKRIGG, A. & COOK, P. R. (1979). Electron microscopy of intact nuclear DNA from human cells. *J. Cell Sci.* **39**, 53–62.

McCREADY, S. J. & COOK, P. R. (1984). Lesions induced in DNA by ultraviolet light are repaired at the nuclear cage. *J. Cell Sci.* **70**, 189–196.

McCREADY, S. J., GODWIN, J., MASON, D. W., BRAZELL, I. A. & COOK, P. R. (1980). DNA is replicated at the nuclear cage. *J. Cell Sci.* **46**, 365–386.

MILLER, O. L. (1975). Fine structure of lampbrush chromosomes. *Nat. Cancer Inst. Monogr.* **18**, 79–100.

MILLER, O. L. & BEATTIE, B. R. (1969). Visualization of nucleolar genes. *Science* **164**, 955–957.

MONTEIL, F. J., NORBURG, C. J., TUITE, M. F., DOBSON, M. J., MILLS, J. S., KINGSMAN, A. J. & KINGSMAN S. M. (1984). Characterization of human chromosomal DNA sequences which replicate autonomously in *Saccharomyces cerevisiae. Nucl. Acids Res.* **12**, 1049–1068.

MULLINGER, A. M. & JOHNSON, R. T. (1979). The organization of supercoiled DNA from human chromosomes. *J. Cell Sci.* **38**, 369–389.

PARDOLL, D. M., VOGELSTEIN, B. & COFFEY, D. S. (1980). A fixed site of DNA replication in eukaryotic cells. *Cell* **19**, 527–536.

ROBINSON, S. I., NELKIN, B. D. & VOGELSTEIN, B. (1982). The ovalbumin gene is associated with the nuclear matrix of chicken oviduct cells. *Cell* **28**, 99–106.

SALDITT-GEORGIEFF, M., HARPOLD, M., CHEN-KIANG, S. & DARNELL, J. E. (1980). The addition of 5' cap structures early in hnRNA synthesis and prematurely terminated molecules are capped. *Cell* **19**, 68–78.

SMETANA, K., STEELE, W. J. & BUSCH, H. (1963). A nuclear ribonucleoprotein network. *Expl Cell Res.* **31**, 198–201.

WARREN, A. C. & COOK, P. R. (1978). Supercoiling of DNA and nuclear conformation during the cell cycle. *J. Cell Sci.* **30**, 211–226.

WEIL, P. A., LUSE, D. S., SEGALL, J. & ROEDER, R. G. (1979). Selective and accurate initiation of transcription at the Ad2 major late promoter in a soluble system dependent on purified RNA polymerase II and DNA. *Cell* **18**, 469–484.

ZBARSKY, I. B., DMITRIEVA, N. P. & YERMOLAYEVA, L. P. (1962). On the structure of tumour cell nuclei. *Expl Cell Res.* **27**, 573–576.

J. Cell Sci. Suppl. 1, 81–93 (1984)
Printed in Great Britain © The Company of Biologists Limited 1984

SOME ULTRASTRUCTURAL ASPECTS OF GENETIC ACTIVITY IN EUKARYOTES

OSCAR L. MILLER, JR

Department of Biology, University of Virginia, Charlottesville, Virginia 22901, U.S.A.

SUMMARY

A brief overview is given of the types of information that have been obtained by chromatin spreading methods regarding the ultrastructure and regulation of genetic units. The examples used are: ribosomal RNA genes of the spotted newt; the silk fibroin gene of *Bombyx mori*; chorion gene amplification in *Drosophila melanogaster*; RNA synthesis patterns during early embryogenesis of *D. melanogaster*; regulation of transcription on homologous non-ribosomal transcription units of *D. melanogaster*; specific nascent transcript cleavage in insects; and nascent polypeptides on insect polyribosomes. The conclusion is drawn that further innovations will be required before significant advances in the use of chromatin spreading techniques to study ultrastructural aspects of genetic activity can occur.

INTRODUCTION

The pioneering work in using isolated material for visualization of ultrastructural aspects of genetic activity was done in the 1950s by J. G. Gall and H. G. Callan with lampbrush chromosomes of various species of amphibians (Gall, 1956 and references therein). Although some quite important information was obtained in these early studies, the state of the art at that time did not allow definitive observations regarding the structure of individual, nascent ribonucleoprotein (RNP) fibrils or estimates of the number of RNA polymerase molecules present on active transcription units (TUs). Further innovations in the technique of dispersing nuclear contents into two dimensions for electron microscopy occurred in the late 1960s with the amphibian oocyte nucleus again being the experimental material (Miller & Beatty, 1969*a*,*b*,*c*). This cell type was optimal for these early studies because of three attributes: first, the thousands of lateral loops of the extended diplotene chromosomes of the lampbrush stage are highly active in RNA synthesis; second, ribosomal DNA is amplified in the zygotene–pachytene stages, giving rise to hundreds of synthetically active nucleoli per lampbrush-stage nucleus that have no physical connection with the chromosomes; and, third, the extremely large size of the nuclei at mid-to-late lampbrush stage allows easy manual isolation and manipulation of the contents of single nuclei.

There were five principal technical advances that allowed definitive observations of the structure of active TUs of amphibian oocytes: (1) specimen-support films made of carbon, which are highly hydrophobic after manufacture, were made hydrophilic by glow-discharge in a partial vacuum, a step that prevents the precipitation effect inherent in drying chromatin spreads on hydrophobic carbon films; (2) nuclear contents were dispersed in distilled water that had been adjusted to pH 9, such very low-salinity conditions causing the relatively dense nucleoli to disperse rapidly and nascent RNP fibrils, which are highly contorted *in vivo*, to become maximally extended; (3) dispersed nuclear contents were fixed and partially attached to the surface of carbon support films by centrifugation through a sucrose/formalin solution in a microcentrifugation chamber; (4) specimens were firmly attached to support films after centrifugation by air-drying out of a low-percentage solution of Kodak Photo-flo (a surface tension-reducing agent), a step that prevents surface-tension distortion by allowing the final surface film of solution to dry almost simultaneously over the area of a grid square rather than moving across the carbon film surface during drying; and (5) electrostatic staining of air-dried chromatin spreads with phosphotungstic acid and/or uranyl acetate in 50 % (v/v) ethanol was used to introduce the needed electron contrast in the specimens.

As other cell types began to be used in studies of gene regulation by chromatin spreading methods in the early-to-mid 1970s, two more modifications were introduced: (1) a detergent mixture was found ('Joy', Proctor & Gamble) that efficiently solubilized cellular membranes while the structure of genetically active chromatin was maintained, a step allowing the analysis of nuclear contents of cells having more typically sized nuclei (Miller & Bakken, 1972); and (2) it was found that soaking carbon support films in 95 % (v/v) ethanol for 1–2 min immediately before use would make the surface sufficiently hydrophilic, obviating the use of glow discharge, which tends to weaken thin carbon films having no plastic backing (McKnight & Miller, 1976).

As will be evident in the following examples, the introduction of chromatin spreading techniques has allowed observation of facets of gene structure and regulation at the single gene level that could not easily be obtained, if at all, by other types of analysis of genetic activity or, alternatively, has provided visual corroboration of interpretations of results obtained by other types of probes.

EXAMPLES   OF   RESULTS   OBTAINED   BY   CHROMATIN   SPREADING METHODS

Visualization of genes coding for specific RNAs

rRNA genes of Notophthalmus (Triturus) viridescens. The first genes coding for a specific RNA to be visualized by chromatin spreading techniques were the tandem arrays of rRNA genes present in the extrachromosomal nucleoli of the oocytes of the common spotted newt of North America (Fig. 1). After preparation for electron microscopy, these genes are easily visualized when active because the genes are maximally loaded with RNA polymerases, with some 80–100 polymerases simultaneously transcribing each gene. Under the spreading conditions used, the nascent RNA chains are still contracted about 10-fold within the extended RNP fibrils. Terminal granules appear on the nascent RNP fibrils after the RNA polymerases have transcribed part of each gene. Such granules have been found on the rRNA genes of all eukaryotes so far examined, but their function remains undetermined. The tandemly repeated rRNA genes of amphibian oocytes are arranged on highly variable-

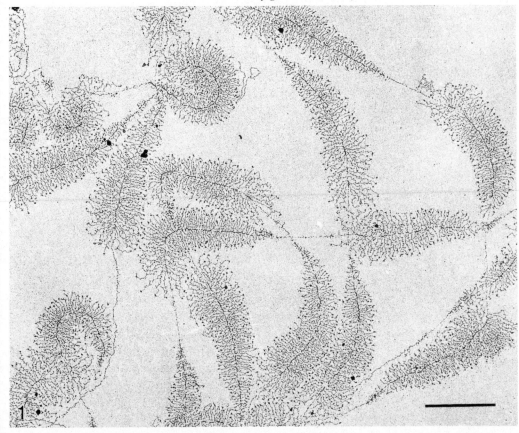

Fig. 1. Electron micrograph of rRNA genes from an extrachromosomal nucleolus isolated from an oocyte of *N. viridescens* (from Miller & Beatty, 1969c). The tandemly repeated genes are maximally loaded with RNA polymerases, are typically separated by transcriptionally inactive DNA segments, have the same polarity and are contained in a circular rDNA molecule. Bar, 1 μm.

sized circles of DNA in the extrachromosomal nucleoli (ranging from a few to several hundred genes per circle). Although there is evidence that the amplification of these genes occurs, at least in part, by a rolling circle mechanism (Hourcade, Dressler & Wolfson, 1973; Rochaix, Bird & Bakken, 1974), the process by which the genes become arranged in simple circles of various sizes remains unknown.

The silk fibroin gene of Bombyx mori. The silk fibroin gene of *B. mori* is a single-copy gene (Lizardi & Brown, 1973) that is very active in the highly polyploid posterior silk gland cells, such genes accounting for over 80 % of the protein synthesis in that portion of the gland (Tashiro, Morimoto, Matsuura & Nagata, 1968). When chromatin spreads were made using portions of the posterior silk gland segment (Fig. 2), distinct TUs some 5–6 μm in length were observed (McKnight, Sullivan & Miller, 1976). These long, polymerase-dense gradients were identified as active silk fibroin genes because: (1) the mean length of the TUs was close to the gene size estimated by biochemical probes; (2) such long gradients were not observed in spreads of the middle portion of the silk gland where little or no fibroin is synthesized; (3) the gene was not tandemly repeated, consistent with the data showing it to be a single-copy gene; and (4) such loci were essentially space-filled with RNA polymerases, consistent with the large number of mRNA molecules synthesized per unit time at the stage examined. These observations marked the first time that definitive ultrastructural details of a eukaryotic gene coding for a specific protein were visualized.

Chorion protein genes of Drosophila melanogaster. The single-copy genes coding for egg shell proteins in the follicle cells of *D. melanogaster* are amplified above the level of polyploidy in such cells. The time-course and degree of amplification of two domains containing major chorion genes have been well documented. A domain in the X-chromosome has several early-acting chorion genes and is amplified 14 to 16-fold. A second domain in chromosome III, containing four genes expressed late in choriogenesis, is amplified some 60-fold (Spradling & Mahowald, 1980; Spradling, 1981; Griffin-Shea, Thireos & Kafatos, 1982). Spradling (1981) determined that each of the domains extends over 90–100 ($\times 10^3$) base-pairs, being maximally amplified in the central region containing the major chorion genes and with the level of amplification gradually decreasing in both directions. The mechanism of amplification,

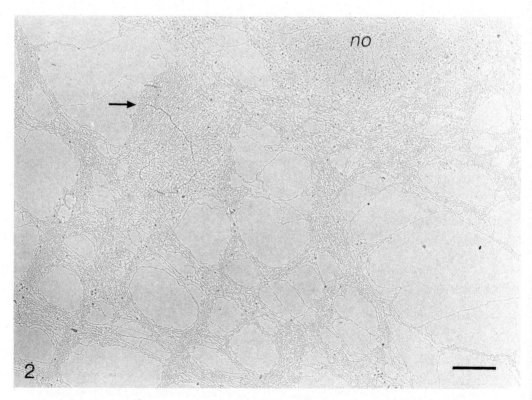

Fig. 2. Electron micrograph of a putative silk fibroin transcription unit exhibiting a 'backbone' of RNA polymerases (arrow) in a chromatin spread of the posterior portion of the silk gland of *Bombyx mori* (from Beyer, McKnight & Miller, 1979). A portion of a nucleolus organizer cluster of rRNA genes (*no*) lies nearby in the spread. Bar, 1 μm.

however, remained obscure. When chromatin spreads were made using appropriately staged follicle cells (Osheim & Miller, 1983), amplification was observed to result from multi-forked chromosomal structures (Fig. 3A,B). Correlation of the bio-chemical and morphological observations indicates that each new round of replication does not start until the previous one has been completed for some time and that the smooth continuum of decrease in amplification may result from variable termination sites for homologous replication forks within the amplified domain. Putative chorion genes were identified by their lengths, relative polarities of transcription, and presence within amplified regions.

Patterns of RNA synthesis during early embryogenesis of D. melanogaster

As the *D. melanogaster* embryo develops from fertilization through the syncytial and cellular blastoderm stages, several dramatic changes occur. During the syncytial stage, the synchronous nuclear division cycles are approximately 10 min in duration

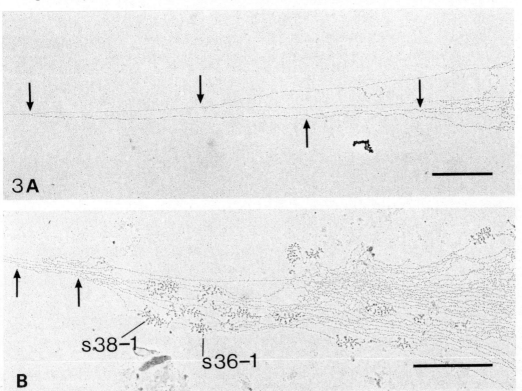

Fig. 3. A. An electron micrograph of an amplified chromatin strand from an early stage 11 follicle cell of *D. melanogaster* (from Osheim & Miller, 1983). Serial rounds of replica-tion have given rise to a complex multi-forked structure. Replication forks are denoted by arrows. Bar, 1 μm. B. An electron micrograph of replication forks (arrows) downstream from active chorion protein genes in a chromatin spread from stage 11 follicle cells (from Osheim & Miller, 1983). The tandemly linked genes, designated s36-1 and s38-1, code for two major egg-shell proteins with molecular weights of 36 and 38 ($\times 10^3$), respectively. Bar, 1 μm.

at room temperature, as opposed to the first cell cycle at cellular blastoderm, which takes more than an hour as cell membranes grow from the periphery of the embryo to form complete cells (Fullilove & Jacobson, 1978). In addition, definitive nucleoli are first detected in cytological preparations of embryos fixed at the early cellular blastoderm stage (Mahowald, 1963). Analysis of transcription during the syncytial and cellular blastoderm stages by chromatin spreading (McKnight & Miller, 1976) revealed the following differences. The relatively low number of TUs in the syncytial stage consisted primarily of short, densely packed gradients of nascent RNP fibrils. Such gradients were still present at the cellular blastoderm stage, but the large majority of non-ribosomal gradients present at this stage were significantly longer, and typically had intermediate densities of RNA polymerases (Fig. 4). Although no specific structural genes could be identified, many of these larger loci presumably code for proteins involved in the various differentiation events beginning at cellular blastoderm. Almost immediately upon the beginning of cell membrane growth at cellular blastoderm, the first rRNA gradients were observed (Fig. 5). The rRNA genes are not activated synchronously but, rather, individual genes of the cluster keep being activated well into the first cell cycle. However, it appeared that no more than about one-half of the genes within a single nucleolus organizer cluster became active during this cell cycle. Since the RNA polymerase density per unit length was maximal on

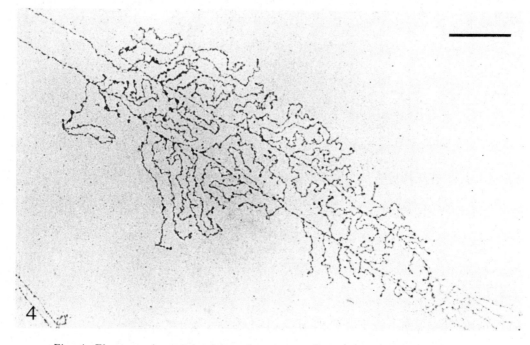

4

Fig. 4. Electron micrograph of homologous non-ribosomal transcription units in a chromatin spread of a cellular blastoderm embryo of *D. melanogaster* (from McKnight & Miller, 1979). The RNA polymerase density is close to 11 molecules/μm of chromatin, as compared to approximately 40 molecules/μm on rRNA genes and the silk fibroin gene. Pairs of homologous loci, with or without nearby replication forks, are often observed side by side in chromatin spreads of early stage embryos. Bar, 1 μm.

both newly activated rRNA genes and genes with fully formed gradients, it seems logical to conclude that the factors controlling the number of rRNA molecules made per unit time at this stage are the number of rRNA genes active at any one time and the speed of transcription.

Regulation of transcription on homologous, non-ribosomal transcription units of D. melanogaster

As noted in the legend of Fig. 4, homologous non-ribosomal genes are often observed lying side by side in chromatin spreads of cellular blastoderm. After observing this phenomenon, Steve McKnight decided that a quantitative assay of such gene pairs would provide a unique opportunity to gain some insight into how precise or imprecise the regulation of the transcription of homologous TUs is (McKnight & Miller, 1979). Such analyses allowed the following conclusions: (1) when one gene is transcriptionally active, the homologous gene also is active, i.e. in all cases in which one or both replication forks of a replicon could be observed adjacent to an active locus, both sister chromatids exhibited nascent transcripts; (2) initiation and termination sites for transcription are the same for homologous TUs; (3) nascent RNP fibre frequency

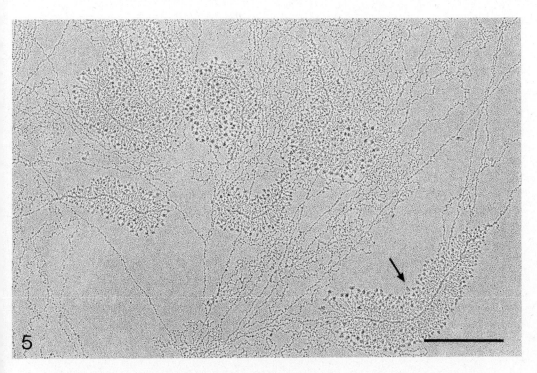

Fig. 5. Electron micrograph of a cluster of rRNA genes in a chromatin spread of an early cellular blastoderm embryo of *D. melanogaster* (from McKnight & Miller, 1976). The longest gradient of RNP fibrils (arrow) is a fully formed one on a gene that has reached a steady state of transcription frequency, whereas most of the other gradients are on recently activated genes that have not reached a steady state. Note, however, that the RNA polymerase density per unit of gradient length is similar on all the genes. Bar, 1 μm.

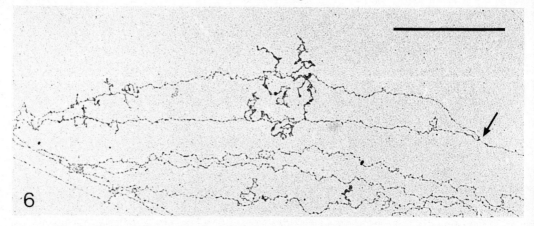

Fig. 6. Electron micrograph of two homologous transcription units in a chromatin spread of an early cellular blastoderm embryo of *D. melanogaster* from McKnight & Miller (1979). A replication fork (arrow) is present downstream from the active loci. Note that the fibre-free gap present on each of the loci occupies essentially the same position. Bar, 1 μm.

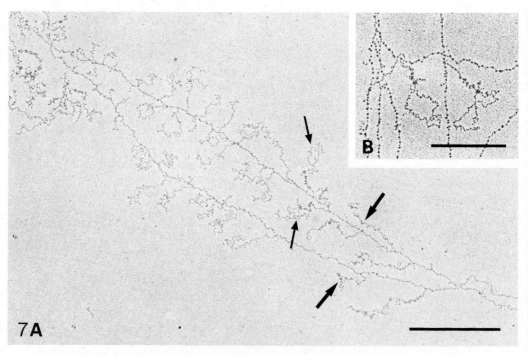

Fig. 7. Nascent transcript cleavage on non-ribosomal transcription units in chromatin spreads of early cellular blastoderm embryos of *D. melanogaster* (from Beyer *et al.* 1981). A. Electron micrograph of sister-chromatid TUs. Thin arrows indicate fibrils in which stable loop formation has occurred. Thick arrows indicate two of the six transcripts that have had such loops excised. Bar, 1 μm. B. Higher magnification electron micrograph of nascent transcripts with stable loops on a different set of sister-chromatid TUs. Bar, 0·5 μm.

varies greatly between different active loci, but the frequency is essentially identical for each member of a pair of homologous TUs; and (4) active loci sometimes exhibit internal fibre-free gaps, which probably result from momentary interruptions in RNA polymerase initiations, but such gaps, when present, occur at the same location on both homologous loci (Fig. 6). Thus, homologous TUs typically have a constant and characteristic RNP fibre frequency, and such frequencies probably vary over several orders of magnitude when all TUs are compared. The precise molecular basis of such a wide range of fine tuning of transcriptional initiation frequency is not yet known. However, some recent, elegant experiments by McKnight and colleagues (McKnight, Kingsbury, Spence & Smith, 1984) have pointed to a possible mechanism. These workers have shown that two distal transcription signals of the herpesvirus thymidine kinase gene share a common hexanucleotide sequence and function in a mutually dependent manner. The signals can function when alone or reiterated, when in either orientation, or when placed at different distances from the 'TATA homology'/mRNA cap region. However, the magnitude of the distal signal effect on transcription is influenced by variation in each of these parameters. McKnight and co-workers suggest that similar modulation of transcription signals might be the basis for the control of a network of cellular genes having different expression levels.

Nascent transcript cleavage in insects

Using embryos of *D. melanogaster*, Laird & Chooi (1976) were the first to describe possible cleavages of nascent RNP fibrils on non-ribosomal TUs. Subsequently, Ann Beyer and colleagues (Beyer, Bouton & Miller, 1981) expanded such observations using embryos and fat body tissues of *D. melanogaster* and *Calliphora erythrocephala*. In chromatin spreads of such material, approximately one in four non-ribosomal TUs exhibits excisions of portions of nascent transcripts (Fig. 7). Such excisions are sequence specific and result in the release of fragments having a smooth fibrillar RNP morphology, while the retained segments have a thicker, particulate morphology. RNP fibril loops occur by association of non-contiguous transcript sequences that correspond to the terminal regions of the segment to be released. This association appears to result from the coalescence of particles formed at the loop base sites before loop formation. The relationship of such cleavages to mRNA production remains obscure; however, these events presumably are not trivial in insects, at least, since they occur on a significant number of TUs at different developmental stages.

Visualization of nascent polypeptides on polyribosomes

The initial reason for doing chromatin spreads of the silk gland of *Bombyx mori* was the hope of visualizing a gene coding for a specific mRNA (McKnight, Sullivan & Miller, 1976). An unexpected fallout from this study was the first visualization of nascent polypeptides on polyribosomes (Fig. 8A). Although direct evidence was lacking, such polyribosomes from the posterior portion of the gland were presumed to contain silk fibroin mRNAs since that gland segment synthesizes silk fibroin almost exclusively in late larval development and the contents of the lumen of the posterior segment primarily consist of molecules having the same morphology and size as the

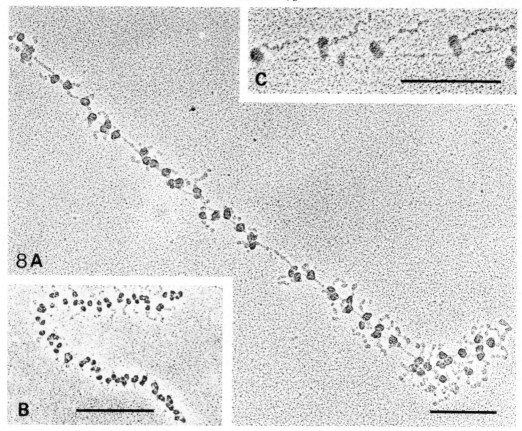

Fig. 8. Electron micrographs of polyribosomes showing nascent polypeptides. A. Putative nascent silk fibroin chains on a polyribosome isolated from the posterior portion of the silk gland of a *B. mori* silkworm (courtesy of S. L. McKnight & O. L. Miller, Jr). Bar, 0·25 μm. B,C. Presumptive nascent chains of secretory proteins on polyribosomes in chromatin spreads of salivary glands of *Ch. tentans* (from Franke *et al.* 1982). Note that in B there are five ribosomes at the 3' end of the mRNA that do not have attached polypeptides. Bars: B, 0·5 μm; C, 0·25 μm.

longest fibrils observed at the 3' end of the polyribosomes. More recently, nascent polypeptides have been visualized on polyribosomes isolated by similar methods from salivary glands of *Chironomus tentans* (Franke, Edström, McDowall & Miller, 1982; Fig. 8B,C). Circumstantial evidence again indicates that such polyribosomes are synthesizing specific proteins, in this case the giant secretory proteins coded for by the large Balbiani rings, BR1 and BR2, of *Ch. tentans* salivary gland chromosomes. An interesting difference between the silk fibroin and salivary gland polyribosomes is the presence in the latter of a small cluster of three to five ribosomes at the 3' end of the mRNA that do not have attached nascent polypeptides.

CONCLUSION

Although a considerable amount of information has been obtained regarding the

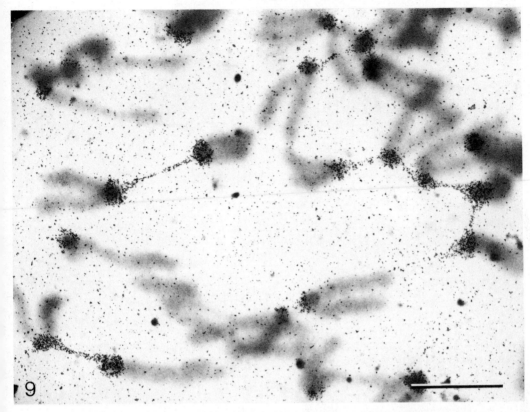

Fig. 9. Electron micrograph of mouse metaphase chromosomes after *in situ* hybridization with a biotinylated mouse A-T satellite probe followed by an antibody sandwich procedure using anti-biotin and secondary antibody/colloidal gold as the electron-opaque tag (courtesy of B. A. Hamkalo). The clusters of colloidal gold particles localize A-T satellite sequences at centromere regions. Bar, 5 μm.

ultrastructure and regulation of several aspects of genetic activity via chromatin spreading methods, there have most often been pre-existing biochemical data on the experimental materials used that allowed putative identification of the genetic elements in question. Advances in using spreading methods to obtain definitive identification of active transcriptional units or specific polyribosomes in circumstances where biochemical data do not allow presumptive identification will require further innovations in methodology. Significant progress has already been made in the use of *in situ* hybridization of nucleic acids plus adjunct antibody procedures at the electron microscope level in the detection of mouse A-T satellite sequences (Hutchison, Langer-Safer, Ward & Hamkalo, 1982) (Fig. 9) and also the detection of 5 S RNA genes and nascent transcripts of rRNA genes (B. A. Hamkalo, personal communication). Further development of *in situ* hybridization techniques should eventually allow the detection and analysis at the ultrastructural level of any active transcription unit for which there is a nucleic acid probe available.

A large majority of the research results reviewed in this article was made possible by research grant GM21020 from NIH, Public Health Services, U.S.A. to O.L.M.

REFERENCES

BEYER, A. L., BOUTON, A. H. & MILLER, O. L. JR (1981). Correlation of hnRNP structure and nascent transcript cleavage. *Cell* **26**, 155–165.

BEYER, A. L., McKNIGHT, S. L. & MILLER, O. L. JR. (1979). IV. Transcriptional units in eukaryotes. In *Molecular Genetics III, Chromosome Structure* (ed. J. H. Taylor), pp. 117–175. London, New York, San Francisco: Academic Press.

FRANKE, C., EDSTRÖM, J.-E., McDOWALL, A. W. & MILLER, O. L. JR (1982). Electron microscopic visualization of a discrete class of grant translation units in salivary gland cells of *Chironomus tentans. EMBO J.* **1**, 59–62.

FULLILOVE, S. L. & JACOBSON, A. G. (1978). Embryonic development: descriptive. In *The Genetics and Biology of* Drosophila, vol. 2c (ed. M. Ashburner & T. R. F. Wright), pp. 105–227. London, New York, San Francisco: Academic Press.

GALL, J. G. (1956). On the submicroscopic structure of chromosomes. *Brookhaven Symp. Biol.* **8**, 17–32.

GRIFFIN-SHEA, R., THIREOS, G. & KAFATOS, F. C. (1982). Organization of a cluster of four chorion genes in *Drosophila* and its relationship to developmental expression and amplification. *Devl Biol.* **91**, 325–336.

HOURCADE, D., DRESSLER, D. & WOLFSON, J. (1973). The amplification of ribosomal RNA genes involves a rolling circle intermediate. *Proc. natn. Acad. Sci. U.S.A.* **70**, 2926–2930.

HUTCHISON, N. J., LANGER-SAFER, P. R., WARD, D. C. & HAMKALO, B. A. (1982). *In situ* hybridization at the electron microscope level: hybrid detection by autoradiography and colloidal gold. *J. Cell. Biol.* **95**, 609–618.

LAIRD, C. D. & CHOOI, W. Y. (1976). Morphology of transcription units in *Drosophila melanogaster. Chromosoma* **58**, 193–218.

LIZARDI, P. M. & BROWN, D. D. (1973). The length of fibroin structural gene sequences in *Bombyx mori* DNA. *Cold Spring Harbor Symp. quant. Biol.* **38**, 701–706.

MAHOWALD, A. P. (1963). Ultrastructural differentiations during formation of the blastoderm in the *Drosophila melanogaster* embryo. *Devl Biol.* **8**, 186–204.

McKNIGHT, S. L., KINGSBURY, R. C., SPENCE, A. & SMITH, M. (1984). The distal transcription signals of the herpesvirus TK gene share a common hexanucleotide control sequence. *Cell* **37**, 253–262.

McKNIGHT, S. L. & MILLER, O. L. JR (1976). Ultrastructural patterns of RNA synthesis during early embryogenesis of *Drosophila melanogaster. Cell* **8**, 305–319.

McKNIGHT, S. L. & MILLER, O. L. JR (1979). Post-replicative nonribosomal transcription units in *D. melanogaster* embryos. *Cell* **17**, 551–563.

McKNIGHT, S. L., SULLIVAN, N. L. & MILLER, O. L. JR (1976). Visualization of the silk fibroin transcription unit and nascent silk fibroin molecules on polyribosomes of *Bombyx mori. Prog. Nucl. Acid Res. molec. Biol.* **19**, 313–318.

MILLER, O. L. JR & BAKKEN, A. H. (1972). Morphological studies of transcription. *Acta Endocrinol. Suppl.* **168**, 155–177.

MILLER, O. L. JR & BEATTY, B. R. (1969a). Extrachromosomal nucleolar genes in amphibian oocytes. *Genetics Suppl.* **61**, 134–143.

MILLER, O. L. JR & BEATTY, B. R. (1969b). Visualization of nucleolar genes. *Science* **164**, 955–957.

MILLER, O. L. JR & BEATTY, B. R. (1969c). Portrait of a gene. *J. cell. Physiol.* **74** (suppl. 1), 225–232.

OSHEIM, Y. N. & MILLER, O. L. JR (1983). Novel amplification and transcriptional activity of chorion genes in *Drosophila melnogaster* follicle cells. *Cell* **33**, 543–553.

ROCHAIX, J. D., BIRD, A. & BAKKEN, A. (1974). Ribosomal RNA gene amplification by rolling circles. *J. molec. Biol.* **87**, 473–487.

SPRADLING, A. C. (1981). The organization and amplification of two chromosomal domains containing *Drosophila* chorion genes. *Cell* **27**, 193–201.

SPRADLING, A. C. & MAHOWALD, A. P. (1980). Amplification of genes for chorion proteins during oogenesis in *Drosophila melanogaster*. *Proc. natn. Acad. Sci. U.S.A.* **77**, 1096–1100.

TASHIRO, Y., MORIMOTO, T., MATSUURA, S. & NAGATA, S. (1968). Studies on the posterior silk gland of the silkworm, *Bombyx mori* I. Growth of posterior silk gland cells and biosynthesis of fibroin during the fifth larval instar. *J. Cell Biol.* **38**, 574–588.

J. Cell Sci. Suppl. 1, 95–101 (1984)
Printed in Great Britain © The Company of Biologists Limited 1984

c-myc GENE ACTIVATION AND CHROMOSOMAL TRANSLOCATION

T. H. RABBITTS, R. BAER*, M. DAVIS†, A. FORSTER,
P. H. RABBITTS‡ AND S. MALCOLM†

Medical Research Council Laboratory of Molecular Biology, Hills Road, Cambridge CB2 2QH, England

SUMMARY

Burkitt's lymphoma cells are characterized by the presence of specific chromosomal translocation bringing the immunoglobulin and the c-myc proto-oncogenes into the proximity of each other. Different translocations involve each of the three immunoglobulin loci but the breakpoint with respect to the c-myc gene is shown to be very variable. In t8/14 the breakpoint occurs upstream from the c-myc gene whilst in the variant lymphomas it occurs downstream from the gene. Possible ways in which the translocation affects the c-myc gene are discussed.

INTRODUCTION

The human c-myc proto-oncogene resides on the long arm of chromosome 8. Its association with the specific, consistent chromosomal translocations observed in Burkitt's lymphoma (BL) involves the immunoglobulin heavy(H) chain locus on chromosome 14 (14q32) in about 90 % of cases, whilst in the so-called variant BL the light(L) chain loci are involved (in about 5 % of cases the lambda (λ) light chain locus on 22q11 and the remaining 5 % the kappa ($\varkappa$) light chain on 2p12). In the predominant 8/14 translocations, the c-myc gene is included in the segment of chromosome 8 that translocates to chromosome 14 (Erikson, Finan, Nowell & Croce, 1982; Davis, Malcolm & Rabbitts, 1984) and the resultant proximity of c-myc and H chain constant region genes (in which the genes are arranged in the opposite transcription orientation) allows the orientation of the respective genes in relation to the chromosomal centromere (i.e. the c-myc gene is present on chromosome 8 with the 5′ end towards the centromere). Fig. 1 illustrates the arrangement of c-myc and $C\gamma_1$ genes in the abnormal chromosome 14 of Raji cells (Hamlyn & Rabbitts, 1983) showing that the breakpoint occurs within an amalgamated switch (S) segment (characteristic of the immunoglobulin (Ig) class switch). Furthermore, this figure demonstrates that the c-myc gene is largely unaffected by the translocation. Recently, studies of both types of variant BL translocation (i.e. t8/22 and t2/8) have shown that

* Present address: Memorial Sloan-Kettering Cancer Center, 1275 York Avenue, New York, NY 10021, U.S.A.

† MRC Human Genetic Diseases Research Group, Biochemistry Department, Queen Elizabeth College, Campden Hill Road, London W8 7AH, England.

‡ Ludwig Institute for Cancer Research, MRC Centre, Hills Road, Cambridge CB2 2QH, England.

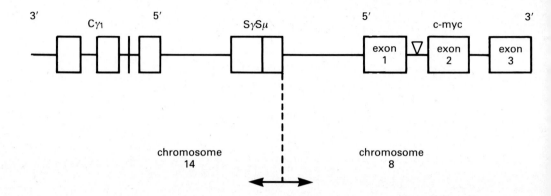

Fig. 1. Structure of the translocated c-myc gene in the Burkitt's lymphoma cell-line Raji (t8/14). The Cγ_1 is the immunoglobulin gamma heavy chain gene and Sμ/Sγ represents switch sequences of the μ and γ genes, respectively. The symbol (∇) between exons 1 and 2 of c-myc gene indicate the occurrence of deletions within this intron.

the breakpoint in these cases occurs to the 3' side or downstream from the c-myc gene (Croce *et al.* 1983; Davis *et al.* 1984; Hollis *et al.* 1984).

The c-myc gene has three exons of which only the second two encode a protein (Colby, Chen, Smith & Levinson, 1983; Hamlyn & Rabbitts, 1983; Watt *et al.* 1983). Studies on cloned DNA segments have shown that, very frequently, in mouse myeloma c-myc translocations the non-coding exon 1 (for which there is no assigned function) is lost from the translocated gene, while it is usually retained in BL c-myc gene translocations (Adams *et al.* 1983; Hamlyn & Rabbitts, 1983; Rabbitts, Hamlyn & Baer, 1983; Stanton, Watt & Marcu, 1983). This apparently conflicting situation between most BL translocations and those in mouse myelomas is one very puzzling aspect of the paradox of c-myc gene translocation. The other intriguing feature of the BL translocations is the great variability of the breakpoint with respect to the c-myc gene (illustrated in Fig. 2) and the rare occurrence of obvious damage to the BL-translocated c-myc gene. We must therefore elucidate a general effect of the transloca-tion on the c-myc gene in generating the putative oncogenic activity of this gene. In this paper we briefly describe results that indicate the possibility that sequence changes within the c-myc gene may be important, such as those found in exon 1, and such alterations (not apparent as gross c-myc gene changes) may affect the control of the c-myc gene. The possibility must also be examined (not mutually exclusive of the above) that the c-myc gene control may be altered by the influence of as yet undeter-mined Ig locus regulators.

TRANSLOCATION IN VARIANT t2/8 BURKITT'S LYMPHOMAS

We have recently demonstrated, using *in situ* hybridization, that the c-myc gene remains on the abnormal chromosome 8 in BL with t2/8 (Davis *et al.* 1984). These

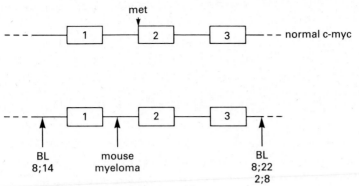

A. Mouse myeloma: invariably exon 1 lost
B. BL: exon 1 usually retained

Fig. 2. BL-mouse myeloma paradox. The top line depicts the three-exon structure of the normal c-myc gene with the protein synthesis initiation codon at the start of exon 2. Exon 1 is a non-coding, transcribed sequence. The lower line shows common breakpoints (indicated by arrows) associated with BL and an analogous translocation present in mouse myeloma. A. Most frequently mouse myeloma translocations involve a break between exons 1 and 2. B. In BL the breakpoint usually does not affect the gross structure of the c-myc gene.

Table 1. *Summary:* in situ *hybridization data*

Cell line: JI t2/8

Probe: V$\varkappa$ HK101/80		*Probe*: λHK101	
102 grains total/14 cells		231 grains total/16 cells	
2p	10	2p	13
2p$^-$	10	2p$^-$	14
8	0	8	1
8q$^+$	1	8q$^+$	0

Probe: C$\varkappa$ pUC R17C$\varkappa$	
113 grains total/23 cells	
2p	7
2p$^-$	1
8	0
8q$^+$	11

The V$\varkappa$ probes λHK101 and HK101/80 were described previously (Bentley & Rabbitts, 1981). The C$\varkappa$ probe (pUCR17C$\varkappa$) was isolated as follows: a genomic library of Raji DNA (Hamlyn & Rabbitts, 1983) was screened with the human C$\varkappa$ cDNA M13C$\varkappa$6 probe (Bentley & Rabbitts, 1983). A positively hybridizing clone λR17 was analysed and found to contain the C$\varkappa$ gene; a subclone was prepared from this in pUC8, which contained a $2 \cdot 5 \times 10^3$ base-pair *Eco*RI fragment with the C$\varkappa$ coding region plus immediate flanking sequences (pUCR17C$\varkappa$). Hybridizations were carried out as previously described (David, Malcolm, Hall & Marshall, 1983), at 43 °C for λHK101 and pUCR17C$\varkappa$, but 37 °C for HK101/80.

---

results therefore show that in this case the breakpoint occurs on the 3′ side of the c-myc gene, as opposed to the 5′ side as in t8/14. We wished to establish whether the ϰ L chain locus was involved in the t2/8 translocation point and, if so, how this locus was affected by the translocation. Accordingly, we used both Cϰ and Vϰ probes to carry out *in situ* hybridization experiments with chromosomes from cells containing t2/8. A summary of the data on grain-counting from these hybridizations is shown in Table 1, which includes only the data for the pairs of chromosomes 2 and 8. With the HK101/80 Vϰ probe there were 102 total grains in 14 cells analysed; with the λHK101 Vϰ probe there were 231 total grains in 16 cells, and with the Cϰ probe there were 113 total grains for 23 cells counted. The normal chromosome 2 shows positive hybridization with both the Vϰ probes (e.g. with HK101/80, 10 grains or 9·8 % of the total) and the Cϰ probe (7 grains or 6·2 % of the total), which is consistent with the previous assignment of this locus to chromosome 2 (Malcolm *et al*. 1982; McBride *et al*. 1982). No significant grains were detected over either normal or abnormal chromosome 8 with any of the Vϰ probes, which shows that the set of V genes detected in the experiment was not included in that part of chromosome 2 that translocated to chromosome 8. However, the possibility that some undetected Vϰ genes are translocated to chromosome 8 cannot be ruled out, especially since somatic cell hybrid experiments indicated that Vϰ genes do move to chromosome 8 (Erikson *et al*. 1983). This is an intriguing difference in the two sets of data, however, as an identical probe (HK101/80; Bentley & Rabbitts, 1983) was used.

Our experiments with the Cϰ probe (pUCR17Cϰ, see Table 1 footnote) show that the Cϰ gene does become translocated onto the $8q^+$ chromosome, since we find significant grains on this long arm (11 grains or 9·7 % of the total). These data show therefore that the Cϰ gene moves into the $8q^+$ chromosome in t2/8, thus finally being positioned to the 3′ side or downstream from the c-myc gene (see Fig. 3). Further-more, it seems that the Vϰ locus remains on the $2p^-$ chromosome with the breakage probably between Vϰ and Cϰ genes or within the Vϰ locus itself (see caveat discussed above). The orientation of Vϰ and Cϰ genes in chromosome 2 may also be deduced from these results (Fig. 3); i.e. the Vϰ genes (at least those detected in these hybridizations) are proximal to the centromere on the normal chromosome 2, while the Cϰ genes are distal or nearer to the telomere. At present we cannot comment on the transcription orientations of these genes. An intriguing feature of these results is the suggestion that the Ig constant region may be required for the effect of transloca-tion to be manifested, as this seems true for t8/14, t2/8 and t8/22.

ARE SEQUENCE CHANGES IN THE c-myc GENE A CLUE TO ONCOGENIC ACTIVATIONS OF THIS GENE?

We have previously reported substantial sequence alterations in the translocated c-myc gene of Raji (Rabbitts *et al*. 1983) in both exons 1 and 2. The latter would be expected to give rise to a substantially altered c-myc protein in this case. This ap-peared not to be so in the translocated gene of Daudi cells, however, as we found no coding sequence alteration in a complementary cDNA clone (Rabbitts *et al*. 1983),

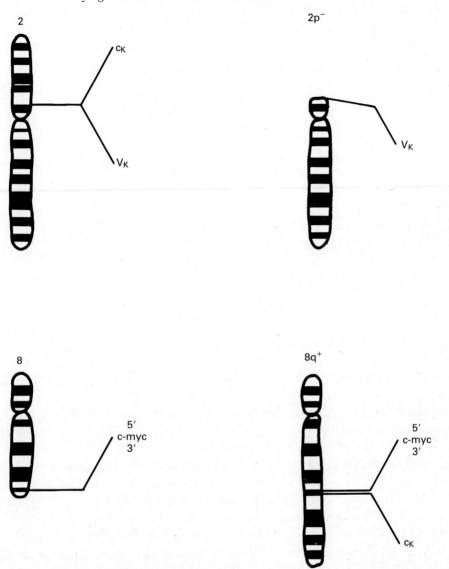

Fig. 3. Diagram of orientations of the various genes involved in translocations of chromosomes 2 and 8 in Burkitt's lymphoma.

which we presume to derive from the abnormal c-myc gene as this gene is preferentially expressed in BL cells (Bernard *et al.* 1983; Nishikura *et al.* 1983). However, we have now sequenced the exon 1 region of the Daudi clone (pUCCD1A) and discovered that, in addition to a 39-base duplication in this exon, there are 7·3 % base differences in exon 1 compared with the normal c-myc gene derived from a genomic cloned DNA segment from Daudi cells. Table 2 outlines the base differences found in the three exons of the translocated c-myc genes of Raji and Daudi cells. As a general rule coding region changes are therefore unlikely to be generally responsible for c-myc gene

Table 2. *Sequence changes in BL translocated c-myc gene*

Cell	Exon 1	Exon 2	Exon 3
Raji t8/14	7·0	3·3	0
Daudi t8/14	7·3	0	0

The Raji exon 1 changes exclude deletions previously noted (Rabbitts *et al.* 1983). Changes are given as percentages.

activation as there are no changes in Daudi cells (either coding or silent) in exons 2 or 3. However, in both cases the sequences of exon 1 have substantial differences from the normal c-myc gene sequenced from the same cell lines; this indicates that sequence changes in this general region may be important for activation of c-myc in BL. Further, we have now a similar observation in the translocated c-myc gene from LY67 (t8/22).

MODEL: LOSS OF c-myc GENE CONTROL RESULTING FROM CHROMOSOMAL TRANSLOCATION

The observation of changes (presumably mutations introduced into the c-myc genes as a consequence of translocation) in exon 1 provides one possible explanation for the c-myc gene paradox. If we assume that exon 1 or an upstream region is the site of action of a repressor protein (a suggestion previously made by Leder *et al.* 1983) that serves to control c-myc gene transcription tightly, this interaction could be altered (i.e. destabilized) by the sequence changes in the translocated c-myc gene in BL. Of course those BL cell lines, and the vast majority of mouse myelomas, in which exon 1 is lost by translocation from the coding part of the gene, will also have this control region removed. Thus we can envisage that a general way in which the c-myc gene is activated in the formation of Burkitt lymphoma and mouse myeloma is by loss or damage of the exon 1 or upstream controlling regions, resulting in constitutive transcription. This in turn would cause the constant presence of the c-myc protein in these malignant cells, whereas normal cells would display controlled c-myc gene transcription. These models offer obvious predictions, which can be readily tested. Such models as these do not of course preclude the possibility that in some cases other mechanisms may operate, such as the protein alteration in Raji (Rabbitts *et al.* 1983).

R. Baer was a recipient of a Lady Tata Memorial Fellowship.

REFERENCES

ADAMS, J. M., GERONDAKIS, S., WEBB, E., CORCORAN, L. & CORY, S. (1983). Cellular myc oncogene is altered by chromosome translocation to an immunoglobulin locus in murine plasma-cytomas and is rearranged similarly in human Burkitt's lymphomas. *Proc. natn. Acad. Sci. U.S.A.* **80**, 1982–1986.

BENTLEY, D. L. & RABBITTS, T. H. (1981). Human Vϰ immunoglobulin gene number: implications for the origin of antibody diversity. *Cell* **24**, 613–633.

BENTLEY, D. L. & RABBITTS, T. H. (1983). Evolution of immunoglobulin V genes. Evidence indicating that recently duplicated human Vϰ sequences have diverged by gene conversion. *Cell* **32**, 181–189.

BERNARD, O., CORY, S., GERONDAKIS, S., WEBB, E. & ADAMS, J. M. (1983). Sequence of the murine and human cellular myc oncogenes and two modes of myc transcription resulting from chromosome translocation in B lymphoid tumours. *EMBO J.* **2**, 2375–2383.

COLBY, W. W., CHEN, E. Y., SMITH, D. H. & LEVINSON, A. D. (1983). Identification and nucleotide sequence of a human locus homologous to the v-myc oncogene of avian myelom cytomatosis virus MC29. *Nature, Lond.* **301**, 722–725.

CROCE, C. M., THIERFELDER, W., ERIKSON, J., NISHIKURA, K., FINAN, J., LENOIR, G. M. & NOWELL, P. C. (1983). Transcriptional activation of an unrearranged and untranslocated c-myc oncogene by translocation of a Cλ locus in Burkitt lymphoma cells. *Proc. natn. Acad. Sci. U.S.A.* **80**, 6922–6926.

DAVIS, M., MALCOLM, S., HALL, A. & MARSHALL, C. J. (1983). Localisation of the human N-ras oncogene to chromosome 1 cen-p21 by *in situ* hybridisation. *EMBO J.* **2**, 2281–2283.

DAVIS, M., MALCOLM, S. & RABBITTS, T. H. (1984). Chromosome translocation can occur on either side of the c-myc oncogene in Burkitt lymphoma cells. *Nature, Lond.* **308**, 286–288.

ERIKSON, J., FINAN, J., NOWELL, P. C. & CROCE, C. M. (1982). Translocation of immunoglobulin VH genes in Burkitt lymphoma. *Proc. natn. Acad. Sci. U.S.A.* **79**, 5611–5615.

ERIKSON, J., NISHIKURA, K., AR-RUSHDI, A., FINAN, J., EMANUEL, B., LENOIR, G., NOWELL, P. C. & CROCE, C. M. (1983). Translocation of an immunoglobulin ϰ locus to a region 3′ of an unrearranged c-myc oncogene enhances c-myc transcription. *Proc. natn. Acad. Sci. U.S.A.* **80**, 7581–7585.

HAMLYN, P. H. & RABBITTS, T. H. (1983). Translocation joins c-myc and immunoglobulin γ1 genes in a Burkitt lymphoma revealing a third exon in the c-myc oncogene. *Nature, Lond.* **304**, 135–139.

HOLLIS, G. F., MITCHELL, K. F., BATTEY, J., POTTER, H., TAUB, R., LENOIR, G. M. & LEDER, P. (1984). A variant translocation places the λ immunoglobulin genes 3′ to the c-myc oncogene in Burkitt's lymphoma. *Nature, Lond.* **307**, 752–755.

LEDER, P., BATTEY, J., LENOIR, G., MOULDING, C., MURPHY, W., POTTER, H., STEWARD, T. & TAUB, R. (1983). Translocations among antibody genes in human cancer. *Science* **222**, 765–771.

MALCOLM, S., BARTON, P., MURPHY, C., FERGUSON-SMITH, M. A., BENTLEY, D. L. & RABBITTS, T. H. (1982). Localisation of human immunoglobulin kappa light chain variable region genes to the short arm of chromosome 2 by *in situ* hybridisation. *Proc. natn. Acad. Sci. U.S.A.* **79**, 4957–4961.

MCBRIDE, O. W., HIETER, P. A., HOLLIS, G. F., SWAN, D., OTEY, M. C. & LEDER, P. (1982). Chromosomal location of human kappa and lambda immunoglobulin light chain constant region genes. *J. exp. Med.* **155**, 1480–1490.

NISHIKURA, K., AR-RUSHDI, A., ERIKSON, J., WATT, R., ROVERA, G. & CROCE, C. M. (1983). Differential expression of the normal and of the translocated human c-myc oncogenes in B cells. *Proc. natn. Acad. Sci. U.S.A.* **80**, 4822–4826.

RABBITTS, T. H., HAMLYN, P. H. & BAER, R. (1983). Altered nucleotide sequence of a translocated c-myc gene in Burkitt lymphoma. *Nature, Lond.* **306**, 760–765.

STANTON, L. W., WATT, R. & MARCU, K. B. (1983). Translocation, breakage and truncated transcripts of c-myc oncogene in murine plasmacytomas. *Nature, Lond.* **303**, 401–403.

WATT, R., STANTON, L. W., MARCU, K. B., GALLO, R. C., CROCE, C. M. & ROVERA, G. (1983). Nucleotide sequence of cloned cDNA of human c-myc oncogene. *Nature, Lond.* **303**, 725–728.

J. Cell Sci. Suppl. 1, 103–122 (1984)
Printed in Great Britain © The Company of Biologists Limited 1984

INTERPHASE NUCLEAR MATRIX AND METAPHASE SCAFFOLDING STRUCTURES

CATHERINE D. LEWIS, JANE S. LEBKOWSKI, ANN K. DALY
AND ULRICH K. LAEMMLI

*Departments of Biochemistry and Molecular Biology, University of Geneva,
30, quai Ernest-Ansermet, Geneva, Switzerland*

SUMMARY

The protein compositions of purified metaphase chromosomes, nuclei and their residual scaffold and matrix structures, are reported. The protein pattern of nuclei on sodium dodecyl sulphate/ polyacrylamide gels is considerably more complex and rich in non-histone proteins than that of chromosomes. Nuclei contain about three to four times more non-histone proteins relative to their histones than chromosomes. Besides the protein components of the peripheral lamina, several protein bands are specific or at least highly enriched in nuclei. Conversely, two proteins X0 ($33\times 10^3 M_r$) and X1 ($37\times 10^3 M_r$) are highly enriched in the pattern of metaphase chromosomes.

We have compared morphologically the previously defined nuclear matrices type I and II. The type I nuclear matrix is composed of the known lamina proteins, which form the peripheral lamina structure, and a complex series of proteins that form the internal network of the matrix as observed by electron microscopy. This internal network is stabilized similarly to the metaphase scaffolding by metalloprotein interaction. Both the scaffolding and the internal network of the matrix dissociate if thiols or certain metal chelators are used in the extraction buffer. Under these conditions the resulting nuclear structure, called matrix type II, appears empty in the electron microscope, with the exception of some residual nucleolar material. This latter material can be extracted from the internal network by exhaustive treatment of the nuclei with RNase before extraction with high salt.

Immunoblotting and activity studies show RNA polymerase II to be tightly bound to the type I, but not to the type II matrix, or to the scaffolding structure. No polymerase II enzyme was detected in isolated metaphase chromosomes. Another nuclear enzyme, poly(ADP-ribose) polymerase is not bound to either of the residual nuclear matrices or to the scaffolding structures. The association of RNA polymerase with the internal network of the nuclear matrix is consistent with the idea that transcription occurs in close association with this structure.

INTRODUCTION

Recent observations have provided evidence that the chromatin fibre is organized into domains or loops, which are constrained by a residual framework both in metaphase chromosomes (Paulson & Laemmli, 1977; Adolph, Cheng & Laemmli, 1977*a*; Adolph, Cheng, Paulson & Laemmli, 1977*b*) and in interphase nuclei (Benyajati & Worcel, 1976; Cook & Brazell, 1976; Igo-Kemenes & Zachau, 1978; Adolph, 1980; Lebkowski & Laemmli, 1982*a*,*b*). The residual framework of metaphase chromosomes has been called a 'scaffolding' (Laemmli *et al.* 1978) since this structure retains some of the morphological features of metaphase chromosomes (Paulson & Laemmli, 1977; Earnshaw & Laemmli, 1983). Recently, we have found that the scaffolding is composed of a subset of non-histone proteins, which include two prominent high molecular weight species, Sc1 and Sc2, of about 170 000 and 135 000 M_r (Lewis & Laemmli, 1982).

The protein framework involved in the organization of the interphase chromatin is thought to correspond to the nuclear matrix, which can be isolated following extraction of nuclei with high salt (Berezney & Coffey, 1974; Comings & Okada, 1976; Herman, Weymouth & Penman, 1978; Long, Huang & Pogo, 1979; van Eekelen & van Venrooij, 1981). Morphologically, this structure is composed of three elements: (1) a peripheral nuclear lamina, (2) an internal protein network, and (3) a residual nucleolar structure. The peripheral lamina is the best-studied component and is composed of three major proteins of $60\,000$–$70\,000 M_r$ (Aaronson & Blobel, 1975; Gerace & Blobel, 1980; Jost & Johnson, 1981).

We have recently been able to distinguish two levels of folding of the chromatin fibre in nuclei (Lebkowski & Laemmli, 1982a,b). One level of organization is thought to result from an attachment of the DNA to the peripheral nuclear lamina structure. We propose that the DNA is stabilized at a second level by a complex set of proteins, which forms the residual network in the interior of the nuclear matrix. A series of recent reports suggest that the nuclear matrix has more than a structural role, and may be involved in DNA replication (Vogelstein, Pardoll & Coffey, 1980; Pardoll, Vogelstein & Coffey, 1980; Dijkwel, Mullenders & Wanka, 1979), transcription (Jackson, McCready & Cook, 1981), and RNA processing (Ciejek, Nordstrom, Tsai & O'Malley, 1982).

MATERIALS AND METHODS

Isolation of nuclei and metaphase chromosomes

HeLa S3 cells were maintained in suspension culture at 37 °C in RPMI-1640 medium supplemented with 5 % (w/v) newborn calf serum, 100 units/ml penicillin and 100 μg/ml streptomycin. For autoradiography, the cells were labelled with [^{35}S]methionine at 1–2 μCi/ml for 48 h before isolation. Metaphase chromosomes were isolated from cells blocked in metaphase at a concentration of 2×10^5 cells/ml with Colcemid at a final concentration of 0·06 μg/ml for 12–16 h. The isolation of metaphase chromosomes in an aqueous, reticulocyte standard buffer (RSB) or in a polyamine buffer system was performed as described by Lewis & Laemmli (1982). Isolation of interphase nuclei by the RSB method was performed as described by Lebkowski & Laemmli (1982b). Isolation of interphase nuclei in a polyamine buffer system was performed as follows. HeLa cells (500 ml) growing exponentially at a concentration of 2×10^5 cells/ml were collected in four tubes (1400 g, 5 min), and washed three times at room temperature with 50 ml/pellet in a buffer containing 20 mM-KCl, 0·05 M-spermine, 0·13 mM-spermidine, 0·5 mM-EDTA, 3·7 mM-Tris·HCl (pH 7·4), (solution I). The pellets were resuspended at 4 °C in 30 ml of solution I containing 0·1 % digitonin and 50 μg/ml RNase A, and homogenized using a type A pestle. Nuclei were pelleted (5 min at 1000 g) in the Clay Adams Dynac centrifuge. The nuclei were vortexed and rehomogenized 7–8 times before a final wash and re-suspension in solution I containing 0·1 % digitonin but no EDTA. All solutions contained 0·1 mM-phenylmethylsulphonyl fluoride (PMSF), 10 KIU/ml Trasylol (Mobay Chemical Co.), 1 % thiodiglycol (Pierce), except during homogenization of the cells when 1 mM-PMSF and 100 KIU/ml Trasylol were used. We will refer to chromosomes and nuclei isolated either in the reticulocyte standard buffer or the polyamine-containing buffer as RSB or polyamine chromosomes and nuclei, respectively.

Isolation of nuclear matrices and metaphase scaffolds

Metaphase scaffolds were isolated from RSB or polyamine chromosomes as described by Lewis & Laemmli (1982). Nuclear matrices types I and II were isolated from RSB nuclei as described by Lebkowski & Laemmli (1982b). Type I and II nuclear matrices from polyamine nuclei were obtained as follows. Isolated polyamine nuclei in 200 μl (10 o.d.$_{260}$ units/ml), were digested with 40 μg/ml of DNase I for 1 h at 4 °C in solution I containing 0·1 % digitonin, 10 mM-MgCl$_2$, but no EDTA. For type I matrices, 0·1 mM-CuSO$_4$ or 0·5 mM-CaCl$_2$ was added, under an N$_2$ atmosphere, to the nuclease-digested nuclei for 10 min at 4 °C or 10 min at 37 °C, respectively. The addition of 5 mM-EDTA was used to stop the reaction. The addition of Cu^{2+} or Ca^{2+} is necessary to stabilize the type I matrix structure if isolated from polyamine nuclei that have been metal-depleted (Lewis & Laemmli, 1982). Histones were extracted from the nuclei by the addition of 4·5 ml of a lysis buffer containing 2 M-NaCl, 10 mM-Tris·HCl (pH 7·4), 10 mM-EDTA, 0·1 % digitonin at 4 °C for 20 min. The lysis mixture containing the nuclei was spun at 15 000 rev./min for 30 min at 4 °C in the SW50.1 rotor (Beckman). Type II matrices were isolated in an identical manner except that the addition of Cu^{2+} was omitted. All solutions contained 0·1 mM-PMSF, 1 % thiodiglycol and 10 KIU/ml Trasylol.

Detection of RNA polymerase II by immunoblotting

Nuclear and chromosomal samples to be tested for RNA polymerase II antibody binding were isolated without thiodiglycol or RNase treatment, electrophoresed on sodium dodecyl sulphate (SDS)/4 M-urea/polyacrylamide gels, and transferred to nitrocellulose filters as described for DNA–protein blotting (Bowen, Steinberg, Laemmli & Weintraub, 1980). The filters with the blotted proteins were processed as described by Stick & Krohne (1982). A monoclonal antibody to *Drosophila* RNA polymerase II, provided by E. Bautz (undiluted mouse ascites fluid, 1·5 mg/ml protein), was used at a dilution of 1 : 500. Antibody binding was visualized by ^{125}I-labelled rabbit anti-mouse antibody (Amersham, 1 μCi/ml, sp. act. 1 μCi/μg) as the secondary antibody.

In vitro *transcription assays*

Polyamine or RSB chromosomes and nuclei were isolated without thiodiglycol or RNase treatment and used either directly or frozen at −80 °C in 20 mM-Tris·HCl (pH 7·9), 75 mM-NaCl, 0·5 mM-EDTA, 8·5 mM-dithiothreitol, 0·125 mM-PMSF and 50 % glycerol. Immediately before use, samples to be tested were washed twice and resuspended in RSB, 0·1 mM-PMSF containing no detergent, at a concentration of 150 o.d. units/ml (A_{260}) at 4 °C. The buffer system of Cox (1976) was routinely used for the assay. Reaction mixtures (0·3–0·5 ml) contained 25 mM-Tris·HCl (pH 7·9), 1 mM-MnCl$_2$, 0·5 mM-dithiothreitol, 0·5 mM of each ATP, CTP and GTP, 30 μM-UTP, 250 mM-(NH$_4$)$_2$SO$_4$, 10 μM-[^{3}H]UTP (20 μCi). Where appropriate, Sarkosyl (0·6 %) or heparin (1 mg/ml) were included. Mixtures were preincubated at 32 °C for 5 min before the addition of nuclei or chromosomes (100–200 μg of DNA in 20 μl or RSB). Samples (50 μl) were removed at 15- to 30-min intervals, and the reaction was stopped in each sample by the addition of 5 mM-EDTA, followed by 200 μg/ml DNase I, 40 μg *Escherichia coli* transfer RNA, 10 mM-MgCl$_2$. The samples were spotted in duplicate onto DE81 filters (Whatman), which were washed three times in 10 % Na$_2$HPO$_4$.12H$_2$O, 0·5 % Na$_4$P$_2$O$_7$, 0·1 % SDS (Gariglio, Llopis, Oudet & Chambon, 1979), three times in water and twice in ethanol. The filters were dried and counted.

Poly(ADP-ribose) polymerase assays

Poly(ADP-ribose) polymerase was assayed by a modification of the method of Ogata, Ueda, Kawaichi & Hayashi (1981). Assays were performed with 1 μM-^{32}P-labelled NAD (850 Ci/mmol, Amersham) at 22 °C in 0·1 mM-Tris·HCl (pH 8·0) 10 mM-MgCl$_2$, 1·25 mM-dithiothreitol. For each assay, 1–2 A_{260} units of nuclei or chromosomes in a volume of 30 μl were added to give a final reaction volume of 100 μl. The reaction was terminated by the addition of 10 μl of reaction mixture to 0·5 ml of absolute ethanol at −20 °C using 25 μl cytochrome *c* (1 μg/ml) as carrier. After 2 h at −20 °C, the solution was centrifuged at 10 000 rev./min for 5 min in the microfuge (Eppendorf). The pellet was resuspended in final sample buffer and electrophoresed as described by Laemmli (1970) with the modifications outlined by Lewis & Laemmli (1982).

For metaphase scaffolds and nuclear matrices, nuclei and chromosomes were digested with DNase I and treated with CuSO$_4$, as described above, before the assay. In this case the polymerase reaction was terminated by the addition of 20 mM-nicotinamide after 10 min of incubation with the ^{32}P-labelled NAD. Samples (10 μl) were treated with 1 ml lysis buffer (2 M-NaCl, 10 mM-Tris·HCl, pH 9·0, 10 mM-EDTA, 0·1 % digitonin) for 20 min, and then pelleted in the microfuge. The supernatants were precipitated with trichloroacetic acid.

Electron microscopy of nuclear matrices

Nuclei isolated the RSB method were resuspended in 10 mM-cacodylate (pH 7·4), 10 mM-NaCl, 5 mM-MgCl$_2$, 0·1 % digitonin, 1·0 % thiodiglycol, 10 KIU/ml Trasylol, 0·1 mM-PMSF, and digested with 40 μg/ml DNase I for 1 h at 4 °C. For type I nuclear matrices, 1 ml of nuclei (5 o.D. units A_{260}) were mixed with 8 ml of 2 M-NaCl, 10 mM-cacodylate (pH 9·0), 10 mM-EDTA, 0·1 % digitonin, 1 % thiodiglycol, 10 KIU/ml Trasylol, 0·1 mM-PMSF and were extracted for 20 min at 4 °C.

Following extraction, glutaraldehyde (Fluka EM grade) was added to each sample to a concentration of 0·2 %, and fixation was allowed to proceed for 60 min at 4 °C. All operations were carried out in glass conical tubes. After glutaraldehyde fixation, the samples were spun at 600g for 20 min in the Clay Adams Dynac centrifuge. The pellets were resuspended gently in 100 mM-cacodylate (pH 7·4), 1·0 % glutaraldehyde and again fixed for 3 h at 4 °C. After this second fixation, the samples were pelleted (600 **g**, 10 min), washed three times with 100 mM-cacodylate (pH 7·4), and were post-fixed with 1 % OsO$_4$ in 100 mM-cacodylate (pH 7·4), overnight at 4 °C. Following post-fixation, the samples were washed three times with 100 mM-cacodylate (pH 7·4) and dehydrated in the following ethanol series (2·5, 5, 10, 20, 30, 40, 50, 60, 70, 80, 90 and 95 %, and three times at 100 %). Each dehydration step was for 15 min at 4 °C. The samples were then kept at room temperature and allowed to be penetrated with increasing concentrations of Epon in 100 % ethanol (10, 25, 50, 75 and 100 %). For each change of Epon, the sample was mixed with the resin and allowed to stand at room temperature until the sample sank to the bottom of the tube. After penetration with 75 % Epon, the samples were centrifuged at 2000 **g** for 10 min in the Clay Adams centrifuge to compact the pellets. The tubes were drained well and the pellets were resuspended in 200 μl of 100 % Epon. The samples in 100 % Epon were transferred to beam capsules and the capsules were filled with 100 % Epon. The samples were allowed to be penetrated with 100 % Epon overnight at 45 °C followed by polymerization for 4 days at 60 °C. The blocks were trimmed with glass knives, and pale gold sections were cut with a diamond knife on the Sorvall Porter Blum microtome. The sections were collected on 200 mesh copper grids that were coated with parlodion and carbon. The sections were stained for 15 min with 0·5 % (w/v) uranyl acetate in 50 % (v/v) methanol and 5 min with 0·5 % uranyl acetate in 50 % methanol and 5 min with lead citrate. The sections were viewed in a Zeiss EM109 electron microscope at 40 kV.

RESULTS

The proteins associated with metaphase chromosomes, nuclei and their residual structures

We have compared the protein pattern of highly purified metaphase chromosomes and nuclei by SDS/polyacrylamide gel electrophoresis. A striking general difference regarding the composition of the non-histone proteins of these two structures is evident. This difference is particularly clear if the samples are loaded so as to have a nearly identical staining intensity of both the core and the H1 histones (Fig. 1). The non-histone protein pattern of nuclei in lane a is considerably more complex and rich compared to that of chromosomes in lane b. We have roughly determined the relative enrichment of the non-histone proteins in nuclei by densitometric scanning of the stained patterns. We find that nuclei are enriched in non-histone proteins by a factor of 3–4 as compared to chromosomes. Examination of the gel patterns permits the identification of many proteins that appear to be specific to nuclei, a representative set of such proteins is observed in the 32 to $42 \times 10^3 M_r$ range indicated in Fig. 1 by dots. Also evident are the well-known major structural components of the peripheral lamina

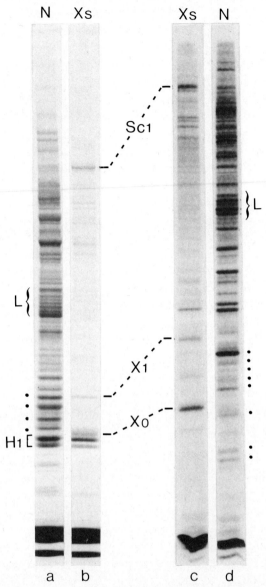

Fig. 1. Protein patterns of nuclei and metaphase chromosomes. Nuclei (N) and metaphase chromosomes (Xs) were isolated from HeLa cells in buffers containing polyamines, treated with DNase I (see Materials and Methods) and the protein patterns were analysed by SDS/polyacrylamide gel electrophoresis. The stained patterns of nuclei (lane a) and chromosomes (lane b) were obtained on linear 5% to 15% gradient gel. The autoradiograph of [^{35}S]methionine-labelled chromosomes (lane c) and nuclei (lane d) was obtained on an 11% gel. L, the cluster of lamina proteins; dots, proteins enriched in preparations of nuclei; H1, histone; Sc1, scaffold protein 1.

structure in a complex cluster of bands labelled L. Many other proteins bands that are enriched in nuclei are observed in Fig. 1.

Conversely, we observe many fewer proteins that are specifically enriched in chromosomes, but two bands X1 ($37 \times 10^3 M_r$) and X0 ($33 \times 10^3 M_r$) are proteins that are characteristic of the pattern of metaphase chromosomes. The protein X0 migrates slightly above histone H1a in a 5 % to 15 % linear gradient gel (Fig. 1, lane b) and it is sometimes difficult to distinguish it from histone H1a in stained gels. However, the autoradiographic pattern derived from [^{35}S]methionine-labelled chromosomes permits easy identification of proteins X0 and X1 (see Fig. 1, lane c). Nuclei, and to a lesser extent chromosomes, are usually contaminated by cytoplasmic components, such as actin and the various intermediate filaments. Comparison of the patterns permits the conclusion that the major differences in protein observed between nuclei and chromosomes are not due to different extents of cytoplasmic contamination.

In Fig. 2 the gel patterns of the residual scaffold structures and the nuclear matrices derived from chromosomes and nuclei, respectively, are shown for comparison. We have previously suggested the existence of metalloprotein interactions important for the structural stability of the metaphase scaffold and part of the nuclear matrices. The metals involved were identified to be Ca^{2+} and or Cu^{2+} (Lewis & Laemmli, 1982; Lebkowski & Laemmli, 1982*a,b*). The biological roles of these metals, if any, are not understood, but they are important parameters, which need to be dealt with since exposure of nuclei to these metals affects the stability and composition of the residual structures. The metaphase scaffold derived from chromosomes stabilized with Cu^{2+} contains 3–4 % of the total chromosomal proteins, the major ones being the proteins Sc1 ($170 \times 10^3 M_r$) and Sc2 ($135 \times 10^3 M_r$) (Lewis & Laemmli, 1982). This pattern is shown in lane f of Fig. 2 for comparison, next to the pattern of unextracted chromosomes in lane e. Included in Fig. 1 is the protein pattern of scaffolds derived from chromosomes exposed to Ca^{2+}, this structure contains about 10 % of the total chromosomal proteins. This latter pattern contains the same major proteins Sc1 and Sc2 but it is more complex regarding the minor proteins (Lewis & Laemmli, 1982). The relatively simple pattern of the chromosomal scaffold needs to be compared to the much more complex pattern of the nuclear matrices. We have defined two types of matrices: the type I matrix derived from metal-containing nuclei, and the type II matrix derived from metal-depleted nuclei (Lebkowski & Laemmli, 1982). The protein pattern of the type I matrix is complex and contains about 10–15 % of the total nuclear proteins (Fig. 2, lane c) if derived from nuclei exposed to Ca^{2+}. Among the most prominent bands are those of the nuclear lamina structure (L) and many high molecular weight proteins. We have included in Fig. 2 (lane b) the matrix type I pattern derived from nuclei exposed to Cu^{2+}; this pattern is even more complex, containing 20–25 % of the total nuclear proteins. A series of prominent nuclear proteins in the 32 to $42 \times 10^3 M_r$ range is particularly evident in the latter pattern.

Fig. 2 shows the pattern of the type II matrix in lane d. This structure is obtained from nuclei by the addition of metal chelators or thiols to the extraction buffers, which results in the solubilization of most of the proteins associated with the type I matrix, with the exception of the lamina proteins (Lebkowski & Laemmli, 1982). The type II matrix is almost exclusively composed of the three lamina proteins (L), a few minor

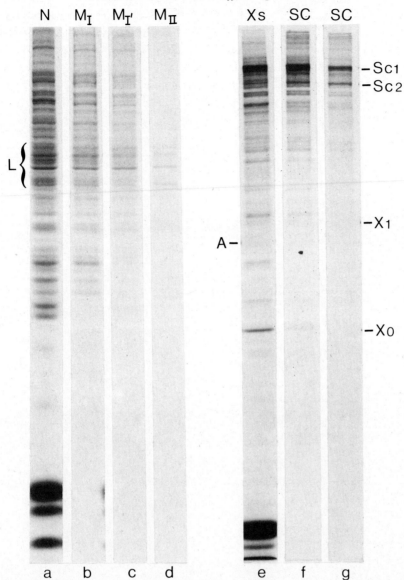

Fig. 2. Comparison of the protein patterns of nuclear matrices types I and II and of chromosomal scaffolds. Nuclear matrices (types I and II) were isolated from nuclei and chromosomal scaffolds were isolated from chromosomes, respectively, as described in Materials and Methods. The stained patterns were obtained by SDS/polyacrylamide gel electrophoresis on a 12·5 % (w/v) gel. Lanes a, unextracted nuclei; b, type I matrices derived from nuclei exposed to Cu^{2+}; c, type I matrices derived from nuclei exposed to Ca^{2+}; d, type II matrices derived from metal-depleted nuclei. Lanes e, chromosomes; f, scaffolds derived from chromosomes exposed to Cu^{2+}; g, scaffolds derived from chromosomes exposed to Ca^{2+}; A, actin; L, lamina protein.

bands and a varying amount of contamination by cytoskeletal proteins, actin and the intermediate filaments. Only 3–5 % of the total nuclear proteins are recovered in the type II structure (Lebkowski & Laemmli, 1982*b*). These and our previous studies have demonstrated that the composition and morphology of the residual structures isolated from chromosomes and nuclei can differ depending on the method of isolation

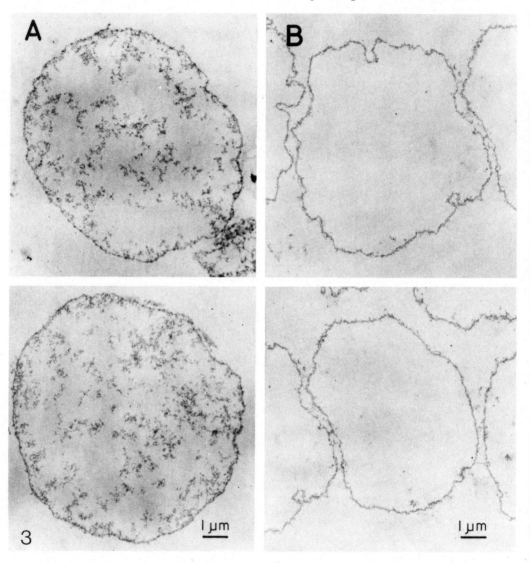

Fig. 3. Electron micrographs of type I and type II nuclear matrices. Interphase HeLa nuclei were isolated, digested with DNase I, extracted with the 2 M-NaCl lysis mixture and fixed for electron microscopy as described in Materials and Methods. During the cell homogenization step of nuclear isolation, the nuclei were digested with 50 μg/ml RNase A at 4 °C. A. Type I matrices after extraction with the 2 M-NaCl lysis mixture; B, type II matrices after extraction in the 2 M-NaCl lysis mixture containing 0·1 % β-mercaptoethanol. ×4400.

(Lebkowski & Laemmli, 1982*a,b*; Lewis & Laemmli, 1982; Earnshaw & Laemmli, 1983). We have identified the metals Ca^{2+} and/or Cu^{2+} as the major parameters that affect the composition and morphology of the residual structures.

Selective dissociation of the internal structures of the nuclear matrix

We have previously examined the morphology of the metaphase scaffold in some detail (Earnshaw & Laemmli, 1983). The residual nuclear matrix has been examined in the electron microscope by various workers (Berezney & Coffey, 1974; Comings

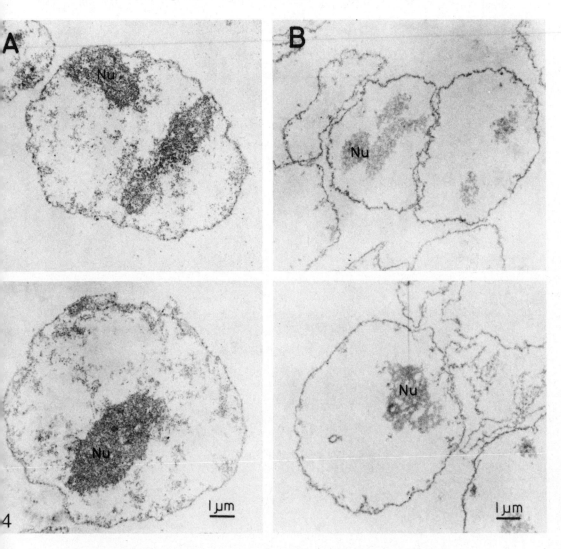

Fig. 4. Electron micrographs of type I and type II nuclear matrices from nuclei not treated with RNase A. Type I and II matrices were isolated from nuclei that were not digested with RNase A during isolation of the nuclei. A. Type I matrices isolated in the 2 M-NaCl lysis mixture; B, type II matrices isolated in the 2 M-NaCl lysis mixture containing 0·1 % β-mercaptoethanol. Nu, residual nucleolar material. ×4400.

& Okada, 1976; Herman *et al.* 1978; Long *et al.* 1979; van Eckelen & van Venrooij, 1981), yet controversy exists regarding the morphology and composition of these substructures (see Kaufman, Coffey & Shaper, 1981; Lebkowski & Laemmli, 1982). Comparison of the nuclear matrices types I and II prepared by our procedure in the light microscope suggests that most of the proteins lost during extraction in the absence of metals are derived from the interior of extracted nuclei. To study the morphology of the nuclear matrices in some detail we have prepared thin sections for the electron microscope. These structures are typically composed of three structural parts: a peripheral nuclear lamina, a residual nucleolar material and an internal network, which spans the space between the nucleolar material and the peripheral lamina. It is possible to extract selectively either the residual nucleolar material or the internal network. Extensive RNase digestion of the nuclei before extraction eliminates the residual nucleolar material (compare Figs 3 and 4). Metal chelation, on the other hand, by thiols before high salt extraction dissociates the internal network. The matrix type II obtained under these conditions is composed of the peripheral lamina and the nucleolar material and contains no visible internal network of protein (Figs 3B, 4B). RNase treatment eliminates the residual nucleolar structure from matrix type II; but is not required to solubilize the internal (non-nucleolar) network. This observation is consistent with our biochemical studies, which show that RNase digestion is not essential for the preparation of either matrix type (Lebkowski & Laemmli, 1982*a,b*).

A comparison of the proteins associated with nuclear matrices types I and II demonstrates that the disappearance of the internal network of the matrix coincides with the loss of many proteins (Fig. 2). We were unable to identify proteins that might be specific to residual nucleolar structure by comparing the gel pattern derived from extracted nuclei that were either treated or not treated with RNase (Laemmli & Lebkowski, 1983*b*). It is of importance to point out that the selective dissociation of either the internal network or the residual nucleolar structure is only reproducibly possible if the isolated nuclei are not exposed to CaCl₂ at 37 °C. We have previously demonstrated that incubation of nuclei with CaCl₂ at 37 °C, but not at 4 °C, leads to a 'toughening' of the nuclei, which prevents solubilization of the internal network to form matrix type II (Lebkowski & Laemmli, 1983*a,b*). We have confirmed the biochemical observation by electron microscopy, finding that nuclei toughened with CaCl₂ generate a structure similar to that shown in Fig. 4A. They contain both the internal network and the residual nucleolar structure despite the presence of thiols and/or metal chelators during extraction (data not shown).

RNA polymerase II but not poly(ADP-ribose) polymerase is bound to nuclear matrix type I

The eukaryotic class II RNA polymerases are large enzymes, composed of 10–15 distinct polypeptides, including two high molecular weight proteins in the range of 130 to $200 \times 10^3 M_r$ (e.g. see Paule, 1981). The engaged RNA polymerase forms very tight complexes with DNA, resisting extraction conditions that solubilize the histones. It was important to determine whether the two scaffolding proteins Sc1 and

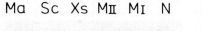

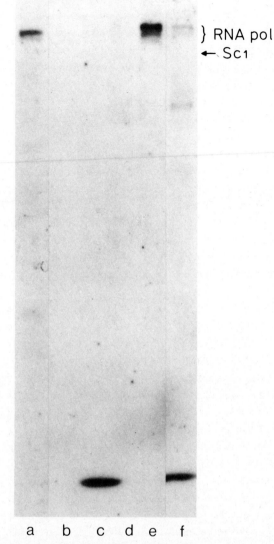

Fig. 5. Detection of RNA polymerase II in nuclei and type I nuclear matrices. Polyamine chromosomes, metaphase scaffolds, RSB nuclei and interphase matrices types I and II were isolated as described by Lewis & Laemmli (1982) and Lebkowski & Laemmli (1982*b*). RNase treatment and thiodiglycol were omitted from the isolation procedures. An extract was isolated from HeLa cells as described by Manley *et al.* (1980). Immuno-blotting was carried out as described in Materials and Methods, using a monoclonal antibody directed against the two largest subunits of RNA polymerase II from *Drosophila*, as described by Kramer *et al.* (1980). Lanes a, 'Manley' extract; b, scaffold; c, chromosomes; d, nuclear matrix type II; e, nuclear matrix type 1; f, whole RSB nuclei. The nuclear matrices types I and II are overloaded by a factor of about 3 relative to the nuclei. The relative positions of the Sc1 protein and the two RNA polymerase II subunits are indicated.

Sc2 are components of the polymerase. Furthermore, it has recently been suggested that the active transcription complexes are associated with the nuclear matrix (Jackson *et al.* 1981; Ciejek *et al.* 1982). If this is correct, polymerase molecules might be found preferentially bound to the nuclear matrix. Finally, the questions of the cellular location of the polymerase during mitosis, as well the physical basis for the absence of transcriptional activity during mitosis, have not been resolved (Matsui, Weinfeld & Sandberg, 1979; Gariglio, Buss & Green, 1974). For these reasons, we have tested metaphase chromosomes and scaffolds, nuclei and nuclear matrices for the binding of RNA polymerase II. Monoclonal antibodies directed against the two largest subunits of RNA polymerase II of *Drosophila melanogaster* were used (kindly supplied by E. Bautz) as probes against various nuclear substructures isolated from HeLa cells. This antibody cross-reacts with the two largest subunits of RNA polymerase II isolated from various organisms (Kramer & Bautz, 1981). The immunoblot in Fig. 5 identifies the two large subunits of the RNA polymerase II in whole nuclei (lane f) and in nuclear matrix type I (lane e), but not matrix type II (lane d). In both nuclei and matrix type I, a doublet of proteins is observed. As a control, we have included in the immunoblot (Fig. 5, lane a) an extract rich in RNA polymerase II prepared from HeLa cells according to the procedure of Manley *et al.* (1980). The binding of the RNA polymerase II subunits to the matrix I structure appears quantitative. We have loaded (in Fig. 5, lane e) three times as many matrices as we have loaded nuclei (in lane f). The immunoreaction is more intense by about this factor in the matrix sample as compared to that in nuclei. In contrast to the detection of the proteins of the large subunit of polymerase II in nuclei, matrix type I and the Manley extract, we detected no reaction in metaphase chromosomes and scaffolds (Fig. 5, lanes b and c). This result indicates that the Sc1 and Sc2 proteins are not the two largest subunits of RNA polymerase II. These data are not affected by the method of isolation of chromosomes or nuclei, since the same results are obtained using chromosomes and nuclei isolated in either aqueous or polyamine buffer systems (data not shown).

From the experiment shown in Fig. 5 it appears that no RNA polymerase II is observed in metaphase chromosomes. In order to verify this result by an alternative method, chromosomes and nuclei were used for *in vitro* transcription assays. In this assay system, engaged polymerase molecules will continue but not reinitiate transcription (Groner, Monroy, Jacquet & Hurwitz, 1975).

Time-course studies of transcriptional activities in both chromosomes and nuclei are presented in Fig. 6. For nuclei, the incorporation of $[^3H]UTP/\mu g$ DNA is shown to be highly dependent upon the inclusion of either the anionic detergent Sarkosyl or the polyanion heparin in the assay buffer. Transcriptional activity is stimulated in polyamine nuclei by as much as factors of 10 and 13 using Sarkosyl and heparin, respectively. These agents have been shown previously to stimulate RNA polymerase activity, presumably by releasing proteins from DNA that repress the polymerase (Gariglio *et al.* 1974; Cox, 1976).

In contrast to nuclei, the incorporation of $[^3H]UTP/\mu g$ DNA into chromosomes (Fig. 6, panel b) indicates a very low level of activity, which is never more than 6 %

of that observed for nuclei. There is some marginal stimulation due to heparin and Sarkosyl. Transcriptional assays carried out with nuclei and chromosomes purified by either aqueous or polyamine buffers gave similar results (data not shown). These results confirm the immunoblotting data shown above. It is clear from both types of assay, *in vitro* transcription and immunoblotting, that very little, if any, polymerase is bound to purified metaphase chromosomes.

The drug α-amanitin, which preferentially inhibits RNA polymerase II activity at

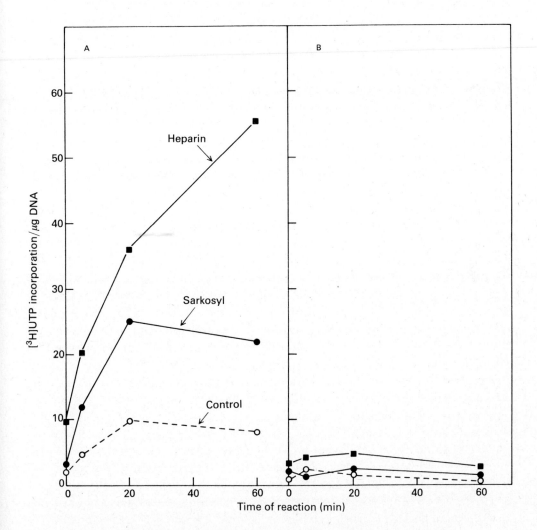

Fig. 6. *In vitro* transcription from chromosomes and nuclei. Polyamine chromosomes and RSB nuclei were isolated as described by Lewis & Laemmli (1982) and Lebkowski & Laemmli (1982*b*), but without RNase treatment and in the absence of thiodiglycol. Transcription assays were carried out according to the method of Cox (1976) and as described in Materials and Methods. A and B show transcriptional activity in nuclei and chromosomes, respectively, in intact nuclei or chromosomes (O----O), or following addition of Sarkosyl (●——●), or 1 mg/ml of heparin (■——■).

a concentration of 0·5 μg/ml (Weinmann & Roeder, 1974), reduces the overall [³H]UTP incorporation in nuclei by 85–90%. In the presence of 1 μg/ml of actinomycin D (Roberts & Newmann, 1966), all transcriptional activity is inhibited. At a concentration of 0·04 μg/ml of actinomycin D, 10–15% activity due to RNA polymerase I is inhibited (data not shown).

It has been suggested that the negligible polymerase activity observed in metaphase chromosomes is due to the highly condensed state of the chromatin in these structures, and that interphase polymerase levels can be obtained from metaphase chromosomes if the enzyme is solubilized by sonication (Matsui et al. 1979). In order to determine the validity of this suggestion, transcription assays were performed with supernatants of sonicated nuclei and chromosomes as described (Matsui et al. 1979). The levels of [³H]UTP incorporation that were obtained (data not shown) indicate that sonication does not release equal amounts of polymerase activity from nuclei and chromosomes; rather, the activities are equivalent to those in the intact structures, respectively.

In order to compare the localization of RNA polymerase II with another nuclear enzyme, we have assayed for poly(ADP-ribose) polymerase activity in nuclei, matrices, chromosomes and scaffolds. Poly(ADP-ribose) polymerase is a nuclear enzyme (Chambon, Weill & Mandel, 1963), which is automodified by the repeated addition of ADP-ribose from the substrate NAD (Yoshinara et al. 1977; Ogata et al. 1981). The enzyme has also been shown to be present in metaphase chromosomes (Hotlund, Kristensen, Ostvold & Laland, 1980). Studies on partially purified and purified preparations of the enzyme have shown that DNA and histones are necessary for its activity (Jump & Smulson, 1980). In addition, nicking of DNA by DNase I has been shown to activate the enzyme in permeabilized cells (Benjamin & Gill, 1980). Automodification enables the enzyme to be detected by autoradiography of SDS/polyacrylamide gels following incubation of nuclei with ³²P-labelled NAD. The major ADP-ribose acceptor in nuclei is a polypeptide of molecular weight 105×10^3 (Fig. 7, lane 1), which corresponds to the molecular weight of poly(ADP-ribose) polymerase (Jump & Smulson, 1980). When longer reaction times are used (lane 2) up to 20 other peptides are also labelled. The nuclei used in this study were treated with micrococcal nuclease, which gives a three to four-fold increase in enzyme activity (data not shown). An identical pattern is obtained for metaphase chromosomes (data not shown).

To determine if poly(ADP-ribose) polymerase is present on metaphase scaffolds and nuclear matrices, micrococcal nuclease-treated nuclei and chromosomes were labelled with [³²P]NAD and extracted with lysis buffers containing a range of salt concentrations (50 mM to 2 M-NaCl). Although the same results were obtained for both chromosomes and nuclei, only those for nuclei are shown (Fig. 7, lanes 2–18). It is clear that salt extraction releases the enzyme from the matrix. Dissociation of poly(ADP-ribose) polymerase is almost complete at a concentration of 0·5 M-NaCl. This extraction condition also solubilizes most of the other ADP-ribose acceptor proteins. The extraction of the poly(ADP-ribose) polymerase and its acceptor proteins is complete following extraction with 1 M-NaCl (lane 7). Thus type I nuclear matrices, which are prepared in a lysis buffer containing 2 M-NaCl (lane 8), contain

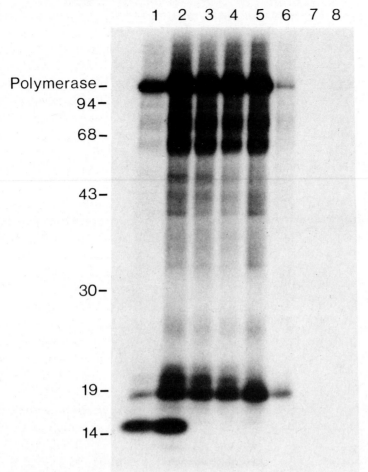

Fig. 7. Salt-dependent dissociation of poly(ADP-ribose) polymerase from nuclei. Polyamine nuclei were assayed for poly(ADP-ribose) polymerase after treatment with micrococcal nuclease. After a 10-min incubation with $1 \mu M$-[^{32}P]labelled NAD, samples were extracted with lysis buffers containing 50 mM to 2 M-NaCl. The resulting matrices were pelleted. Lanes 1 and 2 show nuclei that were incubated for 30 s and 10 min, respectively. Lanes 3–8 show residual nuclear structures prepared following extraction with 50 mM, 100 mM, 200 mM, 500 mM and 2 M-NaCl, respectively.

no poly(ADP-ribose) polymerase. Similar results were obtained for chromosomal scaffolds and for histone-depleted nuclei and chromosomes.

DISCUSSION

Comparison of the total gel pattern of chromosomes and nuclei permitted the identification of protein bands that are specific to or at least highly enriched in either of these structures. Proteins X0 ($33 \times 10^3 M_r$) and X1 ($37 \times 10^3 M_r$) are examples of typical chromosomal proteins while the proteins indicated by dots in Fig. 1 are prominent nuclear proteins. The most characteristic set of proteins of the latter class are observed in the 32 to $42 \times 10^3 M_r$ range, it is tempting to speculate that these proteins may be the structural components of the hnRNP particles (Beyer, Christen, Walter & Stourgeon, 1977). This set of proteins is also observed in matrix type I (Fig. 1), possibly supporting the finding that hnRNA is intimately linked to the nuclear matrix (Herman *et al.* 1978; Miller, Huang & Pogo, 1978; van Eekelen & van Venrooij, 1981).

Nuclei are considerably richer in the content and complexity of their non-histone proteins. Nuclei contain, relative to their histones in weight, three to four times more non-histone proteins than metaphase chromosomes according to our estimate. This finding is not entirely surprising since metaphase chromosomes are inert in terms of transcription and replication. Thus many of the proteins involved in these processes are expected to be released at mitosis. In addition, the nuclear lamina structure dissociates (Gerace & Blobel, 1980) and the hnRNP particles (Martin & Okamura, 1981) are known to be dispersed at mitosis. Our results also show that RNA polymerase is present in nuclei but not in metaphase chromosomes, whereas poly(ADP-ribose) polymerase is present in an active form in both.

We have defined two types of nuclear matrices. Most of the complex set of non-histone proteins observed in the type I but not in the type II structure must be associated with the internal network, which fills the space between the peripheral lamina structure and the residual nucleolar material. Electron micrographs confirm our biochemical observations, showing an internal network in the type I but not in the type II matrix. Residual nucleolar material can be selectively extracted by treatment of nuclei before extraction with RNase A. Thus metal chelation selectively allows solubilization of the internal network, while RNase treatment solubilizes the residual nucleolar material but not the former structure. The classification of the nuclear matrices into types I and II is no doubt an oversimplification. We have observed more subtle compositional differences between matrices depending on various parameters like pH, ionic strength, type of detergent, etc. . . These parameters need to be studied in more detail.

There has been some controversy concerning the composition of the nuclear matrix. Some investigators have found the internal network of fibres to be absent in preparations of nuclear substructures (Aaronson & Blobel, 1975; Dwyer & Blobel, 1978). While others find an internal network and residual nucleolar material (Berezney & Coffey, 1974; Comings & Okada, 1976; Herman *et al.* 1978; Long *et al.* 1979; van Eekelen & van Venrooij, 1981). This and our previous reports (Lebkowski & Laemmli, 1982*a,b*) define conditions under which the filled matrix type I or empty matrix type II structures are obtained. Other reports have also dealt with the questions of the biochemical composition and the morphology of the subnuclear structures (Fisher, Berrios & Blobel, 1982; Kaufmann *et al.* 1981; Adolph, 1980).

Some discrepancy regarding the effect of RNase treatment and the stability of the internal network remains. Kaufmann *et al.* (1981) have recently suggested that the internal network of the nuclear matrix is absent when nuclei are treated with DNase and RNase, and isolated under conditions that minimize formation of disulphide bonds. Under our conditions RNase treatment of nuclei before extraction eliminates only the residual nucleolar material but not the internal network, an observation that is clearly supported by our biochemical studies. We have also suggested that the internal network is stabilized by metalloprotein interaction (Lebkowski & Laemmli, 1982) rather than by extensive disulphide bonding (Kaufmann *et al.* 1981). Additional work is under way, to study these questions in more detail.

RNA polymerase II is bound to the nuclear matrix type I but not to the type II structure, and it is absent from metaphase chromosomes. In contrast, poly(ADP-ribose) polymerase is present in nuclei and chromosomes, but absent in type I and II nuclear matrices. This enzyme is dissociated completely from nuclei and chromosomes following extraction at intermediate salt concentration of about 0·5 M-NaCl.

One of the biochemical events that distinguishes mitosis from the G_1, S and G_2 phases of the cell cycle is the absence in mitosis of any transcriptional activity of RNA polymerase I or II (Johnson & Holland, 1965; Morcillo, de la Torre & Gimenez-Martin, 1976), while continued synthesis of small mitochondrial RNAs by polymerase III has been detected in metaphase cells (Zylber & Penman, 1971). The physical basis for the absence of polymerase II activity has not been explained, but it has been suggested that inactivation of the enzyme might be caused by the dense packing of the chromatin in metaphase chromosomes or by the dissociation of the enzyme from the chromosome as the cell enters mitosis. The results presented here strongly suggest that the second alternative is the correct one.

What is the structural and functional relationship of the metaphase scaffolding and the nuclear matrix? The latter structure is compositionally and structurally much more complex, being composed of the peripheral lamina, a residual nucleolar network and an internal network. The peripheral lamina dissociates during mitosis and is consequently expected to have no major role in metaphase chromosome structure. The internal network of the matrix shares some properties with metaphase scaffolding. The structural stability of both is due to metalloprotein interactions, at least one of the major structural component of the scaffolding, Sc1, is also part of the internal network (J. van Ness, C. Lewis & U. K. Laemmli, unpublished data). Both structures are involved in the folding of the DNA of histone-depleted chromosomes and nuclei, respectively. We have recently presented sedimentation studies, which permitted the identification of two different levels of folding of the DNA in histone-depleted nuclei. One of these levels of DNA folding is due to the interaction of the DNA with the peripheral lamina while a second level is brought about by the internal network (Lebkowski & Laemmli, 1982*a*).

This structural role cannot be the only function of the internal nuclear network; the protein complexity alone suggests additional biological roles. Indeed various reports suggest the possible involvement of the matrix in DNA replication (Berezeney & Coffey, 1975; Vogelstein *et al.* 1980), transcription (Jackson *et al.* 1981) and RNA processing (Ciejek *et al.* 1982). Our finding regarding the association of RNA polymerase II with the matrix is consistent with a role in transcription.

As a possible explanation for the attachment of these processes to the nuclear matrix, one could propose that the matrix is involved in subdividing the nucleus into compartments, which are microenvironments containing and maintaining the various factors, proteins and enzymes needed to carry out each of these biological processes. The elements needed in a given compartment might have a high affinity for the matrix, thus preventing general diffusion and destruction of the compartment.

The association of RNA polymerase II with the nuclear matrix also could be due to an artefactual precipitation of the transcription complexes by the high salt concentration used in these experiments. These transcription complexes might be close to but not directly attached to a subnuclear structural element.

We have recently made progress in studying the DNA sequence organization of the higher-order chromatin loops. We find that the DNA loops are highly organized and the attachment of the DNA to the nuclear matrix occurs at highly specific sites. This specific loop organization is only observed following preparations of nuclear scaffolds by a newly developed method using low salt conditions (J. Mirkovitch, M.-E. Mirault & U. K. Laemmli, unpublished). Conversely, a loss of this specific organization of the loops is observed following exposure of the nuclei to high salt, possibly due to sliding of the DNA along the attachment points. Interestingly, we find that the transcribed regions of active genes are not attached to the matrix under the low salt conditions, whereas attachment of these transcribed regions is found if high salt conditions are used. These observations do not inspire confidence in the hypothesis that all interactions observed in high-salt-extracted matrices are of biological significance.

We are indebted to S. Gasser, F. Keppel and J. van Ness for helpful comments on this manuscript. This work was supported by the Swiss National Science Foundation Grant 3.621.82 and by the Canton of Geneva.

REFERENCES

AARONSON, R. & BLOBEL, G. (1975). Isolation of nuclear pore complexes in association with a lamina. *Proc. natn. Acad. Sci. U.S.A.* **72**, 1007–1011.

ADOLPH, K. (1980). Isolation and structural organization of human mitotic chromosomes. *Chromosoma* **76**, 23–33.

ADOLPH, K., CHENG, S. & LAEMMLI, U. K. (1977a). Role of non-histone proteins in metaphase chromosome structure. *Cell* **12**, 805–816.

ADOLPH, K., CHENG, S., PAULSON, J. & LAEMMLI, U. K. (1977b). The structure of histone-depleted metaphase chromosomes. *Cell* **12**, 817–828.

BENJAMIN, R. & GILL, N. M. (1980). ADP-ribosylation in mammalian cell ghosts. *J. biol. Chem.* **255**, 10493–10501.

BENYAJATI, C. & WORCEL, A. (1976). Isolation and characterization and structure of the folded interphase genome of *Drosophila melanogaster*. *Cell* **9**, 393–407.

BEREZNEY, R. & COFFEY, D. (1974). Identification of a nuclear protein matrix. *Biochem. biophys. Res. Commun.* **60**, 1410–1419.

BEREZNEY, R. & COFFEY, D. (1975). Nuclear matrix: association with newly synthesized DNA. *Science* **189**, 291–293.

BEYER, A. L., CHRISTEN, M. E., WALTER, B. W. & STOURGEON, W. (1977). Identification and characterization of the packaging proteins of core 40S hnRNP particles. *Cell* **11**, 127–138.

BOWEN, B., STEINBERG, J., LAEMMLI, U. K. & WEINTRAUB, H. (1980). The detection of DNA-binding proteins by protein blotting. *Nucl. Acid Res.* **8** (1), 1–20.

CHAMBON, P., WEILL, J. & MANDEL, P. (1983). Nicotinamide mononucleotide activation of a new DNA-dependent polyadenylic acid nuclear enzyme. *Biochem. biophys. Res. Commun.* **11**, 39–43.

CIEJEK, E., NORDSTROM, J., TSAI, J. L. & O'MALLEY, B. (1982). Ribonucleic acid precursors are associated with the chick oviduct nuclear matrix. *Biochemistry* **21**, 4945–4953.

COMINGS, D. E. & OKADA, T. A. (1976). Nuclear proteins. III. The fibrillar nature of the nuclear matrix. *Expl Cell Res.* **103**, 341–360.

COOK, P. & BRAZELL, I. (1976). Conformational constraints in nuclear DNA. *J. Cell Sci.* **22**, 287–302.

COX, R. F. (1976). Quantitation of elongating form A and B RNA polymerase in chick oviduct nuclei and effects of estradiol. *Cell* **7**, 455–465.

DIJKWEL, D., MULLENDERS, L. & WANKA, F. (1979). Analysis of the attachment of replicating DNA to a nuclear matrix in mammalian interphase nuclei. *Nucl. Acid Res.* **6**, 219–230.

DWYER, N. & BLOBEL, G. (1976). A modified procedure for the isolation of a pore complex–lamina fraction from rat liver nuclei. *J. Cell Biol.* **70**, 581–591.

EARNSHAW, W. & LAEMMLI, U. K. (1983). Architecture of metaphase chromosomes and chromosome scaffolds. *J. Cell Biol.* **96**, 84–93.

FISHER, P., BERRIOS, M. & BLOBEL, G. (1982). Isolation and characterization of a proteinaceous subnuclear fraction composed of nuclear matrix peripheral lamina, and nuclear pore complex, from embryos of *Drosophila melanogaster. J. Cell Biol.* **92**, 674–686.

GARIGLIO, P., BUSS, J. & GREEN, M. (1974). Sarkosyl activation of RNA polymerase activity in mitotic mouse cells. *FEBS Lett.* **44**, 330–333.

GARIGLIO, P., LLOPIS, R., OUDET, P. & CHAMBON, P. (1979). The template of the isolated native simian virus 40 transcriptional complex is a minichromosome. *J. molec. Biol.* **131**, 75–105.

GERACE, L. & BLOBEL, G. (1980). The nuclear envelope lamina is reversibly depolymerized during mitosis. *Cell* **19**, 227–287.

GRONER, Y., MONROY, G., JACQUET, M. & HURWITZ, J. (1975). Chromatin as a template for RNA synthesis *in vitro*. *Proc. natn. Acad. Sci. U.S.A.* **72**, 194–199.

HERMAN, R., WEYMOUTH, L. & PENMAN, S. (1978). Heterogeneous nuclear RNA-protein fibers in chromatin-depleted nuclei. *J. Cell Biol.* **78**, 663–674.

HOTLUND, J., KRISTENSEN, T., OSTVOLD, A.-C. & LALAND, S. (1980). On the presence of poly(ADP-ribose) polymerase activity in metaphase chromosomes from HeLa S3 cells. *FEBS Lett.* **116**, 11–13.

IGO-KEMENES, T. & ZACHAU, J. (1978). Domains in chromatin structure. *Cold Spring Harbor Symp. quant. Biol.* **42**, 109–118.

JACKSON, D., McCREADY, S. & COOK, P. (1981). RNA is synthesized at the nuclear cage. *Nature, Lond.* **292**, 552–555.

JOHNSON, T. & HOLLAND, J. (1965). Ribonucleic acid and protein synthesis in mitotic HeLa cells. *J. Cell Biol.* **27**, 565–574.

JOST, E. & JOHNSON, R. (1981). Nuclear lamina assembly, synthesis and disaggregation during the cell cycle in synchronized HeLa cells. *J. Cell Sci.* **47**, 25–53.

JUMP, D. & SMULSON, M. (1980). Purification and characterization of the major non-histone protein acceptor for poly(adenosine diphosphate ribose) in HeLa cell nuclei. *Biochemistry* **19**, 1024–1030.

KAUFMANN, S., COFFEY, D. & SHAPER, J. (1981). Consideration in the isolation of rat liver nuclear matrix, nuclear envelope, and pore complex lamina. *Expl Cell Res.* **132**, 105–123.

KRAKOW, J. (1975). On the role of sulfhydryl groups in the structure and function of the *Azotobacter vinelandii* RNA polymerase. *Biochemistry* **14**, 4522–4527.

KRAMER, A. & BAUTZ, E. (1981). Immunological relatedness of subunits of RNA polymerase II from insects and mammals. *Eur. J. Biochem.* **117**, 449–455.

KRAMER, A., HAARS, R., KABISCH, R., WILL, H., BAUTZ, F. & BAUTZ, E. (1980). Monoclonal antibody directed against RNA polymerase II of *Drosophila melanogaster. Molec. gen. Genet.* **180**, 193–199.

LAEMMLI, U. K. (1970). Cleavage of structural proteins during the assembly of the head of bacteriophage T4. *Nature, Lond.* **227**, 680–685.

LAEMMLI, U., CHENG, S., ADOLPH, K., PAULSON, J., BROWN, J. & BAUMBACH, W. (1978). Metaphase chromosome structure: the role of non-histone proteins. *Cold Spring Harbor Symp. quant. Biol.* **42**, 351–360.

LEBKOWSKI, J. & LAEMMLI, U. (1982*b*). Evidence for two levels of DNA folding in histone-depleted HeLa interphase nuclei. *J. molec. Biol.* **156**, 309–324.

LEBKOWSKI, J. & LAEMMLI, U. (1982*a*). Non-histone proteins and long-range organization of HeLa interphase DNA. *J. molec. Biol.* **156**, 325–344.

LEWIS, C. & LAEMMLI, U. (1982). Higher order metaphase chromosome structure: evidence for metalloprotein interactions. *Cell* **29**, 171–181.

LONG, B. H., HUANG, C.-Y. & POGO, A. O. (1979). Isolation and characterization of the nuclear matrix in Friend erythroleukemia cells: chromatin and hnRNA interactions with the nuclear matrix. *Cell* **18**, 1079–1090.

MANLEY, J., FIRE, A., CANO, A., SHARP, P. & GEFTER, M. (1980). DNA-dependent transcription of adenovirus genes in a soluble whole-cell extract. *Proc. natn. Acad. Sci., U.S.A.* **77**, 3855–3839.

MARTIN, T. E. & OKAMURA, C. S. (1981). Immunochemistry of nuclear hnRNP complexes. In *The Cell Nucleus* (ed. H. Busch), vol. 9, pp. 119–144. New York: Academic Press.

MATSUI, S.-I., WEINFELD, H. & SANDBERG, A. (1979). Quantitative conservation of chromatin-bound RNA polymerase I and II in mitosis. *J. Cell Biol.* **80**, 451–464.

MILLER, T. E., HUANG, C.-Y. & POGO, A. O. (1978). Rat liver nuclear skeleton and ribonucleoprotein complexes containing hnRNA. *J. Cell Biol.* **76**, 675–691.

MORCILLO, G., DE LA TORRE, C. & GIMENEZ-MARTIN, G. (1976). Nucleolar transcription during plant mitosis. *In situ* assay for RNA polymerase activity. *Expl Cell Res.* **102**, 311–316.

OGATA, N., UEDA, K., KAWAICHI, M. & HAYASHI, O. (1981). Poly(ADP-ribose) synthetase, a main acceptor of poly(ADP-ribose) in isolated nuclei. *J. biol. Chem.* **256**, 4135–4137.

PARDOLL, D., VOGELSTEIN, B. & COFFEY, D. (1980). A fixed site of DNA replication in eucaryotic cells. *Cell* **19**, 527–536.

PAULE, M. R. (1981). Comparative subunit composition of the eucaryotic nuclear RNA polymerase. *Trends Biochem. Sci.* **6**, 128–131.

PAULSON, J. & LAEMMLI, U. (1977). The structure of histone-depleted metaphase chromosomes. *Cell* **12**, 817–828.

ROBERTS, W. & NEWMANN, J. (1966). Use of low concentrations of actinomycin D in the study of RNA synthesis in Ehrlich ascites cells. *J. molec. Biol.* **20**, 63–73.

STICK, R. & KROHNE, G. (1982). Immunological localization of the major architectural protein associated with the nuclear envelope of the *Xenopus laevis* oocyte. *Expl Cell Res.* **138**, 319–330.

VAN EEKELEN, CHRIS, A. G. & VAN VENROOIJ, W. J. (1981). hnRNA and its attachment to a nuclear protein matrix. *J. Cell Biol.* **88**, 554–563.

VOGELSTEIN, B., PARDOLL, D. & COFFEY, D. (1980). Supercoiled loops and eucaryotic DNA replication. *Cell* **22**, 79–85.

WEINMANN, R. & ROEDER, R. (1974). Role of DNA-dependent RNA polymerase III in the transcription of the tRNA and 5S RNA genes. *Proc. natn. Acad. Sci. U.S.A.* **71**, 1790–1794.

YOSHIHARA, K., HASHIDA, T., YOSHIHARA, H., TANAKA, Y. & OHGUSHI, H. (1977). Enzyme-bound early product of purified poly(ADP-ribose) polymerase. *Biochem. biophys. Res. Commun.* **78**, 1281–1288.

ZYLBER, E. & PENMAN, S. (1971). Synthesis of 5S and 4S RNA in metaphase-arrested HeLa cells. *Science* **172**, 947–949.

J. Cell Sci. Suppl. 1, 123–135 (1984)
Printed in Great Britain © The Company of Biologists Limited 1984

A STRUCTURAL ANALYSIS OF THE ROLE OF THE NUCLEAR MATRIX AND DNA LOOPS IN THE ORGANIZATION OF THE NUCLEUS AND CHROMOSOME

KENNETH J. PIENTA AND DONALD S. COFFEY

Departments of Urology, Oncology and Pharmacology, Johns Hopkins University School of Medicine, Baltimore, Maryland 21205, U.S.A.

SUMMARY

The interphase nucleus is characterized by a nuclear matrix structure that forms a residual scaffolding composed of approximately 10 % of the total nuclear proteins. The nuclear matrix contains residual elements of the pore-complex and lamina, the nucleolus, and an intranuclear fibrous network that provides the basic shape and structure of the nucleus. In the interphase nucleus this nuclear matrix has been reported to be a central element in the organization of DNA loop domains and to contain fixed sites for DNA replication and transcription. In this study, we have analysed the role of the nuclear matrix and the DNA loop domains in the organization and structure of the number 4 human chromosome. A model is proposed that closely approximates the observed structural dimensions of this chromosome. The model is composed of 30 nm diameter filaments formed from a solenoid of six nucleosomes per turn. This 30 nm solenoid filament is organized as loops of DNA each containing approximately 60 000 base-pairs; each loop is anchored at its base to the nuclear matrix. A radial loop model containing 18 of these loops per turn forms a new unit of chromosome structure termed the miniband. Approximately 106 of these minibands are arranged along a central axis to form the final chromatid. The role of the nuclear matrix in this organization is presented. The accuracy of the proposed model is tested by comparing its features with the known properties of the number 4 human chromosome.

INTRODUCTION

The higher-order organization of DNA within the nucleus and within the metaphase chromosome remains one of the major unsolved problems in molecular biology. At least three higher-order levels of DNA organization have been reported in the past decade, including the nucleosome, the 30 nm solenoid and DNA loops. Cook, Brazell & Jost (1976) proposed that loop structures were involved in the super-helical organization of DNA. In 1980, Vogelstein, Pardoll & Coffey reported that the DNA loop domains were attached at their base to a nuclear skeleton structure termed the nuclear matrix. The nuclear matrix is an insoluble, structural framework that is composed of residual elements of the pore-complex and lamina, residual nucleolus and internal network composed of ribonucleoprotein particles attached to a fibrous protein mesh (see Fig. 1; and Berezney & Coffey, 1974, 1976, 1977; Comings & Okada, 1976; Wunderlich & Herlan, 1977; Hodge, Mancini, Davis & Heywood, 1977; Fisher, Berrios & Blobel, 1982; also see reviews by Shaper *et al.* 1979; and Barrack & Coffey, 1982, 1983). The biological importance of the nuclear matrix is

CEL (S) 1

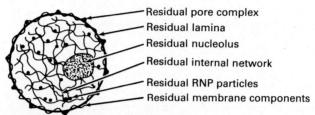

Nuclear matrix
(residual nuclear skeleton)

Residual pore complex
Residual lamina
Residual nucleolus
Residual internal network
Residual RNP particles
Residual membrane components

● Lipid-free
● Represents only 10 % of total nuclear
  proteins contains related proteins
● Site of attachments of DNA loops
● Contains fixed sites for DNA synthesis
● Associated with hnRNA
● Specific binding of hormones
● Proteins phosphorylated
● May have dynamic properties

Fig. 1. A schematic diagram of the structure and properties of the nuclear matrix.

emphasized by its reported role in DNA replication (Berezney & Coffey, 1975; Dvor-kin & Vanyushin, 1978; Dijkwel, Mullenders & Wanka, 1979; Pardoll, Vogelstein & Coffey, 1980; Vogelstein *et al*. 1980; McCready *et al*. 1980; Berezney & Buchholtz, 1981). It appears that the nuclear matrix contains fixed sites for DNA replication (Pardoll *et al*. 1980) and α-DNA polymerase (Smith & Berezney, 1980). In addition to its role in DNA replication, the nuclear matrix also has a central function in transcription in that actively transcribed genes are enriched on the nuclear matrix (Nelkin, Pardoll & Vogelstein, 1980; Robinson, Nelkin & Vogelstein, 1982). Other studies have indicated that over 95 % of the heterogeneous nuclear RNA is associated with the nuclear matrix (Miller, Huang & Pogo, 1978; Herman, Weymouth & Pen-man, 1978; Long, Huang & Pogo, 1979; van Eekelen & van Venrooij, 1981; Jackson, McCready & Cook, 1981; Mariman *et al*. 1982). As well as DNA replication, it has also been reported that RNA is synthesized at fixed transcriptional complexes on the nuclear matrix (Jackson, McCready & Cook, 1981). It is still not known how the functions associated in the nuclear matrix are regulated, but insight has been provided by the reports that the nuclear matrix contains specific receptors for steroid hormones (Barrack *et al*. 1977; Barrack & Coffey, 1980, 1982), as well as the acceptor sites for these steroid receptors (Barrack, 1983).

It is the purpose of this report to analyse the concept of the DNA loop attachment to the nuclear matrix and to determine how these loops can be accommodated into chromosomal structure to meet the known spatial and structural requirements of a given human chromosome.

RESULTS AND DISCUSSION

Vogelstein *et al.* (1980) visualized DNA loop structures attached to the nuclear matrix by releasing the supercoiled loops in the presence of a low concentration of ethidium bromide (5 μg/ml). These loops of DNA extended out beyond the surface of the nuclear matrix structure forming a large DNA halo region that surrounded the periphery of the nuclear matrix. The radius of this halo was approximately 15 μm. This loop length was calculated to contain 90 000 base-pairs for each loop. If the loop of DNA was constrained at its base by attachment to the nuclear matrix, it should be possible to rewind this loop by placing it in high concentrations of ethidium bromide (Benyajati & Worcel, 1976) and this was accomplished by Vogelstein *et al.* (1980), as is depicted in Fig. 2. When the loops of DNA had been nicked, a high concentration of ethidium bromide (100 μg/ml) did not rewind the halo, providing convincing evidence that the loop domains of DNA were anchored at their base to the nuclear matrix. Therefore, an important role of the nuclear matrix is to constrain the loops

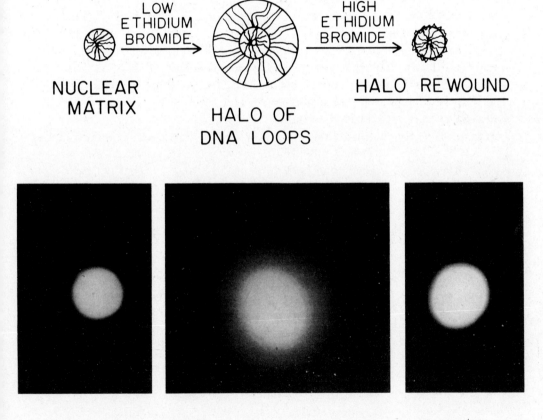

Fig. 2. The release of DNA loops in a low concentration of ethidium bromide (5 μg/ml) to form a DNA halo around the periphery of the nuclear matrix. At high ethidium bromide concentration (100 μm/ml) the halo rewinds if the DNA loops are not nicked (adapted from Vogelstein *et al.* 1980).

of DNA for organization into the superhelical structure. This superhelical loop structure must be maintained even in the chromosome, since Paulson & Laemmli (1977) have observed similar DNA loop domains attached to a residual chromosome core scaffold.

In interphase, another important role of the nuclear matrix is that it contains the fixed sites for DNA replication (Pardoll *et al.* 1980). The loops of DNA observed by Pardoll *et al.* (1980) were demonstrated to be equivalent in size to the replicon units that are the basic lengths of DNA synthesized as continuous units (Huberman & Riggs, 1968). During DNA replication, the loops are reeled down through these fixed sites of synthesis forming two new loops of DNA. It was possible to visualize the rate of movement of this newly synthesized DNA by autoradiography and to determine the distance that the grains ([³H]thymidine) had moved into the DNA halo region with increasing periods of labelling. This is shown schematically in Fig. 3, where the label of the newly synthesized DNA molecules can be monitored with time as it moves into the DNA halo region surrounding the nuclear matrix (Vogelstein *et al.* 1980).

It is apparent that the DNA loop domain is a basic unit of the higher-order structure of DNA in eukaryotic cells. Though the sizes of these DNA loops can vary, the average properties of a major DNA loop domain are shown in Table 1. There are approximately 63 000 base-pairs of DNA per loop contained in 21 μm of DNA double helix. Each loop is large enough to contain 315 nucleosomes that are wound into a solenoid with six nucleosomes per turn as proposed by Finch & Klug (1976). This solenoid is 30 nm in diameter and forms the loop filament. There are approximately 95 000 of these loops in a human diploid cell, and each of these loops of DNA is synthesized in approximately 30–60 min.

It is not known how these loops are organized into chromosomes. Knowing the

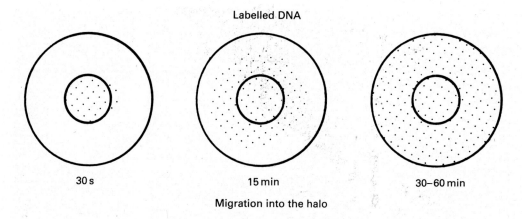

Fig. 3. A schematic diagram of the autoradiography of grains from labelled DNA ([³H]-thymidine incorporation) moving into the DNA halo region surrounding the nuclear matrix. Each cell was labelled for 30 s to 1 h (adapted from original data of Vogelstein *et al.* 1980).

Table 1. *Properties of an average DNA loop domain*

Properties	Average value	Range
Base-pairs/loop	63 000	30 000–100 000
Total length of DNA in loop	21·4 μm	10–34 μm
Total nucleosomes/loop	315	150–500
Diameter of loop filament	30 nm	30 nm
Turns of solenoid/loop	52	25–83
Total length of loop	0·52 μm	0·25–0·83
Height of loop	0·26 μm	0·12–0·41
DNA packing ratio	40	40
Total number of loops per human diploid cell	95 000	60 000–200 000

amount of DNA in a chromatid of the number 4 human chromosome, we attempted to construct models of this chromatid from a 30 nm filament organized into loop domains. Of four previously proposed models of chromosome structure (Bak, Zeuthen & Crick, 1977; Sedat & Manuelidis, 1977; Adolph & Kreisman, 1983; Marsden & Laemmli, 1979; Laemmli, 1979; Dupraw, 1970), we could accommodate these loops into the actual chromatid dimensions only by utilizing the radial loop model suggested by Marsden & Laemmli (1979) and Adolph & Kreisman (1983). The radial loop model proposes that loops are organized in radial structures around the central axis of the chromatid as they are wound and stacked to achieve the overall chromosome length. We then determined how many loops would be required for each full turn of the chromatid (miniband) to fit the known dimensions of the number 4 chromatid. To fit the known chromatid dimensions, we varied the amount of DNA per loop from 30 000 to 80 000 base-pairs as shown in Fig. 4. The observed length and diameter of the chromatid were realized when 18 loops per turn were utilized, with each loop containing 60×10^3 base-pairs.

This model of chromatid of the human chromosome 4 predicts that each level of the chromatid contains 18 loops of 60 000 base-pairs per loop. This 18-loop unit forms another higher-order structure of DNA organization that we termed the miniband. Therefore, the miniband is equivalent to one full turn of loops around the chromatid and contains approximately one million base-pairs. In Table 2 we compare the properties of the human chromosome 4 predicted by our model with those that have been experimentally observed. The 60×10^3 base-pairs in this loop model can be compared to the 62×10^3-base loop reported by Georgiev, Nedospasov & Bakayev (1978); 53×10^3 bases per loop, by Hancock & Boulikas (1982); 54×10^3 base-pairs per loop, by Igo-Kemenes, Horz & Zachau (1982); and $83 \pm 29\times10^3$ base-pairs per loop, by Earnshaw & Laemmli (1983). The average value for all of the above studies is $63 \pm 14\times10^3$ base-pairs per loop, a length of DNA that would be equal to 21·4 μm,

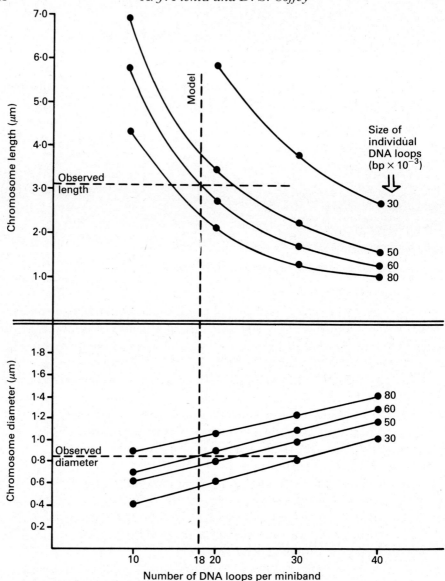

Fig. 4. Human chromosome 4 dimensions as determined by DNA loop size and number of radial loops per miniband (see text). The y-axis is the calculated chromosome length and chromatid diameter in μm that would be required to accommodate the $1·15 \times 10^8$ base-pairs in a chromatid of the chromosome 4 at various loop sizes and number of loops per turn. The horizontal broken lines are the actual observed dimensions of the chromatid. the x-axis is the number of DNA loops per chromatid turn (miniband). The optimal fit to the observed length and diameter was found to be 18 loops of 60 000 base-pairs per loop (see text). We have termed this unit of 18 radial loops per turn a 'miniband'.

assuming 3·4 Å per base-pair. The possibility of 18 loops per miniband in the model was tested by actually counting the number of loops per turn on the chromatids from scanning electron micrographs published in four previous studies. The following

Table 2. *Comparison of experimentally observed values of chromosome properties with those predicted from proposed model*

| | Loop dimensions | | DNA loops/ miniband | Chromatid dimensions Human chromosome 4 | | |
	Base-pairs/ loop ($\times 10^{-3}$)	Length of DNA (μm)/loop		DNA packing ratio	Length (μm)	Chromatid diameter (μm)
Observed	63 ± 14[a]	$21 \cdot 4$[b]	$16 \cdot 9 \pm 1 \cdot 9$[c]	$12\,400$[d]	$3 \cdot 15$[e]	$0 \cdot 85$[e]
Model (predicted)	60	$20 \cdot 4$	18	12260	$3 \cdot 19$	$0 \cdot 84$

[a] Average value ± S.E.M. from the following studies. Georgiev *et al.* (1978); Hancock & Boulikas (1982); Igo-Kemenes *et al.* (1982); Earnshaw & Laemmli (1983).
[b] 63 000 base-pairs $\times$ 3·4 Å per base-pair = 21·4 μm.
[c] Average number of loops per turn on chromatids counted from micrographs published in the following studies: Utsumi (1981); Adolph (1980); Laemmli (1979); Dupraw (1970).
[d] Length of DNA double strand divided by chromatid length ($3 \cdot 91 \times 10^4$ μm divided by 3·15 μm).
[e] Measured by Dr G. F. Bahr of Armed Forced Institute of Pathology, Washington, D.C.

K. J. Pienta and D. S. Coffey

values were determined: $17 \pm 1\cdot4$ from the studies of Utsumi (1981); $17\cdot8 \pm 2\cdot1$, Adolph (1980); $16\cdot8 \pm 3\cdot4$, Laemmli (1979); $16 \pm 1\cdot3$, Dupraw (1970). The average value for loops per turn of the chromatid in the above studies is $16\cdot9 \pm 1\cdot9$. The actual dimensions of the fully condensed chromatid of the human chromosome 4 have been provided by Dr G. F. Bahr of the Armed Forces Institute of Pathology in Washington, D.C., who has determined that the total length of the chromatid is $3\cdot15\ \mu m$ and the diameter is $0\cdot85\ \mu m$. This chromatid contains $1\cdot15 \times 10^8$ base-pairs equivalent to a total length of DNA of $3\cdot91 \times 10^4\ \mu m$. The observed packing ratio for the number 4 chromatid is 12 400 as determined by dividing the length of the free DNA ($3\cdot91 \times 10^4\ \mu m$) by the length of the chromatid ($3\cdot15\ \mu m$). It is apparent from Table 2 that the proposed model agrees closely with all of the observed values.

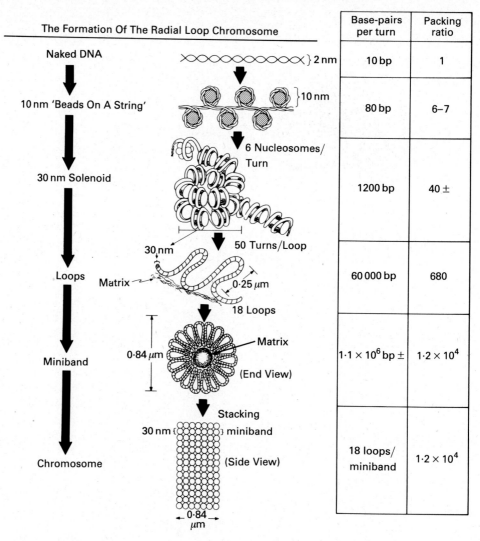

The Formation Of The Radial Loop Chromosome		Base-pairs per turn	Packing ratio
Naked DNA	} 2 nm	10 bp	1
10 nm 'Beads On A String'	} 10 nm	80 bp	6–7
30 nm Solenoid	6 Nucleosomes/Turn	1200 bp	40 ±
Loops — Matrix	50 Turns/Loop — 0·25 μm	60 000 bp	680
Miniband	18 Loops — Matrix (End View)	$1\cdot1 \times 10^6$ bp ±	$1\cdot2 \times 10^4$
Chromosome	Stacking miniband (Side View)	18 loops/miniband	$1\cdot2 \times 10^4$

Fig. 5. A schematic diagram of the higher-order organization of a chromatid of a chromosome.

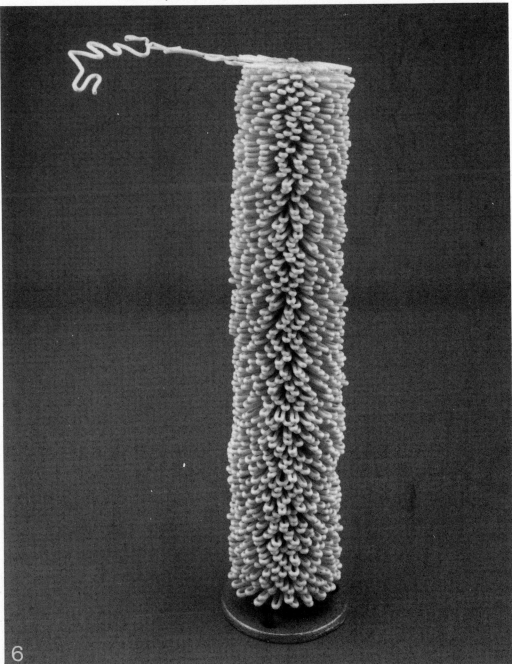

Fig. 6. A scale model of the human metaphase chromatid 4, without centromere, that contains 106 minibands stacked vertically along a central axis in a radial loop model with 18 loops per miniband. The white fibre in the model is equivalent in scale to the 30 nm filament. This fibre forms individual loops each equivalent to 60 000 base-pairs. The model contains a total of 1908 of these loops. The scale model is 26·5 cm in length and is equivalent to an actual chromatid of 3·19 μm.

The various levels of organization of a chromatid of a chromosome and the dimensions of each of the subunits are summarized in Fig. 5. The 20 Å DNA helix is wound twice around the histone octamers that form the well-known 10 nm nucleosomes that each contain 160 base-pairs. These nucleosomes form the beads-on-a-string fibre. These nucleosomes are then wound in a solenoid fashion with six nucleosomes per turn to form the 30 nm filament. The 30 nm solenoid filament forms the 60×10^3 base-pair DNA loops that are attached at their base to the nuclear matrix structure. The loops attached to the nuclear matrix are then wound into the 18 radial loops that form the miniband unit. Approximately 106 of these minibands are arranged along a central axis to form each chromatid of the final human chromosome 4.

We then constructed a scale model of a chromatid of the human chromosome 4, minus the centromere region, based on the structural units outlined above. This scale model is shown in Fig. 6.

Cook *et al.* (1976) and Vogelstein *et al.* (1980) have demonstrated that, even though chromosome structure is not visible during interphase, the loop domains of DNA are preserved. The integrity of these DNA loops is maintained in the interphase nucleus as well as in the chromosomes by attachment to the nuclear matrix. Fig. 7 depicts our concept of the organization of the DNA loops throughout the cell cycle. During DNA synthesis the loops are reeled through their fixed sites located on the

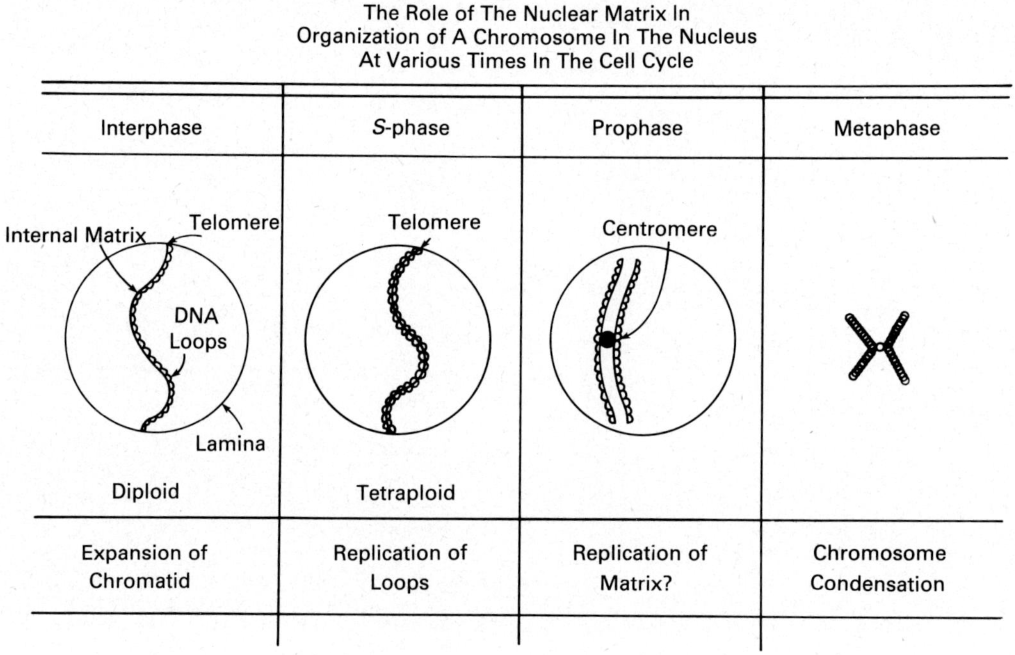

The Role of The Nuclear Matrix In
Organization of A Chromosome In The Nucleus
At Various Times In The Cell Cycle

Interphase	S-phase	Prophase	Metaphase
Internal Matrix, Telomere, DNA Loops, Lamina	Telomere	Centromere	
Diploid	Tetraploid		
Expansion of Chromatid	Replication of Loops	Replication of Matrix?	Chromosome Condensation

Fig. 7. A schematic diagram of the concept of the role of the nuclear matrix in organizing a single chromatid in the interphase nucleus. During *S*-phase the DNA loops replicate. During prophase the matrix separates and disengages the telomere from the lamina. The matrix attached to the DNA loops condenses during metaphase to organize the chromosome.

nuclear matrix and form a new paired loop. During prophase the paired loops with their associated matrix separate and condense to form the metaphase chromosome with elements of the nuclear matrix forming the core portion of the chromosome scaffold. Recently, Laemmli (1984) has reported that the interphase nuclear matrix and the core proteins of the chromosome scaffold contain a similar protein of 170×10^3 molecular weight. Since the DNA loop organization is maintained throughout chromosome expansion and condensation, it would appear that chemomechanical interactions will be required to bring about these events.

In summary, this study has attempted to analyse chromosome structure in relation to the DNA loop model and its attachment to the nuclear matrix. A new unit of hierarchical chromosome structure has been defined, the miniband, which contains approximately 18 radial loops, each composed of approximately 60×10^3 base-pairs of DNA. Insight into the next order of higher structure will require a more complete understanding of how these minibands are clustered to form the well-known chromosomal bands that are visualized at the light microscopic level.

The authors thank Dr Evelyn R. Barrack and Dr Gunter F. Bahr for their critical reading and suggestions. We acknowledge Ruth Middleton for her assistance in the preparation of this manuscript. This work was supported by grant no. AM22000 from HHS, NIADDK. K.J.P. is a Henry Strong Denison Scholar of the Johns Hopkins School of Medicine.

REFERENCES

ADOLPH, K. W. (1980). Isolation and structural organization of human mitotic chromosomes. *Chromosoma* **76**, 23–33.

ADOLPH, K. W. & KREISMAN, L. R. (1983). Surface structure and isolated metaphase chromosomes. *Expl Cell Res.* **147**, 155–166.

BAK, A. LETH, ZEUTHEN, J. & CRICK, F. H. C. (1977). Higher-order structure of human mitotic chromosomes. *Proc. natn. Acad. Sci. U.S.A.* **74**, 1595–1599.

BARRACK, E. R. (1983). The nuclear matrix of the prostate contains acceptor sites for androgen receptors. *Endocrinology* **113**, 430–432.

BARRACK, E. R. & COFFEY, D. S. (1980). The specific binding of estrogens and androgens to the nuclear matrix of sex hormone responsive tissues. *J. biol. Chem.* **255**, 7265–7275.

BARRACK, E. R. & COFFEY, D. S. (1982). Biological properties of the nuclear matrix: steroid hormone binding. *Recent Prog. Horm. Res.* **38**, 133–195.

BARRACK, E. R. & COFFEY, D. S. (1983). Hormone receptors nad the nuclear matrix. In *Gene Regulation by Steroid Hormones II* (ed. A. K. Roy & J. H. Clark), pp. 239–266. New York: Springer-Verlag.

BARRACK, E. R., HAWKINS, E. F., ALLEN, S. L., HICKS, L. L. & COFFEY, D. S. (1977). Concepts related to salt resistant estradiol receptors in rat uterine nuclei: nuclear matrix. *Biochem. biophys. Res. Commun.* **79**, 829–836.

BENYAJATI, C. & WORCEL, A. (1976). Isolation, characterization and structure of the folded interphase genome of *Drosophila melanogaster*. *Cell* **9**, 393–407.

BEREZNEY, R. & BUCHHOLTZ, L. A. (1981). Dynamic association of replicating DNA fragments with the nuclear matrix of regenerating liver. *Expl Cell Res.* **132**, 1–13.

BEREZNEY, R. & COFFEY, D. S. (1974). Identification of a nuclear protein matrix. *Biochem. biophys. Res. Commun.* **60**, 1410–1417.

BEREZNEY, R. & COFFEY, D. S. (1975). Nuclear protein matrix: association with newly synthesized DNA. *Science* **189**, 291–293.

BEREZNEY, R. & COFFEY, D. S. (1976). The nuclear protein matrix, isolation, structure and function. *Adv. Enz. Reg.* **14**, 63–100.

BEREZNEY, R. & COFFEY, D. S. (1977). Nuclear matrix: isolation and characterization of a framework structure from rat liver nuclei. *J. Cell Biol.* **73**, 616–637.

COMINGS, D. E. & OKADA, T. A. (1976). Nuclear proteins. III. The fibrillar nature of the nuclear matrix. *Expl Cell Res.* **103**, 341–360.

COOK, P. R., BRAZELL, I. A. & JOST, E. (1976). Characterization of nuclear structures containing superhelical DNA. *J. Cell Sci.* **22**, 303–324.

DIJKWEL, P., MULLENDERS, L. & WANKA, F. (1979). Eucaryotic chromosome replication. *Annual Review of Genetics*, vol. 9 (ed. E. Roman), pp. 245–284. Palo Alto: Annual Reviews, Inc.

DUPRAW, E. J. (1970). *DNA and Chromosomes*. New York: Holt, Rinehart, Winston.

DVORKIN, V. M. & VANYUSHIN, B. F. (1978). Replication and kinetics of the reassociation of DNA of the nuclear matrix of the regenerating rat liver. *Biochemistry, U.S.S.R.* **43**, 1297–1301.

EARNSHAW, W. C. & LAEMMLI, U. K. (1983). Architecture of metaphase chromosomes and chromosome scaffolds. *J. Cell Biol.* **96**, 84–93.

FINCH, J. T. & KLUG, A. (1976). Solenoid model for superstructure in chromatin. *Proc. natn. Acad. Sci. U.S.A.* **73**, 1897–1901.

FISHER, P. A., BERRIOS, M. & BLOBEL, G. (1982). Isolation and characterization of a proteinaceous subnuclear fraction composed of nuclear matrix, peripheral lamina, and nuclear pore complexes from embryos of *Drosophila melanogaster*. *J. Cell Biol.* **92**, 674–686.

GEORGIEV, G. P., NEDSPASOV, S. A. & BAKAYEV, V. U. (1978). Supranucleosomal levels of chromatin organization. In *The Cell Nucleus*, vol. 6 (ed. H. Busch), pp. 3–34. New York: Academic Press.

HANCOCK, R. & BOULIKAS, T. (1982). Functional organization in the nucleus. *Int. Rev. Cytol.* **79**, 165–214.

HERMAN, R., WEYMOUTH, L. & PENMAN, S. (1978). Heterogeneous nuclear RNA–protein fibers in chromatin-depleted nuclei. *J. Cell Biol.* **78**, 663–674.

HODGE, L. D., MANCINI, P., DAVIS, F. M. & HEYWOOD, P. (1977). Nuclear matrix of HeLa S$_3$ cells. *J. Cell Biol.* **72**, 192–208.

HUBERMAN, J. A. & RIGGS, A. D. (1968). On the mechanism of DNA replication in mammalian chromosomes. *J. molec. Biol.* **32**, 327–341.

IGO-KEMENES, T., HORZ, W. & ZACHAU, M. G. (1982). Chromatin. *A. Rev. Biochem.* **51**, 89–121.

JACKSON, D. A., McCREADY, S. J. & COOK, P. R. (1981). RNA is synthesized at the nuclear cage. *Nature, Lond.* **292**, 552–555.

LAEMMLI, U. K. (1979). Levels of organization of the DNA in eukaryotic chromosomes. *Pharmac. Rev.* **30**, 469–476.

LEWIS, C. D., LEBKOWSKI, J. S., DALY, A. K. & LAEMMLI, U. K. (1984). Interphase nuclear matrix and metaphase scaffolding structures. *J. Cell Sci. Suppl.* **1**, 103–122.

LONG, B. H., HUANG, C.-Y. & POGO, A. O. (1979). Isolation and chracterization of the nuclear matrix in Friend erythroleukemia cells: chromatin and hnRNA interactions with the nuclear matrix. *Cell* **18**, 1079–1090.

MARIMAN, E. C. M., VAN EEKELEN, C. A. G., REINDERS, R. J., BERNS, A. J. M. & VAN VENROOIJ, W. J. (1982). Adenoviral heterogeneous nuclear RNA is associated with the host nuclear matrix during splicing. *J. molec. Biol.* **154**, 103–119.

MARSDEN, M. P. F. & LAEMMLI, U. K. (1979). Metaphase chromosome structure: evidence for a radial loop model. *Cell* **17**, 849–858.

McCREADY, S. J., GODWIN, J., MASON, D. W., BRAZELL, I. A. & COOK, P. R. (1980). DNA is replicated at the nuclear cage. *J. Cell Sci.* **46**, 365–386.

MILLER, T. E., HUANG, C. & POGO, A. O. (1978). Rat liver nuclear skeleton and ribonucleoprotein complexes containing hnRNA. *J. Cell Biol.* **76**, 675–691.

NELKIN, B. D., PARDOLL, D. M. & VOGELSTEIN, B. (1980). Localization of SV40 genes within supercoiled loop domains. *Nucl. Acids Res.* **8**, 5623–5633.

PARDOLL, D. M., VOGELSTEIN, B. & COFFEY, D. S. (1980). A fixed site of DNA replication in eucaryotic cells. *Cell* **19**, 527–536.

PAULSON, J. R. & LAEMMLI, U. K. (1977). The structure of histone-depleted metaphase chromosomes. *Cell* **12**, 817–828.

ROBINSON, S. I., NELKIN, B. D. & VOGELSTEIN, B. (1982). The ovalbumin gene is associated with the nuclear matrix of chicken oviduct cells. *Cell* **28**, 99–106.

SEDAT, J. & MANUELIDIS (1977). A direct approach to the structure of eukaryotic chromosomes. *Cold Spring Harbor Symp. quant. Biol.* **12**, 331–350.

SHAPER, J. H., PARDOLL, D. M., KAUFMANN, S. H., BARRACK, E. R., VOGELSTEIN, B. & COFFEY, D. S. (1979). The relationship of the nuclear matrix to cellular structure and function. *Adv. Enz. Reg.* **17**, 213–248.

SMITH, H. C. & BEREZNEY, R. (1980). DNA polymerase is tightly bound to the nuclear matrix of actively replicating liver. *Biochem. biophys. Res. Commun.* **97**, 1541–1547.

UTSUMI, K. R. (1981). Studies on the structure of chromosomes. II. Chromosome fibers as revealed by scanning electron microscopy. *Cell Struct. Funct.* **6**, 395–401.

VAN EEKELEN, C. A. G. & VAN VENROOIJ, W. J. (1981). hnRNA and its attachment to a nuclear protein matrix. *J. Cell Biol.* **88**, 554–563.

VOGELSTEIN, B., PARDOLL, D. M. & COFFEY, D. S. (1980). Supercoiled loops and eucaryotic DNA replication. *Cell* **22**, 79–85.

WUNDERLICH, F. & HERLAN, G. (1977). A reversible contractile nuclear matrix, its isolation, structure and composition. *J. Cell Biol.* **73**, 271–278.

J. Cell Sci. Suppl. 1, 137–160 (1984)
Printed in Great Britain © The Company of Biologists Limited 1984

ORGANIZATION AND MODULATION OF NUCLEAR LAMINA STRUCTURE

LARRY GERACE, CLAUDETTE COMEAU AND MARY BENSON

Department of Cell Biology and Anatomy, Johns Hopkins University School of Medicine, 725 N. Wolfe St, Baltimore, MD 21205, U.S.A.

SUMMARY

The nuclear lamina is a protein meshwork associated with the nucleoplasmic surface of the inner nuclear membrane, that is suggested to be important for organizing nuclear envelope and interphase chromosome architecture. To investigate the structural organization of the lamina, we have analysed rat liver nuclear envelopes by various chemical extraction procedures. From these studies, we have defined conditions that yield a nuclear envelope subfraction that is both highly enriched in the lamina and devoid of pore complexes. This fraction contains mostly lamins A, B and C, the three major lamina polypeptides that are apparently arranged in a polymeric assembly. Our chemical extraction studies also indicate that lamin B has a stronger interaction with nuclear membranes than the other two lamins, and support the possibility that lamin B is important for attaching the lamina to the inner nuclear membrane.

We have examined the synthesis and assembly of the lamins during interphase in tissue-culture cells to investigate lamina structure by a second approach. We found that all three lamins are synthesized at similar rates throughout the cell cycle in synchronized Chinese hamster ovary cells, and that their biosynthesis is not temporally coupled to DNA replication. Our studies indicate that newly synthesized lamins are rapidly assembled into an insoluble lamina structure but that the apparent half-time for lamina insertion differs for individual lamins. We have also observed that lamin A is synthesized as an apparent precursor molecule that is converted to mature lamin A only after integration into the lamina structure.

The lamina is reversibly depolymerized during cell division, a process that may be mediated by enzymic phosphorylation of the lamins. To investigate this possibility further, we have analysed charge-altering modifications of the lamins on two-dimensional gels, and have found that phosphorylation is the only detectable modification of these proteins that occurs specifically during mitosis. Furthermore, we have determined that when the lamins are disassembled during metaphase, each lamin has approximately 2 moles of associated phosphate/mole lamin, a value that is four to sevenfold higher than the average interphase level. Considering this information, we discuss a model by which depolymerization and reassembly of the lamina can regulate the reversible disassembly of the nuclear envelope during mitosis.

INTRODUCTION

The nuclear envelope is a complex membrane organelle that delimits the boundary of the nuclear compartment in eukaryotic cells (reviewed by Franke, 1974; Fry, 1976; Franke, Scheer, Krohne & Jarasch, 1981). This membrane structure regulates the nucleocytoplasmic movement of large macromolecules (including many protein and RNA species), and may be important for organizing interphase chromosome architecture. The major structural components of the nuclear envelope include inner and outer nuclear membranes, pore complexes and the nuclear lamina.

Pore complexes, which occur at regions where the inner and outer membranes are joined, are elaborate protein assemblies that provide channels through the nuclear envelope for nucleocytoplasmic molecular exchange (Franke, 1974; Maul, 1977). The nuclear lamina (Gerace & Blobel, 1982) is a protein meshwork closely opposed to the nucleoplasmic surface of the inner nuclear membrane that forms a shell-like structure at the nuclear periphery. The lamina is postulated to provide a framework for organization and regulation of nuclear envelope structure (Gerace, Blum & Blobel, 1978; Gerace & Blobel, 1982), and an attachment site in the interphase nucleus (Gerace *et al.* 1978; Hancock & Hughes, 1982; Lebkowski & Laemmli, 1982) for higher order chromatin domains (Benyajati & Worcel, 1976; Cook & Brazell, 1976). In this fashion, the lamina may be a major skeletal component of the interphase nucleus.

A nuclear lamina can be directly visualized by thin-section electron microscopy in a number of eukaryotic cells, where it appears as a discrete 30–100 nm layer interposed between the inner nuclear membrane and chromatin (Fawcett, 1966; for other references, see Gerace *et al.* 1978). In many cell types, however, the lamina is too thin to be detected ultrastructurally in intact cells or nuclei, and can be observed only after partial nuclear subfractionation (e.g. see Aaronson & Blobel, 1975; Scheer *et al.* 1976).

Chemical extraction studies indicate that the lamina of many cell types is a stable supramolecular protein assembly that remains intact during sequential treatment of isolated nuclear envelopes with buffers containing non-ionic detergents and high concentrations of monovalent salts (Dwyer & Blobel, 1976; Shelton *et al.* 1980; Krohne, Dabauvalle & Franke, 1981). A lamina-enriched fraction that has been isolated from rat liver nuclear envelopes by detergent and salt extraction (the 'pore complex–lamina fraction'; Dwyer & Blobel, 1976) contains three prominent 60 000–70 000 molecular weight polypeptides that comprise approximately 40 % of the total protein mass of this fraction. Immunocytochemical localization studies indicate that these polypeptides (lamins A, B and C) occur exclusively at the nuclear periphery during interphase (Gerace *et al.* 1978; Krohne *et al.* 1978*a*; Stick & Hausen, 1980), and that they are localized in the lamina and not in nuclear pore complexes (Gerace & Blobel, 1982; Gerace, Ottaviano & Kondor-Koch, 1982). These three lamins may be organized in a polymeric array that serves as a structural 'core' for the lamina (Gerace & Blobel, 1980).

Three analogous lamins have been detected by immunochemical and biochemical techniques in a variety of vertebrate somatic and tissue-culture cells (Shelton *et al.* 1980; Gerace & Blobel, 1982; Havre & Evans, 1983), indicating that these polypeptides are common constituents of the vertebrate nuclear lamina. The three lamins apparently represent members of a family of related proteins, since two of these polypeptides (lamins A and C) are structurally very similar, as shown by peptide mapping studies (Shelton *et al.* 1980; Gerace & Blobel, 1982; Kaufman, Gibson & Shaper, 1983), and since all three lamins cross-react with certain monoclonal antibodies (Burke, Tooze & Warren, 1983; Krohne *et al.* 1984). However, the functional specializations of individual lamins have not been precisely defined.

In contrast to many vertebrate somatic cells, which have three related lamins, certain higher eukaryotic cell types appear to have a lamina structure that contains only one (in clam oocytes (Maul & Avdaloric, 1980) and amphibian oocytes (Krohne, Franke & Scheer, 1978*b*)) or two (in *Xenopus* erythrocytes (Krohne *et al*. 1981)) major lamin-related polypeptides. The biochemical composition of the lamina in evolutionarily lower organisms has not been precisely described. However, a single (or two closely related) approximately $75\,000\,M_r$ polypeptides found in *Drosophila* cells (Risau, Saumweber & Symmons, 1981; Fisher, Berrios & Blobel, 1982; Fuchs *et al*. 1983) are candidates for being *Drosophila* lamins.

Important information concerning the relationship of the lamina to nuclear archi-tecture has been obtained from studies of tissue-culture cells in mitosis, the period of the cell cycle when the nucleus (and nuclear envelope) of higher eukaryotes is disassembled and subsequently reconstructed (see Fry, 1976). Immunocytochemical (Ely, D'Arcy & Jost, 1978; Gerace *et al*. 1978; Krohne *et al*. 1978*a*) and subcellular fractionation (Gerace & Blobel, 1980) methods have demonstrated that the lamins in these cells are disassembled to a monomeric state and dispersed throughout the cell during mitotic prophase, and subsequently reassembled at the surfaces of the daugh-ter cell nuclei in telophase. These changes occur concomitantly with the processes of nuclear envelope disassembly and reformation, respectively. Based on the biochemi-cal and structural characteristics described for the interphase lamina, the reversible mitotic depolymerization of the lamina is proposed to regulate the disassembly and reconstruction of the nuclear envelope during cell division (Gerace *et al*. 1978). Similarly, growth in the mass or surface area of the lamina during interphase (e.g. by synthesis and insertion of new lamins) may be a major factor in determining the increase in nuclear envelope surface area that occurs during the cell cycle.

In this paper, we describe recent progress that we have made in understanding the biochemical organization of the nuclear lamina and its association with nuclear mem-branes. Furthermore, we consider events associated with synthesis and assembly of the lamins during interphase, and the relationship of lamin phosphorylation to regula-tion of lamina structure during cell division. Finally, we discuss a mechanism by which reversible disassembly of the lamina polymer during mitosis can regulate the major physical events of nuclear envelope disassembly and reconstruction.

MATERIALS AND METHODS

Preparation and fractionation of rat liver nuclear envelopes

All fractionation procedures involving nuclear envelopes were performed at 0–4 °C. Rat liver nuclear envelopes were isolated by digesting purified rat liver nuclei with DNase I (Sigma, DN-EP grade) in a low ionic strength, low magnesium buffer as described (Dwyer & Blobel, 1976), except that all preparative solutions contained 0·0005 M-phenylmethylsulphonyl fluoride (PMSF) (freshly added to buffers from a 0·1 M-PMSF stock solution in ethanol) and 0·001 M-dithiothreitol (DTT). Also, RNase A (Sigma, type XII) was added during the two DNase digestion steps to a final concentration of 1 μg/ml. Stock solutions of DNase I (1 mg/ml) and RNase A (5 mg/ml) were prepared by dissolving enzymes in TKM buffer (Dwyer & Blobel, 1976) containing PMSF and incubating solutions for 1 h at 0 °C before dividing into samples and freezing in liquid N_2.

We refer to the 'D₂p' fraction of Dwyer & Blobel (1976) as 'crude nuclear envelopes' in this paper. Salt-washed nuclear envelopes were prepared by resuspending the crude nuclear envelope pellet to approximately 2 mg/ml protein in 10% (w/v) sucrose, 0·01 M-triethanolamine·HCl (pH 7·4),

0.0001 M-$MgCl_2$ and 0.001 M-DTT and adding an equal volume of 10% sucrose, 0.01 M-triethanolamine·HCl (pH 7·4), 2 M-KCl, 0.0001 M-$MgCl_2$, 0.001 M-DTT. Samples were then centrifuged for 15 min at 2500 rev/min in a Beckman JS 5·2 rotor through a cushion containing 30% sucrose, 0.01 M-triethanolamine·HCl (pH 7·4), 0.0001 M-$MgCl_2$ and 0.001 M-DTT, to yield a pellet of salt-washed nuclear envelopes.

For preparation of a lamina-enriched fraction (Fig. 1), salt-washed nuclear envelopes were resuspended to a concentration of approximately 1 mg/ml protein in 10% sucrose, 0.02 M-triethanolamine·HCl (pH 7·4), 0.005 M-$MgCl_2$ and 0.001 M-DTT, and to this sample was added an equal volume of 10% sucrose, 0.02 M-triethanolamine·HCl (pH 7·4), 0.6 M-KCl, 0.005 M-$MgCl_2$, 0.001 M-DTT. After a 30-min incubation, the sample was centrifuged for 15 min at 5000 rev./min in a Beckman JS 5·2 rotor to yield a pellet of lamina-enriched material. We observed that if a reducing agent such as DTT was omitted from solutions during nuclear envelope preparation and subfractionation, the solubilization of minor nuclear envelope polypeptides by the Triton/0·3 M-KCl step (Fig. 1) was incomplete, presumably due to *in vitro* oxidation of these polypeptides.

Chemical extraction of rat liver nuclear envelopes (Fig. 3) was performed by resuspending pellets of 0.5 M-KCl-washed nuclear envelopes in the appropriate extraction solutions to approximately 1 mg/ml protein, and subsequently centrifuging samples at 48 000 rev./min for 30 min in a Beckman 50 Ti rotor. $MgCl_2$ and sodium carbonate samples were incubated for 30 min before centrifugation, while the remaining samples were centrifuged immediately after resuspension. Extraction solutions contained: (1) 0.05 M-triethanolamine·HCl (pH 7·4), 0.25 M-$MgCl_2$, 0.001 M-DTT; (2) 0.1 M-sodium carbonate (pH 10·5), 0.001 M-DTT; (3) 0.02 M-NaOH, 0.001 M-DTT; or (4) 0.05 M-triethanolamine·HCl (pH 7·4), 1 M-guanidine·HCl.

Electron microscopy

To examine the ultrastructure of material derived from nuclear envelopes treated with Triton X-100 in low or high ionic strength solution (Fig. 2), pellets of crude nuclear envelopes were resuspended in 10% sucrose, 0.02 M-triethanolamine·HCl (pH 7·4), 0.005 M-$MgCl_2$ and 0.001 M-DTT at 2 mg/ml protein. We then added to separate samples of this material an equal volume of: (1) 2% Triton X-100, 0.02 M-triethanolamine·HCl (pH 7·4), 0.005 M-$MgCl_2$ and 0.001 M-DTT (low ionic strength sample) or (2) 2% Triton, 0.02 M-triethanolamine, 0.6 M-KCl, 0.005 M-$MgCl_2$ and 0.001 M-DTT (high ionic strength sample), mixed the capped tubes by gently inverting, and incubated samples for 30 min at 0 °C.

Subsequently, to these samples we added (with gentle mixing as above) an equal volume of solutions containing either: (1) 5% glutaraldehyde, 0.02 M-triethanolamine (pH 7·4), 0.005 M-$MgCl_2$ and 0.001 M-DTT (low ionic strength sample) or (2) 5% glutaraldehyde, 0.02 M-triethanolamine (pH 7·4), 0.3 M-KCl, 0.005 M-$MgCl_2$ and 0.001 M-DTT (high ionic strength sample), and fixed the material for 60 min at 0 °C. Samples were then pelleted at 10 000 *g*, postfixed for 60 min at 0 °C with 1% OsO_4 in veronal acetate buffer (Farquhar & Palade, 1955), stained *en bloc* for 60 min at room temperature with 0.5% uranyl acetate in veronal acetate buffer, dehydrated with a graded ethanol series, and finally embedded in EMBED 812 (Polysciences). Thin sections were stained with uranyl acetate (Watson, 1958) and lead citrate (Venable & Coggleshall, 1965) and examined at 80 kV in a Zeiss 10A electron microscope.

Cell culture and synchrony

Chinese hamster ovary (CHO) cells, obtained from R. Tobey (University of California at Los Alamos, New Mexico), and BRL cells, a rat liver cell line obtained from H. Coon (National Institutes of Health, Bethesda, MD) were grown in monolayer culture at 37 °C in modified (Tobey, Anderson & Petersen, 1967) Ham's F10 medium containing 10% (w/v) foetal calf serum (GIBCO), 0.02 M-HEPES buffer, 100 U/ml penicillin and 100 μg/ml streptomycin. HEPES buffer and antibiotics were also included in all culture media described below.

To obtain synchronized mitotic CHO cells for analysing biosynthesis of the lamins through the cell cycle (Fig. 4), we plated 5×10^6 cells/dish in T-150 culture flasks (Corning) and allowed cells to grow for approximately 30 h. Culture medium was then replaced with Ham's growth medium containing 0.002 M-thymidine (Bostock, Prescott & Kirkpatrick, 1971) to accumulate cells in early–mid *S* phase. After 11 h, the thymidine medium was replaced with normal Ham's growth medium lacking thymidine, and cultures were allowed to grow for another 5 h, when a wave of mitotic cells began to appear. At this point, metaphase cell populations were obtained by selective mechanical detachment ('shake-off', Tobey *et al.* 1967). Cells were harvested from flasks every 15 min and were immediately chilled to 0 °C in an ice bath to arrest cell cycle progress. The pooled metaphase cells obtained over a total period of about 3 h were then divided and placed in 60 mm Petri dishes (Corning) and returned to 37 °C culture. With this synchrony procedure, virtually all cells attached to the Petri dishes and were in early G_1 phase 1 h after return to culture.

For pulse-labelling cells with [^{35}S] methionine, growth medium was aspirated from individual dishes at various times after metaphase, dishes were rinsed with modified Ham's F10 medium (methionine minus) +10 % dialysed foetal calf serum and medium was replaced with modified Ham's F10 medium (methionine minus) +10 % dialysed foetal calf serum +100 μCi/ml [^{35}S]-methionine (Amersham). Dishes were then returned to culture for 30 min, and labelled cells were subsequently harvested by scraping into 1 ml (for 2×10^6 cells) of 0·4 % sodium dodecyl sulphate (SDS), 0·05 M-triethanolamine (pH 7·4), 0·1 M-NaCl and 0·002 M-EDTA. To quantify the rate of total protein synthesis in cell populations at the various times, harvested cell samples were sonicated briefly, and a small portion of each solubilized sample (0·004 ml) was added to 1 ml of 1 mg/ml bovine serum albumin, which was then precipitated at 0 °C by the addition of 1 ml of 20 % tri-chloroacetic acid (TCA). Precipitates were subsequently collected on glass fibre disks (Whatman GF-C filters) for scintillation counting. The remainder of the labelled samples were frozen in liquid N_2 until use for immunoprecipitation.

The rate of DNA replication in cell populations at various times after mitosis was measured by labelling separate cell samples for 30 min with normal Ham's F10 medium +10 % foetal calf serum +1 μCi/ml [^{3}H]thymidine (Amersham). Labelled cells were scraped into phosphate-buffered saline (PBS), precipitated at 0 °C with 10 % TCA, and filtered onto glass fibre discs for scintillation counting as described above.

BRL cells were used for pulse–chase labelling of the lamins (Fig. 7). Exponentially growing cultures in 60 mm Petri dishes (approx. 2×10^6 cells/dish) were incubated in modified Ham's F10 (methionine minus) +10 % dialysed foetal calf serum for 30 min before pulse-labelling. Dishes were then pulse-labelled for 5 min in modified Ham's F10 medium (methionine minus) +10 % dialysed foetal calf serum +500 μCi/ml [^{35}S]methionine, and were subsequently chased for various periods of time (0–240 min) in Ham's F10 medium +10 % foetal calf serum +5 mM-L-methionine. Cells were then harvested by removing the medium, cooling dishes to 0 °C (all subsequent steps were at 0 °C), rinsing well with PBS, and scraping cells directly into 1 % Triton, 0·02 M-triethanolamine-HCl (pH 7·4), 0·13 M-NaCl, 0·0025 M-MgCl$_2$, 0·0005 M-PMSF and 0·005 M-iodoacetamide. After gentle vortexing for approximately 10 s, samples were immediately centrifuged for 5 min in an Eppendorf microfuge (approx.15 000 g_{max}) to obtain supernatants and pellets. These samples were then precipitated for 1 h at 0 °C with 10 % TCA, pelleted, and extracted for 30 min at 0 °C with 90 % (v/v) acetone, 0·1 M-HCl (to remove Triton X-100). Following a second pelleting, samples were solubilized in SDS solution for immunoprecipitation analysis (see below).

Radioactively labelled CHO metaphase cells that were used for two-dimensional gel analysis (Fig. 6) were obtained by maintaining cultures for 11 h in modified Ham's F10 medium (methionine minus) containing 10 % non-dialysed foetal calf serum, 2·5 mg/l L-methionine (half the normal methionine concentration), 10 μCi/ml [^{35}S]methionine and 0·002 M-thymidine. After this period, the thymidine medium was removed and replaced for 5 h with radioactive Ham's medium lacking thymidine. Metaphase populations were then selected by shake-off as described above. Interphase cell populations for this experiment were obtained by maintaining exponentially growing cultures for 16 h in modified Ham's F10 medium (methionine minus) containing 10 % non-dialysed foetal calf serum, 2·5 mg/l L-methionine and 10 μCi/ml [^{35}S]methionine.

The absolute level of phosphorylation of the lamins during interphase and metaphase (Table 1) was determined using CHO cells labelled to steady state with [^{32}P]phosphate. For these experiments, we continuously labelled CHO cells for 48 h in Ham's F10 medium (phosphate minus) containing 20 % dialysed foetal calf serum, $1·7 \times 10^{-4}$ M-sodium phosphate (pH 7·4) and 2·5 μCi/ml [^{32}P]phosphate (Amersham). Metaphase cells were obtained by shake-off synchronization from thymidine presynchronized labelled cultures (see above). In control experiments, we found the same apparent levels of lamin-associated phosphate (see below) in interphase cells that had been labelled for either 36 h or 60 h, indicating that we were at steady state for incorporation of labelled phosphate into the lamins in this experiment (48 h label).

Immunoprecipitation and gel analysis

For immunoprecipitation, we used guinea pig antibodies raised against electrophoretically purified rat liver lamins. Procedures for immunization and antigen preparation were similar to those previously described for chickens (Gerace *et al.* 1978), except that complete Freund's adjuvant was used for only the initial immunization, and incomplete Freund's adjuvant was used for all subsequent injections. Generally, antibodies from animals injected with either lamin A or lamin C reacted strongly on immunoblots with both lamins A and C, but only weakly with lamin B. These antibodies are designated 'anti-lamins (A and C)'. Similarly, antibodies from animals injected with lamin B reacted strongly with lamin B, but only weakly with lamins A and C. These are designated 'anti-lamin B'. All antibodies were affinity-purified by applying serum to a column consisting of SDS-solubilized rat liver pore complex–lamina proteins conjugated to Sepharose 4B, and eluting bound antibodies with glycine·HCl (pH 2·2) (Gerace *et al.* 1982).

Cells or cell fractions used for immunoprecipitation of the lamins in Figs 4, 5, and Table 1 were first solubilized by incubating samples in a boiling water bath for 3 min at a concentration of 4×10^6 cells/ml in a solution containing 0·4 % SDS, 0·05 M-triethanolamine (pH 7·4), 0·1 M-NaCl and 0·002 M-EDTA. Samples were then cooled, sonicated briefly with a Branson sonifier (equipped with a microtip probe) to reduce sample viscosity, and centrifuged for 5 min in an Eppendorf microfuge to remove insoluble material. Next, to each 0·5 ml of solubilized cell sample we sequentially added: 0·05 ml of 20 % Triton X-100, 0·005 ml of Trasylol, 0·001 ml of a 1 mg/ml leupeptin + 1 mg/ml pepstatin solution (in dimethylsulphoxide), 10 μg of affinity-purified anti-lamin (A and C) antibodies and 5 μg of affinity-purified anti-lamin B antibodies. For the experiment shown in Fig. 5, we used anti-lamin (A and C) antibodies only. Samples were incubated for 5–16 h at 4 °C, and were subsequently mixed for 2–4 h at 4 °C with either 0·02 ml of packed protein A–Sepharose beads (Pharmacia), or with 0·02 ml of beads containing rabbit anti-guinea pig immunoglobulin G (IgG) antibodies conjugated to Sepharose 4B at a concentration of 10 mg IgG/ml beads (Gerace *et al.* 1982). Immunoprecipitate beads were then washed batchwise six times with 1 ml of 0·5 % Triton X-100, 0·1 % SDS, 0·05 M-triethanolamine (pH 7·4), 0·1 M-NaCl and 0·002 M-EDTA, and were washed twice more with a solution of 0·01 M-triethanolamine (pH 7·4). Finally, immunoprecipitates were eluted from immunoadsorbent beads by incubating beads for 15 min at 37 °C with 0·06 ml of 15 % sucrose, 3 % SDS, 0·05 M-Tris (pH 8·8), 0·002 M-EDTA and 0·01 % Bromphenol Blue. Beads were then removed by centrifugation, and eluted samples were given an addition of 0·006 ml of 1 M-DTT, incubated for 3 min in a boiling water bath, and electrophoresed on SDS/7·5 % to 15 % polyacrylamide gels (Gerace *et al.* 1978). Gels were visualized by fluorography (Bonner & Laskey, 1974), and radioactivity in individual lamin gel bands from immunoprecipitates (Table 1 and Fig. 4) was quantified as described (Gerace & Blobel, 1980).

To measure the absolute level of lamin phosphorylation in immunoprecipitates of metaphase or interphase CHO cells labelled to steady state with [^{32}P]phosphate (see above), immunoprecipitated lamins from approximately 1×10^7 cells were electrophoresed in a single gel lane. The gel was then stained with Coomassie Blue, the amount of protein in each lamin band was quantified by eluting the bound dye from gel slices with 25 % pyridine and reading the absorbance at 605 nm (Fenner, Trout, Mason & Wikman-Doffelt, 1975). Samples of bovine serum albumin electrophoresed on the same gel were used as protein standards. Following elution of dye from excised gel bands, the ^{32}P radioactivity in each slice was determined as described (Gerace & Blobel, 1980). Based on the specific activity of the [^{32}P]phosphate present in our growth medium, we were able to calculate the moles of phosphate/mole of lamin.

Samples that were immunoprecipitated for two-dimensional gel electrophoresis (Fig. 6) were initially solubilized in the 0·4 % SDS solution (see above) by incubation for 10 min at 60 °C, instead of by boiling. The remainder of the immunoprecipitation procedure up to the final elution step was identical to that described above. Material (from 5×10^6 cells) was eluted from immunoadsorbent beads (0·05 ml) by incubation in 0·1 ml of 0·2 % SDS for 15 min at 37 °C followed by centrifugation to remove the beads. Eluted samples were then brought to a final sample composition (using appropriate stock solutions) of 1 % octylglucoside, 0·1 % SDS, 0·1 M-Tris·HCl (pH 8·0), 0·005 M-MgCl$_2$, 1 % Trasylol, 2 μg/ml leupeptin and 2 μg/ml pepstatin in a final volume of 0·2 ml. To one half of each sample *Escherichia coli* alkaline phosphatase (Sigma type III) was added to 200 μg/ml, using a 2 mg/ml stock solution. Subsequently, both the latter sample and a control sample (minus alkaline phosphatase) were incubated at 37 °C for 3 h. Samples were then cooled to 0 °C, precipitated for 2 h in 20 % TCA and pelleted. After the pellets were rinsed with 5 % TCA, samples were prepared for two-dimensional gels. This involved incubating pellets in 0·025 ml of 1 % SDS, 9·5 M-urea, 2 % LKB ampholines (pH 3·5–10), 0·001 M-EDTA and 0·05 M-DTT for 15 min at 37 °C, followed by adding 0·025 ml of 10 % Nonidet-P40, 2 % ampholines (pH 3·5–10) and 9 M-urea. Samples were applied to the acidic end of a non-equilibrium pH gradient electrophoresis slab gel containing 2 % LKB 3·5–10 range ampholines (O'Farrell, Goodman & O'Farrell, 1977), and were separated at 150 V constant voltage for 21 h (3150 volt-hours). Second-dimensional SDS/polyacrylamide gel electrophoresis and fluorography were performed as described (Gerace & Blobel, 1980).

RESULTS AND DISCUSSION

Chemical fractionation of nuclear envelopes

We have examined the effects of a variety of chemical extraction procedures on isolated rat liver nuclear envelopes to investigate the organization and biochemical composition of the lamina. Previous studies have demonstrated that both nuclear pore complexes and the lamina remain morphologically intact (Aaronson & Blobel, 1974; Scheer *et al*. 1976; Unwin & Milligan, 1982) when treated with low ionic strength buffers containing Triton X-100 (which solubilize the nuclear membrane lipids). Correspondingly, many nuclear envelope polypeptides, including the lamins, are insoluble under these conditions and fractionate completely in the pellet derived from this Triton/low ionic strength treatment, as determined by SDS/polyacrylamide gel electrophoresis (Dwyer & Blobel, 1976). The pore complexes and lamina also appear to retain moderate ultrastructural integrity when treated with buffers containing high concentrations of monovalent salts (e.g. 1 M-NaCl) that lack Triton X-100 (Dwyer & Blobel, 1976; Unwin & Milligan, 1982).

In contrast to these conditions, we have determined that treatment of nuclear envelopes with buffers containing both Triton X-100 and high concentrations of monovalent salts results in preferential solubilization of nuclear pore complex structures, while the lamina remains preferentially intact (Figs 1 and 2). We have defined Triton/high salt extraction conditions (2 % Triton +0·3 M-KCl) under which most nuclear envelope polypeptides are completely solubilized and appear in the supernatant after centrifugation, while the lamins appear almost quantitatively in a 5000 *g* pellet (Fig. 1, 2 % Triton +0·3 M-KCl, s and p lanes). In solutions containing Triton and higher concentrations of monovalent salts (e.g. 0·5–1 M-KCl), the lamins themselves are partially or completely solubilized (data not shown) indicating that the rat liver lamina has a relative but not absolute resistance to chemical solubilization in Triton/high salt solutions compared to pore complexes.

The pellet fraction derived from treatment of nuclear envelopes with Triton +0·3 M-KCl (Fig. 1; 2 % Triton+0·3 M-KCl, p lanes) contains a number of minor bands in the 40 000–55 000 M_r range in addition to the lamins. These minor polypeptides are not insoluble by virtue of being physically associated with the lamina, since certain treatments of the Triton/0·3 M-KCl pellet fraction (e.g. Triton +1 M-KCl) result in preferential solubilization of the lamins, while these other bands sediment in the pellet (data not shown). These solubility characteristics are consistent with the possibility that many or all of these minor bands represent polypeptides of intermediate filaments that contaminate our nuclear envelope fraction (see Fig. 1 legend).

While a supramolecular structure containing nuclear pore complexes attached to the lamina is clearly evident in electron micrographs of nuclear envelopes treated with 2% Triton in a low ionic strength buffer (Fig. 2A,B), only a lamina structure with no identifiable associated pore complexes results from incubation of nuclear envelopes in 2% Triton +0·3 M-KCl (Fig. 2C,D). At high magnification the lamina contained

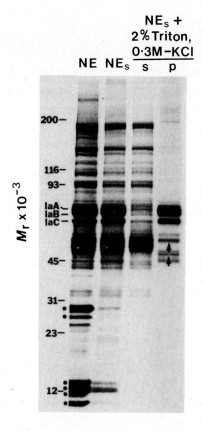

Fig. 1. Isolation of a lamina fraction by chemical extraction of rat liver nuclear envelopes. A crude rat liver nuclear envelope fraction (NE lane) contains numerous polypeptides resolved by SDS/polyacrylamide gel electrophoresis, including the three lamins (1a A, 1a B and 1a C), and histone contaminants (dots to left of NE lane). Extraction of this fraction with a solution containing 1 M-KCl yields salt-washed nuclear envelopes (NE$_s$ lane) from which the histones are largely removed. Salt-washed nuclear envelopes were incubated in a solution containing 2% Triton +0·3 M-KCl and centrifuged at 5000 g_{max} yielding a supernatant and a pellet (NE$_s$+2% Triton, 0·3 M-KCl; s and p lanes, respectively). The three lamins are highly enriched in the pellet fraction, which also contains small amounts of putative intermediate filament polypeptides migrating in the 40 000–55 000 M_r region (see the text). Two of these bands (NE$_s$+2% Triton, 0·3 M-KCl; p lane, arrows) comigrate precisely with major cytokeratins present in samples of rat liver plasma membranes (provided by Dr Ann Hubbard; Hubbard & Ma, 1983). Samples were electrophoresed on a SDS/7·5% to 15% polyacrylamide gel and stained with Coomassie Blue.

in this insoluble fraction appears to comprise a meshwork of short (approx. 10–40 nm) interconnected fibrils when viewed in tangential section (Fig. 2D, double arrows). In transverse section, the lamina is seen as a structure of approximately 10–20 nm diameter (Fig. 2D, single arrows). These characteristic ultrastructural features have been noted previously in the lamina contained in the pore complex–lamina fraction (Dwyer & Blobel, 1976; Scheer *et al*. 1976).

Hence, this biochemical fractionation scheme appears to yield a nuclear envelope subfraction devoid of pore complexes that is highly enriched in a supramolecular assembly composed of the three lamins. These results support our previous immunoferritin-localization results (Gerace & Blobel, 1982; Gerace *et al*. 1982) indicating that the rat liver lamins occur exclusively in the lamina and not in pore complexes. The observation that most or all of the nuclear envelope polypeptides other than the lamins can be solubilized, while an apparently intact lamina structure remains, also supports the possibility that a polymeric assembly of the three lamins serves as a core element of the lamina structure.

In other studies (Krohne *et al*. 1978a), it was shown that treatment of *Xenopus* oocyte nuclear envelopes with Triton plus high concentrations of KCl results in considerable enrichment of a major approximately $66\,000\,M_r$ nuclear envelope band in the insoluble pellet fraction. However, in contrast to our results with rat liver nuclear envelopes, it was argued that oocyte pore complexes are preferentially stable to (and that lamina is preferentially extracted by) this chemical treatment (Krohne *et al*. 1978b, 1981), and that the $66\,000\,M_r$ band (which cross-reacts with the somatic lamins) is present in both lamina and pore complexes (Stick & Krohne, 1982).

The lamina has a tight physical interaction with the inner nuclear membrane (Dwyer & Blobel, 1976), a characteristic that is likely to be important for coordinating the structures of the lamina and nuclear membranes. To investigate the biochemical basis for this interaction, we have investigated whether any of the lamins has a preferentially strong association with the inner nuclear membrane (Fig. 3) by extracting nuclear envelopes with different chemical perturbants in the absence of non-ionic detergents (Steck & Yu, 1973). With the non-detergent chemical conditions that we have used, the lipid bilayer of nuclear membranes remains intact, although the membranes are induced to fragment into small structures that require ultracentrifugation to be completely pelleted. Treatment of nuclear envelope with $0 \cdot 25$–$1 \cdot 0$ M-$MgCl_2$ results in selective extraction of lamins A and C from membranes, while lamin B preferentially occurs in the membrane pellet (Gerace & Blobel, 1982; Fig. 3, $0 \cdot 25$ M-$MgCl_2$, s and p lanes). Similarly, a preferentially strong association of lamin B with nuclear membranes is evident upon incubation of nuclear envelopes with 1 M-guanidine·HCl (Fig. 3, 1 M gu·HCl, s and p lanes), and in a pH $10 \cdot 5$ buffer (Fig. 3; pH $10 \cdot 5$, s and p lanes). Incubation of nuclear envelopes with higher concentrations of each of these protein perturbants, such as $0 \cdot 02$ M-NaOH (Fig. 3; $0 \cdot 02$ M-NaOH, s and p lanes) results in complete extraction of lamin B in addition to the other two lamins.

These results indicate that lamin B has a stronger physical interaction with nuclear membranes than the other two lamins, and may therefore have an important role in attachment of the lamina to the nuclear envelope. In further support of this possibility, when the nuclear envelope is in a physiological state of disassembly during metaphase, biochemical fractionation studies suggest that lamin B may remain associated with membrane vesicles derived from the disassembled nuclear envelope, while lamins A and C are clearly non-membrane-associated (Gerace & Blobel, 1980).

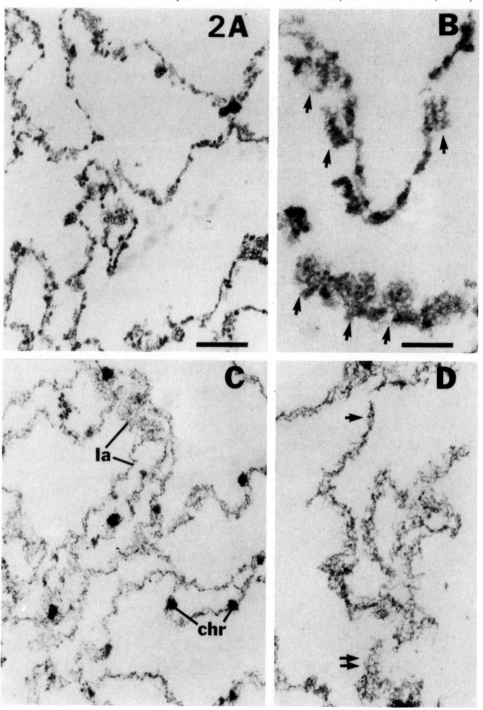

Fig. 2

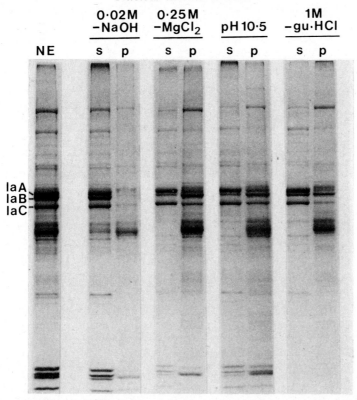

Fig. 3. Extraction of rat liver nuclear envelopes with chemical protein perturbants. Rat liver nuclear envelopes that had been washed with 0·5 M-KCl (NE) were incubated in solutions containing 0·02 M-NaOH, 0·25 M-MgCl$_2$, 0·1 M-sodium carbonate (pH 10·5); and 1 M-guanidine·HCl (1 M-gu·HCl); and sedimented at 200 000 g_{max} to yield supernatants (s) and membrane pellets (p). Samples were electrophoresed on a SDS/7·5 to 15 % polyacrylamide gel and stained with Coomassie Blue. Under the latter three chemical conditions, lamin B is preferentially resistant to extraction, although it can be completely solubilized by more-alkaline pH buffer conditions (0·02 M-NaOH lanes) as well as with 3 M-MgCl$_2$ and 3 M-guanidine·HCl (data not shown).

Fig. 2. Thin-section electron micrographs of rat liver nuclear envelopes extracted with Triton X-100 in low or high ionic strength buffers. A crude rat liver nuclear envelope fraction was incubated in buffers containing 0·02 M-triethanolamine (pH 7·4) and 2 % Triton (A,B) or 2 % Triton +0·3 M-KCl (C,D) and prepared for electron microscopy. Extraction of nuclear envelopes with Triton/low ionic strength conditions (A,B) yields an insoluble supramolecular assembly that contains a morphologically continuous lamina with attached pore complexes (arrows in Fig. 2B). Upon incubation of nuclear envelopes with Triton/high salt solutions (C,D), only the lamina (1a) remains structurally intact, while pore complexes are completely absent. Since we obtain better ultrastructural preservation of pore complexes in samples of crude nuclear envelopes (Fig. 1, NE lane) compared to 1 M-KCl-washed nuclear envelopes (Fig. 1, NE$_s$ lane), we used crude nuclear envelopes for our starting material in this experiment. Chromatin contamination (chr) is visible as irregular darkly staining granular material associated with the lamina in A and B, and is aggregated into larger dense clumps in C and D. On SDS/polyacrylamide gels, the material shown in C and D has a very similar profile to Fig. 1 (NE$_s$ +2 % Triton, 0·3 M-KCl, p lane), except that histone contamination is present (data not shown). A and C: bar, 375 nm; ×40 000: B and D: bar, 150 nm; ×100 000.

Immunofluorescence staining of *Drosophila* metaphase cells with monoclonal antibodies directed against a putative *Drosophila* lamin gives a distinctly punctate staining reaction in the cytoplasm (Fuchs *et al*. 1983), consistent with the possibility that this antigen is associated with partially fragmented nuclear membranes after nuclear disassembly. While lamin B of vertebrates may be primarily responsible for attachment of the lamina to the inner nuclear membrane, it is possible that lamins A and C have physiologically significant membrane interactions as well.

The lamin B–membrane interaction could be mediated either by an association of lamin B with a second intrinsic protein of the inner nuclear membrane, or by the direct physical association of lamin B (possibly through a hydrophobic domain) with the inner membrane bilayer. We have obtained no evidence for the existence of an intrinsic membrane protein associated with lamin B, based on studies of rat liver nuclear envelopes using chemical cross-linking and solubilization approaches (L. Gerace, unpublished). Therefore, we favour the possibility that lamin B itself directly mediates the lamina–membrane interaction. In the future it will be possible to study this question in more detail using a membrane reconstitution approach with purified lamin B.

It has been observed that lamin B in alkaline-extracted nuclear envelopes can be labelled with a hydrophobic photoaffinity reagent (Lebel & Raymond, 1984), which could indicate the presence of a lipid-integrated domain on this polypeptide. However, lamins A and C were apparently labelled to a similar proportional extent in this material, and labelling of native (non-extracted) nuclear envelopes was not described in this study.

Synthesis and assembly of the lamins during interphase

The surface area of the nuclear envelope, as well as the number of pore complexes, increases continuously during the cell cycle (Maul *et al*. 1972; Fry, 1976). Since the lamina forms a skeleton-like protein shell at the nuclear periphery, increase in its mass may be important for regulating growth of nuclear envelope surface area and increase in nuclear volume during interphase. To obtain insight into this question, we have examined the cell cycle timing of lamin biosynthesis. In these experiments we were interested in determining whether synthesis of the lamins occurs continuously throughout interphase (during G_1 and G_2 phases as well as during S), or whether biosynthesis of these proteins (which have a putative role in chromosome structure) is temporally coupled to DNA replication.

Metaphase CHO cell populations were obtained by selective mechanical detachment, and samples of cells were returned to culture for 1–17 h. At 2-h intervals during this period, dishes were pulse-labelled with [^{35}S]methionine, and the lamins were immunoprecipitated from solubilized cells and electrophoresed in SDS/polyacrylamide gels. This permitted quantitation of the relative rate of synthesis of these polypeptides at progressive stages of the cell cycle (Fig. 4).

In these synchronized populations (Fig. 4A), the earliest point at which a significant number of cells has reached S phase is 5 h, and cells begin entering mitosis by 13–15 h. It is evident from this analysis (Fig. 4B) that the lamins are synthesized

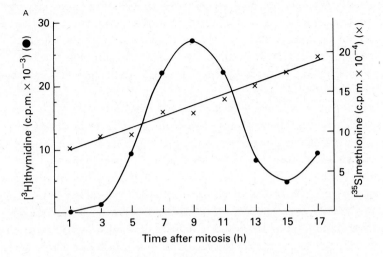

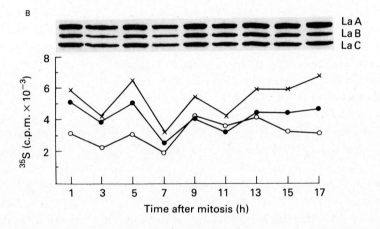

Fig. 4. Biosynthesis of the lamins through the cell cycle in CHO cells. Metaphase CHO cell populations were selected by mechanical shake-off, and cells were sampled and returned to culture. After a 1-h period at 37 °C, and at 2-h intervals thereafter, individual dishes were pulse-labelled for 30 min with either [³H]thymidine or [³⁵S]methionine. [³H]-thymidine-labelled samples (0·9×10⁶ cells each) were precipitated with TCA to measure the rate of DNA replication in cell populations at various times (A). [³⁵S]methionine-labelled cells were directly solubilized in SDS, and a portion of this material (1·5×10⁴ cells) was precipitated with TCA to measure the total rate of protein synthesis at progressive cell cycle stages (A), while the remaining sample (1·8×10⁶ cells) was used for immunoprecipitation of the lamins. Immunoprecipitated material was electrophoresed on an SDS/polyacrylamide gel and visualized by fluorography (B, top). Individual lamin bands were then excised from this gel and ³⁵S incorporation was measured by scintillation counting (B, bottom). Each of the lamin A bands analysed in this experiment is actually a closely spaced doublet comprised of lamin A₀ and lamin A (see Fig. 5). The cell population shows a peak in the rate of DNA replication at 9 h, with a small percentage of cells entering *S* phase of the subsequent cell cycle at 17 h (A). Mitotic cells were first observed in these cultures at 13 h, and reached a peak during the 15 to 17-h period. Each of the lamins has a roughly similar biosynthetic rate at all cell cycle times examined (B). The apparent decreases in lamin biosynthetic rate seen at 3 and 7 h in this experiment were not observed in a subsequent experiment, and were apparently due to incomplete sample recovery.

at similar rates in G_1-enriched (1–3 h) and G_2-enriched (13–15 h) cell populations, compared to S phase cells (e.g. 9 h). Therefore, unlike certain other nuclear structural proteins, such as histones, whose synthesis in many cell types occurs mainly during S phase (Kedes, 1979; Hereford, Osley, Ludwill & McLaughlin, 1981), biosynthesis of the lamins is not temporarily coupled to DNA replication in a rapidly growing tissue-culture line (CHO cells).

While the lamins must be synthesized on polyribosomes in the cytoplasmic compartment and subsequently transported into the nucleus for assembly into a lamina structure, several types of evidence indicate that this 'unassembled' cytoplasmic pool of lamins is small in many types of somatic and cultured cells. First, immuno-fluorescence staining of tissue sections or of growing tissue-culture cells (Gerace *et al.* 1978; Krohne *et al.* 1978a) with anti-lamin antibodies indicates that the lamins occur largely or entirely in a peripheral nuclear localization during interphase (presumably in an assembled lamina), with no clearly detectable levels of these polypeptides in a cytoplasmic configuration. Furthermore, immunoprecipitation studies have shown that when exponentially growing interphase cells are lysed in isotonic Triton-containing buffers (conditions where the isolated lamina is insoluble), the lamins are recovered almost entirely in a high-speed pellet (Gerace & Blobel, 1980). With the same detergent fractionation procedure, the disassembled metaphase lamins are almost quantitatively soluble (Gerace & Blobel, 1980).

Since isotonic Triton fractionation of tissue-culture cells should distinguish, to a first approximation, between unassembled and assembled lamins, we have used this procedure to investigate the average rate of assembly of newly synthesized lamins during interphase (Fig. 5). Exponentially growing cultures of a rat liver cell line (BRL cells) were pulse-labelled with [^{35}S]methionine, and after various chase periods with non-radioactive medium were fractionated by isotonic Triton lysis and centrifugation. The lamins were then immunoprecipitated from supernatants and pellets, and samples were analysed on SDS/polyacrylamide gels. After a 5-min pulse label, an antibody specific for lamins A and C immunoprecipitates two major polypeptides that occur exclusively in the supernatant fraction (Fig. 5; 0 min chase, s and p lanes). Compared to the lamin A and C species found in cells labelled continuously for 36 h (Fig. 5, 36-h lane), the upper of these two bands (designated lamin A_0) migrates approximately 2000 daltons more slowly than the steady state-labelled lamin A species, while the lower band comigrates precisely with lamin C. With progressive periods of chase, the immunoprecipitated lamin A_0 and lamin C species shift to the Triton-insoluble pellet fraction (Fig. 5). The half-time for 'insertion' of lamin A_0 into a Triton-insoluble structure is approximately 5 min, while for lamin C it is approximately 60 min. Finally, subsequent to the time that lamin A_0 appears in the pellet fraction, it shifts in a precursor–product fashion to a faster-migrating form that comigrates with the steady-state labelled lamin A (Fig. 5; 60 and 120 min min chase, p lanes). When monospecific antibodies to lamin B were used to analyse this pulse–chase experiment, we found that the lamin B-reactive species initially appears (0 min chase) entirely in the supernatant fraction as a form that comigrates with steady-state labelled lamin B, and that this species is incorporated

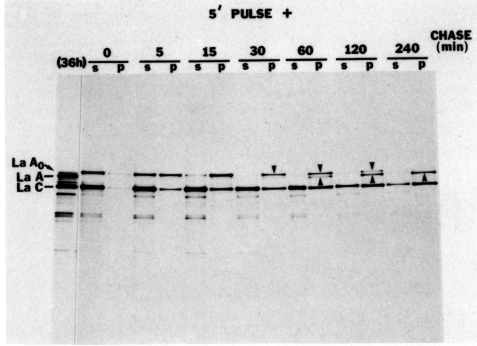

Fig. 5. Assembly of newly synthesized lamins into a Triton-insoluble structure. Exponentially growing cultures of a rat liver cell line (BRL cells) were pulse-labelled with [^{35}S]methionine for 5 min, and subsequently chased with non-radioactive methionine for 0–240 min. Cultures were then lysed in an isotonic Triton-containing buffer, and samples were sedimented in an Eppendorf microfuge to yield supernatants (s) and pellets (p). Lamins A and C were immunoprecipitated from these fractions and electrophoresed on an SDS/polyacrylamide gel before visualization by fluorography. Lamin A initially appears as a form (designated lamin A_0) that migrates approximately 2000 daltons more slowly than 36-h-labelled lamin A (compare 0-min chase lane to 36-h lane), and is gradually converted to a 'mature' lamin A form in a precursor–product fashion after it is integrated into a Triton-insoluble structure (arrows in 30, 60 and 120-min chase lanes).

with a Triton-insoluble structure with a half-time of approximately 60 min in BRL cells (data not shown).

We have examined the characteristics of lamin biosynthesis and assembly in other cell lines (CHO cells and MDBK cells) using this type of pulse–chase analysis, and have observed the same general features described above for BRL cells (L. Gerace & Y. Ottaviano, unpublished). First, lamin A is synthesized as a precursor molecule that migrates approximately 2000 daltons more slowly on SDS/polyacrylamide gels than the principal cellular form of lamin A, and is converted to a species that comigrates with lamin A subsequent to its appearance in a Triton-insoluble fraction. Second, lamin A_0 is incorporated into a Triton-insoluble structure considerably more rapidly than lamins B and C. However, the half-times for insertion of the lamins varied among different cell lines.

In vitro translation of mRNA isolated from BHK cells (Laliberte *et al*. 1984) and from rat liver (L. Gerace, unpublished) also yields an apparent precursor molecule

to lamin A that migrates approximately 2000 daltons more slowly on SDS/
polyacrylamide gels than the major cellular form of lamin A in these cells. Hence, it
is possible that the presence of a lamin A precursor is a widespread phenomenon. The
physiological function for conversion of lamin A_0 to lamin A is unclear, but since it
apparently occurs after insertion of lamin A_0 into the lamina structure, this conversion
is probably not related to intracellular targeting of this polypeptide to the lamina.
Clearly, the processed (mature) lamin A is competent to be assembled into a lamina
structure, since it is quantitatively reutilized in telophase after mitotic disassembly in
tissue-culture cells (Gerace & Blobel, 1980).

While lamins A and C have very similar tryptic peptide maps (Shelton *et al.* 1980;
Kaufman *et al.* 1982), experiments involving *in vitro* translation of mRNA suggest
that lamins A_0 and lamin C are encoded by distinct messenger RNA species (Laliberte
et al. 1984). This result is supported by the pulse–chase experiments described above
(Fig. 5). These two messenger species could be encoded by separate genes or alternatively, could arise from post-transcriptional processing of a single precursor RNA
molecule.

Regulation of lamina structure during mitosis

The lamins are phosphorylated during both interphase and mitosis (Gerace &
Blobel, 1980), but these polypeptides have an approximately four to sixfold higher
level of associated phosphate during metaphase, when they are disassembled, compared to interphase, when they are assembled. Furthermore, they lose much of this
metaphase phosphate by telophase when the lamina has been reconstructed (Gerace
& Blobel, 1980). This correlation suggests that enzymic phosphorylation of the lamins
may be important for regulating mitotic disassembly of the lamina.

To investigate this possibility further, and to establish a framework for studying
disassembly of the lamina *in vitro*, we have analysed CHO cells to compare
phosphorylation of the lamins that occurs during mitotic prophase (the period when
the lamina is disassembled) to that taking place during interphase (Ottaviano &
Gerace, 1985). In these studies, we have found that all of the detectable phosphate
associated with each lamin during interphase and mitosis occurs in a phosphomono-
ester linkage, predominantly as phosphoserine and, to a lesser extent, as phospho-
threonine. Furthermore, lamins A and C are phosphorylated on partially distinct sets
of tryptic peptides during mitosis, compared to interphase.

We have quantified the absolute level of phosphorylation of the lamins from
metaphase and exponentially growing interphase cells by steady-state labelling of
CHO cells with $[^{32}P]$phosphate (Table 1). This determination indicates that each of
the lamins has $1\cdot4$–$2\cdot2$ moles of associated phosphate per mole of lamin during
metaphase, compared to $0\cdot27$–$0\cdot46$ moles of phosphate per mole of protein in the
average interphase state. Since protein mass was quantified in this experiment by
Coomassie Blue dye binding, these values are to be considered approximate. The
results of this analysis agree well with the relative levels of interphase and mitotic
lamin phosphorylation that we determined previously (Gerace & Blobel, 1980).

Most postsynthetic protein modifications including phosphorylation induce

Table 1. *Steady-state levels of phosphate associated with the lamins*

	mol P/mol lamin		
	M	I	M/I
Lamin A	2·2	0·46	4·8
Lamin B	1·9	0·27	7·0
Lamin C	1·4	0·33	4·2

CHO cells were grown in medium containing [^{32}P]phosphate for 48 h, and the lamins were immunoprecipitated from exponentially growing interphase populations (I) or shake-off synchronized metaphase cells (M). After electrophoresis on an SDS/polyacrylamide gel and staining with Coomassie Blue, the protein mass in individual lamin bands was determined spectrophotometrically using bovine serum albumin as a standard (Fenner *et al.* 1975). Subsequently the mol phosphate in each lamin band was determined by scintillation counting. Values represent the average of two separate experiments (which in all cases differed by no more than 15 %).

changes in protein isoelectric point that are detectable on two-dimensional isoelectric focusing SDS/polyacrylamide gels (Wold, 1981). We have used two-dimensional gel electrophoresis of [^{35}S]methionine-labelled lamins to examine phosphorylation and other possible charge-altering modifications of the lamins that occur during interphase and mitosis (Fig. 6). When immunoprecipitates of lamins from interphase cells are analysed on two-dimensional gels (Fig. 6; I,−AP) two predominant charge isomers are detectable for lamins A and C, while a single major form is seen for lamin B. CHO cell lamins A and C are isoelectric at approximately pH 7−7·5, while lamin B has an isoelectric point near pH 6·0 (Gerace & Blobel, 1980). Lamins A and C show minor satellite spots adjacent to major charge species on our pH-gradient electrophoresis gels. (This phenomenon is especially evident in Fig. 6, +AP.) These satellite spots do not necessarily represent charge isomers of these polypeptides, but may be due, for example, to non-uniform binding of ampholytes to the proteins (Cann, 1979).

As previously demonstrated (Gerace & Blobel, 1980), the lamins from mitotic cells migrate as more acidic isoelectric species than those from interphase cells (Fig. 6; M,−AP). This acidic charge shift is consistent with the increased level of mitotic lamin phosphorylation that has been determined (Gerace & Blobel, 1980; Table 1). Mitotic lamin B occurs almost exclusively as a closely spaced doublet (the two components of which have slightly different motilities in both electrophoretic dimensions), while mitotic lamins A and C are predominantly one or two major charge isomers (Fig. 6; M,−AP).

We have determined that the phosphate that becomes associated with pulse-labelled lamins during interphase and mitosis can be almost quantitatively hydrolysed by treatment of immunoprecipitates with bacterial alkaline phosphatase (Ottaviano & Gerace, 1985). Taking advantage of this observation, we have analysed alkaline phosphatase-treated immunoprecipitates of [^{35}S]methionine-labelled interphase and mitotic lamins on two-dimensional gels to determine whether the mitotic

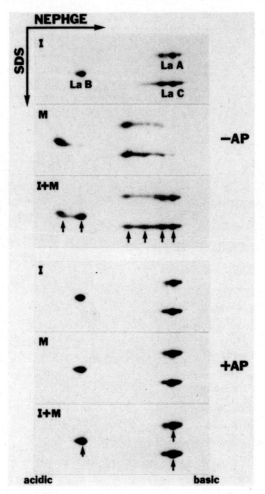

Fig. 6. Two-dimensional gel analysis of interphase and mitotic lamins. CHO cells were labelled with [^{35}S]methionine and metaphase cells were obtained by shake-off synchronization. These mitotic cells (M), and populations of labelled exponentially growing interphase cells (I) were immunoprecipitated with antibodies recognizing the three lamins. Immunoprecipitates were then separated on non-equilibrium pH-gradient electrophoresis (NEPHGE)/SDS/polyacrylamide two-dimensional gels, either without (−AP) or with (+AP) treatment with bacterial alkaline phosphatase before electrophoresis. For both −AP and +AP samples, we electrophoresed mixtures of interphase and mitotic immuno-precipitates (I+M) as well as separate interphase (I) and mitotic (M) samples. Major charge isomers of the lamins that are apparent in mixed immunoprecipitates of interphase and mitotic cells (−AP and +AP) are indicated by arrows. Any pair of adjacent charge isomers probably differs by one phosphate molecule.

charge shift of the lamins is entirely due to phosphorylation (Fig. 6, +AP panels). The interphase lamins A and C treated with alkaline phosphatase shift to a single predominant spot (Fig. 6; +AP, I panel), which comigrates with the more basic of the two charge isomers of these respective polypeptides in the interphase untreated sample (Fig. 6; −AP, I panel). The single interphase lamin B species is not shifted in charge by alkaline phosphatase treatment, compared to lamin B of the untreated sample. All three mitotic lamins undergo a basic charge shift due to alkaline phosphatase treatment, and now occur as single major charge isomers (Fig. 6; +AP, M panel) that precisely comigrate with the corresponding spots of interphase alkaline phosphatase-treated samples. This demonstrates that phosphorylation is the only detectable charge-altering modification of the lamins that occurs specifically during mitosis. Since we find no evidence for other major mitotis-specific postsynthetic modifications of the lamins besides phosphorylation, this result strengthens our hypothesis (Gerace & Blobel, 1980) that phosphorylation of the lamins is important for mediating disassembly of the lamina during cell division. However, our analysis would not detect mitotis-specific modifications of the lamins that affect only a small percentage of the protein population, nor would it necessarily detect protein modifications that are labile in neutral pH buffers. However, the latter are uncommon (Wold, 1981).

Lamina and regulation of nuclear architecture during mitosis

Our working model for the organization of the lamina and its relationship to the mitotic dynamics of the nuclear envelope is shown diagrammatically in Fig. 7. This is an extension of our earlier discussions (Gerace *et al*. 1978; Gerace & Blobel, 1982), and is motivated by the structural, biochemical and physiological properties of the lamins that have been determined. The scheme presented in Fig. 7 depicts the lamina structure of vertebrate cell types that contain three distinct lamins, such as liver and tissue-culture cells (e.g. see Gerace & Blobel, 1982; see Introduction and discussion below).

During interphase, we envisage that the three lamins are organized in a polymeric array of which all three polypeptides are intrinsic components (Fig. 7, Interphase). We suggest that this lamin polymer provides the 'core' element (and probably most of the mass) of the lamina itself. This model is strongly supported by the observation that a lamina-like structure composed almost exclusively of the three lamins can be isolated by chemical extraction of rat liver nuclear envelopes (Figs 1 and 2).

Lamins A and C are depicted as being structurally and functionally similar (Fig. 7, Interphase), based on their extensive immunological and biochemical homology (Gerace *et al*. 1978; Shelton *et al*. 1980; Gerace & Blobel, 1982; Kaufman *et al*. 1982), but these polypeptides may not be functionally identical. Although lamin B has been shown to cross-react with lamins A and C, with certain monoclonal antibodies (Burke *et al*. 1982; Krohne *et al*. 1984), this polypeptide is in part biochemically different from the other two lamins (Shelton *et al*. 1980; Gerace & Blobel, 1982), and is proposed to have a specialized function for mediating the lamina–inner nuclear membrane interaction (Gerace & Blobel, 1982; and Fig. 3). Lamin B may interact with the inner nuclear membrane by virtue of a direct association with the inner membrane bilayer as indicated in Fig. 7, but other possibilities are not excluded at this time.

We also suggest (Gerace *et al*. 1978; and Fig. 7, Interphase) that the lamina functions to attach chromatin to the nuclear envelope (see Franke, 1974; Fry, 1976).

6

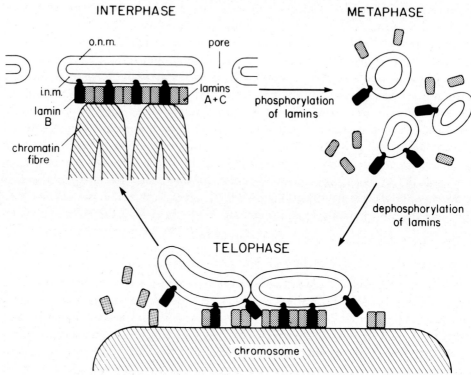

Fig. 7. Proposal for the organization of the interphase lamina, and the relationship between the lamina and the reversible mitotic disassembly of the nuclear envelope. The lamina of many vertebrate cell types is composed mainly of three related polypeptides (lamins A, B and C) that form a shell-like meshwork at the nuclear periphery, and that appear to be organized in a polymeric array (Interphase). The lamina has a strong interaction with the inner nuclear membrane, that may be mediated predominantly by lamin B. In addition, the lamina is proposed to provide a major anchoring site for chromatin in the nucleus, possibly serving as an organizing centre for higher order chromatin domains. By virtue of its dual interaction with the inner nuclear membrane and chromatin, the lamina may be a major skeletal element of the interphase nucleus. During mitotic prophase, the lamins are disassembled to a monomeric form and lose their association with chromatin, so that in metaphase lamins A and C appear to be soluble, while lamin B may retain an association with membrane fragments derived from the disassembled nuclear envelope (Metaphase). The process of lamina depolymerization is proposed to trigger the overall disassembly of the nuclear envelope during prophase, and is suggested to be mediated (at least in part) by enzymic phosphorylation of the lamins. During telophase, the lamina reassembles at the surfaces of mitotic chromosomes, a process that is proposed to result in association of membranes with chromosome surfaces and to promote reassembly of the double-membrane nuclear envelope structure. Lamina repolymerization is suggested to be mediated by dephosphorylation of the lamins during this period.

In this fashion the lamina may provide a major anchoring site for chromatin in the interphase nucleus, and may be important for organization of higher order chromatin domains (Benyajati & Worcell, 1976; Cook & Brazell, 1976). At present, the details of this putative interaction are unknown, and it is not apparent whether it involves an association of one or several of the lamins with DNA directly (Hancock & Hughes,

1982; Lebkowski & Laemmli, 1982), or with some additional chromosomal protein(s) (McKeon, Tuffanelli, Kobayashi & Kirschner, 1984).

This model for the structure of the interphase lamina of vertebrate cells emphasizes three sets of functional interactions for the lamins: those involved in polymeric self-association, those related to interaction with the inner nuclear membrane, and those involved in chromatin attachment. The lamina may in addition provide an anchoring site for pore complexes in the nuclear envelope (not indicated in Fig. 7; Aaronson & Blobel, 1975). While certain vertebrate cell types apparently contain only one or two lamin-related polypeptides (Krohne *et al.* 1981), it is clearly possible that many or all of the functions associated with the three rat liver lamins (which are structurally similar) could be encoded in the structure of a single related polypeptide in other cells of the same organism, as well as in other eukaryotic organisms.

At present the detailed molecular organization of the lamin polymer is not clearly understood. However, small homotypic oligomers of each lamin can be generated in nuclear envelopes by *in vitro* oxidation of intrinsic cysteine sulphydryls (Shelton & Cochran, 1978; Lam & Kasper, 1979; Kaufman *et al.* 1982), consistent with the possibility that a basic 'subunit' of lamina structure may consist of oligomers of each lamin. Considering the ultrastructural appearance of the lamina seen in thin-section electron microscopy, it is conceivable that the short fibrils visible in the isolated lamina structure represent lamin oligomers.

During mitosis, the lamina undergoes dramatic structural reorganizations that temporally coincide with the disassembly and reconstruction of the nuclear envelope (Fig. 7, Metaphase and Telophase). Biochemical and immunocytochemical investigations (Gerace *et al.* 1979; Krohne *et al.* 1978*a*; Gerace & Blobel, 1980) indicate that the lamins are disassembled to an apparently monomeric form during mitotic prophase and lose their interaction with chromatin (Fig. 7, Metaphase). Furthermore, lamin B (but not lamins A and C) may retain an interaction with disassembled nuclear membranes at metaphase (Gerace & Blobel, 1980). Considering the biochemical characteristics described for the metaphase lamins (Gerace & Blobel, 1980; and Table 1, Fig. 6), we suggest that specific enzymic phosphorylation of the lamins is important for mediating prophase lamina disassembly, and possibly for effecting the dissociation of lamins from chromatin. This process of lamina depolymerization is likely to be a major event that controls nuclear envelope disassembly, permitting the processes of nuclear membrane fragmentation to take place.

During telophase (Fig. 7, Telophase), the lamins are reassembled at or near the surfaces of the condensed mitotic chromosomes (Gerace *et al.* 1978; Krohne *et al.* 1978*a*). Studies of mitotic cells by electron microscopy have suggested that nuclear envelope reconstruction involves aggregation and fusion of membrane vesicles in direct contact with the surfaces of telophase chromosomes, which are often fused into a single continuous mass at this period (Robbins & Gonatas, 1964; Murray, Murray & Pizzo, 1965; Erlandsen & DeHarven, 1971; Roos, 1973). Considering the apparent membrane-associated state of lamin B in metaphase cells, lamina reassembly adjacent to chromatin would necessarily result in the association of membrane vesicles with the surfaces of the telophase chromosomes. This would provide appropriate topological conditions for nuclear membrane reconstruction, and could also facilitate the membrane vesicle fusion that apparently results in reappearance of a continuous double membrane structure enclosing the chromosomes (Fry, 1976). We suggest that dephosphorylation of the lamins is important for regulating this reassembly process, with surfaces of chromosomes and, or, membrane vesicles serving as nucleating sites for this reaction. The observation (Forbes, Kirschner & Newport, 1983) that bacteriophage DNA microinjected into *Xenopus* eggs induces assembly of nuclear envelopes and lamina (apparently after the injected DNA is assembled into chromatin) supports the notion that chromatin surfaces are important for directing the topological specificity of lamina reassembly.

In this fashion the processes of lamina disassembly and reformation may be principal factors regulating changes in nuclear envelope architecture occurring during cell division. Our proposals on the relationship of the lamina to nuclear envelope structure are analogous to principles of membrane organization that have derived from study of the red cell membrane (reviewed by Steck, 1974; Branton, Cohen & Taylor, 1981), where it has been demonstrated that a membrane-associated protein meshwork (containing spectrin, actin, etc.) is directly involved in determining the membrane's physical and molecular properties. In the future it will be important to obtain a detailed biochemical understanding of the relationship of phosphorylation to the reversible depolymerization of the lamina during mitosis, and the nature of other processes that affect nuclear envelope structure during this period. This information will undoubtedly help to elucidate the mechanisms that control and coordinate the various mitotic events, and should also promote understanding of interphase nuclear envelope structure and physiology.

We are grateful to Günter Blobel, in whose laboratory the observations on synthesis and assembly of the lamins with pulse–chase experiments were initially made. We also thank Arlene Daniel for assistance with manuscript preparation. This work was supported by a Searle Scholars Award and a U.S. Public Health Services grant to L.G.

REFERENCES

AARONSON, R. & BLOBEL, G. (1974). On the attachment of the nuclear pore complex. *J. Cell Biol.* **62**, 746–754.

AARONSON, R. & BLOBEL, G. (1975). Isolation of nuclear pore complexes in association with a lamina. *Proc. natn. Acad. Sci. U.S.A.* **72**, 1007–1011.

BENYAJATI, C. & WORCELL, A. (1976). Isolation, characterization, and structure of the folded interphase genome of *Drosophila melanogaster*. *Cell* **9**, 393–407.

BONNER, W. & LASKEY, R. (1974). A film detection method for tritium-labeled proteins and nucleic acid in polyacrylamide gels. *Eur. J. Biochem.* **46**, 83–88.

BOSTOCK, C., PRESCOTT, D. & KIRKPATRICK, J. (1971). An evaluation of the double thymidine block for synchronizing mammalian cells at the G1–S border. *Expl Cell Res.* **68**, 163–168.

BRANTON, D., COHEN, C. & TYLER, J. (1981). Interaction of cytoskeleton proteins on the human erythrocyte membrane. *Cell* **24**, 24–32.

BURKE, B., TOOZE, J. & WARREN, G. (1983). A monoclonal antibody which recognizes each of the nuclear lamin polypeptides in mammalian cells. *EMBO J.* **2**, 361–367.

CANN, J. (1979). In *Electrokinetic Separation Methods* (ed. P. Righetti, C. Vanoss & J. Vanderhoff), pp. 369–387. New York: Elsevier.

COOK, P. & BRAZELL, I. (1976). Conformational constraints in nuclear DNA. *J. Cell Sci.* **22**, 287–302.

DWYER, N. & BLOBEL, G. (1976). A modified procedure for isolation of a pore complex–lamina fraction from rat liver nuclei. *J. Cell Biol.* **70**, 581–591.

ELY, S., D'ARCY, A. & JOST, E. (1978). Interaction of antibodies against nuclear envelope-associated proteins from rat liver nuclei with rodent and human cells. *Expl Cell Res.* **116**, 325–331.

ERLANDSON, R. & DEHARVEN, E. (1971). The ultrastructure of synchronized HeLa cells. *J. Cell Sci.* **8**, 353–397.

FARQUHAR, M. & PALADE, G. (1955). Cell junctions in amphibian skin. *J. Cell Biol.* **26**, 263–291.

FAWCETT, D. (1966). On the occurrence of a fibrous lamina on the inner aspect of the nuclear envelope in certain cells of vertebrates. *Am. J. Anat.* **119**, 129–146.

FENNER, C., TRAUT, R., MASON, D. & WIKMAN-DOFFELT, J. (1975). Quantification of Coomassie blue stained proteins in polyacrylamide gels based on analysis of eluted dye. *Analyt. Biochem.* **63**, 595–602.

FISHER, P., BERRIOS, M. & BLOBEL, G. (1982). Isolation and characterization of a proteinaceous sub-nuclear fraction composed of nuclear matrix, peripheral lamina, and nuclear pore complexes from embryos of *Drosophila melanogaster. J. Cell Biol.* **92**, 676–686.

FORBES, D., KIRSCHNER, M. & NEWPORT, J. (1983). Spontaneous formation of nucleus-like structures around bacteriophage DNA microinjected into *Xenopus* eggs. *Cell* **34**, 13–23.

FRANKE, W. (1974). Structure, biochemistry, and functions of the nuclear envelope. *Int. Rev. Cytol. Suppl.* **4**, 71–236.

FRANKE, W., SCHEER, U., KROHNE, G. & JARASCH, E. (1981). The nuclear envelope and the architecture of the nuclear periphery. *J. Cell Biol.* **91**, 39s–50s.

FRY, D. (1976). The nuclear envelope in mammalian cells. In *Mammalian Cell Membranes*, vol. 2 (ed. G. A. Jamieson & D. M. Robinson), pp. 197–265. Boston: Butterworth.

FUCHS, J., GILOH, H., KUO, C., SAUMWEBER, H. & SEDAT, J. (1983). Nuclear structure: determination of the fate of the nuclear envelope in *Drosophila* during mitosis using monoclonal antibodies. *J. Cell Sci.* **64**, 331–349.

GERACE, L. & BLOBEL, G. (1980). The nuclear envelope lamina is reversibly depolymerized during mitosis. *Cell* **19**, 277–287.

GERACE, L. & BLOBEL, G. (1982). Nuclear lamina and the structural organization of the nuclear envelope. *Cold Spring Harbor Symp. quant. Biol.* **46**, 967–978.

GERACE, L., BLUM, A. & BLOBEL, G. (1978). Immunocytochemical localization of the major polypeptides of the nuclear pore complex–lamina fraction. Interphase and mitotic distribution. *J. Cell Biol.* **79**, 546–566.

GERACE, L., OTTAVIANO, Y. & KONDOR-KOCH, C. (1982). Identification of a major polypeptide of the nuclear pore complex. *J. Cell Biol.* **95**, 826–837.

HANCOCK, R. & HUGHES, M. (1982). Organization of DNA in the interphase nucleus. *Biol. Cell* **44**, 201–212.

HAVRE, P. & EVANS, D. (1983). Disassembly and characterization of the nuclear pore complex–lamina fraction from bovine liver. *Biochemistry* **22**, 2852–2860.

HEREFORD, L., OSLEY, M., LUDWILL, J. & MCLAUGHLIN, C. (1981). Cell cycle regulation of yeast histone mRNA. *Cell* **24**, 367–375.

HUBBARD, A. & MA, A. (1983). Isolation of rat hepatocyte plasma membranes. II. Identification of membrane-associated cytoskeletal proteins. *J. Cell Biol.* **96**, 230–239.

KAUFMAN, S., GIBSON, W. & SHAPER, J. (1983). Characterization of the major polypeptides of rat liver nuclear envelopes. *J. biol. Chem.* **258**, 2710–2719.

KEDES, L. (1979). Histone genes and histone messages. *A. Rev. Biochem.* **48**, 837–870.

KROHNE, G., DABAUVALLE, M. & FRANKE, W. (1981). Cell type-specific differences in protein composition of nuclear pore complex–lamina in oocytes and erythrocytes of *Xenopus laevis. J. molec. Biol.* **151**, 121–141.

KROHNE, G., DEBUS, E., OSBORN, M., WEBER, K. & FRANKE, W. (1984). A monoclonal antibody against nuclear lamina proteins reveals cell-type specificity in *Xenopus laevis. Expl Cell Res.* **150**, 47–59.

KROHNE, G., FRANKE, W., ELY, S., D'ARCY, A. & JOST, E. (1978a). Localization of a nuclear envelope-associated protein by indirect immunofluorescence microscopy using antibodies against a major polypeptide from rat liver fractions enriched in nuclear envelope-associated material. *Cytobiologie* **18**, 22.

KROHNE, G., FRANKE, W. & SCHEER, U. (1978*b*). The major polypeptides of the nuclear pore complex. *Expl Cell Res.* **116**, 85–102.

LALIBERTE, J., DAGENAIS, A., FILION, M., BIBOR-HARDY, V., SIMARD, R. & ROYAL, A. (1984). Identification of distinct messenger RNAs for nuclear lamin C and a putative precursor of nuclear lamin A. *J. Cell Biol.* **96**, 980–985.

LAM, K. & KASPER, C. (1979). Electrophoretic analysis of three major nuclear envelope polypeptides. *J. biol. Chem.* **254**, 11713–11720.

LEBEL, S. & RAYMOND, Y. (1984). Lamin B from rat liver nuclei exists both as a lamina protein and as an intrinsic membrane protein. *J. biol. Chem.* **259**, 2693–2696.

LEBKOWSKI, J. & LAEMMLI, U. (1982). Non-histone proteins and long-range organization of HeLa interphase DNA. *J. molec. Biol.* **156**, 325–344.

MAUL, G. (1977). The nuclear and cytoplasmic pore complex. Structure, dynamics, distribution and evolution. *Int. Rev. Cytol. Suppl.* **6**, 75–186.

MAUL, G. & AVDALORIC, N. (1980). Nuclear envelope proteins from *Spisula solidissima* germinal vesicles. *Expl Cell Res.* **130**, 229–240.

MAUL, G., MAUL, H., SCOGNA, J., LIEBERMAN, M., STEIN, G., HSU, B. & BORUN, T. (1972). Time sequence of nuclear pore formation in phytohemagglutinin-stimulated lymphocytes and in HeLa cells during the cell cycle. *J. Cell Biol.* **55**, 433–447.

McKEON, F., TUFFANELLI, F., KOBAYASHI, S. & KIRSCHNER, M. (1984). The redistribution of a conserved nuclear envelope protein during the cell cycle suggests a pathway for chromosome condensation. *Cell* **36**, 83–92.

MURRAY, R., MURRAY, A. & PIZZO, A. (1965). The fine structure of mitosis in rat thymic lymphocytes. *J. Cell Biol.* **26**, 601–619.

O'FARRELL, P., GOODMAN, H. & O'FARRELL, P. (1977). High resolution two-dimensional electrophoresis of basic as well as acidic proteins. *Cell* **12**, 1133–1142.

OTTAVIANO, Y. & GERACE, L. (1985). *J. biol. Chem.* (in press).

RISAU, W., SAUMWEBER, H. & SYMMONS, P. (1981). Monoclonal antibodies against a nuclear membrane protein of *Drosophila*. *Expl Cell Res.* **133**, 47–54.

ROBBINS, E. & GONATAS, N. (1964). The ultrastructure of a mammalian cell during the mitotic cycle. *J. Cell Biol.* **21**, 429–463.

ROOS, U. (1973). Light and electron microscopy of rat kangaroo cells in mitosis. I. Formation and breakdown of the mitotic apparatus. *Chromosome* **40**, 43–82.

SCHEER, U., KARTENBECK, J., TRENDELENBURG, M., STADLER, J. & FRANKE, W. (1976). Experimental disintegration of the nuclear envelope. Evidence of pore-connecting fibers. *J. Cell Biol.* **69**, 1–18.

SHELTON, K. & COCHRAN, D. (1978). *In vitro* oxidation of intrinsic sulfhydryl groups yields polymers of the two predominant polypeptides in the nuclear envelope fraction. *Biochemistry* **17**, 1212–1216.

SHELTON, K., HIGGINS, L., COCHRAN, D., RUFFOLO, D. & EGLE, P. (1980). Nuclear lamins of erythrocyte and liver. *J. biol. Chem.* **255**, 10978–10983.

STECK, T. (1974). The organization of proteins in the human red blood cell membrane. *J. Cell Biol.* **62**, 1–19.

STECK, T. & YU, J. (1973). Selective solubilization of proteins from red cell membranes by protein perturbants. *J. supramolec. Struct.* **1**, 220–231.

STICK, R. & HAUSEN, D. (1980). Immunological analysis of nuclear lamina proteins. *Chromosoma* **80**, 219–236.

STICK, R. & KROHNE, G. (1982). Immunological localization of the major architectural protein associated with the nuclear envelope of the *Xenopus laevis* oocyte. *Expl Cell Res.* **138**, 319–330.

TOBEY, R., ANDERSON, E. & PETERSEN, D. (1967). Properties of mitotic cells prepared by mechanically shaking monolayer cultures of Chinese hamster cells. *J. cell. Physiol.* **70**, 63–68.

UNWIN, P. & MILLIGAN, R. (1982). A large particle associated with the perimeter of the nuclear pore complex. *J. Cell Biol.* **93**, 63–75.

VENABLE, J. & COGGESHALL, R. (1965). A simplified lead citrate stain for use in electron microscopy. *J. Cell Biol.* **25**, 407–408.

WATSON, M. (1958). Staining of tissue sections for electron microscopy with heavy metals. *J. Biophys. biochem. Cytol.* **4**, 475–478.

WOLD, F. (1981). *In vivo* chemical modifications of proteins (posttranslational modification). *A. Rev. Biochem.* **50**, 783–814.

J. Cell Sci. Suppl. 1, 161–186 (1984)
Printed in Great Britain © The Company of Biologists Limited 1984

KARYOSKELETAL PROTEINS AND THE ORGANIZATION OF THE AMPHIBIAN OOCYTE NUCLEUS

RICARDO BENAVENTE, GEORG KROHNE, MARION S. SCHMIDT-ZACHMANN, BARBARA HÜGLE AND WERNER W. FRANKE

Division of Membrane Biology and Biochemistry, Institute of Cell and Tumor Biology, German Cancer Research Center, Im Neuenheimer Feld 280, D-6900 Heidelberg, Federal Republic of Germany

SUMMARY

We have investigated the existence of structural components in the nucleus of the oocyte of *Xenopus laevis* and other amphibia that are insoluble in non-denaturing detergents and buffers of low and high ionic strength. These cells are particularly suitable for such studies as they have a high frequency of extrachromosomal amplified nucleoli and pore complexes of the nuclear envelope. Using biochemical and immunological techniques, we have shown these structures to contain only two major proteins. These are a polypeptide of M_r 145 000, which is located in a meshwork of filaments specific to the nucleolar cortex, and certain nucleoplasmic bodies probably derived therefrom, and a polypeptide of M_r 68 000, which is the predominant constituent of the lamina–pore complex structure. We show that the latter protein is related to, but not identical to, lamina proteins ('lamins') of somatic cells, indicating cell type-specificity of the expression of polypeptides of the lamin family. In addition, we describe a protein of M_r 180 000, which is the major constituent of the dense fibrillar component of the nucleolus. This can be partially solubilized in buffers of moderately high ionic strength. We interpret proteins of this category as karyoskeletal components involved in the architectural organization of specific functional topology within the nucleus. In contrast to previous reports for other cell types we have found no other prominent high-salt-insoluble structures in the nuclear interior, indicating the absence of an extended internal nuclear matrix in this kind of nucleus.

INTRODUCTION

The cytoplasm of most vertebrate cells contains a system of filamentous structures and membrane-associated plaques that are resistant to extraction in buffers of low or high salt concentrations and non-denaturing detergents. This system of insoluble structures is collectively referred to as the cytoskeleton. Considerable progress has been made in the elucidation of the major protein components of the intermediate-sized (7–11 nm diameter) filaments (Ichikawa, Bischoff & Holtzer, 1968; Franke, Schmid, Osborn & Weber, 1978; for reviews see Anderton, 1981; Franke *et al.* 1982*b*; Lazarides, 1982) and the desmosomal plaques (Franke *et al.* 1981*c*, 1982*a*, Mueller & Franke, 1983; Cowin & Garrod, 1983). The biological significance of these structures and their major protein components has been ascertained by immunolocalization *in situ*, using polypeptide-specific antibodies. The cytoarchitectural role of the intermediate filament–desmosome cytoskeleton is reflected by the remarkable stability of this meshwork, which maintains its cell type-specific appearance throughout detergent lysis and extraction of most of the cellular proteins in solutions of high ionic strength. However, structural elements of such high stability are not restricted to the cytoplasm. Extraction studies of isolated nuclei or nuclear envelopes have indicated that similarly resistant structures occur in the nucleus. For example, it has been shown that nuclei that have been demembranated by treatment with detergents, and depleted of chromatin and other components by treatment with nucleases and extraction in high salt buffer, leave a residual structure for which the collective term 'nuclear matrix' has been proposed (Berezney & Coffey, 1974; for reviews see Agutter & Richardson, 1980; Comings & Peters, 1981; Berezney, 1984). The major features of this structurally heterogeneous matrix comprise a peripheral layer, the nuclear lamina–pore complex, residual nucleolar material and an intricate interchromatinic meshwork of filamentous tangles extending throughout the nuclear interior. However, despite considerable effort, with the exception of the nuclear envelope-associated karyoskeletal complex (see below), no defined proteins have been demonstrated in the residual 'matrix' of the nuclear interior. Indeed, it is still uncertain to what extent the fibrillar tangles of the internal nuclear matrix may include nuclear materials, notably ribonucleoproteins, that have been rendered insoluble by rearrangements during exposure to high ionic strength and nucleases (for discussion see Agutter & Richardson, 1980; Kaufmann, Coffey & Shaper, 1981; Bouteille, Bouvier & Seve, 1983).

In the present paper we describe some karyoskeletal proteins that are located in well-defined nuclear substructures as identified by immunolocalization *in situ*. The focus of this study is the nucleus of the vitellogenic amphibian oocyte, termed the 'germinal vesicle'. These oocyte nuclei are advantageous for studies of non-chromatinous nuclear substructures for several reasons. Their large size permits speedy manual isolation of their nuclei and the preparation of two pure nuclear subfractions, the nuclear envelope and the nuclear content (Krohne, Franke & Scheer, 1978*b*; Krohne, Dabauvalle & Franke, 1981; Franke *et al.* 1981*a*). Oocyte nuclei contain relatively little chromatin but have large quantities of amplified nucleoli (Buongiorno-Nardelli, Amaldi & Lava-Sanchez, 1972) and an extensive nuclear envelope with an unusually high frequency of pore complexes (Franke & Scheer, 1970).

MATERIALS AND METHODS

Animals

Females of *Xenopus laevis* were obtained from the South African Farm (Fish Hoek, South Africa). Frogs of the species *Xenopus borealis* were a gift from Dr M. Fischberg (University of Geneva, Switzerland). The salamander, *Pleurodeles waltlii*, was reared in our laboratory. Chickens were obtained from animal farms.

Cell cultures

Cultured cells from kidney epithelium of *X. laevis* (line A6, American Type Culture Collection) were grown as described (XLKE cells; Franke *et al.* 1979*b*).

Antibodies

Mouse antisera. Antibodies against total residual structures of *X. laevis* oocyte nuclei were obtained as described (Stick & Krohne, 1982). Antibodies against the M_r 68 000 and the M_r 145 000 polypeptides were affinity-purified from this serum according to the procedure described by Krohne *et al.* (1982).

Rabbit antisera. For detailed description of these antibodies raised against chicken erythrocyte nuclear lamina proteins see Stick & Hausen (1980) and Stick & Krohne (1982).

Monoclonal antibodies. Monoclonal mouse antibodies were obtained essentially as described by Köhler & Milstein (1975). The PKB8 monoclonal antibody was obtained by immunizing mice with the cytoskeletal fraction of HeLa cells (Krohne *et al.* 1984). Monoclonal antibodies HRS1-105, No-114 and Lo46F7 were obtained after immunizing mice with sedimentable material of homogenates of mass-isolated oocyte nuclei (3500 *g* pellet) of *X. laevis*, containing nuclear envelopes, nucleoli and chromosomal material (for details see Schmidt-Zachmann, Hügle, Scheer & Franke, 1984).

Isolation and fractionation procedures

Nuclear contents were obtained from manually isolated nuclei as described (Krohne & Franke, 1983) using oocytes of stages IV and VI of *X. laevis* (Dumont, 1972). The 'isolation medium' (IM; 83 mM-KCl, 17 mM-NaCl, 10^{-4} M-CaCl$_2$, 10 mM-Tris·HCl, pH 7·2) was used, alternatively, with or without Ca^{2+}. Nuclear contents were fractionated according to the following procedure (see scheme 1).

Alternatively, nuclear contents were isolated in IM containing 10 mM-MgCl$_2$ and fractionated as described in scheme 1 (fractions designated Mg-P$_{1-5}$ or Mg-S$_{1-5}$). In some experiments buffers used for washes of pellets Mg-P$_1$ and Mg-P$_5$ contained 5 mM-EDTA.

In order to examine the effect of Mg^{2+} on the proteinaceous material recovered in supernatant fractions such as S$_1$ we added MgCl$_2$ to a final concentration of 10 mM, incubated this solution for 15 min at room temperature and centrifuged it again at 8000 *g* for 5 min. Pellets thus obtained were designated 'S$_1$-Mg precipitate' and were compared with the corresponding supernatant fraction. As a control, a sample was incubated in IM without addition of MgCl$_2$.

Identical results were obtained in IM with and without 0·5 mM-phenylmethylsulphonyl fluoride (PMSF) or 2·5 mM-dithiothreitol (DTT).

Isolation and fractionation protocols for the preparation of nuclear envelopes and for the M_r 180 000 polypeptide have been described in detail (Krohne *et al.* 1978b, 1981; Krohne & Franke, 1983; Schmidt-Zachmann *et al.* 1984).

Electron microscopy

Nuclear contents and pellet fractions were fixed in 2·5 % glutaraldehyde (in sodium cacodylate buffer, pH 7·2, for 15 min at 4 °C), post-fixed in 2 % OsO$_4$ (same buffer, 15 min, 4 °C) and soaked overnight in a 0·5 % solution of uranyl acetate at 4 °C. After dehydration in graded ethanol solutions the material was embedded in Epon 812 (Fluka). Ultrathin sections were obtained and double stained.

For spread preparations pellets were resuspended in IM and then incubated for 90 s on freshly glow-discarged carbon-coated grids. The grids were then rinsed in distilled water and negatively stained with 1 % uranyl acetate.

Immunolocalization

Immunofluorescence microscopy and electron microscopic immunolocalization experiments were done as described elsewhere (e.g. see Krohne *et al.* 1982, 1984; Benavente, Krohne, Stick & Franke, 1984; Schmidt-Zachmann *et al.* 1984).

Gel electrophoresis and immunoblotting experiments

One-dimensional slab gel electrophoresis in the presence of SDS was according to Laemmli (1970) or Thomas & Kornberg (1975). Two-dimensional gel electrophoresis was according to O'Farrell, Goodman & O'Farrell (1977). Gels were stained with the silver technique (Switzer, Merril & Shifrin, 1979) or with Coomassie Blue. For immunoblotting, polypeptides were partly renatured as described (Bowen, Steinberg, Laemmli & Weintraub, 1980) and then electrophoretically transferred to nitrocellulose paper according to Towbin, Staehelin & Gordon (1979), and incubated with the antibodies (for details see Gigi *et al.* 1982; Krohne *et al.* 1982; Schmidt-Zachmann *et al.* 1984).

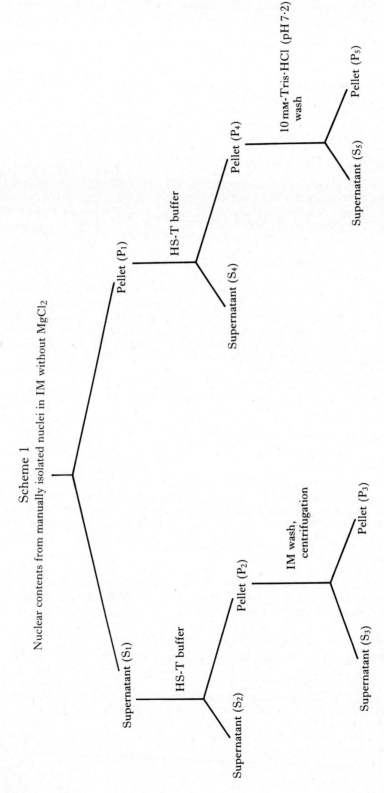

Scheme 1

Nuclear contents from manually isolated nuclei in IM without MgCl$_2$

Supernatant (S$_1$)

Pellet (P$_1$)

HS-T buffer

HS-T buffer

Pellet (P$_2$)

Supernatant (S$_4$)

Pellet (P$_4$)

10 mM-Tris·HCl (pH 7·2) wash

Supernatant (S$_2$)

IM wash, centrifugation

Pellet (P$_3$)

Supernatant (S$_3$)

Supernatant (S$_5$)

Pellet (P$_5$)

Scheme of fractionation of nuclear contents from oocytes of *X. laevis* (centrifugations were for 5 min at 8000 *g*; HS-T buffer was 1 M-KCl, 1 % Triton X-100, 10 mM-Tris·HCl (pH 7·2); fractions were incubated for 30 min in HS-T buffer).

Peptide mapping

Polypeptide spots were excised after two-dimensional gel electrophoresis and used for peptide mapping according to the procedure of Elder, Pickett, Hampton & Lerner (1977).

RESULTS AND DISCUSSION

Karyoskeletal proteins of the nucleolus

In somatic cells, the biochemical identification of structural elements specifically located within the nucleoli is hindered by the intimate association of the nucleoli with other nuclear components such as the perinucleolar heterochromatin and the nuclear envelope. Therefore, in order to avoid this problem of contamination we have chosen to study the nuclei of amphibian oocytes, which contain numerous amplified extra-chromosomal nucleoli (>1000 in *X. laevis*). Since these amplified nucleoli are not in physical connection with the chromosomes they can be easily isolated under physiological conditions with a high degree of purity (Franke *et al.* 1981*a*).

Amplified nucleoli of *Xenopus* oocytes contain a cortical meshwork of 10–12 nm filaments, which appear as beaded chains containing a core filament 3–5 nm in diameter (Franke *et al.* 1979*a*, 1981*a*; Moreno Diaz de la Espina *et al.* 1982). Part of this filament system is resistant to treatment with buffers containing low or high ($\geqq 1 \cdot 0$ M-KCl) salt concentrations, non-ionic detergents, various nucleases and sulphydryl agents, leaving tangles of filament fragments of 3–5 nm diameter. It has been shown that *in situ* these filaments coil into higher-order fibrils (30–40 nm in diameter), which form aggregates at the nucleolar cortex (see Franke *et al.* 1981*a* and below). Filaments of this type have also been found in certain spheroidal bodies with a 'tumbleweed-like organization', which occur in the vicinity of the nucleoli and elsewhere in the nucleoplasm ('medusoid fibril bodies'; Moreno Diaz de la Espina *et al.* 1982). When analysed by polyacrylamide gel electrophoresis (PAGE) this filamentous cortical skeleton of nucleoli is found to contain only one major polypeptide (M_r 145 000). This protein is a major nucleolar polypeptide (Fig. 1, lanes a–c). Incorporation experiments (Fig. 1, lanes d, e) have shown it to be the most intensely synthesized and phosphorylated protein of the 'insoluble residue fraction' (P_5 fraction; see Materials and Methods). By two-dimensional gel electrophoresis the M_r 145 000 nucleolar polypeptide appears as an acidic protein (apparent isoelectric pH approx. $6 \cdot 15$ in the presence of $9 \cdot 5$ M-urea), revealing two isoelectric variants, which probably represent different levels of phosphorylation (Fig. 3; see also Franke *et al.* 1981*a*).

Affinity-purified antibodies specific for the M_r 145 000 polypeptide (Fig. 1c; cf. Stick & Krohne, 1982; Krohne *et al.* 1982) have allowed the identification of this protein in fractions containing either whole nucleoli (P_1) or high salt/Triton X-100 (HS-T) extracted nucleoli (fraction P_5 of the scheme in Materials and Methods) from *X. laevis* and *X. borealis* oocytes. Immunofluorescence microscopy on sections through frozen tissues of *Xenopus* (Krohne *et al.* 1982) and on permeabilized cultured somatic cells of *X. laevis* has located the protein to distinct granular units ('dots') of the nucleolar periphery and to certain smaller nucleoplasmic granules, which probably represent medusoid body equivalents (Fig. 2 presents an example of the kidney epithelial cell line A6). Immunofluorescence microscopy on frozen sections through *X. laevis* and *X. borealis* ovaries shows a strong reaction with the amplified nucleoli (Fig. 4), which is largely restricted to dot-like subunits at the

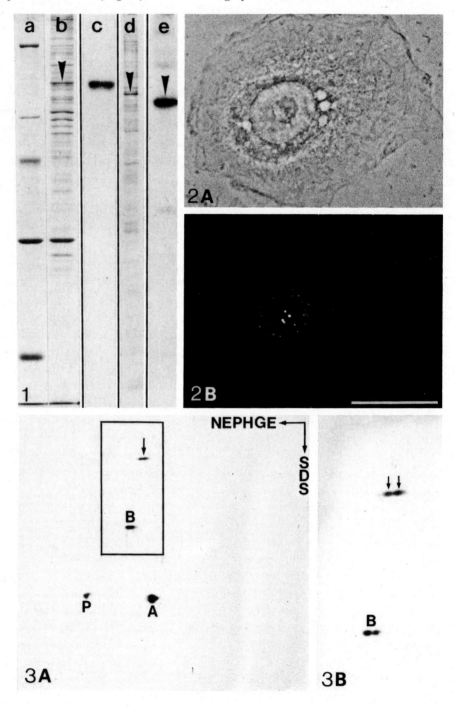

periphery of the amplified nucleoli and seems to coincide with the dense filament aggregates described at the electron microscopic level (Fig. 5). In addition, certain extranucleolar nucleoplasmic bodies ('medusoid fibril bodies', MFBs, *sensu* Moreno Diaz de la Espina *et al.* 1982) are also positive (arrowheads in Fig. 4; cf. Benavente *et al.* 1984). At the electron microscopic level, these antibodies have been located to the cortical filaments of extracted nucleoli and MFBs, suggesting that these karyos-keletal filaments are built up primarily by the M_r 145 000 polypeptide (Fig. 6; cf. Benavente *et al.* 1984). The antibodies also react with small, distinct, spheroidal filament tangles in the nucleolar periphery of somatic cells of *Xenopus* (Benavente *et al.* 1984). These immunological observations suggest the presence of a karyoskeletal protein in nucleoli of somatic cells that is similar, if not identical, to the M_r 145 000 protein of oocytes.

In view of the organization of the M_r 145 000 protein at the periphery of nucleoli and in the MFBs of oocytes and somatic cells, together with the association of these filaments with granular structures that resemble preribosomal particles (Moreno Diaz de la Espina *et al.* 1982), it is tempting to speculate that these karyoskeletal filaments are involved in the functional compartmentalization of the nucleolus and, specifically, in the storage and the nucleocytoplasmic transport of preribosomal particles (Benavente *et al.* 1984).

In addition, we have found another abundant protein present in nucleoli of oocytes and somatic cells of *X. laevis* and *X. borealis* that seems to be involved in the establish-ment of nucleolar suborganization (Schmidt-Zachmann *et al.* 1984). This polypep-tide (M_r 180 000; Fig. 7, lanes b–c) is acidic in nature (apparent isoelectric pH approx. 4·2 in 9·5 M-urea) and resistant to extractions in buffers of physiological and

---

Fig. 1. Biochemical characterization of the major karyoskeletal protein of the nuclear contents of *X. laevis* oocytes (see also Figs 16, 17). Polypeptides after separated by SDS/PAGE (10 % acrylamide) were visualized by Coomassie Blue staining (lanes a, b) and autoradiography (lanes c–e). Lane a, reference proteins: myosin heavy chain (M_r 200 000), phosphorylase a (M_r 94 000), bovine serum albumin (BSA; M_r 68 000), actin (M_r 42 000) and chymotrypsinogen (M_r 25 000). Lanes b, c, in manually isolated and sedimented nuclear contents the M_r 145 000 polypeptide is present in significant amounts (b, arrowhead) and can be identified by the immunoblotting test (c) using specific antibodies (for details see Krohne *et al.* 1982). Lanes d, e, polypeptides of karyoskeletal residues (insoluble in HS-T-buffer; P₅ fraction, see scheme 1) of nuclear contents prepared from oocytes incubated with [³⁵S]methionine (d; 300 μCi/ml, 24 h) or [³²P]-orthophosphate (e; 500 μCi/ml, 24 h). The M_r 145 000 polypeptide is the most intensely labelled protein (arrowheads in d and e) of this fraction.

Fig. 2. Immunofluorescence microscopy of cultured *X. laevis* kidney epithelial cells (line A6) with affinity-purified antibodies against the M_r 145 000 polypeptide. This antibody shows punctate reaction in the periphery of nucleoli and in distinct granules free in the nucleoplasm. A. Phase contrast; B, epifluorescence. Bar, 20 μm.

Fig. 3. A. Two-dimensional gel electrophoresis (first dimension non-equilibrium pH gradient electrophoresis, NEPHGE; second dimension: SDS/PAGE (10%); silver staining) of residual polypeptides (insoluble in HS-T buffer) from *X. laevis* oocyte nuclear contents. The M_r 145 000 polypeptide (arrow) is the major protein of the fraction. Co-electrophoresed reference proteins are BSA (B), phosphoglycerokinase (P) and actin (A). B. An enlarged part of A, showing that the M_r 145 000 polypeptide can be resolved into two isoelectric variants (arrows); B, BSA.

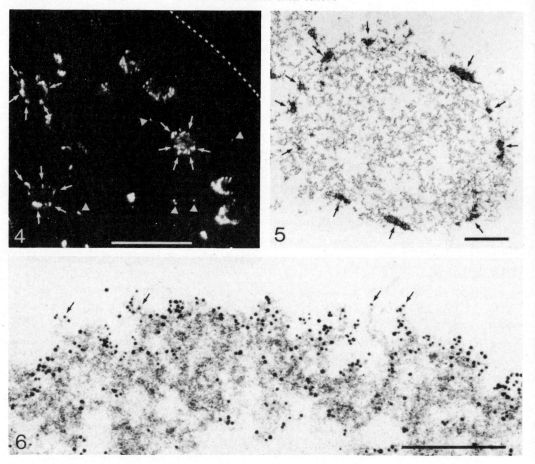

Fig. 4. Immunofluorescence microscopy of a frozen section through a X. laevis ovary after incubation with affinity-purified antibodies against the M_r 145 000 polypeptide. Part of an oocyte nucleus is shown. These antibodies show intense reaction with dot-like areas in the cortices of the amplified nucleoli (arrows) and MFBs free in the nucleoplasm (some are denoted by arrowheads). The position of the nuclear envelope is marked by a broken line. Bar, 50 μm.

Fig. 5. Electron micrograph of an ultrathin section through an extracted nucleolus of X. laevis oocytes obtained after treatment with HS-T buffer (P_5 fraction; for details see Franke et al. 1981a). Nucleolar filaments that tend to form dense aggregates in the nucleolar cortex (arrows) are characteristic of this structure (see Figs 16, lane e and 17, lane a, for biochemical data). Bar, 1 μm.

Fig. 6. Electron microscopic immunolocalization of the M_r 145 000 polypeptide in the nucleolar skeletal structure obtained as described in Fig. 5. Cortical filaments are decorated with 5 nm gold-coupled secondary antibodies (arrows) reacting with primary murine antibodies against the M_r 145 000 polypeptide. Bar, 0·2 μm.

slightly higher ionic strength. However, a large proportion of it can be extracted from isolated nuclear contents and nucleoli at higher ionic strength ($\geq 0·4$ M-NaCl) in an apparently monomeric state (Schmidt-Zachmann et al. 1984). Partial extraction of this protein can also be achieved by digestion of nucleolus-containing structures with

RNase but not with DNase. A monoclonal antibody (No-114) against the M_r 180 000 nucleolar polypeptide from isolated nucleoli of *Xenopus* oocytes (Fig. 7, lane c) shows strong and specific reaction with nucleoli of oocytes (Fig. 8) and of somatic cells, including follicle epithelial cells (Fig. 8), hepatocytes (Fig. 9A,B) and cultured kidney epithelial cells (Fig. 9C–F). Remarkably, the antigen is still present in nuclei of *Xenopus* erythrocytes in which a small residual nucleolar structure is seen that is transcriptionally inactive (Fig. 9A,B). Unlike some other nucleolar proteins such as RNA polymerase I (Scheer & Rose, 1984), but similar to the behaviour of the karyoskeletal protein of M_r 145 000 described above and the nucleolar protein B23 (Ochs, Lischwe, O'Leary & Busch, 1983), the M_r 180 000 polypeptide does not remain in association with the 'nucleolar-organizer region' of mitotic chromosomes but is transiently dispersed throughout the cytoplasm until telophase (Schmidt-Zachmann *et al.* 1984). Immunolocalization at the electron microscopic level reveals that the M_r 180 000 polypeptide is confined to the 'dense fibrillar component' of the nucleolus, thus providing a specific marker for this structure (Fig. 10). This exclusive location in the fibrillar component has been confirmed by experiments using actinomycin D-treated cells in which the fibrillar and granular components of the nucleolus have been segregated (Bernhard, 1971). Under these conditions the monoclonal antibody No-114 recognizes only the phase-contrast 'light' hemisphere of the nucleolus (Fig. 9E,F), which corresponds to the dense fibrillar component.

These observations suggest that the M_r 180 000 protein contributes to the backbone structure of the dense fibrillar component of nucleoli and possibly provides structural support to elements involved in transcription of ribosomal DNA and, or, processing of their products. However, its morphogenetic contribution is not dependent on continuous nucleolar transcription as demonstrated by its conservation in the residual nucleolar structures of the transcriptionally inactive amphibian erythrocytes.

Structural proteins of the nuclear envelope

The nuclear envelope, a characteristic of the eukaryotic cell, is a complex of three prominent components (for reviews see Franke, 1974; Franke *et al.* 1981b). (1) The inner and outer nuclear membrane and the pore walls; (2) the non-membranous pore-complex material; and (3) the nuclear lamina, a thin layer of non-membranous proteinaceous material subjacent to the inner nuclear membrane. The architectural residues of the nuclear pore complexes and the nuclear lamina are the only structural components of the nuclear envelope resistant to treatment with nucleases, non-ionic detergents and high salt concentrations (Aaronson & Blobel, 1975; Scheer *et al.* 1976; Krohne *et al.* 1978b, 1981). This residual 'nuclear pore complex–lamina fraction' contains only a few (1–3) major polypeptides in the M_r range of 60 000–80 000 (Aaronson & Blobel, 1975; Krohne *et al.* 1978a,b, 1981; Gerace, Blum & Blobel, 1978; Shelton *et al.* 1980; Maul & Avdalovic, 1980; Gerace & Blobel, 1980). In order to compare a fraction rich in pore-complex structures with one of exceptionally low pore-complex density we have analysed in detail the composition of pore complex–lamina fraction of *Xenopus* oocytes and those of somatic cells, notably the erythrocytes, of the same species.

Analysis by sodium dodecyl sulphate (SDS)/PAGE shows that the nuclear pore complex–lamina fraction from *X. laevis* oocytes contains only one major polypeptide with an M_r of 68 000 (Fig. 11, lane b). More than 80 % of the total Coomassie Blue-stained protein of this fraction is represented by this polypeptide. In addition, a faint polypeptide band at M_r 100 000 and four minor polypeptides in the M_r range of 180 000–250 000 are detectable by Coomassie Blue staining (Fig. 11, lane b).

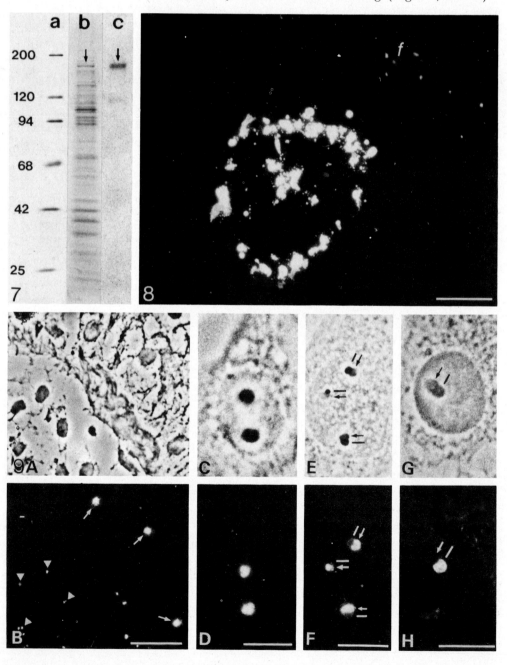

However, these minor high molecular weight components can only be clearly visualized in silver-stained gels (Fig. 11, lane f; for minor components see also fig. 3b, lane 4, of Krohne *et al*. 1981; and Krohne *et al*. 1978*b*). The predominance of only one polypeptide has also been noted in the pore complex–lamina fractions from oocytes of other amphibian species (Krohne *et al*. 1981) and the surf clam, *Spisula solidissima* (Maul & Avdalovic, 1980).

In contrast to that of *X. laevis* oocyte (Fig. 12, lane a), the nuclear pore complex–lamina fraction of somatic cells of this species (Fig. 12, lane b) contains two major polypeptides of M_r 72000 (L_I) and M_r 68000 (L_{II}). In addition, two low molecular weight polypeptides are sometimes found in this fraction in variable amounts (Fig. 12, lane b). The polypeptides L_I and L_{II} of erythrocytes and other somatic cells and the M_r 68000 of oocytes have been studied by using specific antibodies (Fig. 12, lanes a′, b′, a″, b″; and Stick & Krohne, 1982), and all three have been localized in the nuclear lamina (Stick & Krohne, 1982; Krohne *et al*. 1984). In spite of this similarity in molecular size and location, these three polypeptides are clearly different as shown by isoelectric focusing (Krohne *et al*. 1981) and tryptic peptide mapping (Krohne *et al*. 1984). Therefore, we have examined further the difference between both cell types with the aid of different monoclonal antibodies to lamina proteins. Antibody Lo46F7 reacts exclusively with the M_r 68000 polypeptide of the oocyte (Fig. 12, lanes a′, b′; Fig. 13A,B), whereas the reaction of antibody PKB8 is restricted to polypeptides L_I and L_{II} characteristic for somatic cells (Fig. 12, lanes

Fig. 7. Identification of the nucleolar antigen recognized by the monoclonal antibody No-114 (electrophoretical conditions were similar to those in Fig. 1; for details see Schmidt-Zachmann *et al*. 1984). Lane a, reference proteins include, in addition to those shown in Fig. 1, lane a, β-galactosidase (M_r 120000). Lane b, polypeptide pattern of isolated purified amplified nucleoli from *X. laevis* oocytes (Coomassie Blue-staining). Lane c, corresponding autoradiograph after immunoblotting reaction with antibody No-114. This antibody reacts with a protein of M_r 180000 present in the nucleolar fraction (arrows in b and c). M_r are shown ($\times 10^{-3}$).

Fig. 8. Immunofluorescence microscopy of a frozen section through *X. laevis* ovary after incubation with the monoclonal antibody No-114. The large nucleoli of oocytes and the smaller nucleoli of the surrounding follicle cells (f) show intense reaction. Bar, 50 μm.

Fig. 9. Localization of the M_r 180000 protein by immunofluorescence microscopy of frozen sections through liver tissue of *X. laevis* (A,B) and on permeabilized cultured kidney epithelial cells (line A6) grown on coverslips (C–F). A,C,E,G. Phase-contrast optics; B,D,F, H, epifluorescence optics. Nucleoli of hepatocytes (arrows in B) and A6 cells (D) show strong fluorescence. In nuclei of erythrocytes, which are inactive in the synthesis of ribosomal RNA, only one to two small, dot-like areas are stained (arrowheads in B), representing the residual nucleolar structures characteristic of these cells (cf. Schmidt-Zachmann *et al*. 1984). E,F. In actinomycin D-treated kidney epithelial cells (A6) the nucleolar components have segregated (denoted by arrow and pointer; E, 4h AmD), showing that the M_r 180000 protein recognized by monoclonal No-114 is now located in the phase-contrast light hemisphere (F, arrow) which corresponds to the dense fibrillar component. G,H. A6 cells treated for 4h with actinomycin D and incubated then with monoclonal antibody RS1-105. In contrast to the No-114 antibody, the antibody RS1-105 (which recognizes ribosomal protein S_1) binds to the phase-dark hemisphere, which corresponds to the granular component of the nucleolus (pointers in G and H). In addition, the ribosomes of the cytoplasm are stained. Bars: B, 50 μm; D,F,H, 10 μm.

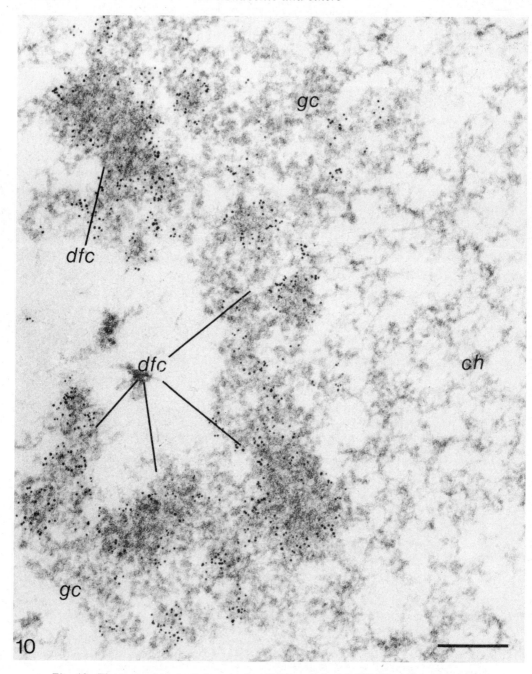

Fig. 10. Electron microscopic immunolocalization of the M_r 180 000 polypeptide in *X. laevis* hepatocyte nuclei using monoclonal antibody No-114 and 5 nm gold-particle-coupled secondary antibodies. The dense fibrillar component (*dfc*) of the nucleolus is labelled. Fibrillar centres (not shown), the granular component (*gc*) and the surrounding chromatin (*ch*) are not significantly labelled. Bar, 0·2 μm.

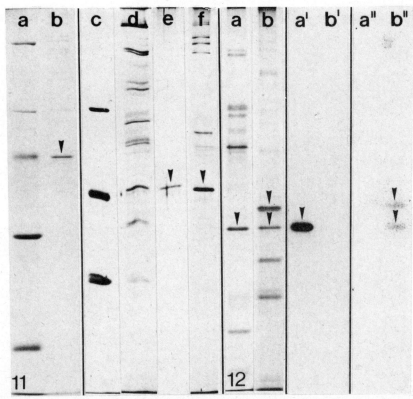

Fig. 11. Characterization of karyoskeletal proteins of the nuclear envelope from *X. laevis* oocytes (SDS/PAGE, 10% acrylamide). Lanes a, b, Coomassie Blue staining; lanes c–f, silver staining. Lane a, reference proteins: myosin heavy chain (M_r 200000), phosphorylase *a* (M_r 94000), BSA (M_r 68000), actin (M_r 42000) and chymotrypsinogen (M_r 25000). Lane b, residual polypeptides of 200 manually isolated nuclear envelopes after treatment with HS-T buffer. The M_r 68000 polypeptide (arrowhead) is the major protein of this fraction. In addition, a minor polypeptide band of M_r 100000 and four faint polypeptide bands in the M_r range of 180000–250000 are detectable. Lanes c–f, characterization of minor karyoskeletal polypeptides associated with the nuclear envelope as detected by silver staining. Lane c, reference proteins: β-galactosidase (M_r 120000), BSA (M_r 68000) and actin (M_r 42000). Lane d, polypeptide pattern of whole unextracted nuclear envelopes (20 manually isolated envelopes). Lanes e, f, residual polypeptides of extracted nuclear envelopes (e, 30 envelopes; f, 150 envelopes; extraction as described in b). In addition to the predominant M_r 68000 protein (arrowheads) four polypeptide bands in the M_r range of 180000–250000 and one polypeptide of approximate M_r 100000 are detectable in silver-stained gels (f; cf. Krohne *et al*. 1981).

Fig. 12. Immunological characterization of the nuclear lamina polypeptides of oocytes and erythrocytes of *X. laevis* (SDS/PAGE according to Thomas & Kornberg, 1975; 12% acrylamide gels). Lane a, karyoskeletal residue of mass-isolated oocyte nuclei (arrowhead; M_r 68000 polypeptide). Lane b, karyoskeletal residue of erythrocytes. Arrowheads denote lamina polypeptides L_I (M_r 72000) and L_{II} (M_r 68000). Lanes a′, b′, corresponding autoradiograph after an immunoblot experiment using monoclonal antibody Lo46F7, which recognizes only the M_r 68000 polypeptide of oocytes (a′, arrowhead), not the related lamina polypeptides of erythrocytes (b′). Lanes a″, b″, autoradiograph of an immunoblot experiment using monoclonal antibody PKB8, which reacts exclusively with the two nuclear lamina polypeptides of erythrocytes (b″, arrowheads), not with the M_r 68000 polypeptide of oocytes (a″; cf. Krohne *et al*. 1984).

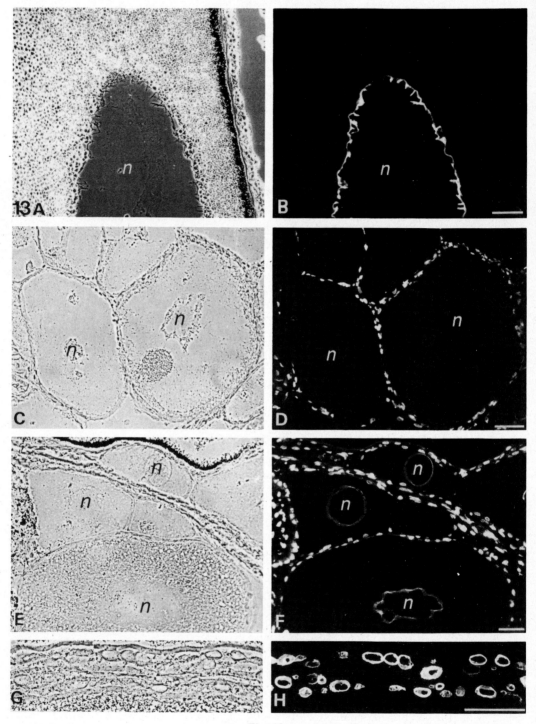

Fig. 13

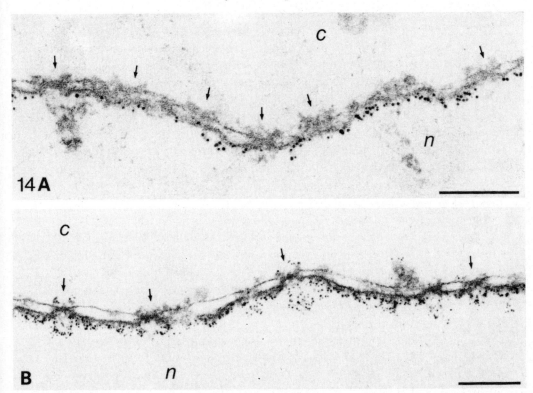

Fig. 14. Electron microscopic immunolocalization of the M_r 68 000 polypeptide in isolated nuclear envelopes of *Xenopus* oocytes. Specifically bound antibodies were visualized by 5 nm gold-coupled secondary antibodies. Monoclonal antibody Lo46F7 shows exclusive reaction with the nuclear lamina (A) whereas polyclonal mouse antibodies (B; Stick & Krohne, 1982) react with both structures, the nuclear lamina and the pore complexes. Nuclear pore complexes are denoted by arrows (A,B). *c*, cytoplasmic side; *n*, nucleoplasmic side. Bars, 0·2 μm.

a″, b″; Fig. 13c,D; cf. Krohne *et al.* 1984). In contrast, polyclonal antibodies from a rabbit antiserum react with the nuclear periphery of both cell types (Fig. 13E–H; for detailed description of this antibody see Stick & Hausen, 1980; Stick & Krohne, 1982), indicating that the nuclear lamina polypeptides of oocytes and somatic cells may share some antigenic determinants (see also Ely, D'Arcy & Jost, 1978; Gerace *et al.* 1978; Krohne *et al.* 1978a).

Fig. 13. Immunofluorescence microscopy of frozen sections through ovaries of *X. laevis* (A–F) and *P. waltlii* (G–H) after incubation with antibodies against nuclear lamina proteins. A,C,E,G. Phase-contrast optics; B,D,F,H, epifluorescence optics. Monoclonal antibody Lo46F7 (A,B) reacts exclusively with the nuclear envelope of oocytes whereas somatic cell nuclei are exclusively stained by the monoclonal antibody PKB8 (c,D). Antibodies to lamina proteins from rabbit antiserum (Stick & Hausen, 1980; Stick & Krohne, 1982) react with the nuclear envelope of both cell types (E,F). In somatic cells nuclear lamina antibodies react exclusively with the nuclear periphery (G,H; follicle cells stained with the rabbit antibodies as used in E and F). *n*, oocyte nucleus. Bars, 50 μm.

Up to now no polypeptide exclusive to the non-membranous part of the nuclear pore complex has been identified. Recently, a glycoprotein of M_r 190 000 has been immunolocalized to the pore walls of nuclear envelopes of rat liver but this component seems to be a membrane constituent (Gerace, Ottaviano & Kondor-Koch, 1982). We have investigated whether the M_r 68 000 protein of the oocyte nuclear membrane is located in the nuclear lamina and, or, in the pore complexes. Under the conditions used, the monoclonal antibody Lo46F7 reacts exclusively with the nuclear lamina (Fig. 14A), whereas the polyclonal antibodies from a mouse antiserum recognize both structures, the nuclear lamina and the pore complexes (Fig. 14B; cf. Stick & Krohne, 1982). This indicates that, at least in *X. laevis* oocytes, the M_r 68 000 polypeptide is not only a structural component of the nuclear lamina but also contributes to the architecture of the pore complex.

The nuclear lamina polypeptides of taxonomically distant vertebrates are immunologically related, as demonstrated by monoclonal antibodies (Krohne *et al*. 1984; a monoclonal antibody to lamina protein has also been described by Burke, Tooze & Warren, 1983; for indications of human anti-lamina antibodies cross-reacting between vertebrates and invertebrates see McKeon, Tuffanelli, Fukuyama & Kirschner, 1983). Apparently these proteins, which have been named 'lamins' by Gerace & Blobel (1980), contain regions highly conserved in evolution. On the other hand, tryptic peptide map analysis reveals that immunologically related lamins of mammals, birds and amphibia are clearly different (Fig. 15; compare with fig. 8 of Krohne *et al*. 1984, and fig. 4 of Kaufmann, Gibson & Shaper, 1983). These and other biochemical data indicate that, at least in birds and mammals, the largest and the smallest lamina polypeptide (lamins A and C, respectively) are closely related, whereas lamin B is clearly different (Lam & Kasper, 1979; Shelton *et al*. 1980; Krohne *et al*. 1984). These results suggest that the lamins represent a family of related polypeptides and that, at least in *Xenopus*, different lamina proteins are expressed differentially in oocytes and somatic cells.

The significance of residual non-nucleolar protein structures in the nuclear interior

The existence of karyoskeletal (nuclear matrix) structures in the nuclear interior other than in nucleoli is still a controversial issue (for discussions see Berezney & Coffey, 1977; Berezney, 1984; Kaufmann *et al*. 1981). Surprisingly, even after a decade of intensive research, no defined protein has been positively localized to a nonnucleolar structure of the high-salt-buffer-insoluble matrix of the nuclear interior. A valuable object for studying this problem is again the *Xenopus* oocyte nucleus, from which nuclear contents can be isolated in high purity and sufficient amount for the biochemical characterization and in times short enough to minimize preparative artifacts such as protein aggregation.

We have fractionated oocyte nuclear contents according to the scheme described in Materials and Methods. After manual removal of nuclear envelopes, nuclear contents are homogenized in isolation medium (IM) and fractionated by centrifugation. More than 95 % of the total protein of nuclear contents are soluble in IM (Fig. 16, lane c, S_1) whereas less than 5 % of the protein are structurally bound and can be pelleted

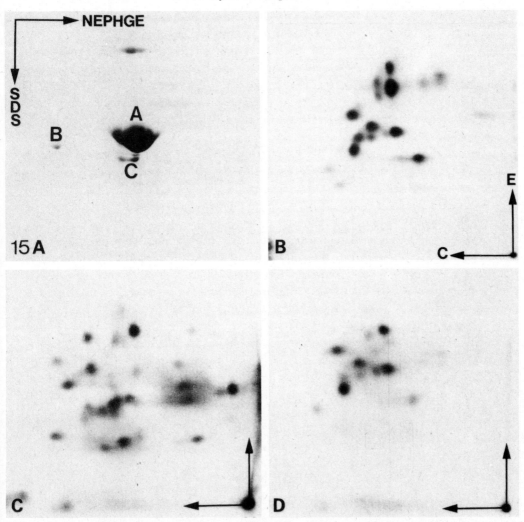

Fig. 15. Biochemical characterization of nuclear lamina polypeptides from chicken erythrocytes. A. Nuclear lamina polypeptides (lamins A,B,C) after separation by two-dimensional gel electrophoresis (for abbreviations see Fig. 3) and staining with Coomassie Blue. B–D. Two-dimensional analysis of ^{125}I-labelled peptides obtained after tryptic digestion of lamin A (B), B (C) and C (D). E indicates electrophoresis in first dimension and C, chromatography in second dimension. Peptide maps of lamins A and C show great similarity and are clearly different from that of lamin B.

(Fig. 16, lane b, P_1). Proteins insoluble in IM (fraction P_1) are then incubated in high salt/Triton/buffer (HS-T) and the solubilized proteins (Fig. 16, lane d, S_4) are separated from the insoluble residue by centrifugation (P_4). The sediment P_4 is then washed once more with Tris-buffer and centrifuged again (S_5 and P_5). In the final pellet (Fig. 16, lane e, P_5) the M_r 145 000 protein is the only major polypeptide detectable by silver staining (for description of this fraction see Fig. 5 and Franke *et al.* 1981*a*), whereas the corresponding supernatant (S_5) does not contain prominent

178   R. Benavente and others

proteins (data not shown). In parallel, soluble proteins of nuclear contents (fraction S_1) have been incubated in HS-T buffer in order to determine whether proteins soluble under physiological conditions can be precipitated by this extraction buffer. Approximately 1 % of total soluble protein has been found to be irreversibly precipitated by the HS-T buffer (Fig. 16, lane i, P_3), whereas 98–99 % of the initial soluble protein remains in the supernatant (Fig. 16, lane h, S_2). Identical results have been obtained when all buffers contain 2 mM-dithiothreitol. These data clearly demonstrate that the M_r 145 000 protein is the only major karyoskeletal protein in the oocyte nuclear content. The vast majority of the polypeptides soluble under physiological conditions remain soluble in the HS-T buffer and no special polypeptides are preferentially enriched in the pelletable material (fraction P_3; Fig. 16, lanes h, i). Practically identical results have been obtained with oocytes of stages IV and VI (Fig. 17, lanes a, b).

   Usually, for the preparation of nuclear matrices from somatic cells nuclei are used that have been isolated in buffers containing considerable concentrations of divalent cations (2–5 mM; e.g. see Berezney & Coffey, 1977; Van Eekelen et al. 1982). Therefore, in order to examine the influence of divalent cations we have isolated the nuclear contents of X. laevis oocytes under similar conditions, i.e. in IM containing 5 or 10 mM MgCl$_2$. The final residual fraction (Mg-P$_5$) reveals, besides the M_r 145 000 protein, a number of polypeptide bands, including a prominent polypeptide that co-migrates with actin (Fig. 17, lanes d, e). This polypeptide has been identified as β- and γ-non-muscle actin by its co-migration, on two-dimensional polyacrylamide gel electrophoresis, with authentic actins (not shown; cf. Vandekerckhove, Franke &

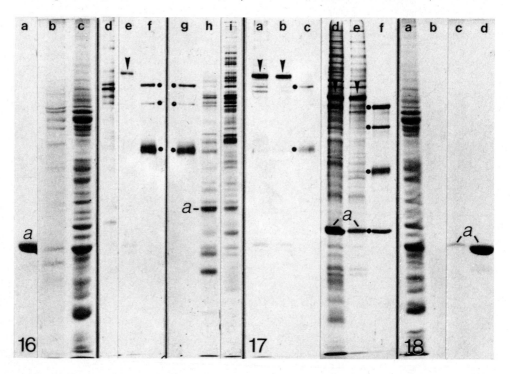

Weber, 1981). Remarkably, the structure-stabilizing effect of Mg^{2+} could not be reversed by repeated washes with buffers containing EDTA (Fig. 17, lanes d, e), indicating that the addition of divalent cations results in an aggregation or re-arrangement irreversible by competition with the chelating agent used.

In order to examine the effect of Mg^{2+} on native soluble nuclear proteins, 10 mM-$MgCl_2$ was added to S_1 fractions (Fig. 18, lane a). This addition resulted in a change in the state of organization of several proteins, including a certain proportion of the actin, and the appearance of a significant pellet (Fig. 18, lane c; Fig. 18, lane b, presents the control showing a pellet from fraction S_1 to which no $MgCl_2$ has been added).

In parallel we have analysed these fractions by electron microscopy. Pellets of nuclear contents isolated in IM without $MgCl_2$ (P_1) contain large amounts of extra-chromosomal nucleoli and MFBs (Moreno Diaz de la Espina *et al.* 1982; see above).

Fig. 16. SDS/PAGE (10 % acrylamide) according to Laemmli (1970) of nuclear content subfractions from *X. laevis* oocytes. The nuclear contents were manually isolated in IM without $MgCl_2$ (for details see scheme 1 in Materials and Methods). Lanes a–c, Coomassie Blue staining; lanes d–i, silver staining. Lane a, reference protein, actin (M_r 42 000; *a*). Lane b, polypeptide pattern of the sediment derived from 50 nuclear contents (P_1). Lane c, polypeptide pattern of the supernatant derived from 50 nuclear contents (S_1). Lanes d, e, results of the extraction of pelletable material of nuclear contents (fraction P_1) with HS-T buffer; d, polypeptides of 10 pelleted nuclear contents solubilized by HS-T buffer (S_4); e, protein that remains pelletable after extraction with HS-T buffer (P_5, residues from 70 nuclear contents). This fraction contains only one major protein, the M_r 145 000 polypeptide (arrowhead; for morphological comparison see Fig. 5). Lanes f, g, reference proteins denoted by dots: β-galactosidase (M_r 120 000), phosphorylase *a* (M_r 94 000) and BSA (M_r 68 000). Lanes h, i, fractionation of proteins of nuclear contents (S_1 fraction) exposed to HS-T buffer; i, pelleted proteins of S_1 fraction from 70 nuclear contents (P_3; fractions P_3 and P_2 were practically identical in composition; no protein was found in the supernatant S_3); h, protein of the S_1 fraction that remains soluble after incubation with HS-T buffer (S_2 fraction; protein corresponding to one nuclear content).

Fig. 17. Polypeptide composition of karyoskeletal residues (insoluble in HS-T buffer; fraction P_5) of nuclear contents of *X. laevis* oocyte isolated in IM without (a, b) and with (d, e) 10 mM-$MgCl_2$. SDS/PAGE (10 % acrylamide) seen after silver staining. Comparison between full-grown (a, d) and stage IV (b, e) oocytes. Lanes a, b, the residual fraction of nuclear contents isolated in IM without $MgCl_2$ contains only one major protein, the M_r 145 000 polypeptide (arrowheads). Lanes d, e, the karyoskeletal residue prepared from oocyte nuclear contents isolated in IM with 10 mM-$MgCl_2$ contains several polypep-tides in addition to the M_r 145 000 protein (arrowheads; Mg-P_5 fraction). This preparation contains large amounts of actin (*a*; for morphological comparison see Fig. 19B–D). Lanes a, b, d, e, each lane contains protein corresponding to the residues from 70 extracted nuclear contents. Lane c, reference proteins (dots): β-galactosidase (M_r 120 000) and BSA (M_r 68 000). Lane f, reference proteins (dots): β-galactosidase, phosphorylase a (M_r 94 000), BSA and actin (M_r 42 000).

Fig. 18. Effect of 10 mM-$MgCl_2$ on protein composition of fraction S_1 of nuclear contents from *X. laevis* oocytes (SDS/PAGE, Coomassie Blue staining). Lane a, protein corres-ponding to the supernatant from 50 nuclear contents (S_1). Lane b, little protein is pelleted in the S_1 fraction (50 nuclear contents) when the incubation (15 min) was performed in IM without $MgCl_2$ (control experiments). Lane c, when $MgCl_2$ (final concentration 10 mM) was added to the S_1 fraction (50 nuclear contents) and incubated for 15 min large amounts of actin appear in a pelletable form. Lane d, actin (*a*) from rabbit skeletal muscle (M_r 42 000).

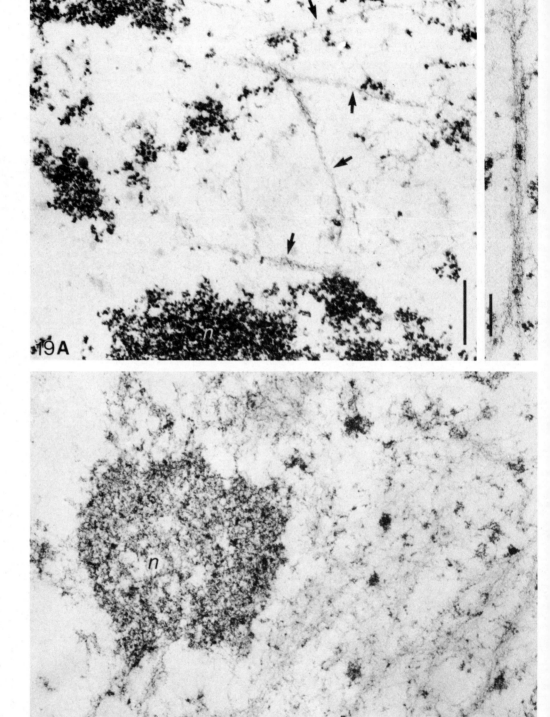

Figs 19A, B. For legend see p. 182.

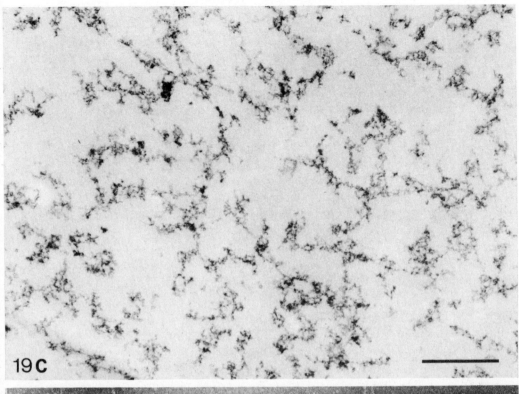

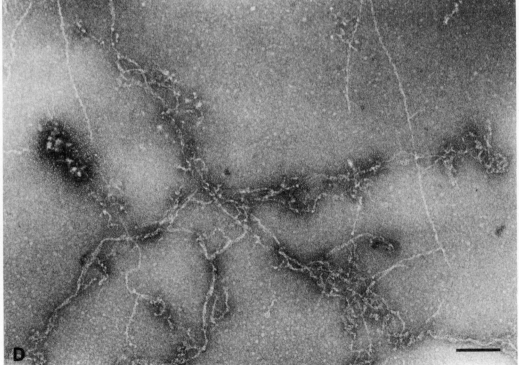

Figs 19c, D. For legend see p. 182.

In contrast, when the nuclear contents are isolated in the presence of $MgCl_2$ large amounts of filament bundles, most probably actin, are found in addition to the nucleolar structures and the nucleoplasmic bodies described above. These filament bundles are not solubilized when $MgCl_2$-treated pellets of nuclear contents are washed in IM with EDTA (Fig. 19A). When pellets of nuclear material obtained after isolation in IM plus $MgCl_2$ are washed with buffer containing EDTA and then further incubated in high salt/Triton buffer (HS-T) the residue fraction (Mg-P_5) consists of a fibrogranular network in which compact residual nucleoli and residual MFBs are embedded (Fig. 19B–D; for the appearance of nucleolar karyoskeleton structures prepared without additions of $MgCl_2$ see Fig. 5, and Franke *et al.* 1981*a*).

These results demonstrate that the biochemical composition and structural appearance of residual fractions obtained after treatment with high salt buffers can depend on the specific ions present in the initial isolation medium. Apparently, addition of divalent cations can induce certain soluble proteins to be included in insoluble aggregates. Our results show that the large nucleus of the oocyte does not contain a considerable internal nuclear matrix when all isolation steps are carried out in isolation media consisting of approximately physiological concentrations of ions.

CONCLUDING REMARKS

Nuclei contain topologically defined 'insoluble' substructures arranged in filaments, membrane-associated layers and more complex structures such as pore complex subunits, which together constitute a nuclear architectural system that we call 'karyoskeleton'.

Our results from amphibian oocytes, together with observations made on diverse somatic cells from diverse vertebrate species (e.g. see Gerace *et al.* 1978; Krohne *et al.* 1978*a,b*, 1984), indicate that the karyoskeletal elements are not distributed throughout the nucleus but constitute specific structural domains such as pore complexes, peripheral lamina and the nucleolar cortex. The data available so far further suggest that these elements form as polymers of proteins of relatively simple composition, which assemble and disassemble in relation to cellular functions such as mitosis (for lamina proteins see also Gerace & Blobel, 1980, 1982; Jost & Johnson, 1983).

The large nucleus of the amphibian oocyte provides a particularly simple system for the study of karyoskeletal elements. It contains only two major polypeptides in the

---

Fig. 19. A. Electron micrograph showing nuclear content material from *X. laevis* oocytes isolated in IM containing 10 mM-$MgCl_2$. In addition to nucleoli (*n*) and MFBs a large number of microfilament bundles are visible (arrows). Insert on the right margin: higher magnification showing a microfilament bundle. B,C. Electron micrographs of ultrathin sections through the Mg-P_5 fraction (see Fig. 17, lane d, for biochemical comparison). Oocyte nuclear contents were isolated in IM containing 10 mM-$MgCl_2$, washed in buffer containing 5 mM-EDTA, and then extracted with HS-T buffer. Compact residual nucleoli (*n* in B) are seen besides an extended fibrogranular meshwork. D. Negative staining of Mg-P_5 fraction, demonstrating the fibrogranular nature of the residual material, including long 5–6 nm filaments. Bars: A–C, 0·5 μm; insert in A and D, 0·2 μm.

structures insoluble in high salt concentrations and detergent: a protein of M_r 145 000, which is contained in filaments specific to the nucleolar cortex and the nucleoplasmic MFBs, and a polypeptide of M_r 68 000, which is the major constituent of the nuclear lamina–pore complex structure. This principle of mutually exclusive location illustrates the topological precision of localized assembly of these proteins and suggests that mechanisms of site-specific nucleation of polypeptide assembly must exist. In addition, some minor polypeptides can be found in the karyoskeletal residues; however, their location has not yet been established. Not all karyoskeletal structures may be resistant to treatment with salt concentrations higher than 1 M-NaCl or KCl. The example of the M_r 180 000 protein specifically located in the dense fibrillar component of the nucleolus shows that this high-salt-extractable proteins contributes to the formation of a specific non-chromatinous nuclear structure.

It is remarkable that the interior of such a large nucleus as that of the amphibian oocyte does not contain a more extensive fibrillar meshwork of an internal nuclear matrix resistant to extraction in high salt buffers. Of course, it cannot be excluded that minor insoluble structural elements may occur in this type of nucleus, such as 'scaffolding proteins' (see the article by Lewis *et al.* in this volume) in the axes of the diplotene lampbrush chromosomes, which are characteristic of these cells. However, our observations strongly suggest that the prominent functions of this nucleus such as transcription, processing and nucleocytoplasmic translocation of macromolecules, and nuclear protein storage, do not require the existence of an extensive nucleoplasmic matrix framework. We find this absence of an insoluble nuclear matrix in the oocyte nucleus a challenging situation in view of the numerous nuclear functions that are at present being discussed as associated with the internal nuclear matrix (see the article by D. Coffey in this issue).

We thank Dr Reimer Stick (Max Planck Institut für Entwichlungsbiologie, Tübingen, FRG) for the rabbit antibodies against chicken lamina proteins, Dr Elke Debus (Max Planck Institut für Biophysikalische Chemie, Göthingen, FRG) for antibody PKB8, and Jürgen Franz (this institute) for providing the peptide maps. We also thank Dr Pamela Cowin (this institute) for reading and correcting the manuscript. Ricardo Benavente was a stipendiate of the Alexander von Humboldt-Stiftung.

REFERENCES

AARONSON, R. P. & BLOBEL, G. (1975). Isolation of nuclear pore complexes in association with a lamina. *Proc. natn. Acad. Sci. U.S.A.* **72**, 1007–1011.

AGUTTER, P. S. & RICHARDSON, J. C. W. (1980). Nuclear non-chromatin proteinaceous structures: their role in the organization and function of the interphase nucleus. *J. Cell Sci.* **44**, 395–435.

ANDERTON, B. H. (1981). Intermediate filaments: a family of homologous structures. *J. Muscle Res. Cell Motil.* **2**, 141–166.

BENAVENTE, R., KROHNE, G., STICK, R. & FRANKE, W. W. (1984). Electron microscopic immunolocalization of a karyoskeletal protein of molecular weight 145,000 in nucleoli and perinucleolar bodies of *Xenopus laevis*. *Expl Cell Res.* **151**, 224–235.

BEREZNEY, R. (1984). Organization and functions of the nuclear matrix. In *Chromosomal Nonhistone Proteins*, vol. 4 (ed. L. S. Hnilica), pp. 119–180. Boca Raton: CRC Press.

BEREZNEY, R. & COFFEY, D. S. (1974). Identification of a nuclear protein matrix. *Biochem. biophys. Res. Commun.* **60**, 1410–1417.

BEREZNEY, R. & COFFEY, D. S. (1977). Nuclear matrix. *J. Cell Biol.* **73**, 616–637.

BERNHARD, W. (1971). Drug-induced changes in the interphase nucleus. In *Advances in Cyto-pharmacology*, vol. 1 (ed. F. Clementini & B. Ceccarelli), pp. 49–67. New York: Raven Press.

BOUTEILLE, M., BOUVIER, D. & SEVE, A. P. (1983). Heterogeneity and territorial organization of the nuclear matrix and related structures. *Int. Rev. Cytol.* **83**, 135–182.

BOWEN, B., STEINBERG, J., LAEMMLI, U. K. & WEINTRAUB, H. (1980). The detection of DNA-binding proteins by protein blotting. *Nucl. Acids Res.* **8**, 1–20.

BUONGIORNO-NARDELLI, M., AMALDI, F. & LAVA-SANCHEZ, P. A. (1972). Amplification as a rectification mechanism for the redundant rRNA genes. *Nature, new Biol.* **238**, 134–137.

BURKE, B., TOOZE, J. & WARREN, G. (1983). A monoclonal antibody which recognizes each of the nuclear lamin polypeptides in mammalian cells. *EMBO J.* **2**, 361–367.

COMINGS, D. E. & PETERS, K. E. (1981). Two dimensional gel electrophoresis of nuclear particles. In *The Cell Nucleus*, vol. 9 (ed. H. Busch), pp. 89–118. New York: Academic Press.

COWIN, P. & GARROD, D. R. (1983). Antibodies to epithelial desmosomes show wide tissue and species cross-reactivity. *Nature, Lond.* **302**, 148–150.

DUMONT, J. N. (1972). Oogenesis in *Xenopus laevis* (Daudin). I. Stages of oocyte development in laboratory maintained animals. *J. Morph.* **136**, 153–180.

ELDER, J. H., PICKETT, R. A., HAMPTON, J. & LERNER, R. A. (1977). Radioiodination of proteins in single polyacrylamide slices. *J. biol. Chem.* **252**, 6510–6515.

ELY, S., D'ARCY, A. & JOST, E. (1978). Interaction of antibodies against nuclear envelope-associated proteins from rat liver nuclei with rodent and human cells. *Expl Cell Res.* **116**, 325–331.

FRANKE, W. W. (1974). Structure, biochemistry, and function of the nuclear envelope. *Int. Rev. Cytol.* **4** (suppl.), 71–236.

FRANKE, W. W., KLEINSCHMIDT, J. A., SPRING, H., KROHNE, G., GRUND, C., TRENDELEN-BURG, M.·F., STOEHR, M. & SCHEER, U. (1981*a*). A nucleolar skeleton of protein filaments demonstrated in amplified nucleoli of *Xenopus laevis*. *J. Cell Biol.* **90**, 289–299.

FRANKE, W. W., MOLL, R., SCHILLER, D. L., SCHMID, E., KARTENBECK, J. & MUELLER, H. (1982*a*). Desmoplakins of epithelial and myocardial desmosomes are immunologically related. *Differentiation* **23**, 115–127.

FRANKE, W. W. & SCHEER, U. (1970). The ultrastructure of the nuclear envelope of amphibian oocytes: a reinvestigation. *J. Ultrastruct. Res.* **30**, 288–316.

FRANKE, W. W., SCHEER, U., KROHNE, G. & JARASCH, E.-D. (1981*b*). The nuclear envelope and the architecture of the nuclear periphery. *J. Cell Biol.* **91**, 39s–50s.

FRANKE, W. W., SCHEER, U., SPRING, H., TRENDELENBURG, M. F. & ZENTGRAF, H. (1979*a*). Organization of nucleolar chromatin. In *The Cell Nucleus*, vol. 7 (ed. H. Busch), pp. 49–95. New York: Academic Press.

FRANKE, W. W., SCHMID, E., GRUND, C., MUELLER, H., ENGELBRECHT, I., MOLL, R., STADLER, J. & JARASCH, E.-D. (1981*c*). Antibodies to high molecular weight polypeptides of desmosomes: specific localization of a class of junctional proteins in cells and tissues. *Differentiation* **20**, 217–241.

FRANKE, W. W., SCHMID, E., OSBORN, M. & WEBER, K. (1978). Different intermediate-sized filaments distinguished by immunofluorescence microscopy. *Proc. natn. Acad. Sci. U.S.A.* **75**, 5034–5038.

FRANKE, W. W., SCHMID, E., SCHILLER, D. L., WINTER, S., JARASCH, E.-D., MOLL, R., DENK, H., JACKSON, B. W. & ILLMENSEE, K. (1982*b*). Differentiation-related patterns of expression of proteins of intermediate-sized filaments in tissue and cultured cells. *Cold Spring Harbor Symp. quant. Biol.* **46**, 431–453.

FRANKE, W. W., SCHMID, E., WINTER, S., OSBORN, M. & WEBER, K. (1979*b*). Widespread occurrence of intermediate-sized filaments of vimentin-type in cultured cells from diverse vertebrates. *Expl Cell Res.* **123**, 633–654.

GERACE, L. & BLOBEL, G. (1980). The nuclear envelope lamina is reversibly depolymerised during mitosis. *Cell* **19**, 277–287.

GERACE, L. & BLOBEL, G. (1982). Nuclear lamina and the structural organization of the nuclear envelope. *Cold Spring Harbor Symp. quant. Biol.* **46**, 967–978.

GERACE, L., BLUM, A. & BLOBEL, G. (1978). Immunocytochemical localization of the major polypeptides of the pore complex–lamina fraction. Interphase and mitotic distribution. *J. Cell Biol.* **79**, 546–566.

GERACE, L., OTTAVIANO, Y. & KONDOR-KOCH, C. (1982). Identification of a major polypeptide of the nuclear pore complex. *J. Cell Biol.* **95**, 826–837.

GIGI, O., GEIGER, B., ESHHAR, Z., MOLL, R., SCHMID, E., WINTER, S., SCHILLER, D. L. & FRANKE, W. W. (1982). Detection of a cytokeratin determinant common to diverse epithelial cells by a broadly cross-reacting monoclonal antibody. *EMBO J.* **1**, 1429–1437.

ISHIKAWA, A., BISCHOFF, R. & HOLTZER, H. (1968). Mitosis and intermediate-sized filaments in developing skeletal muscle. *J. Cell Biol.* **38**, 538–555.

JOST, E. & JOHNSON, R. T. (1983). New patterns of nuclear lamina induced by cell fusion. *Eur. J. Cell Biol.* **30**, 295–304.

KAUFMANN, S. H., COFFEY, D. S. & SHAPER, J. H. (1981). Considerations in the isolation of rat liver nuclear matrix, nuclear envelope, and pore complex–lamina. *Expl Cell Res.* **132**, 105–123.

KAUFMANN, S. H., GIBSON, W. & SHAPER, J. H. (1983). Characterization of the major polypeptides of rat liver nuclear envelope. *J. biol. Chem.* **258**, 2710–2719.

KÖHLER, G. & MILSTEIN, C. (1975). Continuous cultures of fused cells secreting antibody of predefined specificity. *Nature, Lond.* **256**, 495–497.

KROHNE, G., DABAUVALLE, M. C. & FRANKE, W. W. (1981). Cell type-specific differences in protein composition of nuclear pore complex–lamina structures in oocytes and erythrocytes of *Xenopus laevis.* *J. molec. Biol.* **151**, 121–141.

KROHNE, G., DEBUS, E., OSBORN, M., WEBER, K. & FRANKE, W. W. (1984). A monoclonal antibody against nuclear lamina proteins reveals cell type-specificity in *Xenopus laevis. Expl Cell Res.* **150**, 47–59.

KROHNE, G. & FRANKE, W. W. (1983). Proteins of pore complex–lamina structures from nuclei and nuclear membranes. In *Methods in Enzymology*, vol. 96 (ed. S. Fleischer & B. Fleischer), pp. 597–608. New York: Academic Press.

KROHNE, G., FRANKE, W. W., ELY, S., D'ARCY, A. & JOST, E. (1978a). Localization of a nuclear envelope-associated protein by indirect immunofluorescence microscopy using antibodies against a major polypeptide from rat liver fractions enriched in nuclear envelope associated material. *Cytobiologie* **18**, 22–38.

KROHNE, G., FRANKE, W. W. & SCHEER, U. (1978b). The major polypeptides of the nuclear pore complex. *Expl Cell Res.* **116**, 85–102.

KROHNE, G., STICK, R., KLEINSCHMIDT, J. A., MOLL, R., FRANKE, W. W. & HAUSEN, P. (1982). Immunological localization of a major karyoskeletal protein in nucleoli of oocytes and somatic cells of *Xenopus laevis. J. Cell Biol.* **94**, 749–754.

LAEMMLI, U. K. (1970). Cleavage of structural proteins during the assembly of the head of bacteriophage T4. *Nature, Lond.* **277**, 680–685.

LAM, K. S. & KASPER, C. B. (1979). Electrophoretic analysis of three major nuclear envelope polypeptides. *J. biol. Chem.* **254**, 11713–11720.

LAZARIDES, E. (1982). Intermediate filaments: a chemically heterogeneous, developmentally regulated class of proteins. *A. Rev. Biochem.* **51**, 219–250.

MAUL, G. G. & AVDALOVIC, N. (1980). Nuclear envelope from *Spisula solidissima* germinal vesicles. *Expl Cell Res.* **130**, 229–240.

MCKEON, F. D., TUFFANELLI, D. L., FUKUYAMA, K. & KIRSCHNER, M. W. (1983). Autoimmune response directed against conserved determinants of nuclear envelope proteins in a patient with linear scleroderma. *Proc. natn. Acad. Sci. U.S.A.* **80**, 4374–4378.

MORENO DIAZ DE LA ESPINA, S., FRANKE, W. W., KROHNE, G., TRENDELENBURG, M. F., GRUND, C. & SCHEER, U. (1982). Medusoid fibril bodies: a novel type of nuclear filament of diameter 8 to 12 nm with periodic ultrastructure demonstrated in oocytes of *Xenopus laevis. Eur. J. Cell Biol.* **27**, 141–150.

MUELLER, H. & FRANKE, W. W. (1983). Biochemical and immunological characterization of desmoplakins I and II, the major polypeptides of the desmosomal plaque. *J. molec. Biol.* **163**, 647–671.

OCHS, R., LISCHWE, M., O'LEARY, P. & BUSCH, H. (1983). Localization of nucleolar phosphoproteins B23 and C23 during mitosis. *Expl Cell Res.* **146**, 139–149.

O'FARRELL, P. Z., GOODMAN, H. M. & O'FARRELL, P. H. (1977). High resolution two-dimensional electrophoresis of basic as well as acidic proteins. *Cell* **12**, 1133–1142.

SCHEER, U., KARTENBECK, J., TRENDELENBURG, M. F., STADLER, J. & FRANKE, W. W. (1976). Experimental desintegration of the nuclear envelope. Evidence for pore-connecting fibrils. *J. Cell Biol.* **69**, 1–18.

SCHEER, U. & ROSE, K. M. (1984). Localization of RNA polymerase I in interphase cells and mitotic chromosomes by light and electron microscopy immunocytochemistry. *Proc. natn. Acad. Sci. U.S.A.* **81**, 1431–1435.

SCHMIDT-ZACHMANN, M. S., HÜGLE, B., SCHEER, U. & FRANKE, W. W. (1984). Identification and localization of a novel nucleolar protein of high molecular weight by a monoclonal antibody. *Expl Cell Res.* **153**, 327–346.

SHELTON, K. R., HIGGINS, L. L., COCHRAN, D. L., RUFFOLO, J. L. & EGLE, P. M. (1980). Nuclear lamins of erythrocyte and liver. *J. biol. Chem.* **255**, 10978–10983.

STICK, R. & HAUSEN, P. (1980). Immunological analysis of nuclear lamina proteins. *Chromosoma* **80**, 219–236.

STICK, R. & KROHNE, G. (1982). Immunological localization of the major architectural protein associated with the nuclear envelope of the *Xenopus laevis* oocyte. *Expl Cell Res.* **138**, 319–330.

SWITZER, R. C., MERRIL, C. R. & SHIFRIN, S. (1979). A highly sensitive silver stain for detecting protein and polypeptides in polyacrylamide gels. *Analyt. Biochem.* **98**, 231–237.

THOMAS, J. O. & KORNBERG, R. D. (1975). An octamer of histones in chromatin and free in solution. *Proc. natn. Acad. Sci. U.S.A.* **72**, 2626–2630.

TOWBIN, H., STAEHELIN, T. & GORDON, J. (1979). Electrophoretic transfer of proteins from polyacrylamide gels to nitrocellulose sheets: procedure and some applications. *Proc. natn. Acad. Sci. U.S.A.* **76**, 4350–4354.

VANDEKERCKHOVE, J., FRANKE, W. W. & WEBER, K. (1981). Diversity of expression of non-muscle actin in amphibia. *J. molec. Biol.* **152**, 413–426.

VAN EEKELEN, C. A. G., SALDEN, M. H. L., HABETS, W. J. A., VAN DE PUTTE, L. B. A. & VAN VENROOIJ, W. J. (1982). On the existence of an internal nuclear protein structure in HeLa cells. *Expl Cell Res.* **141**, 181–190.

J. Cell Sci. Suppl. 1, 187–201 (1984)
Printed in Great Britain © The Company of Biologists Limited 1984

NUCLEAR PROTEINS THAT BECOME PART OF THE MITOTIC APPARATUS: A ROLE IN NUCLEAR ASSEMBLY?

D. E. PETTIJOHN, M. HENZL* AND C. PRICE

Department of Biochemistry, Biophysics and Genetics, University of Colorado Health Science Center, Denver, Colorado 80262, U.S.A.

SUMMARY

A structure located at the poles of the mitotic spindle is described, which may function as a centre for post-mitotic nuclear assembly. Evidence in support of this function is incomplete, but comes from two different kinds of experiments, which are reviewed here. First, fluorescence microscopy studies show that mitotic chromosomes at telophase or late anaphase are drawn into juxtaposition with this polar structure and second, the structure is made up in part of a non-histone chromosomal protein that in interphase cells can be detected only in the nucleus. Studies of this nuclear–mitotic apparatus protein (NuMA protein) are reported here. Monoclonal antibodies specific for the NuMA protein have been used in immunofluorescence studies to visualize the prenucleus-like polar structure and to identify the NuMA protein by immunoblotting after electrophoretic separation. The NuMA protein is a non-histone chromosomal protein of molecular weight 250 000 relative to standard protein molecular weight markers in sodium dodecyl sulphate/polyacrylamide gel electrophoresis. Experiments are described that indicate several difficulties in studying the possible affinity and association of NuMA protein with mitotic chromosomes. Metaphase chromosomes isolated by the polyamine procedure of Lewis and Laemmli have bound NuMA protein detectable by immunofluorescence or by immunoblotting, but measurements made at different stages of chromosome purification show that most of the NuMA protein is separated from the chromosomes using this purification procedure. Chromosomes purified from mixtures of human and Chinese hamster cells (the latter have none of the human form of NuMA recognized by a monoclonal antibody) have human NuMA protein bound to the hamster chromosomes. Results suggest that in cell extracts exchange reactions of NuMA protein can occur, which must be avoided in the study of its natural function.

INTRODUCTION

Within the past four years a new class of nuclear protein has been identified, which is distinguished from other nuclear proteins by its unusual localization in mitotic cells. During mitosis most of the known nuclear proteins either become part of the mitotic chromosomes or are freely dispersed in the cytoplasm of mitotic cells (for examples, see Smith *et al.* 1978; Gerace & Blobel, 1980). The new protein called nuclear–mitotic apparatus protein (NuMA protein) can be specifically associated with the spindle and particularly with the poles of the mitotic apparatus. The function of this class of protein is not established, but certain of its properties have led us to postulate that it may have a role in post-mitotic nuclear assembly (Lyderson & Pettijohn, 1980;

*Present address: Department of Chemistry, New Mexico State University, Las Cruces, New Mexico.

CEL (S) 1

Van Ness & Pettijohn, 1983). In this article we will briefly review what is known about the NuMA protein and present new data relating to its properties and function.

MATERIALS AND METHODS

Cells and cell culture

HeLa S3 (CCL 2.2) and Chinese hamster ovary CHO-K1 (CCL 61) cells were grown in RMPI 1640 media supplemented with 7·5 % (w/v) foetal calf serum. For preparations of chromosomes or proteins requiring large numbers of cells, the cells were grown in spinner culture to a density of about 5×10^5 cells/ml. Other cultures were grown attached to plastic dishes. Proteins radiolabelled with [^{35}S]methionine were prepared by growing cells in plastic dishes and when cells were nearly confluent media was removed and replaced with methionine-free RPMI 1640 supplemented with 3–20 μCi/ml [^{35}S]methionine (Amersham); growth was then continued for 8–20 h.

Electrophoresis of non-histone chromosomal proteins

Nuclei were purified essentially as described (Lydersen, Kao & Pettijohn, 1980) with 1 mm-dithiothreitol (DTT) and 0·2 mm-phenylmethylsulphonyl fluoride (PMSF) included during Dounce homogenization and centrifugation steps. Nuclei were resuspended in buffer A (0·5 mm-CaCl$_2$ plus 0·1 mm-1,4-piperazine diethanesulphonic acid, pH 6·5) also containing 0·5 % NP40, 0·5 % Triton, 1 mm DTT and 0·2 mm-PMSF and centrifuged for 2500 rev./min in a Sorvall HB-4 rotor at 4 °C. They were then resuspended and washed twice in the same buffer without detergent and finally resuspended in a solution containing 0·05 m-Tris (pH 7·5), 2 mm-MgCl$_2$, 2 mm-CaCl$_2$, 1 mm-DTT and 0·2 mm-PMSF. After centrifuging as above, they were resuspended in the same buffer solution and sonicated with 5·5-s bursts at the top power setting of a Kontes sonicator. DNAase I was added to 50 μg/ml, the mixture was held on ice for 45 min, then sodium dodecyl sulphate (SDS) was added to a final concentration of 0·5 % and the mixture was heated to 97 °C for 5 min. Parts of the mixture were analysed by electrophoresis on SDS/polyacrylamide gel as described by Laemmli (1970). In cases where enhanced resolution of large non-histone chromosomal (NHC) proteins was required, gradient gels of 5 % to 8 % (w/v) polyacrylamide were used. Marker proteins of known molecular weight electrophoresed in a separate lane of the same gel were: thyroglobulin (330 000M_r), large subunit of ferritin (220 000M_r), bovine serum albumin (67 000M_r), catalase (60 000M_r) and lactate dehydrogenase (36 000M_r).

Indirect immunofluorescence microscopy

Cells were grown attached on polylysine-coated 8-well glass slides (Cell Line Assoc.). They were paraformaldehyde/acetone-fixed, treated first with primary mouse antibody then with fluorescein isothiocyanate-conjugated goat anti-mouse immunoglobulin G (IgG) and observed with a Leitz microscope equipped with epi-fluorescence as described (Van Ness & Pettijohn, 1983). Incubation with antibodies was carried out in 30- to 50-μl drops added to the wells containing fixed cells. Isolated metaphase chromosomes were centrifuged onto polylysine-coated coverslips and fixed with paraformaldehyde, then incubated with anti-NuMa monoclonal antibodies and secondary fluorescent antibody as above. In all cases controls in which primary antibody was omitted were carried out in parallel. Such controls for all the immunofluorescence photomicrographs shown here had negligible fluorescence compared to that observed in the experimental observation.

Immunoblot analysis

After electrophoresis, proteins were transferred electrophoretically to nitrocellulose sheets in the presence of SDS according to Towbin, Staehlin & Gordon (1979) as modified by Erickson, Minier & Lasher (1982). The nitrocellulose sheet was washed twice in a tray with two changes of phosphate-buffered saline (PBS) solution containing 0·05 % Tween and then incubated at room temperature for 3 h with agitation, in a sealed plastic bag containing the same buffered Tween solution, plus 25 % foetal calf serum, plus either 25 % spent hybridoma media supernatant containing a monoclonal antibody or a 1/100 to 1/500 dilution of serum containing anti-NuMA polyclonal antibodies. The sheet was then washed for 30 min with two changes of PBS/Tween as before and incubated for 2 h at room temperature in a PBS/Tween mixture containing 25 % foetal calf serum plus a 1/1000 dilution of peroxidase-conjugated goat anti-mouse IgG (Cappel). After washing 3 times in PBS/ Tween and finally in a solution containing 0·05 M-Tris (pH 7·5), the sheet was developed in a solution containing 0·05 M-Tris (pH 7·5), 12·5 μg/ml 3,3'-diaminobenzidine and 0·003 % H_2O_2. Reaction was stopped by replacing the developer with water.

Monoclonal antibodies and polyclonal sera

Anti-NuMa polyclonal antibodies were prepared as described previously (Lydersen & Pettijohn, 1980). Hybridoma production, cloning and preparation of anti-NuMA monoclonal antibodies were as described (Van Ness & Pettijohn, 1983).

Isolation of metaphase chromosomes

Metaphase chromosomes were isolated from HeLa and Chinese hamster ovary (CHO) cells by a modification of the polyamine method described by Lewis & Laemmli (1982). We thank U. Laemmli for the generous hospitality of his laboratory and personal instruction to one of us (D.E.P.). Details of the buffers used in this procedure are given at the end of this section. Approximately 2×10^8 cells were arrested in metaphase by the addition of colcemid, to a final concentration of 0·06 μg/ml, for 15 h. A mitotic index of 80 % of HeLa and 60 % for CHO cells was obtained when the colcemid was added to spinner cultures of logarithmically growing cells. The mitotic cells were harvested and washed twice in buffer PC1. Lysis of the cells was effected by gently douncing the cells in the lysis buffer PC2. This and all subsequent steps were performed at 4 °C. Nuclei were not disrupted by this procedure and were removed by centrifuging at 300 g for 10 min. The chromosome preparations were layered on step gradients constructed in 50-ml centrifuge tubes. The composition of the step gradients is given below. To avoid aggregation of the chromosomes, the chromosomes from not more than 5×10^7 cells were layered on one gradient. The step gradients were centrifuged at 650 g for 15 min. The chromosomes sedimented to the boundary of the two lower steps. The solution above the chromosomes was drawn off and discarded. The chromosome-containing fractions were pooled, the spermine and spermidine concentrations were doubled and the chromosome suspensions were re-homogenized. The chromosome suspension was layered over a Percoll-containing solution (PC4) and centrifuged at 43 500 g for 30 min. The chromosomes banded near the bottom of the tube. The solution above the chromosomes was removed; this portion of the gradient contained much aggregated material. The chromosome suspension was diluted with buffer PC5 and the chromosomes were sedimented at 700 g for 40 min. The chromosomes were resuspended in a small volume of PC5 plus 0·1 % digitonin. At this stage the chromosomes were stable and the tendency to aggregate (as determined by microscopy) was minimal.

Chromosome isolation buffers: all buffers contained 0·1 mM-PMSF, 10 KI units/ml Aprotenin, 1 mM-thiodiglycol. PC1: 7·5 mM-Tris (pH 7·4), 0·1 mM-spermine, 0·25 mM-spermidine, 40 mM-KCl, 1·0 mM-EDTA. PC2: 15 mM-Tris (pH 7·4), 0·2 mM-spermidine, 2·0 mM-EDTA, 80 mM-KCl, 0·1 % digitonin, 10 μg/ml RNase A. Step gradient solutions: (1) 60 % Percoll, 10 % glycerol, 5 mM-Tris (pH 7·4), 2 mM-spermidine, 0·8 mM-spermine, 2 mM-EDTA, 2 mM-KCl, 0·01 % digitonin; (2) 15 % glycerol, 2 mM-Tris (pH 7·4), 2 mM-spermidine, 0·8 mM-spermine, 2 mM-EDTA, 2 mM-KCl, 0·01 % digitonin; (3) 10 % glycerol, 5 mM-Tris (pH 7·4), 0·25 mM-spermidine, 2 mM-EDTA, 2 mM-KCl, 0·1 % digitonin. Percoll solution PC4: 65 % Percoll, 2 M-Tris (pH 7·4), 0·8 mM-spermine, 2·0 mM-spermidine, 2 mM-EDTA, 0·1 % digitonin. PC5: 5 mM-Tris (pH 7·4), 0·25 mM-spermidine, 2·0 mM-EDTA, 2 mM-KCl, 0·01 % digitonin.

Fractionation of anti-NuMA antibodies in polyclonal sera

High molecular weight HeLa NHC proteins (size range 200 000 to about 500 000) were separated from smaller proteins on an agarose bead column (Bio-Gel A5m – Biorad) as described previously (Lydersen & Pettijohn, 1980). The proteins were concentrated in an Amicon pressure filtration apparatus and further fractionated by electrophoresis on a gradient SDS/5 % to 8 % polyacrylamide gel as described above. Proteins were electrophoretically transferred to DPT paper (Bittner, Kupferer & Morris, 1980), and part of the paper was cut away for immunoblotting using the 2E4 monoclonal antibody to identify the 250 000 M_r NuMA protein. Procedures for this immunoblotting were exactly as described by Symington, Green & Brackman (1981). The stained protein was fitted back into the remainder of the blot to identify other parts of the DPT paper containing the unreacted $250\,000\,M_r$ NuMA protein, and that part of the paper was excised as well as sections containing proteins larger than the NuMA protein. These paper strips were then reacted with 1-ml samples of $1/150$ diluted mouse sera obtained from mice immunized with the partially purified $300\,000\,M_r$ human NHC protein. Thus antibodies specific for protein attached to the DPT paper were absorbed out of the serum (Olmsted, 1981). To elute antibody from the DPT paper the strip was incubated with $200\,\mu l$ $0.2\,M$-glycine·HCl (pH 2.8) plus $10\,\%$ dioxane for 1 h, then the solution was separated from the paper and neutralized. The eluted antibodies as well as the absorbed sera were analysed in other immunoblotting experiments to define the specificity of the fractionated antibody and to visualize by immunofluorescence the localization of antigens in cells. For example, sera depleted of antibodies to NuMA protein by incubating with the insoluble $250\,000\,M_r$ NHC protein no longer gave an immunoblot reaction with the NuMA protein, but did with larger NHC proteins.

RESULTS AND DISCUSSION

Identification of NuMA protein

Initial interest in the NuMA protein came about from studies of non-histone chromosomal protein unique to human cells (Lydersen *et al.* 1980; Lydersen & Pettijohn, 1980). Electrophoretic separation of nuclear proteins from different cell types had revealed a prominent high molecular weight protein (about 300 000 in solvents containing SDS) present in all human cell types that were examined but absent in cells of other mammals (Fig. 1). This large protein was purified to the point where only trace contaminants could be observed in electrophoretic analysis and the purified protein was used to raise polyclonal antibodies in mice. Immunoprecipitation experiments showed that these sera precipitated the $300\,000\,M_r$ NHC protein specifically, so it was concluded that the sera were monospecific for the large NHC protein. Immunofluorescence studies of fixed human cells using these sera showed that the antibodies reacted exclusively with nuclear components in interphase cells and the poles of the mitotic apparatus in mitotic cells (Lydersen & Pettijohn, 1980). Moreover, non-human cells lacking the $300\,000\,M_r$ protein did not react with the antibodies nor could protein be immunoprecipitated from non-human cells. These immunofluorescence experiments identified a nuclear antigen (defined as NuMA antigen), which became part of the mitotic apparatus during mitosis and seemed to indicate that this antigen was the rather abundant $300\,000\,M_r$ human specific NHC protein.

Subsequent studies have used monoclonal antibodies made from splenocytes of mice, which had been immunized with the same partially purified high molecular weight (300 000) nuclear protein (Van Ness & Pettijohn, 1983). Recently these monoclonal antibodies have enabled more precise identification of the NuMA antigen. Hybridomas were screened using immunofluorescence techniques to detect those secreting mouse antibodies specific for the nucleus of human cells, and which bound the mitotic apparatus of metaphase cells. A group of such hybridomas were identified and cloned, and antibodies were obtained in both ascites fluid and supernatant media. Antibodies from eight distinct hybridomas have been studied that seem to react with the same antigen. These are referred to as the 2E4-type monoclonal antibody. The immunofluorescence pattern obtained with fixed permeabilized HeLa cells using one

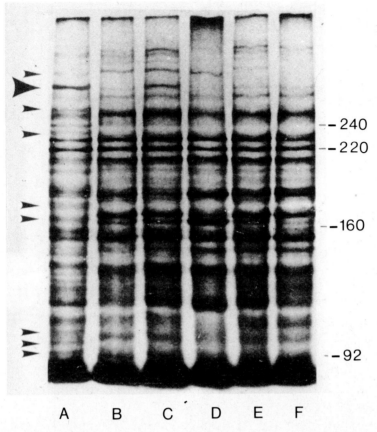

Fig. 1. Electrophoresis of high molecular weight nuclear proteins of different mammalian cells and cell hybrids. Nuclei were isolated from: lanes A, human (HeLa); B, hamster (CHO); and C through F, several human/hamster hybrids, which had been grown with [^{35}S]methionine to label proteins. The nuclear proteins were solubilized in 0·3 % SDS, DNA was removed, and the proteins were separated by electrophoresis in different lanes of a slab polyacrylamide gel containing SDS. An autoradiogram of the gel is shown. Only proteins of molecular weight greater than 90 000 are resolved, smaller proteins were deliberately allowed to pass through the gel. The large arrowhead indicates the largest abundant NHC protein present in human cells and in some hybrid cells (depending on their content of human chromosomes), but not in CHO cells. Smaller arrowheads denote other apparently human-specific NHC proteins (see Lydersen *et al.* 1979). Numbers on the right show positions of stained molecular weight markers ($\times 10^{-3}$) in the same gel (see Materials and Methods). (Reproduced from Lydersen *et al.* 1980.)

of these antibodies (an IgG$_1$ subclass) is shown in Fig. 2. The other seven give indistinguishable immunofluorescence, which is also similar to that previously seen using the anti-NuMA sera. In the metaphase cell seen in the centre of the field the poles of the mitotic apparatus are prominently fluorescent, while the nuclei of inter-phase cells scattered about the mitotic cell are fluorescent. As previously reported the fluorescence at the mitotic poles is coincident with the poles observed directly by phase-contrast or differential interference contrast microscopy (Van Ness & Pettijohn, 1983). There is no fluorescence detectable above background in the cytoplasm, associated with cytoplasmic microtubules in interphase cells, or on the intercellular bridge of telophase cells (see also Lydersen & Pettijohn, 1980), showing that the 2E4 antigen is different from proteins known to be microtubule-associated (MAPs).

Electrophoretic separations of NHC proteins were designed to resolve the largest proteins better and were combined with immunoblot analysis to investigate more precisely which protein reacts with the spindle-pole-specific monoclonal antibodies (Fig. 3). In this experiment total nuclear ^{35}S-labelled proteins from HeLa and CHO cells were resolved in separate lanes of the same gel so that the major $300\,000\,M_r$ human NHC protein present in the former but absent in the latter could be unambiguously identified by autoradiography. It was then possible to compare directly an immunoblot of the same gel after reaction with 2E4 antibody to identify its NuMA antigen. This analysis clearly showed that the monoclonal antibody does *not* react with the major $300\,000\,M_r$ protein previously thought to be the NuMA protein, but rather with a somewhat smaller protein with a molecular weight of about $250\,000$. Since the proteins analysed in the immunoblot were the same as those analysed by autoradiography, the possibility that the $250\,000\,M_r$ antigen is a degradation product

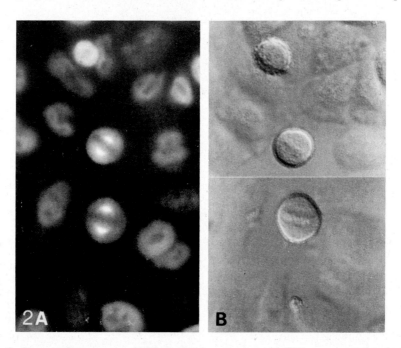

Fig. 2. Immunofluorescence of HeLa cells after reaction with 2E4-type monoclonal antibody. Cells growing attached to a glass slide were fixed with paraformaldehyde, rinsed with PBS, permeabilized with acetone, rinsed again and incubated first with antibody 2E4, then with fluorescein-conjugated goat anti-mouse IgG, all as previously described (Van Ness & Pettijohn, 1983). Cells were photographed through a Leitz microscope equipped with epi-fluorescence. A. Immunofluorescence; B, differential interference contrast microscopy of the same cells as in A (only the mitotic cells are in focus but the more elongated interphase cells can be seen in background corresponding to the cells with fluorescent nuclei in A). ×400.

of the $300\,000\,M_r$ protein can be excluded. All other independently derived monoclonal antibodies that show the immunofluorescence pattern of Fig. 2 also react exclusively with the $250\,000\,M_r$ protein.

While these results indicate that the NuMA protein recognized by the panel of 2E4-type monoclonal antibodies is distinct from the $300\,000\,M_r$ protein, the possibility remains that the larger protein is also a NuMA-type protein bound at the spindle poles during mitosis. To investigate this possibility the polyclonal antibodies obtained by immunizing mice with the partially purified $300\,000\,M_r$ protein were fractionated, using methods described by Olmsted (1981), into antibody fractions binding the $250\,000\,M_r$ NuMA protein and fractions binding larger NHC proteins. Immunoblot

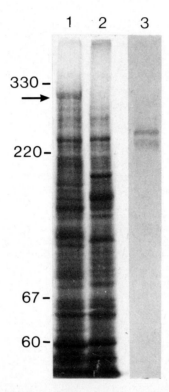

Fig. 3. Immunoblot of NuMA protein following electrophoresis. Nuclear proteins were solubilized from nuclei isolated from cells grown with [^{35}S]methionine and electrophoretically separated on a gradient 5 % to 8 % polyacrylamide/SDS gel as described in Materials and Methods. Proteins were then transferred to a nitrocellulose sheet and part of the sheet was analysed by autoradiography and part was reacted with 2E4 anti-NuMA monoclonal antibody followed by peroxidase-conjugated rabbit anti-mouse IgG to identify the NuMA antigen. Lanes 1 and 2 show the autoradiogram of [^{35}S]methionine-labelled HeLa and CHO nuclear proteins, respectively. Lane 3 is an immunoblot of the same HeLa proteins analysed in lane 1; the lower band is a degradation product of the higher occasionally seen in such analysis and also observed after incubation of the larger protein with trypsin (Price *et al.* 1984). The arrow on the left shows the prominent $300\,000\,M_r$ protein present in HeLa but absent from CHO nuclei. Markers denote position of ^{125}I-labelled molecular weight markers ($\times 10^{-3}$) detected on the same autoradiogram (see Materials and Methods).

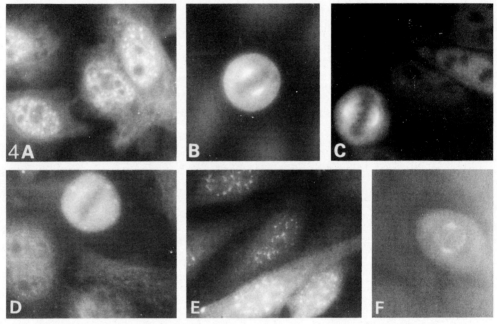

Fig. 4. Immunofluorescence photomicrographs of HeLa cells treated with antibodies from fractionated anti-NuMA protein sera. Sera from a mouse immunized with the purified 300 000 M_r human NHC protein was separated into fractions with antibodies specific for NHC proteins larger than the 250 000 M_r NuMA protein and fractions with antibodies specific for proteins of the size of the NuMA protein (see Materials and Methods). These antibodies were then applied to fixed, permeabilized HeLa cells and followed with fluorescein-conjugated goat anti-mouse IgG as in Fig. 2 to visualize the attachment sites of the primary antibody. A. Control interphase cells after reaction with total, unfractionated sera; B, a mitotic cell reacted with the total sera as in A; C, cells reacted with sera depleted of antibodies specific for NHC proteins in the range from 290 000 to 500 000 M_r; note the spindle pole fluorescence of the mitotic cell in the lower left is maintained, but the nuclear speckling has disappeared in the nucleus on the right; D and E, mitotic and interphase cells, respectively, after incubation with sera depleted of antibodies specific for NHC proteins of 250 000 ± 40 000; note that the spindle pole fluorescence is very faint, but that bright speckled nuclear fluorescence persists; F, a mitotic cell incubated with the recovered antibodies that had been absorbed out from the sera used in D and E (see Materials and Methods for details). ×500.

analysis of the polyclonal sera done by the method described for Fig. 3 showed that antibodies were present that recognize a protein having the same electrophoretic mobility as the 250 000 M_r 2E4 antigen as well as antibodies that recognize several larger proteins, including that having the mobility of the 300 000 M_r protein. When the polyclonal sera were depleted of antibodies reacting with the 250 000 M_r protein, the remaining antibodies assayed by immunofluorescence microscopy reacted with human nuclear antigens but not with the mitotic apparatus (Fig. 4). Sera depleted of antibodies reacting with NHC proteins larger than the 250 000 M_r NuMA protein continued to bind to spindle poles in mitotic cells, but in some cases the pattern of nuclear fluorescence was changed (compare Fig. 4A and C). Antibodies eluted from complexes with immobilized 250 000 M_r NuMA protein stained the spindle pole in mitotic cells while those eluted from proteins of higher molecular weight did not (C. Price, Ph.D. thesis, University of Colorado, in preparation). Thus this analysis failed to detect antibodies specific for the mitotic apparatus having specificity for any NHC protein except the 250 000 M_r NuMA antigen. However, studies from other laboratories have identified another NHC protein that seems to be distinct from the 250 000 M_r NuMA protein, yet is also a nuclear–mitotic apparatus protein (Izant, Weatherbee & McIntosh, 1982).

Attachment of NuMA protein to metaphase chromosomes

Previous immunofluorescence studies of human and other primate cells using 2E4 monoclonal antibodies demonstrated that the antibody could bind specifically to the mitotic chromosomes (Van Ness & Pettijohn, 1983). After fixing the mitotic cells using certain procedures, the chromosomes examined by the methods described for Fig. 2 were brightly fluorescent and few mitotic cells had fluorescent spindle poles. Cells fixed only with acetone or ethanol did not exhibit fluorescent chromosomes after binding 2E4 antibodies. In this case only mitotic spindle poles were fluorescent, while cells fixed with paraformaldehyde/acetone demonstrated a transition during which mitotic cells with initially fluorescent chromosomes gradually lost this chromosomal staining while acquiring fluorescent spindle poles. Control experiments showed that the transition was induced by the 2E4 antibody and was independent of other conditions of the immunofluorescence procedure. The results indicated that the 2E4 antibody might induce a dissociation of antigen from chromosomes and that the antigen–antibody complex subsequently bound specifically at spindle poles. The findings suggested that the NuMA protein could bind specifically to both chromosomes and mitotic spindle poles (the site of post-mitotic nuclear assembly) and led to the proposal that the NuMA protein could have dual binding sites involved in linking chromosomes into the assembling nucleus.

While the decoration of mitotic chromosomes with 2E4-type antibodies in fixed cells has been observed in many separate experiments over a three-year period, recently it has often not been reproducible. In the later case only the spindle poles of metaphase and anaphase cells attach the anti-NuMA monoclonal antibodies as shown in Fig. 2. Consistently in all experiments telophase chromosomes became fluorescent after application of NuMA-specific antibodies, although as noted previously (Van Ness & Pettijohn, 1983), the significance of this is not clear since at telophase the spindle poles and chromosomes are closely linked. This uncertainty has prompted the development of new experimental approaches to define the possible chromosomal attachment of NuMA protein.

Human metaphase chromosomes have been isolated from colcemid-treated HeLa cells and examined for reaction with a 2E4 monoclonal antibody specific for NuMA protein, using the immunofluorescence assay (Fig. 5). The metaphase chromosomes bound the antibody, indicating the presence of the 2E4 antigen. Chromosomes isolated from other mammals that lack the 2E4 antigen did not bind significant amounts of the 2E4 antibody, assayed by immunofluorescence (see, e.g., Fig. 7). The distribution of the NuMA protein on the chromosome as indicated from the immunofluorescence

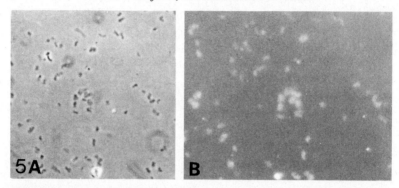

Fig. 5. Immunofluorescence of isolated HeLa metaphase chromosomes after reaction with 2E4 monoclonal antibody. Metaphase chromosomes were isolated using the polyamine procedure of Lewis & Laemmli (1982), centrifuged onto coated coverslips, and incubated first with 2E4 antibody (approx. concn 1 μg/ml) then with fluorescein-conjugated goat anti-mouse IgG. A. A phase-contrast photomicrograph of a field of chromosomes; B, a fluorescence photomicrograph of the same field. A control in which primary 2E4 antibody was omitted was too dark to photograph (see Materials and Methods for details). ×1000.

could take two forms. As shown in Fig. 5, the chromosomes sometimes appeared nearly uniformly fluorescent with no regions of apparent concentration of the antibody. In other cases the centromeric region tended to be more brightly fluorescent, indicating a possible localization of the NuMA antigen at that site (see, e.g., Fig. 7A).

Immunofluorescence experiments done on whole fixed cells have the potential for revealing the sites in the cell where an antigen is concentrated and thus for indicating sites of its specific binding. In contrast, experiments with isolated organelles or complexes, such as those with the metaphase chromosomes, indicate only the presence and distribution of the antigen and not whether it is specifically bound or even if the chromosome is a major site of concentration of the antigen. To investigate more quantitatively the relative amounts of NuMA protein bound to isolated metaphase chromosomes, immunoblots using antibody 2E4 were made of proteins obtained from the isolated chromosomes (Fig. 6). The measurements were organized so that constant numbers of chromosomes (constant DNA content) were analysed at different stages of chromosome purification. A band corresponding to the molecular weight of NuMA was recognized by the NuMA-specific monoclonal antibody in proteins obtained from chromosomes at all stages of purification. Thus the immunofluorescence studies showing association of NuMA with isolated chromosomes were confirmed. However, it is apparent from the analysis of Fig. 6 that relatively little of the NuMA protein is attached to the most highly purified chromosomes, as indicated by the intensity of immunoblot reaction. There is much more NuMA protein in fractions containing the same number of partially purified chromosomes. Recovery of chromosomes in the preparations is consistently poor (about 1 % recovery), so it is not clear whether the elimination of NuMA from the final chromosomes is the result of preferential loss of chromosomes with greater amounts of bound NuMA protein or whether NuMA is eliminated as a contaminant weakly bound to the chromosomes. In

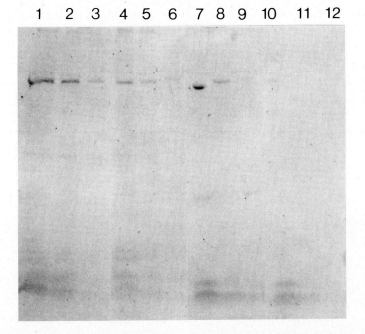

Fig. 6. Immunoblot of electrophoretically separated proteins from isolated metaphase chromosomes using anti-NuMA monoclonal antibody. HeLa cells (approx. 5×10^6) growing exponentially were labelled for 48 h with $20\,\mu\text{Ci}$ of [^{3}H]thymidine and cells were collected, washed and mixed with a 1·0-l culture of the same unlabelled cells. After 24 h growth, colcemid was added to final concentration $0·06\,\mu\text{g/ml}$ and after 16 h cells were collected and metaphase chromosomes were isolated as described in Materials and Methods. Mitotic index was about 0·8 and specific activity of DNA was about 700 c.p.m./ μg DNA. At different steps in the purification procedure samples of the partially purified chromosomes containing constant amounts of ^{3}H-labelled DNA were removed, heated in SDS-containing buffer, and prepared for electrophoresis of the chromosomal-associated protein. Following electrophoresis the proteins were transferred to a nitrocellulose sheet and immunoblotting using antibody 2E4 and peroxidase-conjugated secondary antibody carried out as described in Materials and Methods. Shown above is a photograph of the immunoblot. Lanes 1–3 contain crude lysate of the disrupted cells; 4–6, partially purified chromosomes after centrifuging away nuclei and cell debris, 35 % recovery of ^{3}H label; 7–9, partially purified chromosomes after glycerol gradient centrifugation, 7·4 % recovery of ^{3}H label; 10–12, purified chromosomes after Percoll gradient and final resuspension, 1·0 % recovery of ^{3}H label. Amounts of radioactive DNA applied per lane were: lanes 1, 4, 7, 10 ($1·2 \times 10^3$ c.p.m.); 2, 5, 8, 11 ($0·58 \times 10^3$ c.p.m.); 3, 6, 9, 12 ($0·29 \times 10^3$ c.p.m.). The staining at the bottom of the paper is due to limited non-specific attachment of the secondary peroxidase-conjugated antibody to histones, as also observed when primary antibody was omitted.

any case it is clear that it is possible by at least one procedure to prepare human chromosomes that have a relatively low content of NuMA protein.

The previous experiment suggests the possibility that the NuMA protein may be weakly associated with chromosomes and perhaps other cell organelles in lysates of mitotic cells and may undergo reassociation reactions. The following experiment was designed to test this possibility more definitively. Chromosomes were isolated from mixed Chinese hamster and HeLa cells and the association of NuMA protein with the isolated chromosomes was studied by the immunofluorescence procedure (Fig. 7). Chinese hamster cells have no protein recognized by the 2E4 antibodies that are specific for human NuMA protein (Lydersen & Pettijohn, 1980; Van Ness & Pettijohn, 1983). Therefore, as expected chromosomes isolated from these cells alone gave only weak background fluorescence after reaction with 2E4 antibodies. When coisolated with human chromosomes from mixed cell populations, however, the Chinese hamster chromosomes were also fluorescent. The Chinese hamster chromosomes could be recognized because the larger chromosomes were bigger than any HeLa cell chromosome; they were also identified by a specific Geimsa 11 staining procedure (Friend, Chen & Ruddle, 1976; Alhadeff, Velivakakis & Siniscalo, 1977). The results described in this section indicate that at least some reassociation of NuMA protein is possible in lysates used to prepare mitotic chromosomes. It will be necessary

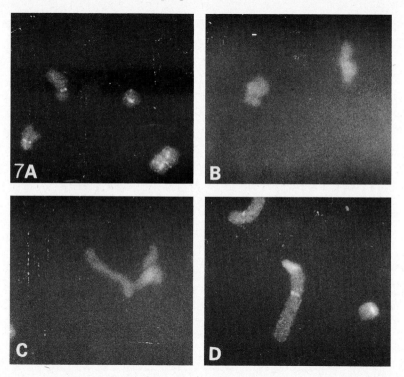

Fig. 7. Immunofluorescence of mixed chromosomes from HeLa and CHO cells using 2E4 monoclonal antibody. HeLa and CHO cells growing separately were treated with colcemid to align them in mitosis and 3×10^7 CHO cells were mixed with 3×10^7 HeLa cells. Chromosomes were isolated from the cell mixture as well as from the unmixed cell types and prepared for immunofluorescence after incubation with the monoclonal antibody specific for NuMA protein. A. Purified HeLa chromosomes (note particularly the fluorescence at the centromere). B. Purified HeLa chromosomes; reactions omitted the primary 2E4 antibody but included the secondary fluorescent antibody. A longer photographic exposure was used to detect background fluorescence and absence of centromeric fluorescence. C. Isolated CHO chromosomes. A longer photographic exposure was used to detect background fluorescence. D. A mixture of purified HeLa and CHO chromosomes. The large chromosome with fluorescent centromere is a CHO chromosome. ×1000.

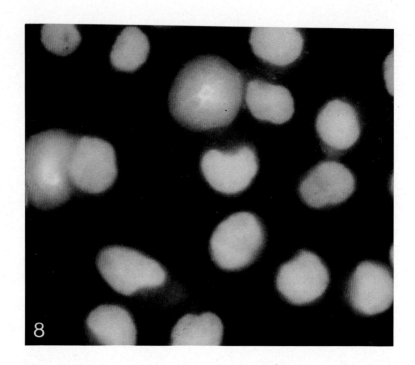

to re-examine the significance of chromosomal associations of NuMA protein.

Species specificity of NuMA proteins

As noted above the 2E4-type monoclonal antibodies recognize an epitope present on human NuMA protein and not present in the cells of other mammals. Recently, it was shown that the antibodies recognize a NHC protein in African Green monkey cells, which is similar in size to the human protein (Van Ness & Pettijohn, 1983). The epitope and its associated NuMA protein are therefore primate-specific. Cells of other animals have been screened by the immunofluorescence assay and their NHC proteins screened by immunoblotting. Mouse, rat, hamster, rabbit, chicken, certain fish species, *Drosophila* and *Dictyostelium* were all negative. Recently, however, we have obtained antibodies that recognize the primate form of NuMA as well as a NHC protein in many of the above species including all mammals that have been tested. The intracellular distribution of NuMA in fixed cells of these other animals assayed by immunofluorescence is similar to that found in human cells. However, the NuMA proteins are electrophoretically distinct. These studies will be described in detail elsewhere (C. Price & D. Pettijohn, unpublished). Thus is appears that NuMA proteins exist in many different species, but that the structure of the NHC protein has greatly diverged in evolution.

It is also interesting to note that the $300\,000\,M_r$ NHC protein found in primate cells appears in cell types in correlation with the primate form of NuMA. Different cell types that lack the primate form of NuMA also lack the major $300\,000\,M_r$ protein, which was confused for some time with NuMA protein. There may therefore be a set of NHC proteins as divergent in structure as NuMA protein.

NuMA protein is a human autoantigen

Studies done in colaboration with G. McCarty of Georgetown University Medical School have shown that a group of patients with connective-tissue disorders produce antibodies specific for NuMA protein (Price, McCarty & Pettijohn, 1984). In some cases the antibody is the major or only detectable autoantibody in the patients' sera. Immunoblots using these sera indicate a detectable reaction only with a NHC protein of the size of human NuMA. The specificity of the human autoantibody was unambiguously demonstrated when it was shown that a set of high molecular weight proteolytic degradation product of NuMA identified by reaction with 2E4 monoclonal antibody are also recognized by the autoantibodies. These autoantibodies will be most useful in future studies of the NuMA protein.

The polar structure and NuMA protein in nuclear assembly

Of all the known exclusively nuclear proteins, NuMA protein is apparently the

Fig. 8. Immunofluorescence of mitotic spindle poles using 2E4 monoclonal antibody. HeLa cells were fixed and incubated with 2E4 and fluorescein-conjugated goat anti-mouse IgG as described for Fig. 2. Shown at the top and bottom of the photomicrograph are two mitotic cells orientated with one pole behind the other viewed along the spindle axis. Fluorescent nuclei from interphase cells surround the two mitotic cells. ×500.

earliest to attach at or near the site where the post-mitotic nucleus will assemble in the cell. Thus we have previously speculated that the NuMA protein might have some role in the assembly. Although it is not established that the structure at the poles of the mitotic spindle provides an organizing centre for nuclear assembly, photomicrographs taken at late anaphase and early telophase showing chromosomes closely associated with the polar structure suggest such a relationship (see Van Ness & Pettijohn, 1983). If the polar structure is *not* the pre-nucleus then the NuMA protein must leave the polar structure and reattach later to the true nucleus. Detailed examination by fluorescence microscopy of post-mitotic cells and cells during telophase has failed to reveal intermediates or other evidence of such a transfer (Van Ness & Pettijohn, 1983). However, studies at higher resolution using electron microscopy are needed to probe this question further.

Visualization of the polar prenucleus-like structure has been greatly aided by the 2E4 anti-NuMA monoclonal antibodies, which specifically bind to it. However, with the aid of fluorescent images to orient the viewer, the structure can also be seen with phase and differential interference microscopy. When viewed from a point perpendicular to the spindle axis the two polar structures are seen as concave disks focused towards the chromosomes (for examples, see Figs 2 and 4), but when viewed from a point along the spindle axis with one pole behind the other the structure is often seen as a ring shape with a hole of roughly $0.5\,\mu$m diameter (Fig. 8). The anti-NuMA monoclonal antibodies should be useful in future studies to investigate the possible function of this polar structure in nuclear assembly.

As emphasized above, the earlier evidence that NuMA protein could bind to both mitotic chromosomes and the mitotic pole structure was compatible with the possibility that this protein might link telophase chromosomes to the polar structure. However, results of the present work indicate that caution is required in interpreting evidence of NuMA protein association with metaphase chromosomes. Dissociation of NuMA protein and reassociation to other sites may complicate experiments done with cell extracts or disrupted cells. Our studies in progress using microinjection procedures with living cells may help establish the function of NuMA protein.

This research was supported by grants from the U.S. National Institutes of Health (GM 182432-12), from the U.S. National Science Foundation (PCM-7921406).

REFERENCES

ALHADEFF, B., VELIVAKAKIS, M. & SINISCALO, M. (1977). Simultaneous identification of chromatid replication and of human chromosomes in metaphases of man–mouse somatic cell hybrids. *Cytogen. Cell Genet.* **19**, 236–239.

BITTNER, M., KUPFERER, P. & MORRIS, C. (1980). Electrophoretic transfer of proteins and nucleic acids from slab gels to diazobenzyloxymethyl cellulose or nitrocellulose sheets. *Analyt. Biochem.* **102**, 459–471.

ERICKSON, P., MINIER, L. & LASHER, R. (1982). Quantitative electrophoretic transfer of polypeptides from SDS polyacrylamide gels to nitrocellulose sheets: A method for their use in immunoautoradiographic detection of antigens. *J. immun. Meth.* **51**, 241–249.

FRIEND, K., CHEN, S. & RUDDLE, F. (1976). Differential staining of interspecific chromosomes in somatic cell hybrids by alkaline Giemsa stain. *Som. Cell Genet.* **2**, 183–188.

GERACE, L. & BLOBEL, G. (1980). The nuclear envelope lamina is reversibly depolymerized during mitosis. *Cell* **19**, 277–287.

IZANT, S., WEATHERBEE, J. & McINTOSH, J. (1982). A microtubule associated protein in the mitotic spindle and the interphase nucleus. *Nature, Lond.* **295**, 248–250.

LAEMMLI, U. (1970). Cleavage of structural proteins during the assembly of the head of bacteriophase T4. *Nature, Lond.* **227**, 680–685.

LEWIS, C. & LAEMMLI, U. (1982). Higher order metaphase chromosome structure: Evidence for metalloprotein interactions. *Cell* **29**, 171–181.

LYDERSEN, B., KAO, F. T. & PETTIJOHN, D. (1980). Expression of genes coding for non-histone chromosomal proteins in human/Chinese hamster cell hybrids: An electrophoretic analysis. *J. biol. Chem.* **255**, 3002–3007.

LYDERSEN, B. & PETTIJOHN, D. (1980). Human-specific nuclear protein that associates with the polar region of the mitotic apparatus: Distribution in a human/hamster hybrid cell. *Cell* **22**, 489–499.

OLMSTED, J. B. (1981). Affinity purification of antibodies from diazotized paper blots of heterogeneous protein samples. *J. biol. Chem.* **256**, 11955–11957.

PRICE, C., McCARTY, G. & PETTIJOHN, D. (1984). NuMA protein is a human autoantigen. *Arthritis Rheum.* **27**, 774–779.

SMITH, B., ROBERTSON, D., BIRBECH, M., GOODWIN, G. & JOHNS, E. (1978). Immunochemical studies of high mobility group non-histone chromatin proteins HMG 1 and HMG 2. *Expl Cell Res.* **115**, 420–423.

SYMINGTON, J., GREEN, M. & BRACKMAN, K. (1981). Immunoautoradiographic detection of proteins after transfer from gels to diazopaper: Analysis of adenovirus encoded protein. *Proc. natn. Acad. Sci. U.S.A.* **78**, 117–181.

TOWBIN, H., STAEHLIN, T. & GORDON, J. (1979). Electrophoretic transfer of proteins from polyacrylamide gels to nitrocellulose sheets: Procedure and some applications. *Proc. natn. Acad. Sci. U.S.A.* **76**, 4350–4354.

VAN NESS, J. & PETTIJOHN, D. (1983). Specific attachment of nuclear–mitotic apparatus protein to metaphase chromosomes and mitotic spindle poles: possible function in nuclear reassembly. *J. molec. Biol.* **171**, 175–205.

J. Cell Sci. Suppl. 1, 203–221 (1984)
Printed in Great Britain © *The Company of Biologists Limited 1984*

THE ULTRASTRUCTURAL ORGANIZATION OF PREMATURELY CONDENSED CHROMOSOMES

SUSANNE M. GOLLIN[1],[*], WAYNE WRAY[1],[*],
STEVEN K. HANKS[2],[*], WALTER N. HITTELMAN[2] AND
POTU N. RAO[2]†

[1] *Department of Cell Biology, Baylor College of Medicine, Houston, Texas 77030, U.S.A.*

[2] *Department of Chemotherapy Research, The University of Texas M. D. Anderson Hospital and Tumor Institute, Houston, Texas 77030, U.S.A.*

SUMMARY

In an effort to understand the arrangement of the basic 30 nm chromatin fibre within metaphase chromosomes, changes in the organization of prematurely condensed chromosomes (PCC) were examined as a function of progression through the cell cycle. The structural features of PCC observed under the light microscope were compared with those obtained by scanning electron microscopy. PCC with varying levels of condensation were obtained by fusing mitotic HeLa cells with interphase cells synchronized at different times in the cell cycle. PCC from G_1 cells are composed of rather tightly packed bundles of tortuous chromatin fibres. The density of fibre packing along the longitudinal axis of G_1-phase PCC is lower and less uniform than that of metaphase chromosomes. Early G_1 PCC exhibit gyres suggesting a despiralized chromonema. The condensed domains in G_1 PCC appear to be organized as supercoiled loops; whereas fibre-sparse domains consist of longitudinal fibres running along the chromosome axis. As cells progressed towards S phase, a greater proportion of highly extended regions containing prominent longitudinal fibres became evident in the PCC. The pulverized appearance of S-phase PCC under the light microscope corresponded to the highly condensed, looping fibre domains separated by more extended segments containing longitudinal fibres that are visualized using the scanning electron microscope. Active sites of DNA synthesis are implicated to be localized within extended longitudinal fibres. Post-replicative chromosome maturation extends through the G_2 period and appears to involve rearrangement of the extended longitudinal fibres into packed looping-fibre clusters, which then coalesce.

These observations support the model for packing DNA into chromosomes proposed in 1980 by Mullinger & Johnson. Briefly, this model suggests that the chromonema of each metaphase chromatid contains regions composed of folded longitudinal chromatin fibres as well as looping fibres that emerge from the axis at distinct foci. The final level of chromatin packing in metaphase chromosomes is attained by spiralization of the chromonema.

INTRODUCTION

Metaphase chromosomes and interphase chromatin are constructed from 10 nm nucleosome fibres coiled in the form of a 30 nm solenoid, stabilized by histone H1 and divalent cations (Finch & Klug, 1976; Worcel & Benyajati, 1977; Ris & Korenberg, 1979; Hamkalo & Rattner, 1980). Despite numerous investigations, the arrangement

---

* Present addresses: S. M. Gollin, Cytogenetics Laboratory, Department of Pediatric Pathology, Arkansas Children's Hospital, Little Rock, AR72202, U.S.A.; W. Wray, Biology Department, The John Hopkins University, Baltimore, Md 21218, U.S.A.; S. K. Hanks, Division of Cellular Biology, Department of Basic and Clinical Research, Scripps Clinic and Research Foundation, La Jolla, Calif. 97037, U.S.A.

† Author for correspondence.

of the 30 nm chromatin fibre within metaphase chromosomes remains unclear. The nature of this higher order organization has been difficult to ascertain due to the compact packaging of chromatin fibres within metaphase chromosomes. Techniques designed to loosen the structure of metaphase chromosomes and thus reveal the underlying fibre organization are fraught with a spectrum of problems ranging from extensive dispersal of chromosomes beyond recognition to aggregation of non-histone chromosomal proteins.

One approach to understanding the arrangement of the 30 nm chromatin fibre within metaphase chromosomes is to visualize the chromosome condensation cycle, which is tightly coupled to the mammalian cell cycle. According to the model for the chromosome condensation cycle proposed by Mazia (1963), chromosomes begin to decondense during the telophase stage of mitosis, and gradually continue this process throughout G_1 and into S phase until maximum dispersion is reached at the time of DNA replication. Following replication, chromosomes begin a gradual recondensation process, which culminates in the formation of metaphase chromosomes. This model is supported by results from a number of investigations using a variety of experimental methods (Ringertz, Darzynkiewicz & Bolund, 1969; Pederson & Robbins, 1972; Zetterberg & Auer, 1970; Alvarez, 1974; Moser, Muller & Robbins, 1975; Hildebrand & Tobey, 1975; Nicolini, Ajiro, Borun & Baserga, 1975). The phenomenon of premature chromosome condensation provides direct visual evidence for cell-cycle-specific changes in the higher order arrangement of chromatin fibres within interphase chromosomes. Fusion of mitotic cells with interphase cells results in a rapid breakdown of the interphase nuclear framework and organization of interphase chromatin into prematurely condensed chromosomes (PCC) (Johnson & Rao, 1970). The process of premature chromosome condensation closely resembles the entry of the nucleus of a cycling cell into mitotic prophase (Johnson & Rao, 1970; Matsui, Yoshida, Weinfeld & Sandberg, 1972; Obara, Chai, Weinfeld & Sandberg, 1974). The only apparent difference is that the morphology of PCC is determined by the position of the interphase cell in the cell cycle at the time of fusion (Johnson & Rao, 1970; Stenman & Saksela, 1971).

Prematurely condensed chromosomes are an elegant model system for ultrastructural analysis of the organization of interphase chromatin. In the process of premature chromosome condensation, the nuclear membrane breaks down and the chromatin condenses, so that the resulting PCC may reflect the actual intranuclear organization before fusion. This characteristic permits investigation of changes in the arrangement of the chromatin fibre within PCC as a function of progression through the cell cycle. Previous electron-microscope studies of PCC were not specifically designed to address this question. Matsui *et al.* (1972) studied thin sections of CHO cells during PCC formation in order to compare the events associated with the disruption of the nuclear framework during premature chromosome condensation with the events occurring during normal mitotic prophase. Schwarzacher, Ruzicka & Sperling (1974) and Ruzicka (1977) investigated ultrastructural features of metaphase chromosomes and PCC from unsynchronized human fibroblasts following G-banding of methanol/acetic acid-fixed, air-dried chromosome spreads. They demonstrated that PCC are composed of the same 30–100 nm fibrils as metaphase chromosomes and interphase chromatin, and that G-bands appear thicker and contain relatively more tightly packed fibrils than R-bands. Mullinger & Johnson (1983) studied the organization of chromatin fibres in *S*-phase PCC and discussed the relationship between condensed fibre aggregates and replication clusters.

Changes in the ultrastructural arrangement of the basic 30 nm chromatin fibre that parallel the well-characterized changes in PCC morphology during the cell cycle by light microscopy have been analysed in our laboratories (Hanks, Gollin, Rao, Wray & Hittelman, 1983). We used high-resolution scanning electron microscopy (SEM) to examine the three-dimensional relationship of chromatin fibres within chromosomes prepared from synchronized HeLa cells using standardized, conventional cytogenetic spreading techniques.

METHODS

Preparation of chromosome spreads for light and electron microscopy

These studies were performed on HeLa cells grown in monolayer cultures. Procedures for cell culture, synchronization and fusion to induce PCC have been described (Hanks *et al*. 1983). Analysis of PCC morphology by light microscopy was performed on chromosome spreads prepared using classical cytogenetic procedures. Briefly, cells were fixed in methanol/acetic acid (3:1, v/v), dropped on wet microscope slides, air-dried and stained with Giemsa. Chromosome spreads were prepared for electron microscopy using the same procedures, except that cells were dropped onto glass coverslips and immediately immersed in fresh methanol/acetic acid (3:1) fixative to avoid the drastic alterations in specimen structure produced by air-drying. The chromosomes were then stabilized in 2% aqueous uranyl acetate, dehydrated in a graded series of acetone solutions, critical-point dried, sputter-coated with 15–20 nm gold/palladium, and observed using a JEOL JEM-100CX scanning-transmission electron microscope operating at 40 kV (for details, see Hanks *et al*. 1983).

Technical problems in the preparation of PCC for scanning electron microscopy

PCC induction and preparation of chromosomes for SEM are characterized by occasional technical problems. The capricious step in PCC induction is that of fusion of mitotic with interphase cells. The amount of fusion, that is, the number of cells that fuse to each other (from two to ten, for example) varies between different lots of Sendai virus or polyethylene glycol and also fluctuates for reasons that remain unclear. The difficulty in the preparation of chromosomes for SEM is based on the necessity to preserve the fragile, three-dimensional structure of chromosomes. Air-drying damages the ultrastructure of specimens due to fierce surface-tension forces inherent in the process. Standard chromosome-spreading techniques utilize air-drying as a means of achieving flat chromosome spreads that adhere to microscope slides. In the interest of preserving chromosome ultrastructure, we chose not to air-dry the chromosomes and consequently, our chromosome spreads were often incomplete.

The ultrastructure of chromatin fibres observed within chromosomes might depend on other factors in the method of preparation. Two potential artifacts inherent in our method of chromosome preparation should be mentioned. First, fixation of chromosomes with methanol/acetic acid (3:1) is known to extract some histone proteins (Dick & Johns, 1968; Brody, 1974; Burkholder & Duczek, 1982). In addition, methanol/acetic acid is a coagulant fixative, and therefore not generally useful for extremely high-resolution transmission electron-microscopic analyses of structures such as macromolecules. However, methanol/acetic acid has been widely used for ultrastructural studies of chromosomes, since it is the only fixative that preserves chromosomes *in situ* and also permits chromosome spreading (Burkholder, 1977; Ruzicka, 1977; Harrison, Allen, Britch & Harris, 1982). Cheung, Gollin & Wray (1981 and unpublished observations) found that fixation with methanol/

acetic acid does not alter the arrangement of the basic 30 nm chromatin fibre within PCC or metaphase chromosomes compared to fixation with the Wray-Stubblefield hexylene glycol buffer, although it decreases chromatin fibre diameter. These results confirm those of Ris (1978), who suggested that methanol/acetic acid is extremely useful for investigating the arrangement of the basic chromatin fibre in chromosomes although it is not suitable for the study of nucleohistone structure. The second potential artifact is that the hypotonic treatment used to swell cells before fixation and chromosome spreading may affect chromosome structure. Barnitzke, Bullerdiek & Schloot (1981) have shown a strong correlation between chromosome length and increasing hypotonicity. This finding suggests that the PCC we observed may have an extended morphology relative to their state *in situ*. This extension of length is most probably achieved at the level of chromomere clustering or uncoiling of the chromonema (Jorgensen & Bak, 1982). To avoid this potential artifact, we have prepared all chromosomes for examination using standard cytogenetic techniques and have attempted to limit discussion of our data to a description of changes in the arrangement of chromatin fibres associated with changes in PCC morphology during the cell cycle.

Other methods have been used to prepare PCC for SEM. Most recently, Mullinger & Johnson (1983) used a technique adapted for chromosome preparation by Harrison *et al.* (1982). The procedure involves preparation of standard, air-dried chromosome spreads after fixation in methanol/acetic acid, followed by trypsin–Giemsa banding, fixation in glutaraldehyde and osmium tetroxide, sequential incubations in sodium thiocarbohydrazide, distilled water, osmium tetroxide and distilled water, dehydration in a graded series of acetone solutions and, finally, critical-point drying. This technique eliminates the need to coat the specimen with a conductive layer of metal, since the sodium thiocarbohydrazide–osmium tetroxide complex imparts conductivity to the specimen. This feature would permit resolution of finer surface details.

Problems may be associated with the following steps in this preparative technique. Treatment with hypotonic solution and fixation in methanol/acetic acid may have inherent problems as previously discussed. Air-drying may distort the fine surface structure of the chromosomes leading to inability to distinguish individual chromatin fibres and the paths they traverse. Trypsin–Giemsa banding is known to alter chromosome morphology, primarily by extraction of chromosomal proteins. However, this step is necessary to visualize surface details of chromosomes prepared by this procedure.

Thus, it is apparent that a completely satisfactory method of preparing chromosomes for analysis by scanning electron microscopy has not been developed. Therefore, the results of SEM analysis of chromosomes must be interpreted cautiously in the light of the artifacts that can be produced by current preparative techniques.

RESULTS AND DISCUSSION

The structure of prematurely condensed chromosomes

G_1-*phase PCC.* Under the light microscope, PCC of G_1 phase cells appear as single chromatids. A closer analysis of G_1 PCC morphology reveals a relationship between chromatid length and thickness, and the degree of advancement of the cell toward S phase at the time of fusion (Schor, Johnson & Waldren, 1975; Hittelman & Rao, 1976, 1978; Rao, Wilson & Puck, 1977; Rao & Hanks, 1980; Sperling, 1982). As a cell progresses through G_1, its PCC become more extended. The early stages of this decondensation process appear to involve an uncoiling of the chromonema, resulting in gyred chromatids characteristic of those produced after specific treatments of chromosomes (Manton, 1950; Ohnuki, 1968; Goradia & Davis, 1977) (Fig. 1A). Immediately before entry into S phase, the PCC are highly extended and individual chromosomes are no longer distinguishable. This decondensation process appears to be necessary, although not sufficient for the initiation of DNA synthesis (Hanks & Rao, 1980).

At the ultrastructural level, early G_1-phase PCC are composed of a rather tightly packed bundle of highly tortuous chromatin fibres with a diameter of about 30 nm (Fig. 2). G_1 PCC show a general resemblance to individual metaphase chromatids. However, the density of fibre packing along the longitudinal axis of PCC is lower and less uniform than that of metaphase chromatids. The fibres composing the more condensed domains of the early G_1 PCC often appear to be organized as supercoiled loops that emerge from within the chromosome axis, while in fibre-sparse domains, longitudinal fibres running along the chromonemal axis are often visible (Fig. 2). In more extended regions along the longitudinal axis of early G_1-phase PCC, gyres are apparent (Fig. 2, closed arrows). The coiled appearance seems to arise from a uniform unwinding of the chromosome. The packing of the basic chromatin fibre within this uncoiled chromosome appears much less dense than in the more highly condensed PCC domains.

As cells progress to late G_1, the PCC appear more attenuated, as revealed by light microscopy (Fig. 1B). SEM analysis reveals that late G_1 PCC have a greater proportion of highly extended regions containing prominent longitudinal fibres (Fig. 3, open arrow). Domains composed of tightly packed looping fibres are diminished in size. In some regions, small clusters of loops are observed that appear to arise from a single point of origin (Fig. 3, closed arrow).

S-phase PCC. PCC from *S*-phase cells exhibit a characteristic 'pulverized' morphology. This appearance results from variable levels of condensation in different chromosome segments and is precisely related to their position in *S* phase and to their replicative state at the time of fusion (Johnson & Rao, 1970; Sperling & Rao, 1974; Sperling, 1982).

During early *S* phase, PCC reach their overall minimum level of condensation (Figs 1c, 4). Mid-*S*-phase PCC are characterized at the light-microscopic level by the presence of many condensed segments, often appearing double, which represent regions of the chromosome that have completed replication (Figs 1D, 5A, boxed regions). The highly condensed segments are separated by more extended domains, which represent regions that have not yet initiated replication as well as 'gap' regions. Autoradiographic analyses of PCC spreads from *S* phase cells pulse-labelled with [³H]thymidine immediately before fusion clearly reveal a heavy localization of silver grains within the gap regions of the PCC (Sperling & Rao, 1974; Lau & Arrighi, 1981; Mullinger & Johnson, 1983). Thus, the sites of active DNA replication at the time of fusion appear as gaps in the continuity of the chromosome when viewed under the light microscope.

Ultrastructurally, mid-*S*-phase PCC consist of alternating domains of sparse longitudinal fibres and packed looping fibres. Regions of low-density longitudinal fibres correspond to the gap regions detected using light microscopy. Presumably, the gaps represent sites where the density of nucleoprotein fibres is too low to be resolved, rather than actual breaks in the continuity of the chromosome (Rohme, 1975). In some cases, the continuity of PCC is apparently maintained by a single longitudinal fibre linking two looping-fibre domains (Fig. 6, bracketed region). Looping-fibre

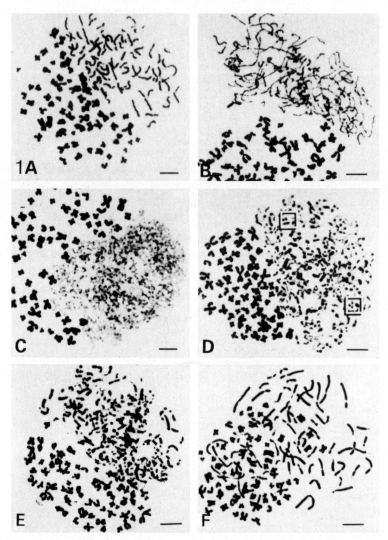

Fig. 1. Light micrographs of PCC spreads at various phases of the cell cycle. A. Early G_1; B, late G_1; C, early S; D, mid-S; E, late S; F, G_2. The darkly stained, highly condensed metaphase chromosomes at the left of each figure are from the mitotic cell used to induce premature chromosome condensation. Bars, 5 μm. (From Hanks *et al.* (1983).)

domains show various degrees of compaction (Fig. 6). In some cases, clusters of looping fibres appear to emerge from a single point of origin (Fig. 6, arrow *b*). Many parallel longitudinal fibres can be seen within larger clusters (Fig. 6, arrow *a*).

The light-microscopic morphology of late-S-phase PCC differs from that of mid-S-phase PCC in that the condensed, replicated chromosome segments are much longer and thus constitute a greater fraction of the total chromosome length (Figs 1E, 7). Ultrastructural analysis of late S PCC indicates that the long stretches of condensed,

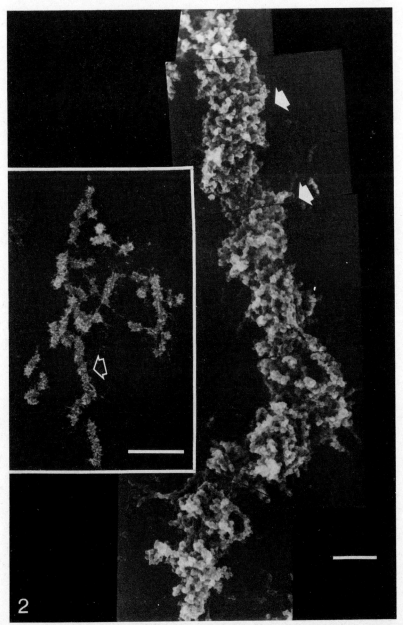

Fig. 2. Ultrastructure of early G_1 PCC showing features suggesting chromonema spiralization (indicated by closed arrows). Bar, $0.5 \, \mu m$. Inset illustrates position of enlarged chromosome in spread (open arrow). Bar, $5 \, \mu m$. (From Hanks *et al.* (1983).)

replicated chromosomes are composed of nucleoprotein fibres organized primarily as packed loops (Fig. 8). The fibres are packed together much more loosely than in metaphase chromatids, however, and some degree of longitudinal organization is observed. In regions where single, unreplicated segments merge into condensed,

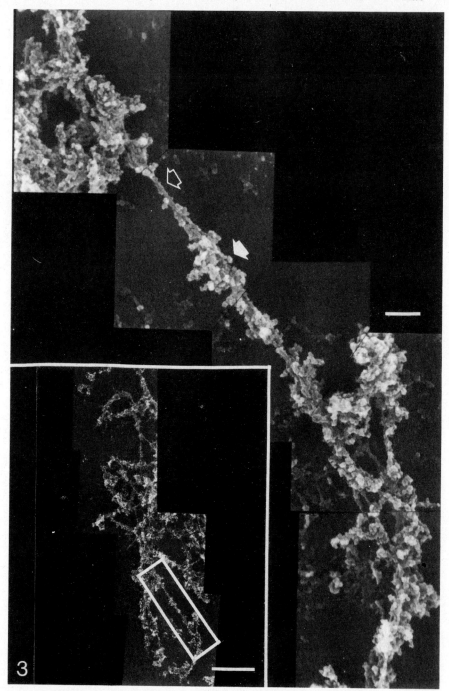

Fig. 3. Ultrastructure of late G_1 PCC. The region shown is an enlargement of the boxed area of the inset. Bars, 0·5 μm; inset, 5 μm. (From Hanks *et al*. (1983).)

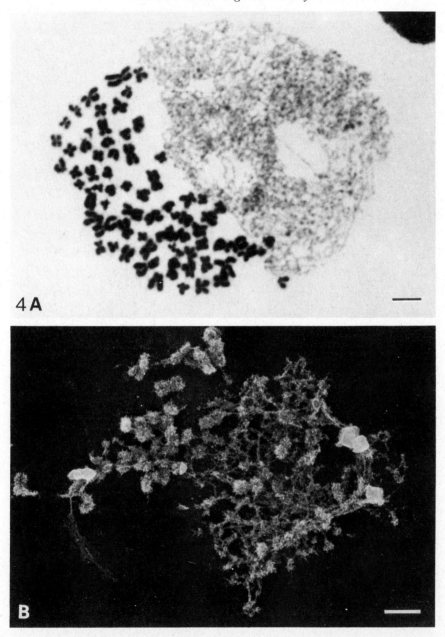

Fig. 4. Light (A) and SEM (B) micrographs of early *S* PCC spreads. Bars, 5 μm.

replicated domains, the unreplicated chromatid appears to be contiguous with one of the doubled segments, while the other replicated chromatid segment appears to be situated laterally (Fig. 8, inset).

G_2-*phase PCC*. When viewed by light microscopy, G_2 PCC resemble early prophase chromosomes and are characterized by extended double chromatids of rather uniform

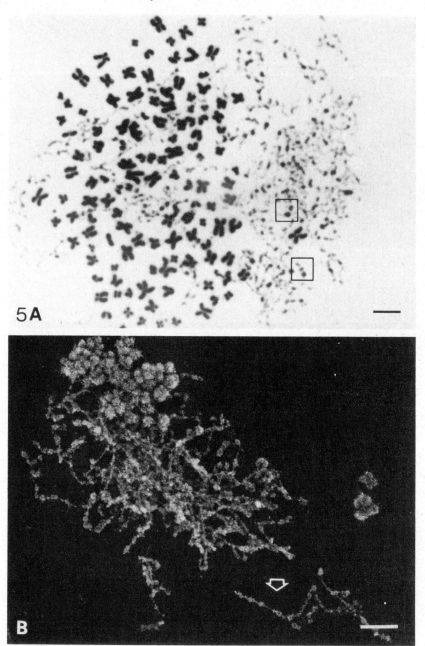

Fig. 5. Light (A) and SEM (B) micrographs of mid-*S* PCC spreads. Bars, 5 μm.

thickness throughout the length of the chromosome (Fig. 1F). At the ultrastructural level, G_2 PCC appear to consist primarily of packed looping fibres very similar to the replicated segments of late *S* PCC (Fig. 9). In contrast to late G_1 and *S*-phase PCC, the fibre density is quite uniform throughout the length of the G_2 chromosome.

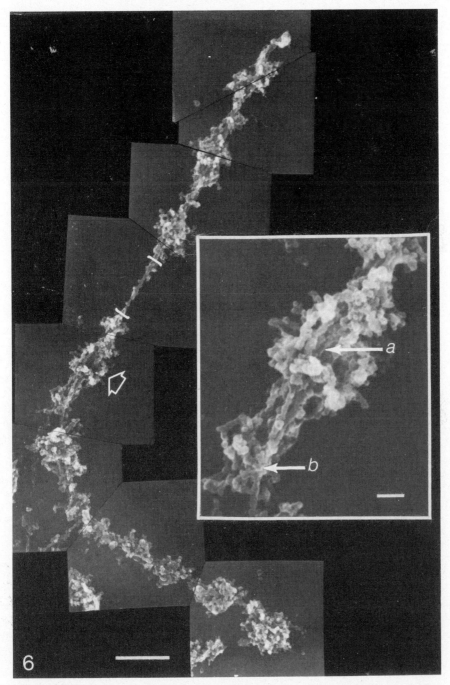

Fig. 6. Ultrastructure of mid-*S* PCC illustrating continuity of a single longitudinal fibre. The chromosome shown is indicated by an arrow in Fig. 5B. Bar, 1 μm. The inset is a further magnification of the region indicated by the arrow in the main part of the figure. Arrow *a* indicates a cluster with many parallel fibres; arrow *b*, a cluster of looping fibres with a common origin. Bar, 0·2 μm. (From Hanks *et al.* (1983).)

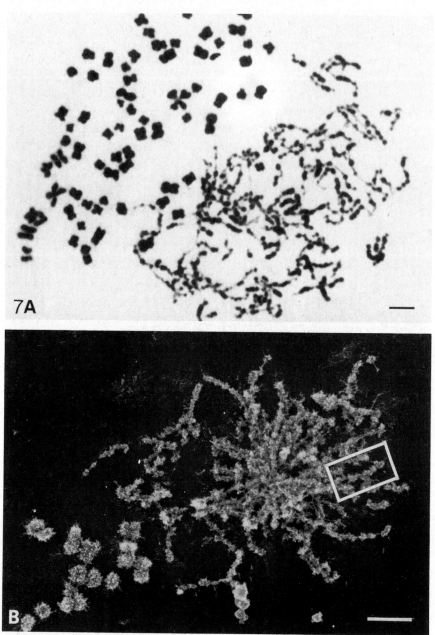

Fig. 7. Light (A) and SEM (B) micrograph of late S PCC spreads. Bars, 5 μm.

Metaphase chromosomes appear much more tightly packed than G_2 PCC (Fig. 1F). The width of G_2 PCC chromatids is narrower than metaphase chromatids. The loose packing of G_2 PCC allows a limited view of the internal fibre organization, and longitudinal fibres can be observed running for rather short stretches within the G_2 chromatids.

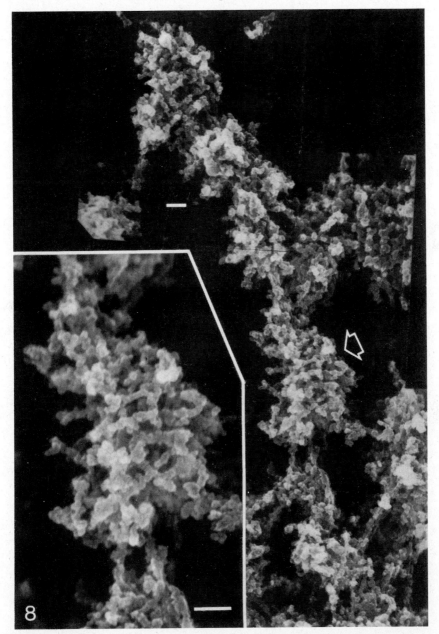

Fig. 8. Ultrastructure of late *S* PCC. The main part of the figure is an enlargement of the boxed region in Fig. 7B. The inset is an enlargement of the segment indicated by the arrow. Bars, 0·2 μm. (From Hanks *et al.* (1983).)

Progressive changes in the arrangement of the chromatin fibre during the cell cycle

The 30 nm chromatin fibre appears to be present in two forms in PCC: (1) looping fibres, and (2) longitudinal fibres. The relative fractions of tightly packed looping fibres and more extended longitudinal fibres vary during the cell cycle. The level of

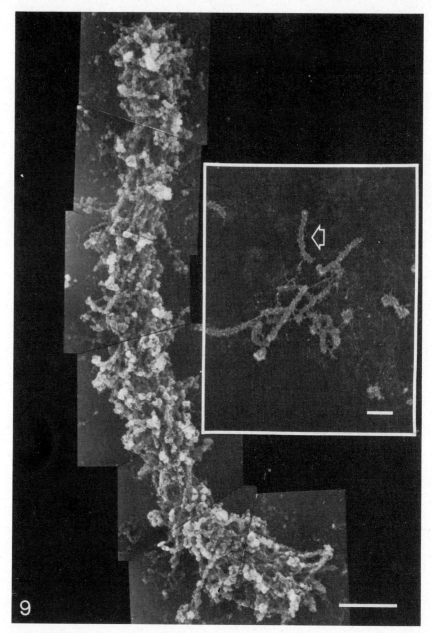

Fig. 9. Ultrastructure of G_2 PCC. The chromosome shown is an enlargement of the chromosome indicated by the arrow in the inset. Bars, 1 μm; inset, 5 μm. (From Hanks *et al.* (1983).)

chromosome extension appears directly related to the ratio of longitudinal to looping fibres within the chromosome. PCC decondensation during G_1 traverse is associated with despiralization of the chromonema, followed by a gradual transition from packed, looping fibres to prominent longitudinal fibres. Autoradiographic studies at the light-microscopic level have clearly demonstrated that the gaps in S-phase PCC are the regions undergoing active DNA replication (Sperling & Rao, 1974; Lau & Arrighi, 1981; Mullinger & Johnson, 1983). We and others have shown that the gaps correspond to sparse, extended longitudinal chromatin fibres (Rohme, 1975; Hanks *et al.* 1983).

Progression through S phase is associated with a transition from a highly decondensed to a highly condensed morphology (compare Fig. 1c–F), which corresponds to the reorganization of sparse, extended longitudinal fibres to packed, looping-fibre domains. Lau & Arrighi (1981) have shown that this transition occurs soon after completion of DNA replication within a chromosome segment. Analysis of our electron micrographs of S-phase PCC reveals the presence of both single longitudinal fibres (pre-replicative and actively replicating chromatin) and packed looping fibres (post-replicative chromatin). The data suggest that post-replicative chromosome maturation includes the formation of looping-fibre clusters that may arise from a single point of conjunction (Fig. 6, arrow b), followed by the coalescence of these clusters into larger looping-fibre domains (Fig. 6, arrow a; Fig. 8, insert). The formation of packed looping domains is apparently associated with an increase in the number of longitudinally oriented fibres lying within them (Fig. 6, arrow a).

G_2-phase PCC contain numerous looping-fibre domains with longitudinal fibres apparent only in more loosely packed regions of the chromosome. In general, however, the double chromatids of G_2 PCC are organized as packed looping fibres that have a rather uniform density throughout their length (Fig. 9). Longitudinal fibres are not apparent in the highly condensed metaphase chromosomes obtained after Colcemid arrest.

These observations allow us to describe the chromosome condensation cycle in terms of the arrangement of the basic, 30 nm chromatin fibre within PCC. Chromosome decondensation during G_1 is accomplished by uncoiling the spiralized chromonema followed by a gradual transition from packed looping fibres to extended longitudinal fibres. Active sites of DNA replication are thought to be localized within single longitudinal fibres – the maximum level of PCC decondensation. Post-replicative chromosome maturation appears to involve rearrangement of the extended longitudinal fibres into packed looping-fibre clusters. This process begins during S phase, soon after replication of a chromosome segment, and appears to be associated with the assembly of a chromosome axis composed of multiple longitudinal fibres. Further compaction of replicated chromosome segments is achieved by coalescence of looping-fibre domains and by spiralization of chromonema, resulting in the formation of a highly compact metaphase chromosome.

PCC versus *metaphase chromosomes*

The results of our studies on the ultrastructural organization of PCC in conjunction with those of numerous investigations on metaphase chromosome structure shed light on the arrangement of chromatin fibres within metaphase chromosomes.

Early ultrastructural studies of whole-mount metaphase chromosomes revealed the presence of loops at the periphery of metaphase chromosomes (Gall, 1963; DuPraw,

1970). Stubblefield & Wray (1971) examined metaphase chromosomes that had been isolated and then treated with distilled water to loosen the packaging of the condensed chromatin and thus reveal the details of fibre arrangement. They observed longitudinally oriented fibres and looping-fibre domains, and proposed the concept of distinct axial and peripheral chromatin components. Golomb & Bahr (1974) used scanning electron microscopy to examine mitotic chromosomes and interphase nuclei. They observed both looping and longitudinal fibres in interphase chromatin and prophase chromosomes; whereas metaphase chromosomes appeared to consist solely of tightly packed looping fibres. Yunis & Bahr (1979) noted that human prophase chromosomes were composed of alternating looping and longitudinal-fibre domains. Laemmli and co-workers examined histone-depleted, surface-spread metaphase chromosomes (Adolph, Cheng & Laemmli, 1977; Paulson & Laemmli, 1977) and observed a 'halo' of looping DNA strands attached to a residual proteinaceous core or scaffold. Further ultrastructural studies of metaphase chromosomes suggested that the chromatin fibre loops are arranged in a radial fashion about the central axis of the chromatid (Marsden & Laemmli, 1979; Adolph, 1980, 1981; Earnshaw & Laemmli, 1983). More recent SEM studies of isolated metaphase chromosomes in conjunction with thin-sectioning studies provide strong evidence for the presence of both radial loops and longitudinal fibres along the chromosome axis (Adolph & Kreisman, 1983). Alternatives, such as the helical-coil model have been proposed on the basis of analysis of chromosomes in intact and disrupted nuclei (Sedat & Manuelidis, 1978). Mullinger & Johnson (1980) studied protein-depleted, Kleinschmidt-spread metaphase chromosomes and proposed an elegant model for chromosome fibre organization. They suggested that the chromatid consists of a chromatin fibre that folds back on itself several times over short regions to form multiple longitudinal fibres. Lateral loops of chromatin emanate from distinct regions (chromomeres) along the chromatid axis. These 'chromomeric blocks' are sites of fibre constraint and are interspersed with regions of the chromonemal axis that contain fewer fibres. They suggested that chromonema compaction at metaphase may occur by shortening the inter-loop axis, by creating new loops or by packing the inter-loop DNA in order to bring looped inserts together. Further shortening would be achieved by spiralization or helical coiling of the chromonema.

In addition to the observations discussed above, the data of Laughlin, Wilkinson-Singley, Olins & Olins (1982), and our data strongly support the Mullinger & Johnson model for chromosome organization. We clearly demonstrate the presence of looping-fibre domains interspersed with regions containing multiple longitudinal fibres. Our observations of late S PCC suggest that compaction of replicated chromosome segments is achieved by coalescence of looping-fibre domains. Our data further imply that spiralization of chromonema may be the final step in mitotic chromosome compaction, since despiralization appears to be the first level of chromosome decondensation observed in G_1-phase PCC.

The authors thank Dr Bill R. Brinkley for the generous use of his JEOL JEM–100CX electron microscope. This work was supported in part by NIH grants CA-27544 and CA-34783 to P.N.R.; NIH grants GM-26415, CA-18455, R.C.D.A. CA-00532, and NSF PCM 79-05428 to W. W.; NIH grants CA-28153 and CA-27931 to W.N.H.; and a Rosalie B. Hite award to S.K.H.

REFERENCES

ADOLPH, K. W. (1980). Organization of chromosomes in mitotic HeLa cells. *Expl Cell Res.* **125**, 95–103.

ADOLPH, K. W. (1981). A serial sectioning study of human mitotic chromosomes. *Eur. J. Cell Biol.* **24**, 146–153.

ADOLPH, K. W., CHENG, S. M. & LAEMMLI, U. K. (1977). Role of nonhistone proteins in metaphase chromosome structure. *Cell* **12**, 805–816.

ADOLPH, K. W. & KREISMAN, L. R. (1983). Surface structure of isolated metaphase chromosomes. *Expl Cell Res.* **147**, 155–166.

ALVAREZ, M. R. (1974). Early nuclear cytochemical changes in regenerating mammalian liver. *Expl Cell Res.* **83**, 225–230.

BARTNITZKE, S., BULLERDIEK, J. & SCHLOOT, W. (1981). Effects of hypotonic treatment on human metaphase chromosome length. *Cytobios.* **31**, 75–80.

BRODY, T. (1974). Histones in cytological preparations. *Expl Cell Res.* **85**, 255–263.

BURKHOLDER, G. D. (1977). Electron microscopy of banded mammalian chromosomes. In *Principles and Techniques of Electron Microscopy. Biological Applications*, vol. 7 (ed. M. A. Hayat), pp. 323–340. New York: Van Nostrand Reinhold.

BURKHOLDER, G. D. & DUCZEK, L. L. (1982). The effect of chromosome banding techniques on the histone and nonhistone proteins of isolated chromatin. *Can. J. Biochem.* **60**, 328–337.

CHEUNG, P. P., GOLLIN, S. M. & WRAY, W. (1981). Isolation and scanning electron microscopy of prematurely condensed chromosomes. *J. Cell Biol.* **91**, 68a.

DICK, C. & JOHNS, E. W. (1968). The effect of two acetic acid containing fixatives on the histone content of calf thymus deoxynucleoprotein and calf thymus tissue. *Expl Cell Res.* **51**, 626–632.

DuPRAW, E. J. (1970). *DNA and Chromosomes*. New York: Holt, Rinehart and Winston.

EARNSHAW, W. C. & LAEMMLI, U. K. (1983). Architecture of metaphase chromosomes and chromosome scaffolds. *J. Cell Biol.* **96**, 84–93.

FINCH, J. T. & KLUG, A. (1976). Solenoidal model for superstructure in chromatin. *Proc. natn. Acad. Sci.* **73**, 1897–1901.

GALL, J. G. (1963). Chromosome fibers from an interphase nucleus. *Science* **139**, 120–121.

GOLOMB, H. M. & BAHR, G. F. (1974). Human chromatin from interphase to metaphase. A scanning electron microscopic study. *Expl Cell Res.* **84**, 79–87.

GORADIA, R. & DAVIS, B. K. (1977). Banding and spiralization of human metaphase chromosomes. *Hum. Genet.* **36**, 155–160.

HAMKALO, B. A. & RATTNER, J. B. (1980). Folding up genes and chromosomes. *Q. Rev. Biol.* **55**, 409–417.

HANKS, S. K., GOLLIN, S. M., RAO, P. N., WRAY, W. & HITTELMAN, W. N. (1983). Cell cycle-specific changes in the ultrastructural organization of prematurely condensed chromosomes. *Chromosoma* **88**, 333–342.

HANKS, S. K. & RAO, P. N. (1980). Initiation of DNA synthesis in the prematurely condensed chromosomes of G1 cells. *J. Cell Biol.* **87**, 285–291.

HARRISON, C. J., ALLEN, T. D., BRITCH, M. & HARRIS, R. (1982). High-resolution scanning electron microscopy of human metaphase chromosomes. *J. Cell Sci.* **56**, 409–422.

HILDEBRAND, C. E. & TOBEY, R. A. (1975). Cell cycle-specific changes in chromatin organization. *Biochem. biophys. Res. Commun.* **63**, 134–139.

HITTELMAN, W. N. & RAO, P. N. (1976). Conformational changes of chromatin associated with phytohemagglutinin stimulation of peripheral lymphocytes. *Expl Cell Res.* **100**, 219–222.

HITTELMAN, W. N. & RAO, P. N. (1978). Mapping G_1 phase by the structural morphology of the prematurely condensed chromosomes. *J. cell. Physiol.* **95**, 333–342.

JOHNSON, R. T. & RAO, P. N. (1970). Mammalian cell fusion: Induction of premature chromosome condensation in interphase nuclei. *Nature, Lond.* **226**, 717–722.

JORGENSEN, A. L. & BAK, A. L. (1982). The last order of coiling in human chromosomes. *Expl Cell Res.* **139**, 447–451.

LAU, Y. F. & ARRIGHI, F. E. (1981). Studies of mammalian chromosome replication: II. Evidence for the existence of defined chromosome replicating units. *Chromosoma* **83**, 721–741.

LAUGHLIN, T. J., WILKINSON-SINGLEY, E., OLINS, D. E. & OLINS, A. L. (1982). Stereo electron microscope studies of mitotic chromosomes from Chinese hamster ovary cells. *Eur. J. Cell Biol.* **27**, 170–176.

MANTON, I. (1950). The spiral structure of chromosomes. *Biol. Rev.* **25**, 486–508.

MARSDEN, M. P. F. & LAEMMLI, U. K. (1979). Metaphase chromosome structure: Evidence for a radial loop model. *Cell* **17**, 849–858.

MATSUI, S. I., YOSHIDA, H., WEINFELD, H. & SANDBERG, A. A. (1972). Induction of prophase in interphase nuclei by fusion with metaphase cells. *J. Cell Biol.* **54**, 120–132.

MAZIA, D. (1963). Synthetic activities leading to mitosis. *J. cell. comp. Physiol.* **62** (suppl. 1), 123–140.

MOSER, G. C., MULLER, H. & ROBBINS, E. (1975). Differential nuclear fluorescence during the cell cycle. *Expl Cell Res.* **91**, 73–78.

MULLINGER, A. M. & JOHNSON, R. T. (1980). Packing DNA into chromosomes. *J. Cell Sci.* **46**, 61–86.

MULLINGER, A. M. & JOHNSON, R. T. (1983). Units of chromosome replication and packing. *J. Cell Sci.* **64**, 179–193.

NICOLINI, C., AJIRO, K., BORUN, T. W. & BASERGA, R. (1975). Chromatin changes during the cell cycle of the HeLa cells. *J. biol. Chem.* **250**, 3381–3385.

OBARA, Y., CHAI, L. S., WEINFELD, H. & SANDBERG, A. A. (1974). Prophasing of interphase nuclei and induction of nuclear envelopes around metaphase chromosomes in HeLa and Chinese hamster homo- and heterokaryons. *J. Cell Biol.* **62**, 104–113.

OHNUKI, Y. (1968). Structure of chromosomes. I. Morphological studies of the spiral structure of human somatic chromosomes. *Chromosoma* **25**, 402–428.

PAULSON, J. R. & LAEMMLI, U. K. (1977). The structure of histone-depleted metaphase chromosomes. *Cell* **12**, 817–828.

PEDERSON, T. & ROBBINS, E. (1972). Chromatin structure and the cell division cycle: Actinomycin binding in synchronized HeLa cells. *J. Cell Biol.* **55**, 322–327.

RAO, P. N. & HANKS, S. K. (1980). Chromatin structure during the prereplicative phases in the life cycle of mammalian cells. *Cell Biophys.* **2**, 327–337.

RAO, P. N., WILSON, B. & PUCK, T. T. (1977). Premature chromosome condensation and cell cycle analysis. *J. cell. Physiol.* **91**, 131–142.

RINGERTZ, N. R., DARZYNKIEWICZ, Z. & BOLUND, L. (1969). Actinomycin binding properties of stimulated human lymphocytes. *Expl Cell Res.* **56**, 411–417.

RIS, H. (1978). Preparation of chromatin and chromosomes for electron microscopy. *Methods Cell Biol.* **18**, 229–246.

RIS, H. & KORENBERG, J. (1979). Chromosome structure and levels of chromosome organization. In *Cell Biology: A Comprehensive Treatise* (ed. D. M. Prescott & L. Goldstein), pp. 268–361. New York: Academic Press.

ROHME, D. (1975). Evidence suggesting chromosome continuity during the *S*-phase of Indian muntjac cells. *Hereditas* **80**, 145–149.

RUZICKA, F. (1977). G banding of chromosomes. In *Principles and Techniques of Electron Microscopy. Biological Applications*, vol. 7 (ed. M. A. Hayat), pp. 144–162. New York: Van Nostrand Reinhold.

SCHOR, S. L., JOHNSON, R. T. & WALDREN, C. A. (1975). Changes in the organization of chromosomes during the cell cycle: Response to ultraviolet light. *J. Cell Sci.* **17**, 539–565.

SCHWARZACHER, H. G., RUZICKA, F. & SPERLING, K. (1974). Electron microscopy of human banded and prematurely condensed chromosomes. *Chromosomes Today* **5**, 227–234.

SEDAT, J. & MANUELIDIS, L. (1978). A direct approach to the structure of eukaryotic chromosomes. *Cold Spring Harbor Symp. quant. Biol.* **42**, 331–350.

SPERLING, K. (1982). Cell cycle and chromosome cycle: morphological and functional aspects. In *Premature Chromosome Condensation. Application in Basic, Clinical and Mutation Research* (ed. P. N. Rao, R. T. Johnson & K. Sperling), pp. 43–78. New York: Academic Press.

SPERLING, K. & RAO, P. N. (1974). Mammalian cell fusion. V. Replication behavior of heterochromatin as observed by premature chromosome condensation. *Chromosoma* **45**, 121–131.

STENMAN, S. & SAKSELA, E. (1971). The relationship of Sendai virus-induced chromosome pulverization to cell cycles in HeLa cells. *Hereditas* **69**, 1–14.

STUBBLEFIELD, E. & WRAY, W. (1971). Architecture of the Chinese hamster metaphase chromosome. *Chromosoma* **32**, 262–294.

WORCEL, A. & BENYAJATI, C. (1977). Higher order coiling of DNA in chromatin. *Cell* **12**, 83–100.

YUNIS, J. J. & BAHR, G. F. (1979). Chromatin fiber organization of human interphase and prophase chromosomes. *Expl Cell Res.* **122**, 63–72.

ZETTERBERG, A. & AUER, G. (1970). Proliferative activity and cytochemical properties of nuclear chromatin related to local cell density of epithelical cells. *Expl Cell Res.* **62**, 262–270.

J. Cell Sci. Suppl. 1, 223–234 (1984)
Printed in Great Britain © The Company of Biologists Limited 1984

SPATIAL ORGANIZATION OF THE *DROSOPHILA* NUCLEUS: A THREE-DIMENSIONAL CYTOGENETIC STUDY

Y. GRUENBAUM, M. HOCHSTRASSER, D. MATHOG,
H. SAUMWEBER*, D. A. AGARD and J. W. SEDAT

Department of Biochemistry and Biophysics, University of California at San Francisco, San Francisco, California 94143, U.S.A.

SUMMARY

The combination of optical fluorescence microscopy with digital image processing and analysis has been used to examine the three-dimensional organization of chromosomes within intact polytene nuclei. Although the arrangement indicates a high degree of flexibility, there are many conserved features between nuclei at the same developmental state. For example, chromosome arms are loosely coiled with centromeres clustered at the opposite end of the nucleus from the telomeres. Individual chromosome arms are not interwoven but occupy different spatial domains. Chromosomal sites that contact the envelope correlate with intercalary heterochromatin. Connections are observed between actively transcribing regions.

INTRODUCTION

Optical section microscopy uniquely allows the analysis of the three-dimensional arrangement of cellular and sub-cellular components in intact tissues. As part of a continuing investigation into the structure and function of eukaryotic chromosomes, we have used this powerful method to map the spatial organization of the giant polytene chromosomes in *Drosophila melanogaster* salivary gland nuclei. Although aspects of this work have already been reported (Agard & Sedat, 1983; Mathog *et al.* 1984), in this paper we present the conclusions obtained from an analysis of chromosomal folding in 10 nuclei as well as preliminary findings on both the spatial association of transcriptionally active regions and the correlation between transcriptional activity and three-dimensional location. In addition we report on the use of improved algorithms for removal of out-of-focus information during the analysis of optical section images.

DATA COLLECTION AND ANALYSIS

Although details of the preparation of glands for microscopy (Mortin & Sedat, 1982; Sedat & Manuelidis, 1977) and the computer-controlled microscope and data collection hardware (Mathog, Hochstrasser & Sedat, 1985) are described elsewhere,

---

* Present address: Abteilung fur Physikalische Biologie, Max-Planck Institut fur Virusforschung, D-7400 Tubigen 1, FRG.

the salient features will be briefly mentioned. Salivary glands from late third-instar *D. melanogaster* larvae are carefully hand-dissected into a buffer optimized for the preservation of chromosome structure (Sedat & Manuelidis, 1977) and subsequently stained with the DNA-specific, non-intercalative fluorescent dye DAPI (4′, 6-diamidino-2-phenylindole). By using such a fluorescent dye, only the DNA-containing structures are imaged, largely unencumbered by proteinaceous or membraneous material. Using this approach it is possible to examine chromosome organization in intact cells located within a whole salivary gland.

Fluorescent images were recorded using a 100× 1·3 N.A. oil-immersion lens on an inverted Zeiss Axiomat microscope set up for epi-fluorescence. Under computer control, the focal plane was increased by small amounts (1·2–1·4 μm), and pixel 512×512 images were acquired from a SIT video camera and digitized. At each focal position, 256 digital images were averaged (each taken in 1/30 s) to reduce noise. A typical data set consisted of 24, 512×512 digital images.

Because of the finite depth-of-focus of the microscope's objective lens, each image represents the sum of in-focus information from a narrow plane within the specimen and out-of-focus information from the remainder of the sample. From a knowledge of the specific objective lens parameters it is possible to determine the precise relationship between the 'true' three-dimensional image and what is actually recorded by the microscope. A comprehensive discussion of the image-forming properties of a microscope as well as an analysis of reconstruction algorithms is presented elsewhere (Agard, 1984; Castleman, 1979). Because of the rather coarse sampling used here, relatively simple approaches can substantially remove the out-of-focus component that contaminates each image.

The approach chosen is a modification of that of Weinstein & Castleman (1971). For any section j, the reconstructed image i_j is calculated from the observed section o_j and the ones immediately above it o_{j+1} and below it o_{j-1}. The adjacent sections are first blurred by an amount corresponding to one focal step, scaled by an empirically determined constant and subtracted from the current section. The resultant image is then de-blurred by the in-focus contrast-transfer function in order to sharpen the image. For simplicity and ease of calculation these operations are all done in Fourier space:

$$I(u,v)_j = (O(u,v)_j - s_1(r)[O(u,v)_{j-1} + O(u,v)_{j+1}])/s_0(r),$$

where $I(u,v)_j, O(u,v)_j$ are the two-dimensional Fourier transforms of the observed $(o(x,y)_j)$ and final $(i(x,y)_j)$ images, $r = (u^2 + v^2)^{\frac{1}{2}}$. The in-focus contrast-transfer function $s_0(r)$ and the out-of-focus contrast-transfer function $s_1(r)$ are calculated from the theory of Stokseth (1969) as described by Castleman (1979) and shown in Fig. 1. The final enhanced image stack is calculated by inverse Fourier transformation of the $I(u,v)_j$ values. Examples of several sections before and after processing are shown in Fig. 2. The improvement in image quality due to de-blurring greatly facilitates the reading of cytology. This is especially true of glands from other developmental stages that are less transparent and show more light scattering. However, the data discussed in this communication were collected from nuclei which were sufficiently clear that no image processing was required.

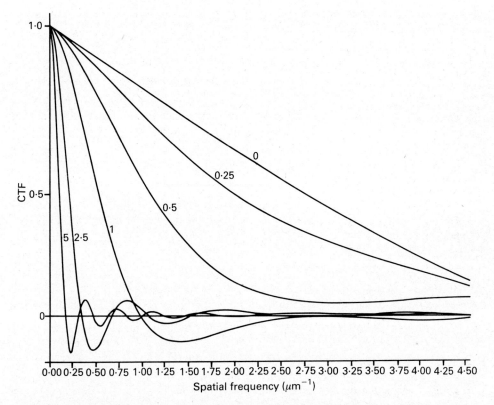

Fig. 1. A family of calculated contrast transfer functions (CTF) is shown for a 100×
1·3 N.A. Planapochromat oil-immersion objective lens. The degree of defocus (in μm) is
shown by each curve.

EVALUATION OF CHROMOSOME ORGANIZATION WITHIN THE NUCLEUS

The initial aim of this work was a description of the manner in which polytene
chromosomes are packaged within the cell nucleus. Because the three-dimensional
folding pattern of the chromosomes within the nucleus is neither simple nor identical
between different nuclei, it has been necessary to find objective methods for evaluating these structures and for assessing the degree of similarity between different nuclei.
What is desired is the ability to quantitate and compare the functionally significant
aspects of structural organization. Unfortunately, it is by no means obvious what the
most relevant structural description might be. Our approach has been to compare a
set of nuclei in a single tissue at a specific time in development and determine if any
regularities can be recognized, the assumption being that similarities reflect functionally important structural aspects of the nucleus (Mathog *et al.* 1984). This work
represents an extension of the original data set (Mathog *et al.* 1984) to ten nuclei.

The three-dimensional chromosomal layout can be studied at several levels of
detail. First of all, the optical section data set itself can be inspected. It is possible to
draw several broad conclusions based on such observations. First, the bulk of the
chromosomes are found in the peripheral shells of the nuclear volume, leaving a

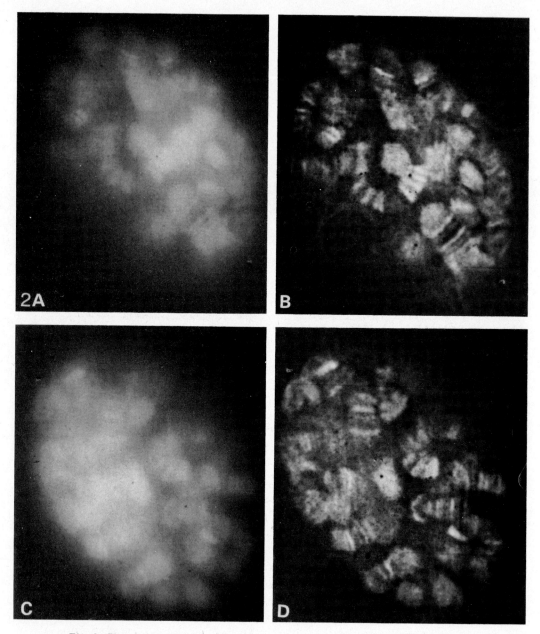

Fig. 2. Two optical sections from a stack of 24 are shown before (A,C) and after (B,D) processing to remove out-of-focus information. Note that the fine banding detail is considerably more apparent in the processed images. After processing, some of the intrinsic aberrations in the current SIT video camera also become more apparent. The use of better detectors will avoid this problem. These data come from a gland which has been fixed and embedded in Spurr and subsequently optically sectioned.

central zone largely free of chromatin. Second, the chromosome pathway does not always trace a smooth curve but is marked by a number of kinks. These sharp changes

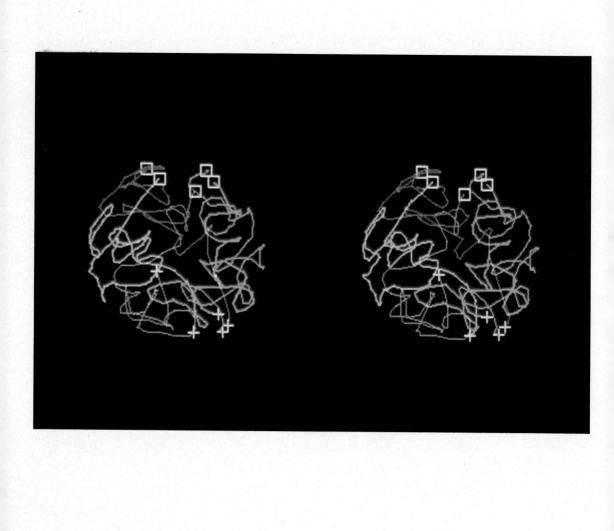

in direction are found most frequently at chromosomal weak points or at puffs. Finally, certain regions are marked by an unusual degree of contortion, and in favourable circumstances can be seen to give rise to ectopic fibres (for a discussion on ectopic fibres see Kaufmann & Iddles, 1963).

The complicated folding of chromosomes and the wealth of detail available in the images demands the abstracting of this information into a more readily analysable form. A software package has been created (Mathog *et al*. 1985) that allows the pathways of the different chromosome arms to be traced out within the three-dimensional data set. By careful examination of the optical section data it has been possible to recognize the characteristic banding patterns revealed by fluorescence staining. With reference to maps made from squashed preparations, precise cytogenetic locations can be assigned along the chromosome path. The resulting stick-figure model, complete with cytogenetic information (an example is shown in Fig. 3), is then examined for various folding features. The analysis at this level has revealed additional insights into nuclear organization. (1) The most common folding motif is the loop. Chromosome arms often coil into three to four successive gyres, and these irregular helices are almost always right-handed. (2) The centromeres are aggregated into a single chromocentre, which is invariably in contact with the nuclear envelope. (3) The chromosome arms do not usually fold into tight globular units but are more or less extended, with telomeres at the opposite end of the nucleus from the chromocentre. This is the classical Rabl orientation (Rabl, 1885) noted previously in diploid cells, particularly those of plants (Fussell, 1975). (4) Most surprisingly, the chromosome arms are each restricted to a different region of the nucleus; no inter-woven arms have ever been observed in salivary gland nuclei.

Structural information can be further abstracted from the three-dimensional chromosome models in the form of quantitative plots. We have tested a variety of rotationally invariant structural parameters and have used them to quantitate various organizational features (Mathog, 1985). One means of representing three-dimensional data in two-dimensional form is the intradistance diagonal plot, which has been used extensively in evaluating protein crystal structures (Rossman & Liljas, 1974). Fig. 4 shows a representative diagonal plot derived from chromosome arm 3L in one of the reconstructed nuclei. Each axis represents cytogenetic position along the chromosome, beginning in each case with the centromere at the origin. The graph depicts a contoured set of distances displayed as intensity values, the brighter values representing chromosome points that are close together in space. The contour steps are $1\,\mu m$; any intradistance value greater than $8\,\mu m$ is set to black. The distances between any two cytogenetic points on the chromosome can be found by locating each point on the x and y axes, respectively, and finding the intersection of the orthogonals

---

Fig. 3. Stereo pair of a model derived from one polytene nucleus. There are five major chromosome arms: X (green), 2L (orange), 2R (blue), 3L (purple) and 3R (light green). The centromere of each is marked by a square while each telomere is denoted by a +. The centromeres are actually aggregated to form a single chromocentre; the telomeres are located in a more dispersed manner at the opposite end of the nucleus (Rabl orientation).

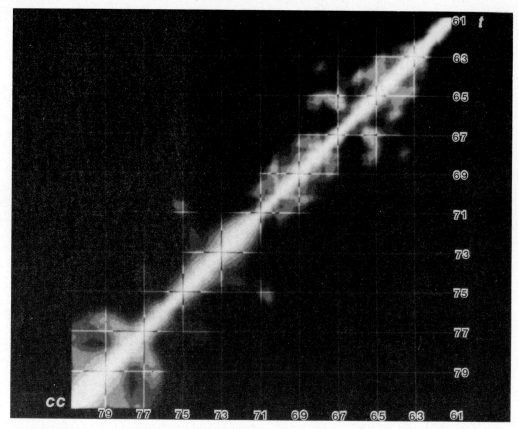

Fig. 4. An intradistance plot of the 3L chromosome from one nucleus. Each axis represents a cytological position, starting with the centromere at the lower left; 20–30 bands from the cytogenetic sequence have been used to normalize the plot onto a standard grid. Each subdivision of the grid represents two divisions (out of 20) on the cytological map (Bridges, 1935), with the telomere, t, 61A at the two extrema and of the chromocentre, cc, 80F at the origin. Intensities, which are inversely proportional to the absolute distance between any two chromosomal points, are contoured in steps of 1 μm. Chromosome points further apart than 8 μm are shown in black.

drawn from them. The intensity value at this position is inversely proportional to the absolute distance between the two loci.

These intradistance maps are used to assess the folding of each arm and to facilitate the comparison of corresponding arms in different nuclei. The loop motifs mentioned above can be seen in the plot in Fig. 4 as bars of intensity extending at right angles from the diagonal. Their position within the cytogenetic sequence is now easily determined. This work is still in a preliminary stage and further details will be published elsewhere.

In attempting to compare chromosome structures in different nuclei two principal problems have been encountered. Most importantly, we have found it necessary to have a set of guide-marks along each chromosome to ensure that precisely corresponding regions are compared. As it is possible to follow the banding pattern *in situ*, this requirement is readily met. The second general difficulty is in the quantitative comparison itself. Only a moderate number of nuclei have been reconstructed so far, and the chromosome packaging is sufficiently flexible to make it difficult, in some cases, to distinguish statistical noise from significant differences. A rank order parameter has previously been used to compare the diagonal plots from multiple nuclei (Mathog *et al.* 1984). With the increase in the number of data sets, other statistical methods are now possible.

A particularly informative quantitative measurement has been the minimum distance between the nuclear envelope and loci along a chromosome (Mathog *et al.* 1984). This revealed a set of highly conserved 'contacts' with the nuclear envelope. We have expanded the initially reported data set by another four nuclei from the same salivary gland, and essentially all of the loci identified previously as conserved nuclear envelope contact sites remain so classified. Fig. 5A shows the superimposed plots of 10 2L chromosomes; in B the average distance to the surface is plotted, along with the standard deviations. As seen previously, the correlation of these surface contact sites with regions of intercalary heterochromatin (loci with high frequencies of ectopic pairing and rearrangement, and which have late-replicating properties shared with centric heterochromatin; Zhimulev, Semeshin, Kulichkov & Belyaeva, 1982) is very strong.

PRELIMINARY ANALYSIS OF TRANSCRIPTIONALLY ACTIVE LOCI

In an effort to better understand the significant functional properties of chromosomal organization, we have begun a series of experiments to probe the correlation of

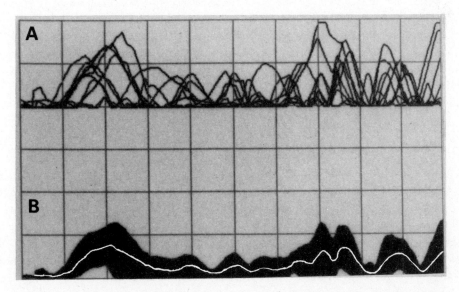

Fig. 5. The distance-to-surface plots of ten 3L chromosomes. A. The 10 plots superimposed. The abscissa is the same as for Fig. 4. The ordinate represents the minimum distance to the nuclear surface and is scaled to 5 μm per division, starting at 0 for each plot. Points on the curves that touch the x axis are loci that are at the surface of the nucleus. Peaks on the curves denote chromosomal points that extend furthest into the nuclear interior. B. The average of the 10 plots, shown within an envelope of ± 1 standard deviation.

structure with transcriptional activity. We have directly analysed the three-dimensional distribution of actively transcribing DNA in salivary gland nuclei by labelling the DNA with the fluorescent dye DAPI and the nascent RNA with a short pulse of tritiated uridine.

Salivary glands were again hand-dissected from third instar larvae and pulsed for 4 min in modified Shield & Sang (1970) medium that contained the RNA precursor [5-^{3}H]uridine (29 Ci/mmol). Following fixation with formaldehyde and permeabilization with Triton X-100, the glands were stained with DAPI, refixed in formaldehyde, embedded in Spurr's resin and serially sectioned. The 0·7 μm thick sections were prepared for autoradiography and exposed for 12 days. Images of both the fluorescent chromosomes and the silver grains from each section were digitized and aligned, using the algorithm of Agard & Sedat (1980), to form two registered image stacks. Using this approach, and our interactive modelling programs (Mathog, et al. 1985), we have been able to reconstruct two complete nuclei from physical sections. In both cases, the paths of the chromosomes complete with their cytogenetic markers have been determined.

Since only two nuclei have been examined, any conclusions drawn at this point are necessarily very speculative. However, two very interesting observations have been made. First, it appears that the spatial distribution of active loci is very heterogeneous. That is, there are regions of the nucleus in which highly active transcribed regions are located, as well as regions relatively devoid of transcriptional activity. In addition, there seems to be some correlation between intense transcriptional activity and proximity to the nuclear membrane, as there is between chromosome position and proximity to the envelope. This remains to be analysed rigorously.

Another interesting observation from the pulse-labelling experiments is that connections of silver grains between spatially close puffs are frequently seen. These extensions from the edge of the puff are decidedly asymmetric, and are only seen on the edge that is adjacent to another puff. This suggests that there might be some link between active regions on different chromosomes or between different regions on the same chromosome (Fig. 6A,B).

The existence of RNA connections suggested by the pulse-labelling experiments is strongly supported by experiments using another approach to label active genes. Whole salivary glands have been stained by indirect immunofluorescence using monoclonal antibodies X4 or S5 that had previously been shown to be specific for different classes of ribonucleoprotein (RNP) particles (Risau, Symmons, Saumweber & Frasch, 1983; Saumweber et al. 1980). Following staining with rhodamine-conjugated second antibody, the chromosomes were stained with DAPI. Nuclei prepared in this manner were either physically or optically sectioned. Results from physical sectioning of an embedded gland labelled with the X4 antibody are presented in Fig. 6C,D. Similar results were obtained using the S5 antibody. Connections between different chromosome loci that have these RNP antigens can be seen at many locations within each nucleus using either antibody. Similar fluorescent antibody connections can be viewed in optical sections of whole glands as well as in isolated nuclei from the same tissue (data not shown). The equivalence of the antibody and grain connections is now being rigorously established.

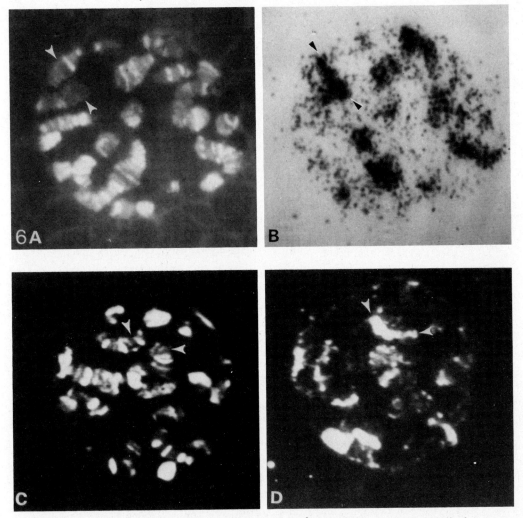

Fig. 6.A,B Salivary glands were pulse-labelled with [5-³H]uridine for 4 min as described in the text. The DAPI-stained image of a section is shown in A and the autoradiography image in B. C,D. Fluorescent images of the DNA and hnRNP antigens, respectively, from the same physical section. The antibody used here was X4. Some of the connections here are indicated by arrowheads.

Great care has been taken to ensure that these connections links are not preparation artifacts. Several different regimes of fixation and sample preparation have been tried, and in all cases connections were seen. Labelling with other monoclonal antibodies that are not directed against heterogeneous nuclear RNP (hnRNP) antigens, which also stain multiple sites along the polytene chromosome, did not give rise to such connections.

CONCLUSIONS AND SPECULATIONS

Several features of the present results are particularly striking. First is the fact that

the polytene chromosome arms remain, in most cases, in the polarized Rabl orientation. This configuration is seen in dividing cells and is thought to result from the
traction of the previous anaphase movement (Fussell, 1975). The salivary gland
nuclei, however, underwent their last division early in embryogenesis, yet they continue to maintain their polarized chromosome configuration. A precedent for this
long-term positional stability is the finding by Sperling & Luedke (1981) that quiescent muntjack lymphocytes also retain the Rabl orientation for extended periods of
time. However, in the case of the polytene chromosomes the result is still surprising
as there have been some 10 rounds of DNA replication, during which time the
mechanical properties of the chromosomes as well as the physical properties of the
nuclei might be expected to change considerably.

The presence of topological boundaries observed between chromosomes is an even
more unexpected example of long-range positional stability. It is somewhat reminis-
cent of the separation of individual chromosomes into vesicles or karyomeres seen in
the early stages of nucleus reformation in rapidly dividing embryonic cells (Ito, Dan
& Goodenough, 1981; Wilson, 1925). It is possible that nuclear architectural elements such as the matrix may remain organized in subnuclear domains that isolate
each chromosome. In any case, the simplest interpretation of the absence of inter-
twining of different arms seems to be that they too reflect the positions of the preced-
ing mitotic chromosomes. For dividing nuclei, this would allow the straightforward
condensation of each chromosome arm during the transition from interphase to
metaphase.

The chromosomal sites that appose the nuclear envelope in all or virtually all the
nuclei have been shown to correlate very well with regions of intercalary
heterochromatin (IH). As argued previously, these sites may also serve as
envelope–chromosome anchorage sites (Mathog et al. 1984). It is worth pointing out,
however, that there are many more IH loci than conserved envelope contact regions;
in other words, there are many 'unused' anchorage loci. Since it is known that centric
heterochromatin can be arranged differently in nuclei of different cell types (Hsu,
Cooper, Mace & Brinkley, 1971), it is conceivable that the other IH loci are used as
anchorage points in other tissues, generating alternative nuclear arrangements of
chromosomes. Perhaps in different tissues different functional requirements may be
met by a different chromosomal architecture. Several other tissues in D. melanogaster
are sufficiently polytenized to test this hypothesis, and such work is under way. It
should be noted that when Zhimulev et al. (1982) compared IH characteristics in
different tissues, the IH loci all mapped to the same sites as found in salivary glands.

The striking observation of connections between actively transcribing regions suggests a possible metabolic link between heterologous chromosome sites. Whether this
represents a sharing of transcriptional or RNA-processing machinery, or has a structural or regulatory role, or is merely fortuitous is, as yet, unclear. Any functional
purpose would have to be linked to the three-dimensional folding of the chromosomes
inside the interphase nucleus. Further experiments to clarify this point are now under
way.

All of the studies reported here involved relatively few sections separated by rather large intervals. We are currently exploring the use of considerably higher-resolution data sets (128 images, each separated by $0.3\,\mu$m). The hope is to be able to extend these studies to diploid prophase and possibly interphase nuclei. It should also be possible to examine directly ectopic fibre locations in intact salivary gland nuclei. In addition to using more data, it is essential that more-accurate reconstruction (out-of-focus removal) algorithms are used. Two methods that appear to provide the requisite accuracy have been analysed in detail (Agard, 1984) on mock data and are now being tried on real data.

In addition to providing new insights into chromosome architecture, these powerful new approaches for studying structure at the cellular level in intact tissues should prove quite useful in other areas of cell biology. Possible areas include: analysis of spatial organization of actin or tubulin, or secretory components, or possibly even neuron interconnections within the nervous system.

This work was supported by NIH grants GM25101 (J.W.S.) and GM31627 (D.A.A.). Y.G. is supported by a postdoctoral fellowship from the Fogarty International Center (NIH 3F05 TW03270-01S1); M.H. is supported by an NSF predoctoral fellowship. D.A.A. is a Searle Scholar.

REFERENCES

AGARD, D. A. (1984). Optical sectioning microscopy: cellular architecture in three dimensions. *A. Rev. Biophys. Bioengng* **13**, 191–219.

AGARD, D. A. & SEDAT, J. W. (1980). Three dimensional analysis of biological specimens using image processing techniques. *Proc. Soc. photo-opt. Instr. Engng* **264**, 110–117.

AGARD, D. A. & SEDAT, J. W. (1983). Three-dimensional architecture of a polytene nucleus. *Nature, Lond.* **302**, 676–681.

BRIDGES, C. B. (1935). *Salivary chromosome maps. J. Hered.* **26**, 60–64.

CASTLEMAN, K. R. (1979). *Digital Image Processing*, pp. 351–360. New Jersey: Prentice-Hall.

FUSSELL, C. P. (1975). The position of interphase chromosomes and late replicating DNA in centromere and telomere regions of *Allium cepa* L. *Chromosoma* **50**, 201–210.

HSU, T. C., COOPER, J. E. K., MACE, M. L. JR & BRINKLEY, B. R. (1971). Arrangement of centromeres in mouse cells. *Chromosoma* **34**, 73–87.

ITO, S., DAN, K. & GOODENOUGH, D. (1981). Ultrastructure and [^{3}H]thymidine incorporation in chromosome vesicles in sea urchin embryos. *Chromosoma* **83**, 441–453.

KAUFMANN, B. P. & IDDLES, M. K. (1963). Ectopic pairing in salivary gland chromosomes of *Drosophila melanogaster*. I. Distributional patterns in relation to puffing. *Port. Acta biol. A*, **7**, 225–248.

MATHOG, D. (1985). Light microscope based analysis of three-dimensional structure: Applications to the study of *Drosophila* salivary gland nuclei. II. Algorithms for model analysis. *J. Microsc.* (in press).

MATHOG, D., HOCHSTRASSER, M., GRUENBAUM, Y., SAUMWEBER, H. & SEDAT, J. W. (1984). Characteristic folding pattern of the polytene chromosomes in *Drosophila* salivary gland nuclei. *Nature, Lond.* **308**, 414–421.

MATHOG, D., HOCHSTRASSER, M. & SEDAT, J. W. (1985). Light microscope based analysis of three-dimensional structure: Applications to the study of *Drosophila* salivary gland nuclei. I. Data collection and analysis. *J. Microsc.* (in press).

MORTIN, L. & SEDAT, J. W. (1982). Structure of *Drosophila* polytene chromosomes: evidence for a toroidal organization of the bands. *J. Cell Sci.* **57**, 73–113.

RABL, C. (1885). *Morph. Jb.* **10**, 214–330.

RISAU, W., SYMMONS, P., SAUMWEBER, H. & FRASCH, M. (1983). Nonpackaging and packaging proteins of hnRNA in *Drosophila melanogaster*. *Cell* **33**, 529–541.

Rossman, M. G. & Liljas (1974). Recognition of structural domains in globular proteins. *J. molec. Biol.* **85**, 177–181.

Saumweber, H., Symmons, P., Kabisch, R., Will, H. & Bonohoeffer, F. (1980). Monoclonal antibodies against chromosomal proteins of *Drosophila melanogaster. Chromosoma* **80**, 253.

Sedat, J. W. & Manuelidis, L. (1977). *Cold Spring Harbor. quant. Biol.* **42**, 331–350.

Shield, G. & Sang, J. H. (1970). Characteristics of five cell types appearing during *in vitro* culture of embryonic material from *Drosophila melanogaster. J. Embryol. exp. Morph.* **23**, 53–69.

Sperling, K. & Luedke, E.-K. (1981). Arrangement of prematurely condensed chromosomes in cultured cells and lymphocytes of the Indian muntjac. *Chromosoma* **83**, 541–553.

Stokseth, P. A. (1969). Properties of a defocused optical system. *J. opt. Soc. Am.* **59**, 1314–1321.

Weinstein, M. & Castleman, K. R. (1971). Reconstructing 3-D specimens from 2-D section images. *Proc. Soc. photo-opt. Instr. Engng* **26**, 131–138.

Wilson, E. B. (1925). In *The Cell in Development and Heredity*, 3rd edn, pp. 215–225. New York: Macmillan.

Zhimulev, I. F., Semeshin, V. F., Kulichkov, V. A. & Belyaeva, E. S. (1982). Intercalary heterochromatin in *Drosophila*. I. Localization and general characteristics. *Chromosoma* **87**, 197–228.

INFORMATION FOR CONTRIBUTORS

1 Manuscripts should be sent to The Editors, *Journal of Cell Science*, Department of Zoology, Cambridge CB2 3EJ, England.

2 Manuscripts must be typewritten, *in double spacing throughout (including tables, references and legends)*. Each table should be typed on a separate sheet. Legends to figures should be typed in a single series and placed at the end of the manuscript. Two complete copies of the manuscript should be submitted. Manuscripts must be fully corrected by the author, and a charge will be made for excessive alteration in proof.

3 A short title of not more than 40 characters, for use as page headings, should be supplied and at least **3 key words** for indexing papers.

4 Manuscripts must contain a **Summary** of not more than 500 words, placed immediately after the title page. This must be intelligible without reference to the main text and contain no references.

5 The list of **References** must be given in alphabetical order of authors' names. The titles of journals should be abbreviated in accordance with the *World List of Scientific Periodicals*, 4th edn (1963) and *Short Titles of Commonly Cited Scientific Journals*, Royal Society, London (1980). The following style is used:

> GRAY, E. G. & WILLIS, R. A. (1968). Problems of electron stereoscopy of biological tissue. *J. Cell Sci.* **3**, 309–326.
> MAZIA, D. (1961). Mitosis and physiology of cell division. In *The Cell*, vol. 3 (ed. J. Brachet & A. E. Mirsky), pp. 77–412. New York, London: Academic Press.

Citations in the text are given in the following form: Jones & Smith (1960) or (Jones & Smith, 1960). Where there are more than two authors and less than five the first citation should include all the names and subsequent citations should be in the form (Jones *et al.* 1960). Where more than one paper by the same author(s) have been published in the same year they are cited as Jones (1960*a*), Jones (1960*b*) etc.

6 Footnotes should be avoided wherever possible.

7 SI units should be used throughout in the preparation of manuscripts.

8 Text figures and **photographs** should be numbered in a single series, in the order in which they are referred to in the text. Each individual drawing or photograph should be numbered separately (Fig. 1, Fig. 2 and so on).

9 Text figures should preferably be not more than twice final size; very large drawings should be avoided. Original drawings are needed for reproduction as photographic copies cannot always be used. The maximum printed size of a drawing is 200 mm by 125 mm. Lettering will be inserted by the printers and should be indicated on a tracing-paper overlay or a duplicate copy.

10 Photographs should preferably be submitted the same size as they are to appear. The maximum for a plate is 200 mm by 140 mm. Where several photographs make up a plate they should be mounted accurately on one sheet of cardboard and irregular shapes avoided wherever possible. Lettering on plates will be inserted by the printers and should be indicated either on a duplicate, marked set of prints or on a tracing-paper overlay bearing accurately marked outlines of the objects indicated.

11 Authors should retain a complete set of labelled figures for checking against proofs. The originals will not be returned to authors with proofs.

12 Authors will receive 200 offprints free of charge and may order additional copies when proofs are returned.

13 In order to give the Company of Biologists authority to deal with matters of copyright, authors will be required to assign to them the copyright of any article published in the journal.

The Company of Biologists Limited is a non-profit-making organization whose members are active professional biologists. The Company, which was founded in 1925, is the owner and publisher of this and Journal of Experimental Biology and Journal of Embryology and Experimental Morphology.

Journal of Cell Science is devoted to the study of cell organization. Papers will be published dealing with the structure and function of plant and animal cells and their extracellular products, and with such topics as cell growth and division, cell movements and interactions, and cell genetics. Accounts of advances in the relevant techniques will also be published. Contributions concerned with morphogenesis at the cellular and sub-cellular level will be acceptable, as will studies of micro-organisms and viruses, in so far as they are relevant to an understanding of cell organization. Theoretical articles and occasional review articles will be published.

Subscriptions

Journal of Cell Science is published nine times a year, in February, March, April, June, July, August, October, November and December. Each issue is a complete volume. The subscription price of volumes 65–73, 1984, is £150.00 (U.S.A. and Canada US $405.00, Japan £165.00) post free. Individual volumes may be purchased at £28.00 (U.S.A. and Canada US $77.00) each, plus postage. Orders for 1984 may be sent to any bookseller or subscription agent, or to The Biochemical Society Book Depot, P.O. Box 32, Commerce Way, Colchester CO2 8HP, U.K. Copies of the journal for subscribers in the U.S.A. and Canada are sent by air to New York for delivery with the minimum delay. Second class postage paid at New York, N.Y., and at additional mailing offices, Postmaster, send address corrections to: Journal of Cell Science, c/o Expediters of the Printed Word Ltd, 527 Madison Avenue, New York, N.Y. 10022, U.S.A.

Back numbers of the *Journal of Cell Science* are available from Messrs William Dawson & Sons, Cannon House, Folkestone, Kent, U.K. at £46.00 each for volumes 1–22 and £25.00 each for volumes 23–64. This journal is the successor to the *Quarterly Journal of Microscopical Science*, back numbers of which are also obtainable from Messrs William Dawson & Sons at £8.00 per volume.

Copyright and reproduction

1. Authors may make copies of their own papers in this journal without seeking permission from The Company of Biologists Limited, *provided that such copies are for free distribution only: they must not be sold*.
2. Authors may re-use their own illustrations in other publications appearing under their own name, without seeking permission.
3. Specific permission will *not* be required for photocopying copyright material in the following circumstances.
    (a) For private study, provided the copying is done by the person requiring its use, or by an employee of the institution to which he/she belongs, without charge beyond the actual cost of copying.
    (b) For the production of multiple copies of such material, to be used for bona fide educational purposes, provided this is done by a member of the staff of the university, school or other comparable institution, for distribution without profit to student members of that institution, provided the copy is made from the original journal.
4. ISI Tear Service, 3501 Market Street, Philadelphia, Pennsylvania 19104, U.S.A., is authorized to supply single copies of separate articles for private use only.
5. For all other matters relating to the reproduction of copyright material written application must be made to Dr R. J. Skaer, Company Secretary, Company of Biologists Limited, Department of Zoology, Downing Street, Cambridge CB2 3EJ, U.K.

© The Company of Biologists Limited 1984

Journal of **CELL SCIENCE**

Editors:

A. V. GRIMSTONE   HENRY HARRIS

R. T. JOHNSON

Editorial Board:

W. B. AMOS   B. E. S. GUNNING

M. D. BENNETT   R. A. LASKEY

D. BRAY   H. C. MACGREGOR

G. M. W. COOK   C. J. MARSHALL

V. DEFENDI   J. C. METCALFE

H. G. DICKINSON   R. B. NICKLAS

G. A. DUNN   J. D. PITTS

D. R. GARROD   N. J. SEVERS

G. GERISCH   L. SIMINOVITCH

I. R. GIBBONS   D. C. SMITH

D. M. GLOVER   J. TAYLOR-PAPADIMITRIOU

S. GORDON

Published by

THE COMPANY OF BIOLOGISTS LIMITED

CAMBRIDGE